Companion Spider

Companion Spider

WESLEYAN UNIVERSITY PRESS

E S S A Y S

Clayton Eshleman

Foreword by Adrienne Rich

MIDDLETOWN, CONNECTICUT

Published by Wesleyan University Press, Middletown, CT 06459

Text copyright © 2001 by Clayton Eshleman

Foreword copyright © by Adrienne Rich

Printed in the United States of America

5 4 3 2 1

LIBRARY OF CONGRESS CATALOGING-IN-PUBLICATION DATA

Eshleman, Clayton.

Companion spider : essays / Clayton Eshleman ; foreword
by Adrienne Rich.

p. cm.

ISBN 0-8195-6482-6 (alk. paper)—ISBN 0-8195-6483-4
(pbk. : alk. paper)

1. Eshleman, Clayton—Aesthetics. 2. Translating and
interpreting. 3. Poetry—Translating. I. Title

PS3555.S5 C66 2002

418'.02—dc21   2001004218

for Lindsay Hill—without whose comradeship
this book could not have been completed.

Contents

Foreword

There is very little around today, certainly in the literary essay genre, that possesses the depth and substance of this book.

This is the accumulated prose-work of a poet and translator who has gone more deeply into his art, its process and demands, than any modern American poet since Robert Duncan or Muriel Rukeyser. As a poet, Eshleman has wrestled with his vocation and, in some senses, created himself through poetry. At the same time, he has offered poetry his inspired and tireless service. He is the translator of such essential world poets as César Vallejo, Aimé Césaire, Antonin Artaud, and Arthur Rimbaud, and the founder and editor of two important magazines of innovative literature and art, *Caterpillar* (1967–1973) and more recently *Sulfur* (1981–2000). He has written on the self-making and apprenticeship of the poet and of poet as translator, as no one else in North America in the later twentieth century. He has written perceptively about visual art in its relation to contemporary poetics. And he has delivered stinging critiques of mediocrity and cautiousness in the standardizing of poetic canons.

Eshleman's integrity as a translator has demanded meticulous searching of texts, glossaries, dictionaries, and intense collaborations. In "The Lorca Working," "At the Locks of the Void," and "Tribute to Américo Ferrari," among other pieces, he lays open the cartography of the poet-translator's work. Anyone wanting to study live, pulsing poetry will find these essays illuminating and contagious.

"Novices" and "Remarks to a Poetry Workshop" directly engage the nascent poet and introduce the concept of "apprenticeship"—to the work of earlier poets, to powerful living poets if possible: an apprenticeship that is a deep immersion, a recognition that art is difficult and exigent, an ocean and not a swimming pool, a calling and not a career path.

Through the variety of poets and visual artists whom he addresses, Eshleman evokes a community of no one place or time or language, where a younger poet might hang around to overhear conversations, absorb the individual gestures of certain remarkable practitioners. The reader is made aware of a complex of artistic practices to be explored, not to mention arguments and conflicts within the gathering.

A running criticism by Eshleman himself has to do with the exclusionary maleness of this tradition, its error in gendering concepts like muse or mentor, the defacement of Western tradition by misogyny. Eshleman clearly understands the meaning of entitlement—and of its lack. So I would unhesitatingly urge these essays upon women poets. Too little has been asked of us—by our peers, by feminist criticism, by the university workshop and the feminine ghetto. Eshleman writes of "blocks and chasms," of "strife and destruction" in the making of poetry, which are of the deep psyche, not the stuff of limited personal observation or attractive style. Eshleman's stormy and rigorous claims for the art belong to whoever needs them, whoever has felt "there must be more than this."

Crucial to this book is the idea of a lifelong commitment of self to art. There are novices who want poetry to enhance *them* by making them careers; there are others who vaguely or keenly sense that it's the vocation that matters, the long accountability to the word and the oceans and deserts around it. In several places, notably in the clear-eyed and compassionate essay on Artaud, or the Celan essay, Eshleman refers to the *stamina of poetry* (which is, of course, the stamina of the poet in the face of disaster). This stamina, along with prodigious empathetic capability, is embodied in Eshleman's own life/work. I am glad to see these essays entering a new form of accessibility, for those of our dazed and enraged era who surely have need of them.

Adrienne Rich
December 2000

I

Novices: A Study of Poetic Apprenticeship

Thou hast a lap full of seed,
And this is a fine country
Why dost thou not cast thy seed
And live in it merrily?
—*William Blake, 1793*

I came to see that art, as it was understood until 1800, was henceforth finished, on its
last legs, doomed, and that so-called artistic activity with all its abundance is only the
many-formed manifestation of its agony.
—Attributed (falsely it turned out) to Picasso, and
probably written by Giovanni Papini, in the early 1950s

These two "statements" drove lightning and rain through me as an apprentice to poetry, in Kyoto, in the early 1960s. It was as if I worked daily under the spell of personal potency and transpersonal impotency. Today still looking at the statements I see a propeller twist and then whirr, and in the haze of bladed motion the melding of yes and no that probably every young artist in most ages and places has had to stare at for many years, as he flexes in place, extending and contracting his claws . . .

For years I have wanted to make a trenchant declaration to those who are on the verge of an apprenticeship to poetry. I am not interested in being prescriptive, or rehearsing poetic terminology. I want to do here what the Introduction to Poetry textbooks *don't* do: to address the initial chaos as well as the potential coherence involved in making a commitment to poetry, and suggest that blocks and chasms are not to be avoided but are to be worked through and assimilated.

Chapters of "Novices" have appeared in the following publications: *Agni, Antiphonal Swing: Selected Prose 1962–1987* by Clayton Eshleman (McPherson & Co., Kingston, N.Y., 1989), and *Sulfur*. Again, my gratitude to my closest reader, Caryl Eshleman, for constructive criticism and suggestions during the writing of this study. *Novices* was first published in book form by Mercer & Aitchison (Los Angeles, 1989), which ceased to distribute it in 1990. It was dedicated to George Butterick.

On one level, we are all belated comers to that labyrinth in whose folds struggle between self and other is said to lead to the transformation of personality and significant art. On another level, the world now seems deeper and wider and more vector-permeated than ever before. Through the efforts of such multiply-based writers as Ezra Pound, Antonin Artaud, and Charles Olson, the image of the poet has been densified and removed from the academic-literary niche that had come to mean that the poet was merely a clever manipulator of his own sensitivity rather than a man or woman of knowledge.

What I intend to stress here is the most soulful and open image of the poet that I can grasp—an image that is involved with years of apprenticeship within the confines of a social structure that offers superficial handouts and massive undermining. These pages are for the young person who desires that impossible state identified by Artaud in the asylum at Rodez: "The great total dimension is to become as a simple man strong as all infinity."

CHAPTER I

(Charles Olson to Cid Corman, January 26, 1953)

"you must cease to think of a poem as anything but an expression of
THAT WHICH YOU ARE A SPECIALIST—which has to be, if it is a
poem, YRSELF, YR THINGS, no one else's, nothing else but that
which you are sure of
          and you must be prepared to find that you have
LITTLE to speak of: that, surprisingly enuf, is what we all find—that—
as The Confuser sd—it's all/as much/as on the back of a postage
stamp
      CLEARLY, you are writing abt what you think are the proper sub-
jects of writing—not at all abt one CID CORMAN:
                                  please *hear* me. I
am giving you a present. It's yrself.
                        We Americans have nothing but our
personal details. Don't let anyone fool you, any poet, any body. There is
nothing but all the details, sensations, facts which are solely known
to Cid Corman. And you must stick to them—get them straight—even
if (AS IT DAMN WELL IS) NOTHING. Understand? It will seem—
does seem to you—NOTHING: that is
                     why you are writing abt anything
but CORMAN. Because Corman to Corman is ZERO
                        what you don't
know is, that that is as it is for anyone but the pseudo-whatever:
                                that we
begin with ZERO—are O."[1]

Olson's ZERO is also the filled pot of yourself. You are stuffed as well as
empty. Perhaps you approach poetry, desirous of being affected by it,
because the friction between your impaction and your emptiness has
become unbearable—because you seek to bear it, bear the friction and
as in the image of giving birth, be reborn, bear yourself—

Artaud:

> And there is only one sun, one moon and stars because everyone yielded on this point about universal light to the conceptions of that phenomenal hood named god, instead of doing as in the real world where each individual enlightens himself on himself, as did van Gogh in order to paint the night with his 12 candled hat.
>
> None will initiate me into anything.
>
> All experience is resolutely personal.[2]

A few years earlier, Artaud had also written:

> We have never written anything except against a backdrop of the incarnation of the soul, but the soul already is made (and not by ourselves) when we enter into poetry.[3]

The charge is to enlighten yourself on yourself, to refuse continuing initiation by parents and teachers, but the contradiction (to be ingested, not stopped before) is that the discovery of poetry is also the discovery that the soul of the world has already been formed—it is an immense and detailed rose window made up of all the initiations and stories of imaginative art. It in fact includes stories and figures you will never know about because they are in languages (or places) that you will never read (or see). The cathedral was built way before you arrived. But you are not here to worship—

Robert Kelly:

> The typical mistake of religion has been to assume that what the priest does at the altar is somehow transmittable to me, poor dumb me sitting in the pew, kneeling there with my mouth open, that somehow some magic that he can perform in Latin or with his hands or in Mithra with a cut bull can transform me. And the superstition that lies there forgets that I must do something too; even if the magic part works I am transformed, but 10 minutes later my transformation falls off me just as I dry out after coming in from the rain. I mean, it may be real rain in that church, maybe that's real blood, but somehow my habits are sufficient to drain that out again, purify my animal nature. I think the poem gets harder in the way that a religion, if it were a real thing, would be a hard thing because it would inevitably be personal, it would inevitably be something *you* have to *do* & *I* have to do. That if I'm given a poem which tells me the whole thing I have no work to do with it. It can't save me then. I don't know exactly what I have to be saved from, but let's allow salvation for a moment—I can't be saved unless I do it myself. And I think poems become hard exactly as religion fades away—because we've

got to get the sense that nothing is really easy. There's a certain kind of person who will inevitably go to *The Cantos* or the *Maximus Poems* or some other ballbuster and make that his destiny for a year or two years, who recognizes however dumb he is when he starts out, there is something in this complexity that if he just go through it, if he follows the dance or the pattern or climbs the rock, he will have passed through a process which is not just a process of perception or critical judgement but a process of transformation.[4]

NOTES

1. Charles Olson, Letters for Origin (1950–1956), NYC, 1970, pp. 119–120. This edition, which contains only portions of Olson's letters to Cid Corman, and none of Corman's to Olson, is now out of print, and has been superseded by *Charles Olson & Cid Corman: The Complete Correspondence, 1950–1964*, Volume 1 (Orono, Maine, 1987), edited and annotated by George Evans (Volume 2 is due out spring 1989). In Olson's body of work (as in Rilke's and van Gogh's, for example) correspondence is a major element; in fact, at many points there is no genre difference between his poetry, letters, and essays. Concerning other important Olson correspondences, see footnote 1, chapter 13, and *Charles Olson & Robert Creeley: The Complete Correspondence*, edited and annotated by George Butterick, eight volumes of which have been published by Black Sparrow Press.

2. Antonin Artaud, *Letter to André Breton*, Sparrow 23, Santa Barbara, 1974. See the Note prefacing this letter for the particular initiation that occasioned Artaud's protest against all initiations.

3. *Antonin Artaud Anthology*, San Francisco, 1965, p. 100.

4. "Ta'wil or How to Read," *Vort* # 5, 1974, p. 140.

CHAPTER 2

In alchemical terminology, which also applies to writing poetry, prime or first matter is to be found in yourself. It is the uncreated, the *masa confusa*.[1] To be confused is to be inert; inertia is the primary sin, the dragon to be slain. You cut apart to name, to say that it is this and not that. In the *masa confusa* (your self, your ZERO = your uroboros, the swamp of your attempts at thought and emotional clarity) are all the seeds of what is to come.

The desire to write poetry leads first to seeing the *vilifigura*, the reviled face, the shame of your own face.[2] To embrace your soul may be to experience the extent to which you despise your soul, the extent to which whatever this soul is feels despised—for what have you actively asked of it before? Isn't it true that it has been left in the corner for years, collecting dust like a castaway doll? Loathing itself, its first motion upon suddenly being awakened may be to claw out at the one who has disturbed its remorseful holding pattern (and the clawed one may very well claw out at others; to suddenly wake up may mean fury at having been asleep so long e.g., Malcolm X in prison).

When I considered attempting to evade this turbulent, sickening confusion in Kyoto, 1963,[3] I saw I was faced with an alternative worse than confronting it, for that alternative seemed to consist in my attaching myself to another poet's leavings and saying: this will be my poem. Had I settled for this, I would have been proclaiming that my soul was so sick that I had to mask it with the soul of another, a soul-mask tried and successful (published, heralded, anthologized, consecrated by critics and scholars). With a lot of hard, unsatisfying, imitative work, this might have led to becoming a spoken cipher (instead of a ZERO), a diminution of another's energies.

It is natural to feel competitive with one's peers. But one is essentially not in competition with other poets. One is essentially only in competition with one's own death.

Alchemy suggests that to not evade the *masa confusa* is to search for that which can withstand dissolution and fire, that which experiences events as psychic process. Just to discover one's own resistances is something—to feel something push back when one pushes out (Olson later in the quoted-from letter to Corman writes: "that's what a poem is, a conjecture abt an experience we are, for what reason, seized by— BUT I MEAN SEIZED. It has to be something on our mind, really on our mind, at the heart of us—where it hurts").

> *Moonset, Gloucester,*
> *December 1, 1957, 1:58 AM*
>
> Goodbye red moon
> In that color you set
> west of the Cut I should imagine
> forever Mother
>
> After 47 years this month
> a Monday at 9 AM
> you set I rise I hope
> a free thing as probably
> what you more were Not
> the suffering one you sold
> sowed me on Rise
> Mother from off me
> God damn you God damn me my
> misunderstanding of you
>
> I can die now I just begun to live[4]

It is the unpoetic, the anti-poetic, that encloses the precious material—your actual thoughts while writing, what you want to overlook, the awkward, the ugly, thoughts that make you feel ashamed. What *do* you resist while writing? Does your mother swim forth and call you to bed? Do you recall with pleasure a perverse humiliation that took place when you were three? Do "bad words" mosquito your working space? Do you *want* to write and *need* to shit?

César Vallejo:

> *Intensity and Height*
>
> I want to write, but out comes spume,
> I want to say so much and I lurch in mud;

there's no spoken cipher which is not a sum,
there's no written pyramid, without interior bud.

I want to write, but I feel puma;
I want to laurel myself, but I utter onions.
There's no sproken cough which doesn't end in brume,
there is no god nor son of god, without evolution.

Because of this let's go, then, and feed on grass,
lamentation flesh, ululation fruit,
our melancholy soul preserve.

Let's go! Let's go! I'm wounded;
let's go and consume that already consumed,
let's go, blackbird, and fecundate your ladybird.[5]

Vallejo's resolution of this sonnet is less based on the idea of abandoning the frustrations of writing for sexual release (or death, if one reads "blackbird" as a death emblem), than it is on calling upon the animal powers of his imagination to redirect the physical blockage. The underpinning of this piece, as well as much of Vallejo's mature poetry, is the poet's acute sensitivity to the suffering of others, and his refusal to forget about it while writing.

Reflecting on the figure of Enion, in Blake's *The Four Zoas*, Northrop Frye writes:

> She is the "vain shadow of hope" which finds everything short of a complete apocalypse hopeless. She is the part of our minds which dimly realizes that all pleasure is at least partly a dream under an anesthetic. Something is always suffering horribly somewhere, and we can only find pleasure by ignoring that fact. We must ignore it up to a point, or go mad; but in the abyss of consciousness, to which Enion has been banished, there lurks the feeling that joy is based on exclusion, that the Yule log can blaze cheerfully only when the freezing beggars in the streets are, for the moment, left to freeze.[6]

The peristalic body of a poetry, visionary *and* critical (of its own insights as well as of the world), cannot be regularly rhythmic, cannot simply "flow," as long as the innocent suffer. I break my teeth on Apollo as long as my taxes issue forth as a blowtorch into the face of a Latin-American peasant. I swallow and I break. Broken and loaded. Symmetry implies perfection and is a lie as long as the world body is broken, tortured, in separation, and utterly (now) imperiled. "Fighting World War II took the equivalent of three megatons of TNT: all that and more now fits into the business end of a single MX missile."[7]

NOTES

1. Material on alchemy is taken from notes made listening to a James Hillman seminar on alchemy, Los Angeles, 1985; during Hillman's two days of lectures, I jotted down the basic outline for *Novices*. The key work on psychology and alchemy is C. G. Jung's *Mysterium Coniunctionis*. For material on the uroboros, see the first chapter of Erich Neumann's *The Origins and History of Consciousness*. For a critique of Neumann and an enlarged sense of the uroboros, see Wolfgang Giegerich's "Deliverance from the Stream of Events: Okeanos and the Circulation of the Blood," *Sulfur* # 21, 1988.

2. Diane Wakoski evokes the insidious strength of the *vilifigura* in "I have had to learn to live with my face" (from *The Motorcycle Betrayal Poems*, NYC, 1971):

> I want to go to sleep and never wake up.
> The only warmth I ever feel is wool covers on a bed.
> But self-pity could trail us all, drag us around on the bottom
> of shoes like squashed snails so that
> we might never fight / and it is anger I want now, fury,
> to direct at my face and its author,
> to tell it how much I hate what it's done to me,
> to contemptuously, sternly, brutally even, make it live with
>   itself,
> look at itself every day,
> and remind itself
> that reality is
> learning to live with what you're born with,
> noble to have been anything but defeated . . .

Another more transpersonal engagement with the sourness of self and background, as they thrust themselves upon the novice, is illustrated in Section V of Robert Kelly's "The Exchanges" (*origin* # 5, second series), as an omnipresent "black flower" that accompanies the poet everywhere.

3. See my *Coils* (Los Angeles, 1973). In his 1972 Preface to *Caesar's Gate*, Robert Duncan writes:

> I had, and still have—for again and again the apprehension returns—essential to my art, a horror of creation, as if beauty were itself the sign of an immanent danger. The announcement then of an imminent disclosure. It is the grue, the sense of coming near to grief, that signifies in the lore of Scotch folk, the weird of poetry. My art sought to spell that moment, even as I saw Peggy Linnet [an artist whose drawings were the symptom or flowering of a schizophrenic breakdown] in her art sought to dispel. In her house the vividness of that borderline of spelling and dispelling was felt as a kind of sea-sickness, a vertigo at the heart of the continent, the discovery of a discontinuity in the mass we would take experience to be, a poetic nausea.
>
> I had come to the pass in 1949 when I committed myself to Poetry, even as if to a madhouse or a religion. Yet it was a madness I had to make up, a conviction that I came to know only as I went into the depths of its invention in which I stood convicted of being its author. In the fiction of that authority I was without the guarantees of the authenticity I saw in madness. What Peggy Linnet suffered I projected. The grue was there, yes. A suspicion in poetry was growing in me. I would have, ultimately, to name the grief myself.

In another context, commenting on Artaud's ability to articulate excitations intolerable to his imagination, Duncan wrote: "We can entertain what he suffered." (*Letters*, Highlands, North Carolina, 1958).

4. Charles Olson, *The Distances*, NYC, 1960.

5. *Conductors of the Pit: Major Works by Rimbaud, Vallejo, Césaire, Artaud, and Holan* (translated by Clayton Eshleman), NYC, 1988, p. 43, with slight revisions.

6. Northrop Frye, *Fearful Symmetry*, Princeton, 1969, p. 279.

7. *Newsweek*, March 2, 1987, p. 72.

CHAPTER 3

In a "visionary moment dramatic" of the 7th Night of *The Four Zoas*, Blake writes:

> Los embrac'd the Spectre, first as a brother,
> Then as another Self, astonish'd, humanizing & in tears,
> In Self abasement Giving up his Domineering lust.

You are not who you think you are, you are something to be imagined. Your inertia, your *masa confusa*, is your spectre, and your spectre is not only to be scrutinized and cut apart, it is to be accepted and embraced. I am not my background, the novice cries, I am not merely a mass of assignments, restrictions, impulses, and black thoughts about others—but once I subtract all these—what do I have? At this point, poetry intensifies its glow on the horizon. I am that, the novice cries out again, I am those words of e. e. cummings, Dylan Thomas, Pablo Neruda, Rimbaud.

But in practice, to believe that one is the words others have found in the struggle to say themselves, is to screw one's ZERO onto the nozzle of a hose through which only others are pouring. At this point, there is the possibility of turning back to what of oneself has been rejected and saying: but I am that, on one important level, I am what I have been given and shaped into. This is the only wood I really have to put into the fireplace.

Then the novice possibly turns again to the smoldering horizon and understands something about the enormity of his task. His possible small fire is a joke compared to the dragon of flames emanating from the multi-chambered sun of achieved imagination—but at least he is holding his own log, and seeing that in essence his tiny fire may be of the same nature as the great one out there.

It all smarts so much, this burning water, this "thing" made up of ir-resolvable contradictions, this "thing" that is so much bigger than any combed-out "truth." The liquid spilling through the hose is flame; the most distant fire can be tapped right here. As he squats by the blazing red drops, this novice glimpses that making use of another's poetry is a double if not a triple bladed gesture. Since he only has his background to draw upon, he tries to think through its interstices, and hears himself murmuring, as if between waking and sleep:

> Come forth that I may slay you, father, and, slung across my shoulder, may your blood drip into my lute. I will call my slaying an embrace, and as I slay-embrace you, I will pocket a few of your organs, and reject the rest. I will call your marbles gems, and your gems marbles. And I will try to shuffle you into the deck of what I call my experience in the context of my times.

As he attempts to read "between the lines," to induct a poem's full connotational field, he notices that the lines do not want to yield, there seems to be no place for him between lines 1 and 2, or between 2 and 3, or 3 and 4. Perhaps he recalls, in his frustration, having read a version of the beginning of everything, with God separating the heavens from the waters of the deep. That God now seems to be a little like him, a son of God, a second-comer, trying to separate the lines from their own intense embrace—to push up a heaven line and pull an earth line down a bit, to make a place for little Me. Each act of reading as a writer be-comes for this novice an attempt at incision into a primal scene.

He begins to realize, this novice I am dreaming of, that he must look long and hard at coitus in order to escape intellectual inhibition, for co-itus is everywhere he looks—in bridge and windmill, furnace and vault—it is the recombining magma into which as a dreamer he is dipped, as if by animal tongs. In comparison to most poets, the Freu-dian ethnographers look bold—but then again, this novice thinks, they are not watching their own hands dissolve in burning liquid as I am—they have a distance—I am up against my own body as my hedge and hinge. And he continues to think: why do most poets appear to fear the lower body? Why does he have to go to N. O. Brown's *Love's Body* to find a clot like

> One of Melanie Klein's discoveries in the world of the unconscious is the archetypal—primordial and universal—fantasy of (parental) coitus as a process of mutual devouring—oral copulation; or rather, cannibalistic; and therefore combining in one act the two Oedipal wishes, parental

murder and incest; and including sexual inversion, since the male member is always seen as a breast sucked.[1]

To dwell on the grotesque with its chambers of warped, self-distorting mirrors, may be to increase the possibility of passing through a bottleneck that ultimately leads back to the world outside the novice, but a world which now has the novice inside it, as if he is in what he is looking at. For the primal scene parents are the "secretaries" of two sets of parents, the four grandparents, etc. From this viewpoint, the primal scene is buried at the base of the pyramid upon whose peak the novice thinks of himself as an individual. Turn the pyramid on its side, novice, and enter its peak. Who knows what you will find at the back wall—deified ancestors, human beings with animal heads, or roaring nothingness? And streaming out from the base, like giant squid tentacles, are those not the pyramid's roots connecting it to the kingdoms of the non-human other?

Gaston Bachelard, pondering Lautréamont, writes: there is "a *need* to *animalize* that is at the origins of imagination. The first function of imagination is to create animal forms."[2]

N. O. Brown, digesting Sandor Ferenczi's *Thalassa* as an aspect of *Love's Body:*

> Copulation is uterine regression. "The purpose of the sex act can be none other than an attempt to return to the mother's womb." "The sex act achieves this transitory regression in a three-fold manner: the whole organism attains this goal by purely hallucinatory means, somewhat in sleep; the penis, with which the organism as a whole has identified itself, attains it partially or symbolically; while only sexual secretion itself possesses the prerogative, as representative of the ego and its narcissistic double, the genital, of attaining in *reality* to the womb of the mother."
>
> Life itself is a catastrophe, or fall, or trauma. The form of the reproductive process repeats the trauma out of which life arose, and at the same time endeavors to undo it. The "uterine regressive trend in the sex act" is an aspect of the universal goal of all organic life—to return to the lifeless condition out of which life arose.[3]

NOTES

1. N. O. Brown, *Love's Body*, NYC, 1966, p. 25.
2. Gaston Bachelard, *Lautréamont*, Dallas, 1986, p. 27.
3. *Love's Body*, pp. 47 and 53. I refer to the novice as "he" because I am writing out of my male experience. I mention this at this point for several reasons. Most of the sources here come from male writers because, as a novice myself in 1960, the

artistic international field seemed overwhelmingly rich and it did not occur to me at that time to question the fact that this richness was also overwhelmingly male. I became aware while studying the *I Ching* in Kyoto in 1962 that the yin/yang differentiation associated man with day/clarity/good and woman with night/opaqueness/bad. This made me doubt its wisdom and it also helped me to start opening myself to "the darkening of the light," i.e., to powers that my critique of the *I Ching* made me realize I had previously been unaware of. I was so pent upon myself at the time that it did not occur to me to start investigating the implications of all this in terms of culture and society. Since the early 1970s, my poetry has hammered at patriachal sexuality, constantly attempting to block reader-escape from the fact that men usurp "self," misuse their strength against women (and against themselves), equate terror with glory and heroism, and control nearly all the power junctures in society. In this regard, I am in near agreement with Andrea Dworkin in her compelling book, *Pornography*. The reader might therefore inquire: why do you quote Ferenczi, then, where he not only restricts coitus to a male viewpoint, but treats women as no more than a conduit by which man attempts "to return to the mother's womb?" [And while their feel for the human is quite different, Ferenczi's view is not incompatible with that of Aleister Crowley for whom woman's body is no more than a "pylon" through which man might make contact with the infinite. In this regard, Tantrik sexuality might seem to exploit while Christian sexuality represses.] My response to the question above is the following: Ferenczi is still valuable because whether he intends to or not he unmasks male fantasy, and contributes his own speck of information about the nature of that living midden called the self. To what extent primordial impulses to penetrate/attack/fantasize belong to the male sphere I cannot and would not say. And while all of us should encourage women to explore realms that have previously (i.e., in historical time) been dominated by masculine compulsions and maps, men should not simply evade these truly loaded words, such as "masculinity" and "phallus" etc. All of us, I feel, are still in the rudimentary stages of exploring (and when necessary, dismantling) that gargantuan "I" that is not only a landmine but also the repository for much of our feeling of love and public trust. Too much avant-garde or experimental art appears to regard this grotesque "combined object" in a way that is evoked (in a different context, of course) by John Ashbery in his poem "Soonest Mended":

> And Angelica, in the Ingres painting, was considering
> the colorful but small monster near her toe, as though wondering whether forgetting
> The whole thing might not, in the end, be the only solution.

CHAPTER 4

Everything is material. You must learn to turn any flinch or fantasy into grist so as not to be bound to your own backside. You make a gain on your material when you are able to express that which you do not know, which, at the same time, seems welded to that which you feel you are. To pull up a fistful of crabgrass and feel the whole yard tremble. To lift a rock and see deep into the iguana's eyes.

The imagination as I understand it is synthesis in melee, melee in synthesis. Images are winding windows.

Arthur Rimbaud argued in 1871 that the poet via an ordered derangement of the senses must make himself monstrous[1] (here I read not only "freakish," but "marvelous," "prodigious," based on the Latin *monstrare*, to show—suggesting that the poem is a full or amplified showing, to the extent that it becomes grotesque, beyond observational limits). I would footnote Rimbaud's statement with: and the imagination must become mongrel, freed of racial stratification, released from the prism of white supremacy,[2] whose self-reflecting facets include purity, sanctity, spirituality, sublimity, forever, and God.

You sit down with the intention of saying something nice about someone you love. Before your fingers can touch the keys an inversion takes place: a worm peers out of the apple, or something merely irrelevant falls like a veil across your intended address. Psyche has cautiously opened her bedroom door and glanced into the hallway; she has responded to your intention by turning it upside down, or by making it sound irrelevant, or dumb. She will stay in the doorway for a moment, seeing if you bite. If you can absorb and immediately assimilate her inversion, she may smile, and her smile may crack your line in two. Chances are you will disregard her query, and she will shut the door, at which point you will mush on through your intended program, the prisoner of your intention, going through its paces, resolute, predict-able, over before it has begun. You will have a limited number of chances with Psyche and her door. Too many initial closures and she will abandon you to *closure as a routine*, which might be defined in the following way: poetry as reification/reinforcement of what has taken place in the past. The past as a citadel, imagination its court life—the present as heretical, that which is to be swept out of sight, the refuse. The door Psyche opens is a breach between walled-off present and walled-off past. Her desire is to have intercourse with the poet, to slip out the Puritan plank between her resting place and his.

Linear time, Puritanic time. The "light at the end" to justify this struggle, this now. But such "light" is a haze, is nothing, is distraction from the here and now. When I focus on my literal death, my glance drifts to a vanishing point. Tunnel vision is no vision. Instead, populate the tunnel with bathing shelves, bring in the rats. Let's gnaw into a bask, corrode the relaxed sides of the image, set in stained glass, alcoves with access to the Hitlers of the heart, our dread of vanishing, our need to plug up our hole and by doing so, banish all difference, all otherness . . . all that does not reinforce our uniqueness. Alas, but hooray, we are not unique. Unlike trees, we are adrift in a breath bowl, rootless algae, wings searching for angelic bodies.

NOTES

1. Best summation of Rimbaud's achievement I know of is Kenneth Rexroth's five pages on him in *Classics Revisited*.
2. See James Hillman's "Notes on White Supremacy," *Spring* 1986.

CHAPTER 5

My first poem was called "The Outsider," and was a timid, versified re-enactment of the feelings I had picked up reading Colin Wilson's *The Outsider*, a book which introduced me to the visionary figure on the periphery of societal centers, in 1957. However, my first engagement with poesis took place when I was a freshman at Indiana University, 1953, in Herbert Stern's Freshman Composition class. After having given us several assignments (which I had done poorly with), he said: write anything you want to.

I wrote a kind of prose-poem, in the voice of an aging prostitute, standing at her hotel window, watching newspaper and rubbish blow down a deserted street at 4 AM. Stern gave me an A– and under the grade wrote: *see me*. When I sat down in his office, he told me that the piece was excellent but that I was in trouble because I had not written it. I still recall his words: "the person who wrote this did not write your other themes." I protested and in the end he believed me, and said: "if you can write like that, there are a couple of books you should read." On a scrap of paper, which he handed me, he wrote: *The Metamorphosis*, and under it, *Portrait of the Artist as a Young Man*. To what extent Stern himself was conscious of the significance of this particular juxtaposition, I will never know—but by citing the Kafka story (which I waited two years to read), he had identified what had happened to me in my "free theme," and by citing Joyce (which I read nine years later), had he offered me the challenge to become an artist?

In my theme I had aged myself, changed my sex, and dressed up as a parody of my mother. The figure was utterly fictional—I knew nothing about prostitutes, and that was probably part of the point too: contra Olson, I had entered imagination by speaking out of a place I had never personally experienced. I had left the confines of an "assignment"—my entire life up to that time and then some was framed by assignments—and wandered into an "other." *Je est un autre*, Rimbaud had written when he was 17. I am a metaphor. Clayton is a prostitute, Clayton is not merely Clayton. Clayton does not merely live in the Phi Delta Theta fraternity house and take abuse daily as a "pledge." Clayton is a 55 year old woman looking out on a street that does not exist.

A move toward origin. Toward our so-called "face before birth." Toward that which we are but will never be. Toward what we were but are not. The initial fascination with writing poetry is similar to a visit to an astrologer and a request for a horoscope. My aged whore positioned me toward a past in the present, indicating (though I did not realize it then) continuity and depth. The street was empty except for blowing (unreadable) newspapers, yesterday's news. It was empty and I was to populate it with my own news—I was to learn how to read the street, and to get used to not being myself. I was, like a tree still rooted in Indiana earth, to learn how to twist within my own bark and observe "other" things around me.

CHAPTER 6

When I was teaching at the California Institute of the Arts in 1971, I had writing students who were smoking a lot of dope and taking LSD. I wanted to move them further in and further out,[1] to help them become more inward and more outward, because conventional recognitions (the enemy of imaginative perceptions) live on a threshold between careful observation and proprioceptive awareness, drugs or no drugs. Ultimately, as the phrase "imaginative awareness" is intended to suggest, poetic mind moves so rapidly between the inner and the outer that in many cases (Montale and Vallejo come immediately to mind) the distinction appears to be eliminated.

The outer-oriented exercise at Cal Arts made use of objects in conjunction with texts by Francis Ponge.[2] I brought fruit, paintings, and things like an art-nouveau ashtray, into the classroom, put them one at a time on the table, and asked the students to simply look at the object for 15 minutes and then to write a paragraph of what they had seen. We read and discussed Ponge's prose-poems on a boat, an oyster, wine, or rain, etc., as examples of permeative observation. Initially, many student paragraphs were so disoriented that the object itself was not present. Some students who applied themselves and took the course a second semester improved considerably. One day I brought a bottle of 1962 Brane-Cantenac to class; we all went outside and sitting in a circle, sipping the wine, commented on what it said to us when we rolled it in our mouths; then I asked the students to write down what they associated with the taste of the wine.

The inner-oriented exercise was more complicated, and almost impossible to do in class. I had been struck by a phrase that the painter Francis Bacon used in a BBC conversation with David Sylvester. When asked how he arrived at his images, Bacon responded that they often came from "semi-conscious, or subliminal scanning." I understood this to mean that Bacon worked in a kind of trance between waking and dreaming, where things decompose, merging and fraying with memories and sensations. I have trained myself to write in such a state, encouraging image-chains to proliferate, so as to not will the poem but in a way that is hard to explain, to accompany it on its way. There is an alchemical image of a man semi-reclined, watching with intense interest a tree which has grown out of his groin. That image is a stunning example of the self-connectedness *and* otherness of art as I understand it.

One problem at Cal Arts was: how to get the students to notice and to articulate psychic processes?[3] I asked them to try free-associating out loud in class, and to follow the associations as well as the sounds of the words. Everyone began by stammering out disconnected gerunds and/or nouns, like "sun . . . clouds . . . flying . . . dreaming . . . moon . . . bird . . ." which indicated to me that censorship was extremely active in the intervals between the words, and that the uttered words were ones which had passed the acceptable-as-images-of-myself test. It was impossible for anyone to keep the exercise going, even in a halting state, for more than a minute. When I asked people to put in "I/s," to encourage a more self-involved participation, most students would stop after a few seconds and say they couldn't continue. The few that kept at it uttered clichés and pieces of advertising jargon and expressed amazement that when they tried to free-associate out loud clichés and jargon were what came out. They seemed to have no ability to put together word combinations that were in any sense spontaneously unusual. We discussed Allen Ginsberg's little aphorism, "First thought, best thought," and spent a lot of time pondering what was and what was not a thought.

To a certain extent, it was the *vilifigura* thumbing its nose at the silences between stammered out words, a fear of revealing material to peers and to me. I think this touches on the core problem of the creative writing workshop: peer pressure encourages the throwing up of defenses—justifications, rationalizations, hurt feelings—rather than the lowering of them so as to enable Psyche to make some unexpected gestures in the poems-to-be. I asked the students to try the exercise alone at home on a cassette recorder and try to detect "holes" in patterns, ways in to their concerns, as if they were a halfback, the football suddenly snapped into their hands; the play has misfired and they must immediately find an alternative hole in the wall of advancing defense.

From 1969 to 1973, I practiced this exercise myself, alone with a cassette. While I never used taped sequences per se in poems, I think the practice loosened me up and made me more daring in admitting fascinating *and* irrelevant (at the moment of presentation) words while writing. Such chains as "ale the heil in to roo the bovine sky over what roots," or "hear the ore masted in the world Ulyssean siren wax," made me more flexible and porous to sounds and associations (bovine sky, ore masted) which enable poems to veer and recharge, making little leaps between "the clashing rocks" of the conventional and the insignificant (that defensive wall in which holes must be found in order to really run and, as Robert Duncan once put it, exercise one's faculties at large).

NOTES

1. The idea that conventional poetry fails to thrust in or thrust out was brought to my attention by Olson's "*Outside, Inside:* Notes on Narrative, provoked by Mr. Creeley's stories," which appeared in *New Directions* annual # 13, 1951.

2. At Cal Arts I used Cid Corman's Ponge versions (*Things*, NYC, 1971); since then, Beth Archer's translation of some of the same poems as well as others has appeared (*The Voice of Things*, NYC, 1974). Both translations are acceptable, and rather than choosing between them, it is more useful to read a Corman version and an Archer version of the same poem together with a French-English dictionary, looking up words the translators disagree upon. In this connection, see the issues of *Caterpillar* magazine (1967–1973), where 10 "Tests of Translation" (modeled upon Louis Zukofsky's *A Test of Poetry*) appeared.

3. Besides the two exercises discussed here, there was a third, in the form of a reading/writing notebook that I have continued to make use of for over 15 years. Students are asked to draw a horizontal line across each page of a large notebook, and to keep the notebook open by any book of poetry they are reading. Quotations go in the top half; response in the bottom half. The idea here is to break down the distance between reading and writing, and to encourage the student to start poems while reading as well as to turn from a stalled piece of his own writing back to a text he had previously been reading.

CHAPTER 7

The alchemist Fulcanelli:

> The picture of the labyrinth is thus offered to us as emblematic of the whole labour of the work, with its two major difficulties, one the path which must be taken in order to reach the centre—where the bitter combat of the two natures takes place—the other the way which the artist must follow in order to emerge. It is there that *the thread of Ariadne* becomes necessary for him, if he is not to wander among the winding paths of the task, unable to extricate himself.[1]

Anton Ehrenzweig:

> Any creative search, whether for a new image or idea, involves the scrutiny of an often astronomical number of possibilities. The correct choice between them cannot be made by a conscious weighing up of each single possibility cropping up during the search; if attempted it would only lead us astray. A creative search resembles a maze with many nodal points. From each of these points many possible pathways radiate in all directions leading to further crossroads where a new network of high- and by-ways comes into view. Each choice is equally crucial for further progress. The choice would be easy if we could command an aerial view of the entire network of nodal points and radiating pathways still lying ahead. This is never the case. If we would map out the entire way ahead, no further search would be needed. As it is, the creative thinker has to make a decision about his route without having the full information needed for his choice. This dilemma belongs to the essence of creativity.[2]

From the 1950 *Webster's New International Dictionary:*

> panopticon (pan + Gr. *optikon*, neut. of *optikos* of or for sight). 1. A kind of optical instrument, as a combination of a telescope and microscope. 2. A prison built so radially that the guard at a central position can see all the prisoners. 3. A place where everything can be seen; an exhibition room for novelties.[3]

There is an archetypal poem, and its most ancient design is probably the labyrinth. One suddenly cuts in, leaving the green world for the apparent stasis and darkness of the cave. The first words of a poem propose and nose forward toward a confrontation with what the writer is only partially aware of, or may not be prepared to address until it emerges, flushed forth by digressions and meanders. Poetry twists toward the unknown and seeks to realize something beyond the poet's initial awareness. What it seeks to know might be described as the unlimited interiority of its initial impetus. If a "last line," or "conclusion," occurs to me upon starting to write, I have learned to put it in immediately, so it does not hang before me, a lure, forcing the writing to constantly skew itself so that this "last line" continues to make sense as such.

As far as poetry is concerned, "the bitter combat of the two natures" can be understood as the poet's desire to discover something new or unique vs. the spectral desire of tradition to defeat the new and to continue to assert its own primacy. It is a "bitter" combat because the realization which writing a poem may provide is inevitably partial. The Minotaur is at best crippled, never slain, and the poet never strides forth from the labyrinth, heroic and intact. At best he crawls forth, "wounded" as in the cry of Vallejo in *Intensity and Height;* more often than not, he never emerges at all. The poet never leaves this combat with a total poem, because such a poem would confirm that the discrepancy between desire and the fulfillment of desire had been eliminated. But since my desire is ultimately to create reality and not merely to observe it, I am bound to be defeated if reality is at stake in my poem's ambition. As I emerge from my poem, regardless of what I have realized while in the poem, I am back in the observable biological continuum, and part of it, part of its absolute mortality. I suspect that I am always aware of *this* closure, and that it underwrites (asunder-writes) what I envision while inside the poem.

Harold Bloom's "Six Revisionary Ratios,"[3] which propose to identify "intra-poetic relationships" among the poets that for Bloom constitute an Anglo-American Romantic tradition, may be most useful to poets themselves as a reading of the stages involved in working through a particular poem. Bloom of course intends his "ratios" to challenge current critical attitudes, and as such, it is a book that could only offend poets who are not named as part of the center stage action of Bloom's "tradition," which becomes increasingly arbitrary as it approaches the present. Its argument in which an earlier poet becomes the focus of a struggle on the part of a later poet, who must wrest mana from the former in order to assert himself, is actually depicted by Blake in his vision of his struggle with Milton in *Milton: A Poem.* My idea here is to regard this "struggle" in the context of Fulcanelli's and Ehrenzweig's images of the labyrinth as a symbol of the creative process, in which much more than literary combat takes place. The nodes, or advance positions, that send out radial possibilities everywhichway, are charged with the poet's personal life as well as the context of his times, to mention two considerable influential powers that lie outside Bloom's sense of influence.

Here are Bloom's Six Ratios, followed by the keyword he focuses them with:

1. Clinamen, or Swerve
2. Tessera, or Completion
3. Kenosis, or Emptying
4. Daemonization, or Counter-Sublime
5. Askesis, or Curtailment
6. Apophrades, or Holding Open to the Dead

Is it possible that these terms double Fulcanelli's three-beat rhythm of the labyrinth, offering a more complex and assymetrical sense of the contractions and expansions involved in solving the burden many but not all poems take on?

The poet Swerves into the poem by redirecting his attention from the utilitarian world to one in which "precise subjectivity"[4] is constantly at stake. Or think of the poet as a falling angel who refuses at the last moment to continue to fall and become one of the fallen (= unimaginative man, the literal minded, one for whom the objective world is the real world). He Swerves, beating his wings up, up, up, and enters a new space.

The Swerve into imaginative space together with the first few words or lines, determine mode, tone, direction, and some of the difficulties to be undertaken. Once all of this is in place the poem runs the risk of lapsing into a conventional handling of its direction, in effect Completing itself before it has even gotten underway (as a joke poorly told may imply its punchline and thus be "over" before its actual punchline falls). While the taking on of direction is necessary, if the direction takes its theme or subject matter for granted, the reader has "heard it before," and the poem no longer belongs to itself. Thus the initial move toward Completion must be redirected, or complexed, in order to build up steam, or availability to the unknown that is beyond the poem's initial knowing. Such a move is a contractive one, and would be the Empty-ing, or willingness to introduce contradiction and/or obscurity via sound-oriented or associational veers.

Emptying makes it possible for the poem to have space for the other or the otherness that can be the most single compelling moment in composition. Daemonization (in contrast to demonization) is the ad-mitting of unconscious material into the composition-in-process, the point at which the poet weds himself, consciousness and unconscious-ness fuse—the poet is the world, no separation between his skin and everything else. The eagle of inspiration has sunk its talons into the poet's shoulders and he is borne aloft. There are many ways to ap-proach this moment: in Blake it would be the moment in which the au-thors in eternity communicate to mortal secretary William. In D. H. Lawrence, the moment that the wind does blow through him (Law-rence states the archetypal daemon plea in: "Not I, not I, but the wind that blows through me!"[5]). García Lorca, weary of hearing critics and conventional poets prattle about the Muse and the angel, borrowed from the world of flamenco dancing the figure of the "duende," which translates into English rather poorly as "imp." It is a figure of the blood for Lorca,[6] an uprushing or seizure, in which the dancer and poet is momentarily possessed, or incubated (as if by a dream succubus, who lays a psychic egg in the dreamer's body as she fucks him, and "steals" his semen).

Daemonization is perilous because as such it cannot complete the poem (when we are stoned, daemons seem to rush through us, but when we try to articulate their message-sensations, we have nothing—if not less than nothing, for the Daemon of Marijuana loves to gobble up imaginative potential, eating the poem on the spot that had we not got-ten stoned might have been *written* the following day). Curtailment is similar to Emptying, in that both are experienced as severe, contractive moments—however, Curtailment is more complex, because the poem has taken on much more burden and possibly unmanageable material than earlier. If the poet does not successfully separate himself from the Daemon's embrace or claws, one result is that inspiration turns into ego-inflation (nearly always just around the corner in Whitman or Gins-berg). In Curtailment (Bloom's Ratio term, Askesis, is based on "as-cetic"), the poet must cut into his own beanstalk, bringing the drama tumbling down or seeing into the meaning of the action in Giant Castle through a narrowing, densifying perception. Or to put it another way: in

Curtailment, I step outside the poem and in a sense become my own critic, looking for loose ends, ego-inflations that have gotten into the Daemonization, gaps to be plugged—while at the same time I must stay with the shape of the energy recast by the Daemonization.

Bloom's Apophrades is a marvelous image. The dead, the great dead, return to inhabit our houses—life returns to before that fall in which a Swerve was a possibility. The dead return—the poem is over, *the way things are* overwhelms metaphor. The poet, like a streaker now, shows himself to the dead, a phantomic act the dead could care little about. The dead return, life returns to its deadliness, its obliviousness to poetry. Our poems end because at Curtailment we know we cannot escape the product of the poem if we are to have art at all; we know we cannot sustain the poem against the desire of the dead to reinhabit the *temenos* they believed they inhabited in their own time. In a great closure (Wallace Stevens' "Each person completely touches us / with what he is and he is / In the stale grandeur of annihilation."[7]) there is a shadowed Daemonization, an embrace at the edge of here and not-here.

The dead are now back in our houses. We are outside, outsiders to the poem, peripheral, schizophrenic, caught up in the physical need to reconnect. Every completed poem collects its rejected children, bundles them into its immense laundry-basket and takes off. Images of its huge ass, in peasant shoes, hurrying away from van Gogh's corn field.

NOTES

1. Fulcanelli: Master Alchemist, *Le Mystère des Cathédrales*, London, 1974, p. 48. On the following page, Fulcanelli offers an alchemical definition of Ariadne. "Placements II," in my *The Name Encanyoned River: Selected Poems 1960–1985*, explores the resonance of Ariadne as the "mistress of the labyrinth."

2. Anton Ehrenzweig, *The Hidden Order of Art*, Berkeley, 1971, pp. 35–37. Ehrenzweig's drawing of "the maze (serial structure)" on p. 36, reminds me of shattered glass more than of the concentrically infolding/outfolding labyrinth. See also van Gogh's *Starry Night*, with its two milky flows of light, one curling down to tuck into the other curling up—a figure Wilhelm Reich identified as "Cosmic Superimposition." The so-called "serial poem" (Whitman's "Song of Myself," Jack Spicer's "Books") attempts to make use of nodal discontinuities, viewing sections as corresponding rather than connecting.

3. Harold Bloom, *The Anxiety of Influence*, NYC, 1973, pp. 14–15. The novice must decide to what extent Bloom's highly exclusionary study (in which only several 20th century American poets appear in a context that presents them as representing the end of an essentially English literary tradition) is a projection of his own anxious desire to be with poets, one of them, a poet himself. Is it possible that in failing to realize himself as a poet, he envisions the end of a great tradition in his

own time, and appoints himself as the eagle-surveyor on a crag overlooking a bat-tlefield of his own construction that stretches narrowly back to Milton?

4. Robert Kelly's phrase, which will appear in his own context later in *Novices*.

5. *The Complete Poems of D. H. Lawrence*, Vol. 1, NYC, 1964, p. 250.

6. "Theory and Function of the Duende," *Lorca*, The Penguin Poets, London, 1960. See Robert Duncan's novice encounter with Lorca elaborated in the 1972 Preface to *Caesar's Gate*. For distinctions between "daemon" and "demon," see James Hillman's *The Dream and the Underworld*, NYC, 1979, especially the "Bar-riers" section, which considers Materialism, Oppositionalism, and Christianism. Emily Dickinson's # 754, written around 1863, is as severe a description as I know of Daemonization and the extent to which its possession can become a life posses-sion, a living out of an alien other's commands. Lawrence emphasizes unconscious message over the poet's willing; in Dickinson's visionary description, the poet is seen as a tool (a gun), at the trigger-mercy of an owner-duende who can fire her at whim (see Susan Howe's thoughtful and differing consideration of this poem in *My Emily Dickinson*, Berkeley, 1985):

> My Life had stood—a Loaded Gun—
> In Corners—till a Day
> The Owner passed—identified—
> And carried Me away—
>
> And now We roam in Sovereign Woods—
> And now We hunt the Doe—
> And every time I speak for Him—
> The Mountains straight reply—
>
> And do I smile, such cordial light
> Upon the Valley glow—
> It is as a Vesuvian face
> Had let its pleasure through—
>
> And when at Night—Our good Day done—
> I guard My Master's Head—
> 'Tis better than the Eider-duck's
> Deep Pillow—to have shared—
>
> To foe of His—I'm deadly foe—
> None stir the second time—
> On whom I lay a Yellow Eye—
> Or an emphatic Thumb—
>
> Though I than He—may longer live
> He longer must—than I—
> For I have but the power to kill,
> Without—the power to die—

7. Wallace Stevens, *The Collected Poems*, NYC, 1957, p. 505.

CHAPTER 8

My sense of poetic labyrinth here is very flexible—for one writer "the bitter combat" at the center may fill the stage, and for another opening and/or closure may be so difficult that the other stages seem to be non-existent. And too, there are experiences of the labyrinth which are not engaged by the use I have made of Bloom's "Ratios." To some extent, the elaboration of any vision is labyrinthine. Olson's vision of Homer's *Odyssey* as a dance-drama, in which a shaman-hero dances his way through a gauntlet of monsters to be reunited with a human other,[1] suggests how labyrinthine a 20-year voyage can be. While a single poem may be experienced as working through a maze, such a poem may also be a mere knot in a network that comprises all the writer's poems as well as his unwritten life. In relation to the labyrinth, I would like to consider one of several existent poetic Curriculums for novices. Unlike the others I will mention later, it is not a set of proposals or even an argument, but a tilting assembly of names, subjects, and ideas that evokes the accesses and restrictions of the labyrinth itself.

Charles Olson's "A Plan for a Curriculum of the Soul" may be especially baffling for the novice accustomed to poetry anthologies that for the most part contain poems which the editors feel are self-contained, and can be examined and taught as discrete objects. Poets who tend to write discrete lyrics (Robert Herrick, Emily Dickinson, Robert Frost) can be fairly represented in such anthologies. Poets whose work is primarily constellational—in which individual poems refer not only to themselves but are part of the diagram of a larger constellation—are poorly represented. This is a primary reason, in my opinion, for by-passing anthologies and reading all poets in terms of individual books that in most cases they themselves organized.[2] This does not mean that such poets as William Blake, Ezra Pound, and Charles Olson only write poems that are referential to their own systems—all three, in fact, have written superb self-contained lyric poems. What it does mean is that to appreciate a passage in *The Four Zoas*, or *The Cantos*, or *The Maximus Poems*, you need to know the way in which the entire poem relates to what has come before and after it in the poet's body of work. Poets who attempt to increase the responsibilities of poetry by drawing upon the materials of non-literary disciplines—who in effect strive for a vision big enough to combat the resistance of their times to poetry—are almost inevitably pedagogical.

On February 9, 1968, Olson sent his student George Butterick a two-page "outline" that on the one hand was probably spontaneous (reflecting current preoccupations) and on the other the result of twenty years of research and writing. Such a "Plan" suggests a mysterious correspondence between terrestrial labyrinths, star maps, and the human mind. Not only does this "Plan" fail to follow the steps of most outlines, it treats its "subjects" as if they were pick-up sticks that had suddenly been loosed from the poet's grip, falling everywhichway on the page. The only "direction" is that indicated by the fact that the title, one third of the way down on the right-hand page, is under a phrase ending in the word "completion," suggesting that the "Plan" is to be read as a kind of asymmetrical swirl, working down from the title on the right-hand page, crossing over to the left-hand page and following it upward, then crossing back to the right-hand page and ending with "completion." The problem with following such a direction is that the left-hand page has obviously been written from the top down. Another reading possibility is to disperse with direction entirely, and take the subjects and suggestions as "free bodies" brought together in a single double-page arena. If they are taken as a set of leads, the novice can follow them out himself. By coming to terms with "Alchemy—rather by plates [as connected to dreams]" or with what Olson might mean by "Bach's *belief*," he can (often by arguing with Olson) start to develop his own assembly of intersecting subjects or directions.

how to live as a
single natural being
the dogmatic nature of
(order of)
experience

how many?
& how each
made known,
exercised,

as _____

organs &
function—activity
of the soul
or psyche or
Heaven or God

Ismaeli muslimism

&, all together,
create
organism

Alchemy—rather by plates

⌊as connected to dreams⌋

pictorialism

as in Earth, "View"

& perspective

/cf. Weyl on ocular

power

Vision

✗

Messages

technically, Analytic Psychology, as only technical study I
know of modern Western man under enough mental
control

jazz playing

dance as individual
body-power

equally say Homer's art
Bach's belief
⌊ cf. Novalis'
"subjects"

the Norse & the Arabs

- locally, American
Indians

Egyptian hieroglyphs
drawing

(gesture, speech
habits condition
mental

<u>matter</u>

<u>Phenomenological</u>

<u>Sensation</u>   and   <u>Attention</u>   ∕training in exhaustion &
                                                      completion

A Plan for a Curriculum of the Soul

	(Intuition	
	& Feeling	one's own
the Mushroom	dream woman	mind ∧ language

<u>Earth</u>   as a
     geology ∧ comprehension like archeology
     geography - equally, though here maps & experience of
human history ⌐   walking

                    in this connection, as habitat
          inhabitation of, rather than as politics say
              or national. Instead, <u>physical</u>, &
              <u>vertically incremental</u>   physical

     man as animal ∕ praxis of - as Earth as a

emotional mental experience

Poets   as such, that is disciplined lives not
       history or for any "art" reasons <u>example,</u>

Blake ⌐

          └the same, say, medicine men

     & like theologians: example, Dante - Giotto

Charles Olson

Butterick objected to the word "drugs" in the copy sent to him by Olson, and apparently made other objections to the "Plan." In a letter of February 26, Olson replied:

> Just for further accuracy please change words drugs in 1st line of Plan for a Curriculum of the Soul to the Mushroom. I find your objection, that there is nothing new in the above, a curious demand, and not actually relevant, I don't think, to the proposal. That is, the need, in fact—or at least what seemed to me the gain of this particular spreading was to have a congestin [*sic*] which ought to be including and likewise exclusive. Or at least that, so placed, it can then be tested for thoroughness. In fact what new is as interesting now as condensation?[3]

It is fascinating to follow out what has been done to date with Olson's "Plan." It was first published in *Magazine of Further Studies* #5, 1968, and was subsequently taken up as an investigative poetic "working" by another Olson student (and the editor of *Further Studies*), Jack Clarke, who selected twenty-eight words from the total 223, and after consulting two other students, Albert Glover and Fred Wah, assigned these words to twenty-eight members of the Olson community, with the proposal that each would write a twenty- to fifty-page "fascicle" off of that word. All but five fascicles have been written and published (for the most part in the early 1970s). When all twenty-eight are completed, along with Olson's *Pleistocene Man* (letters to Clarke, during October 1965), to be included in the set without a number, the "Curriculum" will be bound and published as a single volume, each fascicle becoming a chapter.

It is difficult to say to what extent the individual fascicles are successful; most are novice work, writing by Olson-allied students who by the early 1970s had only a fragmentary sense of Olson's body of work and who had not, at least at that time, found their own footing.[4] Only a handful represent significant research contributions to Olson's subjects or could be considered engaging collections of poetry. However, more important than achievement in this instance is the extent to which the fascicles demonstrate that there was a circle of novices around a single poet who cared enough for his vision to contribute up to fifty pages on a single word of it. Olson did not *assign* the fascicles; they were generated by the students themselves. In response to my letter inquiring as to what use had been made of the "Plan" and the fascicles, Clarke replied:

> Actually, there has been no thought of "use" of it, only a place to be together, the O-community i.e., those living in his "world," his "soul."

After his death in 1970, we all needed something to survive the boredom of what was to follow i.e., *before the war*, as Duncan says. We will soon publish the definitive text of *Dante* [Duncan's fascicle, #8], replacing both the earlier fascicle and [the poem in] *Groundwork*, to be sold modestly as "book," i.e., that will be Glover Publishing *for* the Institute of Further Studies.

NOTES

1. For Olson's perceptive notes on the Upper Paleolithic, see *Olson* #10, 1978, Storrs, CT. Ten issues of *Olson* were researched, edited, and annotated by George Butterick as part of his own poetic apprenticeship. Butterick, who also edited and annotated over 4,000 pages of Olson's poetry, prose, and correspondence, died of cancer in July, 1988, at 46. While he wrote poetry at many points over the two decades of his full-time Olson scholarship, he gave Olson all the front burners, modestly placing his own poems on back ones. Butterick's gesture is tragically moving and perhaps unique in a world in which most novices, sidestepping the risks of a prolonged apprenticeship, only find time for themselves.

2. Other reasons to avoid anthologies: teachability is a prime consideration (how much Stein, Zukofsky, and Spicer do you find in current anthologies?)—especially as the selections move toward the present, easy-to-read poems that follow in the wake of the established teachable masters are the rule. The editors are not entirely to blame (though nearly all of them go along with the situation), as trade publishers rely considerably on reports from the field (who the professors want to teach) when they decide whether or not a particular anthology (after production and often high permission fees) will make a profit. While minority poets appear with increasing regularity, many appear to be selected on two bases: they will give the anthology a democratic appearance, and they will not offend Professor X because the poems selected read like the poems of their mainstream male writing-workshop contemporaries.

3. When looking at someone's outline or program for others, it is important to decide if their own poetry and poetics back it up. Olson's concern with "spreading," "congestin'," and "condensation" has underpinnings in his work at large. The "Plan" is one of many manifestations of Olson's attempt to revision life as turning on a single center, with the poet as integral to a will to cohere. The "Plan" thus embodies the tension between his extensive "spread" of historical and interdisciplinary materials, and his ongoing "condensation" of his findings. See "The Gate and the Center" essay in *Human Universe*, NYC, 1967. Unfortunately, like most poets of his generation (Robert Duncan being a striking exception), he assumed a male reader. Thus in the "Plan," men are identified as individuals e.g., Bach, Blake, Dante, Novalis, Weyl—and women generically as Woman.

4. The Institute of Further Studies fascicles are as follows:
   1. *The Mushroom*, by Albert Glover, 1972.
   2. *Dream*, by Duncan McNaughton, 1973.
   3. *Woman*, by John Wieners, 1972.
   4. *Mind* (assigned to Robert Creeley).
   5. *Language* (assigned to Edward Dorn).
   6. *Earth*, by Fred Wah, 1974.

7. *Blake*, by John Clarke, 1973.
8. *Dante*, by Robert Duncan, 1974.
9. *Homer's Art* (reassigned to Alice Notley).
10. *Bach's Belief* (assigned to Robin Blaser).
11. *Novalis' "Subjects,"* by Robert Dalke, 1973.
12. *The Norse*, by George Butterick, 1973.
13. *The Arabs*, by Edward Kissam, 1972.
14. *American Indians*, by Edgar Billowitz, 1972.
15. *Jazz Playing*, by Harvey Brown, 1977.
16. *Dance*, by Lewis MacAdams, 1972.
17. *Egyptian Hieroglyphs*, by Edward Sanders, 1973.
18. *Ismaeli Muslimism*, by Michael Bylebyl, 1972.
19. *Alchemy*, by David Tirrell, 1972.
20. *Perspective*, by Daniel Zimmerman, 1974.
21. *Vision*, by Drummond Hadley, 1972.
22. *Messages*, by James Koller, 1972.
23. *Analytic Psychology*, by Gerrit Lansing, 1983.
24. *Organism*, by Michael McClure, 1974.
25. *Matter*, by John Thorpe, 1975.
26. *Phenomenological* (assigned to Joanne Kyger).
27. *Sensation*, by Anselm Hollo, 1972.
28. *Attention*, by Robert Grenier, 1985.

CHAPTER 9

Gary Snyder:

What You Should Know to Be a Poet

all you can about animals as persons.
the names of trees and flowers and weeds.
names of stars, and the movements of the planets
                and the moon.

your own six senses, with a watchful and elegant mind.

at least one kind of traditional magic:
divination, astrology, the *book of changes*, the tarot;

dreams.
the illusory demons and illusory shining gods;

kiss the ass of the devil and eat shit;
fuck his horny barbed cock,
fuck the hag,
and all the celestial angels
                and maidens perfum'd and golden—

& then love the human: wives   husbands   and friends.

children's games, comic books, bubble-gum,
the weirdness of television and advertising.

work, long dry hours of dull work swallowed up and
    accepted
and livd with and finally lovd.   exhaustion,
                hunger, rest.

the wild freedom of the dance, *extasy*
silent solitary illumination, *enstasy*

real danger. gambles. and the edge of death.[1]

The lack of capitals and the presence of periods give this page of Snyder's a modest notational quality, a man sharing his thoughts with you, without broadcasting their importance. At the same time, *What You Should Know* is a tool-kit, a Poetic Curriculum, a several-year study program in nucleus that if followed, in disciplined "ordered derangement" on one's own, might represent a meaningful compromise between the oversocialized university writing programs and Artaud's stark command of no enlightenment other than oneself on oneself, no initiation *period*. Artaud made this statement after having put himself through his own equivalent of Snyder's Curriculum, and after he had been incarcerated in asylums for nearly nine years, where he had been "initiated" by therapy and electroshock.

I would like to draw three nodes from Snyder's piece—experience, research, self-regulation—and suggest that becoming a poet is involved with working out a balance, or rhythm, between these three multi-radial activities—

EXPERIENCE: having the courage of your own impulses, getting in "water over your head"; acting out curiosities and responsibilities whenever possible—confronting a friend, telling off an unfair superior, having the abortion etc., rather than non-action that subsequently possesses or leaks into poems.

(In Kyoto, 1963), Snyder seemed to me to live like a monk during the week and like a libertine on the weekend—he rose at 4 AM and had a day's study and writing done by late morning; as I recall, afternoons were given to chores, shopping, teaching English as a foreign language. Early rising probably Zen practice, which permeated but did not curtail—)

Snyder at a ranger station in Mt. Baker National Forest, twenty-one years old:

> Discipline of self-restraint is an easy one; being clear-cut, negative, and usually based on some accepted cultural values. Discipline of following desires, *always* doing what you want to do, is hardest.[2] It presupposes self-knowledge of motives, a careful balance of free action and sense of where the cultural taboos lay—knowing whether a particular "desire" is instinctive, cultural, a product of thought, contemplation, or the unconscious. Blake: if the doorways of perception were cleansed, everything would appear to man as it is, infinite. For man has closed himself up, 'til all he sees is through narrow chinks of his caverns. Ah.
>
> > the frustrated bumblebee turns over
> > clambers the flower's center upside down

furious hidden buzzing
near the cold sweet stem.

In a culture where the aesthetic experience is denied and atrophied, genuine religious ecstasy rare, intellectual pleasure scorned—it is only natural that sex should become the only personal epiphany of most people &
the culture's interest in romantic love take on staggering size.[3]

RESEARCH: is of course a kind of experience too, but here I stress
finding contemplative territories that have not been mined (or strip-
mined) by other poets, and making them your own, bringing them into
contemporary writing, by poetry or by prose, in order to increase its
range of responsibilities.

This should involve travel, when such territory is visitable. Olson
could have gone to the library and read up on Maya research (in fact, he
did, but was so dissatisfied by what was available that he became all the
more obsessed with going to Yucatán on his own)—however, nearly
penniless, he went to Mérida and picked up shards rather than merely
examining photos of them.[4]

Penelope Shuttle and Peter Redgrove write that they went to their
College Librarian seeking information on menstruation because of
Shuttle's cramps and depression. They found nothing that they could
use, and thus began their own research on an area of every woman's experience that has become an endless lode of discovery for both of them.[5]

There is something embedded in the nature of poetry itself that
yearns to travel and to translate, not merely a foreign text, but the experience of otherness. "The most sublime act," Blake wrote, "is to set another before you." Thus Bashō's physical urge to get roving one spring
morning in 1689 led to his famous *Oku-no-Hosomichi*,[6] the last of several haibun-haiku hiking journals, a model of layered cultural awareness, acute observation, and a heart open to transiency and "the modest
proportions of human destiny." "What Bashō doesn't say," writes translator Cid Corman, "moves at least as much as what he does. One knows
his silences go deeper than reasons. And when his eyes plumb words for
heart—when the heart holds the island of Sado, locus of exile, at the
crest of a brimming sea, and the eye lifts from that pointed violence and
loneliness on the horizon to the stars flowing effortlessly up and over
and back into the man making vision, who has not at once felt all language vanish into a wholeness and scope of sense that lifts one as if one
weighed nothing?" (Here it is appropriate to note especially in the

context of *Novices* the distance Corman has traveled from being an apprentice pounded by Olson's injunctions to the author of the just-quoted sentence.)

In 1965 I hitched, bused, and flew to Lima, Peru, to study the worksheets for the poetry of César Vallejo that I had been attempting to translate from error-riddled editions. While the Vallejo part of the trip was utterly frustrating (his widow denying me and all others access to materials that would have enabled translators and scholars to make his achievement available on an international scale), the spirit of Vallejo led me into days of wandering the worst of Lima's barriadas, and my need to pay my way into experiencing USIS censorship of a bilingual literary magazine I was hired to edit. The context in which poetic research takes place can become as valuable in regard to learning as the project itself.

To only have yourself as subject, novice, is undermining, and it will tend to push you toward an "academic" (= conventional, diminutional) imitation of other poetries. If your attentions are not partially given over to the non- or foreign-literary, the temptation is to read, with blinders, the work of friends and teachers, and to operate under a single canopy of current literary taste.

At twenty-four, Snyder saw experience and research ultimately as irreconcilable opposites: "Comes a time when the poet must choose: either to step deep in the stream of his people, history, tradition, folding and folding himself in the wealth of persons and pasts; philosophy, humanity, to become richly foundationed and great and sane and ordered. Or, to step beyond the bound onto the way out, into horrors and angels, possible madness or silly Faustian doom, possible utter transcendence, possible enlightened return, possible ignominious wormish perishing."[7]

In *What You Should Know*, written when he was in his mid-thirties, Snyder implies that such opposites are contraries (a Blakean perception: two-way traffic without collisions).

It is risky to go to college and remain there more or less for the rest of one's life and expect to write significant poetry. For the poet, the library is a more intimidating place than a foreign city, and to spend one's life nursing in a library is not only to remain an "eternal adolescent" as far as the alleys of Calcutta are concerned, but to become so overwhelmed by what one does not know—can never know—that what one intuits, or does at least deeply feel, gets trashed. Great writing involves protecting one's intuitions, even one's ignorance. Knowing, as such, is not always an advantage to making significant art. Acknowledging one's ignorance, and learning to respect personal as well as human limitations, *while* one works with the welter of fantasies that tumble between certainty and helplessness, is not learnable in school, and can probably best be dealt with in what I would call "neutral solitude" (Rilke's little château in the Swiss mountains, Blake's flat in "fourfold" London, Artaud's cell at Rodez). For a poet, ignorance is as deep a well as knowing, and lifelong adherence to institutions of higher learning (with travel contingent upon awards) not only wrecks any possible balance between the two, but puts the poet, daily, class-wise, office-wise, library-wise, before the dragons of respectability and caution.[8]

The poetry and prose of William Bronk is a testimonial of the extent to which ignorance can be frugally held in an imaginative frame.

Again, Artaud (he is contemplating van Gogh): "No one has ever written, painted, sculpted, modeled, built, or invented except literally to get out of hell.

"And I prefer to get out of hell, the landscapes of this quiet convulsionary to the teeming compositions of Brueghel the Elder or Hieronymous Bosch, who are, in comparison with him, only artists, whereas van Gogh is only a poor dunce determined not to deceive himself."[9]

SELF-REGULATION: I take the term for this third "node" from the psychology of Wilhelm Reich, who believed that "the function of the orgasm" was to enable an individual to respect and take responsibility for his own energy household. Reich envisioned a world that did not need regulation from without (the police, the state, the nation), but a world in which people enjoyed their work because they had chosen it as an outgrowth of what Snyder refers to as "the discipline of following desires" (in contrast to negative self-restraint). In contemplating an ideal world made up of self-regulatory people, Reich was elaborating one of the core perceptions in Blake's poetry:

> What is it men in women do require?
> The lineaments of Gratified Desire.
> What is it women do in men require?
> The lineaments of Gratified Desire.[10]
> (1793)

—a way of erotically grounding the Golden Rule, as it were; physical gratification as a *requirement* (note how trenchantly this word clings in the line, in contrast to "want" or "need") of the human, identical for both sexes, a reciprocity. Neither Blake nor Reich saw Gratified Desire or self-regulation as an end in itself—both saw it as a requirement for giving oneself wholeheartedly to one's work, whether that work be farming or sculpture. In my own life (partially through two years of Reichian therapy, 1967–1969), I have discovered that there is an "antiphonal swing" (I coin the phrase off the last line in Hart Crane's *The Bridge*) between gratificational love-making and imaginative release, that these two "acts" are contraries, not opposites, and that as in the alchemical image of the "double pelican," they both feed each other in contrast to sapping strength from each other.

That which helps us define what we are also marks out boundaries. What we are not, artistically speaking, is a limitation. The challenge is to create a self that is up to, and imaginatively includes, all the selfhood and selves one has experienced. Even if we are able to allow contradiction and flow of contraries in our work, each assertion, each placement, carries, like an aura, its unstated qualification or exception. In my own case, this challenge is: how accommodating can I be to material that flies in the face of my "antiphonal swing?"

Crane's "Havana Rose" recalls a conversation with the bacteriologist Hans Zinsser over dinner at a restaurant in Havana, 1931:

> And during the wait over dinner at La Diana,
> the Doctor had said—who was American also—
> "You cannot heed the negative—, so might go on
> to undeserved doom . . . must therefore loose yourself
> within a pattern's mastery that you can conceive, that
> you can yield to—by which also you
> win and gain that mastery and happiness which
> is your own from birth."[11]

For thirty years, I have thanked Crane for having the savvy to write down Zinsser's words (whose "undeserved doom" Crane met within a year of that dinner), which offer yet another image of the labyrinth, as a pattern one masters and works (dances) within (Olson's: "how to dance/sitting down"). My own attempt at a "pattern's mastery" is sounded by the three words I have been mulling over in this section, words that make up a kind of web, or trampoline, I have constructed between sky and earth, and one which, against which, by which, I have lived and worked since the late 1960s. To these three words, I would now add a fourth: EXPERIMENT, the poetic engagement with the sustaining mesh of experience-research-self-regulation. One's eyes bouncing off one's sheet of typing paper, one's mind against the trampoline, hurling one's self-in-process at it again and again, aware that often one smacks and loses balance, falls through a hole and probably wrongly scrambles to get back to what one knows—

<pre>
                    work swallowed and accepted
     and livd with and finally lovd.   exhaustion,
                    hunger, rest.
</pre>

NOTES

1. Gary Snyder, *Regarding Wave*, NYC, 1970, p. 40.
2. The discipline of self-restraint vs. the discipline of following desires is taken up by the German painter Max Beckmann in one of a series of open letters that he wrote "to a woman painter" in 1948 while he was in residence at Stephens College, in Columbia, Missouri. Beckman writes:

It is necessary for you, you who now draw near to the motley and tempting realm of art, it is very necessary that you also comprehend how close to danger you are. If you devote yourself to the ascetic life, if you renounce all worldly pleasures, all human things, you may, I suppose, attain a certain concentration: but for the same reason you may also dry up. Now, on the other hand, if you plunge headlong into the arms of passion, you may just as easily burn yourself up! Art, love, and passion are very closely related because everything revolves more or less around knowledge and the enjoyment of beauty in one form or another. And intoxication is beautiful, is it not, my friend?

Have you not sometimes been with me in the deep hollow of the champagne glass where red lobsters crawl around and black waiters serve red rumbas which make the blood course through your veins as if to a wild dance? Where white dresses and black silk stockings nestle themselves close to the forms of young gods amidst orchid blossoms and the clatter of tambourines? Have you never thought that in the hellish heat of intoxication amongst princes, harlots, and gangsters, *there* is the glamour of life? Or have not the wide seas on hot nights let you dream that we were glowing sparks on flying fish far above the sea and the stars? Splendid was your mask of black fire in which your long hair was burning—and you believed, at last, at last, that you held the young god in your arms who would deliver you from poverty and ardent desire?

Then came the other thing—the cold fire, the glory.

Never again, you said, never again shall my will be slave to another. Now I want to be alone, alone with myself and my will to power and to glory.

You have built yourself a house of ice crystals and you have wanted to forge three corners or four corners into a circle. But you cannot get rid of that little "point" that gnaws in your brain, that little "point" which means "the other one." Under the cold ice the passion still gnaws, that longing to be loved by another, even if it should be on a different plane than the hell of animal desire. The cold ice burns exactly like the hot fire. And uneasy you walk alone through your palace of ice. Because you still do not want to give up the world of delusion, that little "point" still burns within you—the other one! And for that reason you are an artist, my poor child! And on you go, waking in dreams like myself. But through all this we must also persevere my friend. You dream of my own self in you, you mirror my soul.

Perhaps we shall awake one day, alone or together. This we are forbidden to know. A cool wind beyond the other world will awake us in the dreamless universe, and then we shall see ourselves freed from the danger of the dark world, the glowing fields of sorrow at midnight. Then we are awake in the realm of atmospheres, and self-will and passion, art and delusion are sinking down like a curtain of grey fog . . . and light is shining behind an unknown gigantic gleam.

There, yes there, we shall perceive all, my friend, alone or together . . . who can know?   [Tr. by Mathilde Q. Beckmann and Perry T. Rathbone]

Art, then, for Beckmann, seems to spring from between self-restraint and following desires in at times a nearly helpless way to make contact with "the other," not as a love slave, but on a spiritual plane. Snyder's *discipline* of following desires proposes a "way"—Snyder is a Buddhist—that would be flexible enough to include art and a living other.

3. Snyder, *Earth House Hold*, NYC, 1969, p. 19.

4. For Olson in Yucatán, see *Letters for Origin*, and Vols. 5 and 6 of *Charles Olson & Robert Creeley: The Complete Correspondence*, Santa Barbara, 1983 and 1985, as well as the essay "Human Universe," in *Human Universe*, NYC, 1967.

5. Penelope Shuttle & Peter Redgrove, *The Wise Wound: Menstruation and Everywoman*, London, 1986.

6. *Back Roads to Far Towns*, Bashō's *Oku-no-Hosomichi*, NYC, 1968. A landmark in the translation of Japanese haibun and haiku. For improvisations on haibun in English, see the six haibun in John Ashbery's *A Wave*, NYC, 1984. Direct imitations of haiku in English are generally of little interest; however, many of Corman's very short poems are keen workings off haiku sensibility and form, e.g.,

> The cicada
> singing isnt:
> that sound's its life

(from *for granted*, New Rochelle, NY, 1967). Haiku suggests that all event is spontaneous and that dramatic narrative is an accordion-expansion of a shakahachi flute-shriek moment.

7. Snyder, *Earth House Hold*, p. 39.

8. In his *The Life of John Berryman* (London, 1982), John Haffenden wrote: "He belongs to what has become known as the Middle Generation of American poets, a group that includes Delmore Schwartz, Robert Lowell, Randall Jarrell, and Theodore Roethke." While "confessional" (a term I believe coined by the poet and critic M. L. Rosenthal) is a fuzzy identifying term for these poets, much of their writing is characterized by personal trauma felt as *the* centripetal force that whirls all other considerations of myth, learning, and daily observation, into its vortex. Refusing la vie bohème, expatriotship, and engagement by non-English European literary movements—Berryman it seems might have improved his lot by becoming a Dadaist—these poets stayed home, looked up to Yeats, Auden, and Frost, and established the image of the American poet as a teacher sharing an office with his academic colleagues, a very tactile member of a middle-class professional community. Because of the congruity of these poets to the teaching profession itself, and be-

cause their writing for the most part does not provide any challenging difficulties, it is natural that they have been taught a great deal, identified by teacher-critics as *the* poets of their generation, and are presented in the majority of textbook poetry anthologies as the creators of post WWII American poetry.

9. *Antonin Artaud Selected Writings*, NYC, 1976, p. 497.

10. *The Complete Writings of William Blake*, London, 1957, p. 328. For Reich on self-regulation, see *The Function of the Orgasm*, NYC, 1961, pp. 143–61.

11. *The Poems of Hart Crane*, NYC, 1986, pp. 200–201.

CHAPTER 10

Snyder's *What You Should Know* is the child of post–WWII interdisciplinary, experimental, experience-oriented poetics, a new American poetry, open to (and often weakened by) cross-cultural appropriations. In his broad and thoughtful essay "The Poet & the City" (1962), W. H. Auden proposed a more traditionally Western curriculum, what he called his "daydream College for Bards":

1. In addition to English, at least one ancient language, probably Greek or Hebrew, and two modern languages would be required.
2. Thousands of lines of poetry in these languages would be learned by heart.
3. The library would contain no books of literary criticism, and the only critical exercise required of students would be the writing of parodies.
4. Courses in prosody, rhetoric, and comparative philology would be required of all students, and every student would have to select three courses out of courses in mathematics, natural history, geology, meteorology, archaeology, mythology, liturgics, cooking.
5. Every student would be required to look after a domestic animal and cultivate a garden plot.[1]

Auden's "College," with its emphasis on memorization, which has become archaic in our time, is a model for poet as Man of Letters, a Jack of All Literary Trades, who elaborates his life in poetry, letters, reviews, essays, possibly editing and translating etc. Relative to Snyder's *What You Should Know*, it is Ivory Towerish; at the same time, it implicitly believes in a continuity of Western literature and humanities that has become suspect to Snyder with his Eastern focus aligned with Zen Buddhism and underscored by a belief in a usable shamanic deep past. Snyder's program is thus more tied to present-day consumer society and to the deep past than is Auden's, which spreads out in the immense Western "interval" between. Snyder's poet is a ronin (a masterless samurai) with his house on his head; Auden's a broadcaster at the console of the great Western Library, with a house or cottage to stroll home to in the evening. Broken down into the most rudimentary forms, Snyder is a hunter, Auden a planter.

While pondering poetic Curriculums, I recalled Robert Graves' *The White Goddess*, a scholarly Fantasia on the nature of "true poetry," in which Graves' picture of ancient Celt and Irish poets carries not only Auden's erudition but also Snyder's shadow of "the dancing sorcerer," the Upper Paleolithic shaman of 15,000 BC (a figure involved with the whole rope of a clan's knowledge and ability to survive, in contrast to the contemporary American poet who at best represents one strand of a rope unraveled throughout the humanities, medicine, magic and law):

> The ancient Celts carefully distinguished the poet, who was originally a priest and judge as well and whose person was sacrosanct, from the mere gleeman. He was in Irish called *fili*, a seer; in Welsh *derwydd*, or oak-seer, which is the probable derivation of "Druid." Even kings came under his moral tutelage. When two armies engaged in battle, the poets of both sides would withdraw together on a hill and there judiciously discuss the fighting. . . . The gleeman, on the other hand, was a *joculator*, or entertainer, not a priest: a mere client of the military oligarchs and without the poet's arduous professional training.
>
> In ancient Ireland the *ollave*, or master-poet, sat next to the king at table and was privileged, as none else but the queen was, to wear six different colors in his clothes. The "bard," which in medieval Wales stood for a master-poet, had a different sense in Ireland, where it meant an inferior poet who had not passed through the "seven degrees of wisdom" which made him an ollave after a very difficult twelve-year course.
>
> Who can make any claim to be a chief poet and wear the embroidered mantle of office which the ancient Irish called the *tugen*? Who can even claim to be an ollave? The ollave in ancient Ireland had to be master of one hundred and fifty Oghams, or verbal ciphers, which allowed him to converse with his fellow-poets over the heads of unlearned bystanders; to be able to repeat at a moment's notice any one of three hundred and fifty long traditional histories and romances, together with the incidental poems they contained, with appropriate harp accompaniment . . . to be learned in philosophy; to be a doctor of civil law; to understand the history of modern, middle and ancient Irish with the derivations and changes of meaning of every word; to be skilled in music, augury, divination, medicine, mathematics, geography, universal history, astronomy, rhetoric, and foreign languages; and to be able to extemporize poetry in fifty or more complicated meters. That anyone at all should have been able to qualify as an ollave is surprising; yet families of ollaves tended to

intermarry; and among the Maoris of New Zealand where a curiously similar system prevailed, the capacity of the ollave to memorize, comprehend, elucidate and extemporize staggered Governor Grey and other early British observers.[2]

Graves will go ahead through his charming, questionable, vexing, and thoroughly labyrinthine work to argue that all "true poetry" celebrates some incident or scene of a particular story, identified in the chapter entitled "The Single Poetic Theme":

> Originally, the poet was the leader of a totem-society of religious dancers. His verses—*versus* is a Latin word corresponding to the Greek strophe and means "a turning"—were danced around an altar or in a sacred enclosure and each verse started a new turn or movement in the dance. The word "ballad" has the same origin: it is a dance poem, from the Latin *ballare*, to dance. All the totem-societies in ancient Europe were under the dominion of the Great Goddess, the Lady of the Wild Things; dances were seasonal and fitted into an annual pattern from which gradually emerges the single grand theme of poetry: the life, death and resurrection of the spirit of the Year, the Goddess's son and lover.
>
> Poetry began in the matriarchal age, and derives its magic from the moon, not from the sun. No poet can hope to understand the nature of poetry unless he has had a vision of the Naked King crucified to the lopped oak, and watched the dancers, red-eyed from the acrid smoke of the sacrificial fires, stamping out the measures of the dance, their bodies bent uncouthly forward, with a monotonous chant of: "Kill! kill! kill!" and "Blood! blood! blood!"
>
> Constant illiterate use of the phrase 'to woo the Muse' has obscured its poetic sense: the poet's inner communion with the White Goddess, regarded as the source of truth. Truth has been represented by poets as a naked woman: a woman divested of all garments or ornaments that will commit her to any particular position in time and space. The Syrian Moon-goddess was also represented so, with a snake head-dress to remind the devotee that she was Death in disguise, and a lion crouched faithfully at her feet. The poet is in love with the White Goddess, with Truth: his heart breaks with longing and love for her. She is the Flower-goddess Olwen or Blodeuwedd; but she is also Blodeuwedd the Owl, lamp-eyed, hooting dismally, with her foul nest in the hollow of a dead tree, or Circe the pitiless falcon, or Lamia with her flickering tongue, or the snarling-chopped Sow-goddess, or the mare-headed Rhiannon who feeds on raw flesh. *Odi atque amo:* "to be in love with" is also to hate. Determined to escape from the dilemma, the Apollonian teaches himself to despise woman, and teaches woman to despise herself.[1]

If poetry did begin in a matriarchal age, and if the first poets were women, how could their source be the Muse Graves identifies as *the*

Muse for the heterosexual male poet? Graves would of course argue that regardless of cultural gender-priority the first poets were male—in fact, he goes a good deal further, by stating that "woman is not a poet: she is either Muse or she is nothing."[4] But since men are the guardians of attitudes and laws in a patriarchal culture, it is reasonable to assume that women would be the guardians, and shamans, of what appears to be ancient Indo-European matriarchal culture.

I suspect that the matter is much more complex than this, and offer the following suggestion: in an Upper Paleolithic semi-nomadic hunting-based clan, the magic of the kill would be primarily man-determined and the domain of a male shaman. On the other hand, the magic of generation (fecundity, birth, the hearth) would be primarily woman-determined and the domain of a female shaman. The gender emphasis of Upper Paleolithic image-making is clearly matriarchal, and is associated with cave shelter (the so-called Venuses were found in rock shelters, either as a carved part of the shelter, or stuck into the shelter floor) or deep-cave sanctuary; it stresses fecundity and the "Demeter delta," or yonic triangle. There are, however, male images too: more often than not animal-garbed, dancing figures whose animal attributes or associations appear to be tied up with the hunt and power over hard-to-kill beasts.[5]

Graves' book is, in fact, an amazing mish-mash of personal projections and ollave-like research, and I would not reject all of his detailed evidence for a view of poetry based on a White Goddess, who at one time may have been as cogent a source for imagination as Jesus Christ was for Renaissance painters. But always White? Whiteness is but a portion of the spectrum attributed to The Triple Goddess (the precursor figure for the Christian Trinity), a "Goddess in three aspects—as a young woman, a birth-giving matron, and an old woman. This typical Virgin-Mother-Crone combination was Parvati-Durga-Uma (Kali) in India, Ana-Babd-Macha (the Morrigan) in Ireland, or in Greece Hebe-Hera-Hecate, the three Moerae, the three Gorgons, the three Graece, the three Horae, etc. Among the Vikings, the three-fold Goddess appeared as the Norns; among the Romans, as the Fates or Fortunae; among the druids, as Diana Triformis. The Triple Goddess had more than three: she had hundreds of forms."[6] In the margin of the "Fates" entry page of Barbara G. Walker's *The Woman's Encyclopedia of Myths and Secrets*, I scribbled various attributes of the three phases of the Triple Goddess:

1. lily dove white purity spinner frog spider silver fish white stag silver wheel white-flower virgin creator

2. rose passion red measurer heifer serpent dragon preserver

3. darkness black cutter sow vulture sphinx black bitch mare destroyer [Homer's black ewe which Odysseus sacrifices in order to speak with Tiresias in the 11th book of the *Odyssey*]

Relative to the amazing rainbow of The Triple Goddess, to simply call her White is to remove her from the dimensionality of red and black (the Venus of Laussel, carved in the prow of a tiny rock shelter in the French Dordogne at around 20,000 BC, was originally painted red). And might there not be Brown Goddesses? Yellow Goddesses? Blue Goddesses? "The White Etc Goddess," Olson is said to have commented.

And the homosexual poet? In Graves' categorical patriarchal (matriarchally veiled) thinking, he is Apollo-bound, and without a "true" source, or figure, of inspiration. Yet for both García Lorca and Robert Duncan, to mention two homosexual *and* Dionysian poets, the source is neither Muse nor angel, but the figure so compellingly described by Lorca as the "duende," the daemonized thought of the blood.

And lest Apollo be implicitly dismissed by Graves' dismissal of him from the "truth" of poetry, the novice should consider Walker's entry on "Abaddon" in her *Encyclopedia*, which describes the first spirit-pits, which seem to float in time between the Upper Paleolithic cave-sanctuaries and the pagan temples, of which medieval cathedrals and modern churches appear to be the final "installments":

> The god Apollo was a solar king in heaven during the day, and a Lord of Death in the underworld at night. His latter form became the Jewish Apollyon, Spirit of the Pit (Revelation 9:11). Apollo-Python was the serpent deity in the Pit of the Delphic oracle, who inspired the seeress with mystic vapors from his nether world. The Greek word for Pit was *abaton*, which the Jews corrupted into Abaddon—later a familiar Christian synonym for hell.
>
> Also called a *mundus* or earth-womb, the *abaton* was a real pit, standard equipment in a pagan temple. Those who entered it to "incubate," or to sleep overnight in magical imitation of the incubatory sleep in the womb, were thought to be visited by an "incubus" or spirit who brought prophetic dreams. Novice priests went down into the pit for longer periods of incubation, pantomiming death, burial, and rebirth from the womb of Mother Earth. Once initiated in this way, they were thought to gain the skill of oneiromancy: the ability to interpret dreams.
>
> The Old Testament Joseph earned his oneiromantic talent by incubation in a Pit. The "brothers" who put him there seem to have been fellow

priests. He could interpret Pharaoh's dreams only after he had submitted to the ritual. Assyrian priests derived similar powers from a sojourn in the Pit. They then assumed the priestly coat of many colors, signifying communion with the goddess under her oneiromantic name of Nanshe, "Interpreter of Dreams." It seems likely that Joseph's coat of many colors would have been given him originally not before the initiation, but afterward, by a "father" who was actually the high priest.[7]

The Irish ollave in his six-colored garb, priest Joseph in his many-colored coat, against the backdrop of a primordial spore in which clear skies and the moon, night and the bottomlessness of source, fire and the blood of renewal as well as the blood of destruction, are "the deeds done and suffered by light."[8]

NOTES

1. Auden's essay is from *The Dyer's Hand and Other Essays* (NYC, 1962); it is reprinted in *Poetry and Politics*, NYC, 1985, pp. 36–51.
2. Robert Graves, *The White Goddess*, NYC 1969, pp. 21, 22, and 457.
3. Graves, *The White Goddess*, pp. 422 and 448. Graves' dancers, turning and twisting as we poets intend our lines to imaginatively turn and twist, are also figures of the labyrinth, an out-in-the-open version of its interior action: after the elevation of Dionysus and Ariadne as a divine couple into the night sky, Theseus and his companions are said to have danced a swirling in and out dance around a horned altar, which recalls the actual bull horns through which Cretan bull-dancers flipped in a sacred marriage of the sun-king and the moon-goddess.
4. Graves, *The White Goddess*, p. 446.
5. S. Giedion's *The Eternal Present*, Vol. 1, *The Beginnings of Art*, NYC, 1957, is an excellent introduction to Upper Paleolithic imagination. See also Olson's lectures in *Olson* # 10, and my *Fracture*, Santa Barbara, 1983.
6. *The Woman's Encyclopedia of Myths and Secrets*, NYC, 1983, p. 1018.
7. *The Woman's Encyclopedia*, pp. 2–3.
8. Goethe is said to have stated: "Colors are deeds done and suffered by light."

When I briefly notice a comment or gesture, and then dream a variation of it, I feel there is something nourishing going on. Caught up in
the flux of consciousness, the figure has been encouraged to perform a
version of itself in a way I failed to imagine until my rational intentionality and its attendant guards fall asleep. Merely noticed, or overheard,
the figure was a black spot. The dream tells me that such a spot is a
spore with fungus potential, like one of those firecracker worms, a small
keg that upon ignition curls out several inches. Such a spot, placed on
the warmer of Psyche, is capable of its own elaboration.

Another kind of dreaming seems to be an intensification of ordinary
dreaming, capable of hallucinatory welding of waking imagination and
dreaming. If there is a pattern to such dreams, they seem to occur
around dawn after I have awakened from an ordinary dream. I find myself wondering if I am awake or still dreaming. I am suddenly as if
awake in a dream, or dreaming awake, and I have only to reclose my
eyes to see what is behind my consciousness at that instant. Since there
seems to be nothing on my mind, the spurt of images feels completely
spontaneous (as if I were projecting a movie onto a screen out of my
head, a movie of unconscious action that bypassed conscious censorship). I find myself in a corridor or tunnel of parthenogenesis, in which
being there is sufficient to produce "the whole show." There is the sensation of head as camera projecting a tunnel of light in which it creates
its own action, of rapid passage around bend after bend (it is, I think, on
this basis that I referred to images as winding windows earlier). There
is a curious wholeness or freedom in poetry that seems contingent upon
consciously/unconsciously recreating these conditions while writing.

Such dreaming evokes a line of Pound's in Canto 92 in which he
states that while Paradise is not artificial it *is* jagged (and a line or two

later, indicates that the jaggedness is the jaggedness of lightning, which recalls a line of Dylan Thomas': "The meaning of miracle is unending lightning"). Such dreaming is extremely physical—it pours through my body like tons of grain through a sieve in a way that recalls the second hour of LSD sensation. It suggests that the tough material world is actually highly porous, combustible, and that anything can become something else instantaneously. It is redolent of both day and night, and while it occurs the partition between desire and fulfillment of desire is momentarily down.

My first "visionary" dream took place in Kyoto, 1963, when my first wife and I were living on tatami in two rooms of a nineteenth-century Japanese house. I was daily in the throes of trying to find out what counted for me *and* to articulate it at the same time. I had no confidence in my imagination, so what took place in those long mornings was mainly the typing out of a line or two, and then, blocked, staring at it on the page. A grinding against no self in the hope that a speakable self could be sparked or driven into existence. I often had nauseating headaches and was so tense that I once passed out while reading Blake's *The Book of Urizen*.

I recall at one point a young Japanese man was in the news for having crossed the Pacific Ocean in a small boat. I was struck by this, without knowing why, and typed out:

Kenichi Horie, across the Pacific, alone

I must have stared at the line for a week, unable to push on. I felt that I knew nothing about the ocean, or sailing, or who Horie was, or what his act *meant*. It did not occur to me that I had some things in common with the line—I had crossed the Pacific to find myself in a foreign world facing a long and perhaps very lonely voyage. Looking at such a line, it was as if heavy tongs gripped my head from behind, paralyzing my mind while they held me in position before it.

In April of that year, I became aware of the following pattern when I stretched out on the futon to sleep: as I was about to doze off, I would hear a sharp PING that rang in or was struck off my forehead between my eyes. At first this "bell" was more frightening than I can describe. In an effort to escape it, I would concentrate on falling asleep. In doing so, a second thing would happen: as if from about 100 feet away, there was the sound of a window being slammed shut, as if someone with both hands had slammed a window as hard as possible. I curled tighter into myself and awaited the nightmare. The third phase was the rerun of a "visionary" dream: I was in a twisting tunnel moving at high speed, head first, with a sense of impending collision, as if the only culmination could be shattering. The tunnel was smoking, and in attempting to see through the fumes, and in effect to get to the tunnel's end before it got to me, I would conjure my father's face. The dream would always end before I reached the end of the tunnel and I seemed to be in the tunnel a bit longer each time the dream occurred. It was as if I was on some sort of psychic hamster-belt being run through my paces night after night until a certain charge exhausted itself.

Was I repeating emerging from my mother to instantly become dependent upon my father to catch my "fall"? My father, who had whipped me, and was never, after infancy, a loving companion? There was a peristaltic ambivalence in the dream, roller-coaster exhilaration and fright. I began to realize that for the psychological background of the dream to be activated, there had to be a present condition to supply its terrible energy. Besides the mental tension of sitting blocked before a page, there was a concomitant physical tension/distraction: I would often become sexually aroused, or feel a need to defecate. Since I did not desire my wife or feel it was right (or have the nerve) to be unfaithful, I tried to swallow the sexual sensation and keep concentrating on the page in the typewriter. At one point for several months, I spent time at the Kyoto University Library, making use of a huge Spanish dictionary, in order to check hundreds of words in the poetry of Vallejo which I had begun to translate daily in the fall of 1962. In 1965, back in Indiana for the year, I tried to simply say what those days in the library had been:

The Library

Either masturbate or sleep—
that's how it was translating Vallejo those days,
an interlude coming along the railing back
looking down into the court. A pine
low-flung & stately. Below it benches
a student or two. But the book, the
heavy leather Spanish dictionary
I could not crack. Nor "the book is
the life blood of a master spirit." It was
reliving days I never got in then,
days that could not be relieved,
days & days, & the past came up,

without my present how alone I was,
how singular & horny. Love was not
given at home. Stiff at night I was
swollen in the morning. I ached
& Vallejo lay mute. The john
walls stared What do you want
coming here? Why are you not
at home without literature
and life?[1]

The traditional Japanese toilet is what is referred to in the West as a
"Turkish toilet"—one squats over a rectangular porcelain trench.
When I got up from sitting cross-legged on the tatami by my typewriter table to relieve myself, I would find, once crouched in the benjo,
that I did not have to go at all. It occurred to me that there was a bizarre
relationship between the position assumed by the Aztec goddess of
childbirth and filth, Tlazolteotl-Ixcuina, squatting in the tension of
birth, with a little male figure emerging between her knees, and my
own position, caught up in attempting to birth myself, which on a
psychic level had become a caricature of projecting a poem onto the
page. To find the Aztec metaphor obviously did not solve my problems,
but it helped me to realize that in making a life-commitment to poetry
I had brought to the surface lower-body tensions that I had been unaware of before. It slowly began to dawn on me that everything was at
stake in the creative act, that what I did or did not do with myself away
from working on a poem was going to attach itself to the writing process, and, furthermore, it was best to try and work through these problems away from the writing table so as to not ultimately have to
transcend them in the act of writing (and thus live with them unresolved) if for no other reason than that I could not stand facing them
day after day while attempting to write.

About six months before the bell-slammed-window-roller-coaster
nightmare, I had a hallucinatory experience that seemed to loosen me
up to the extent that such a nightmare could occur. Snyder, who was
living half an hour north of us with his wife, the poet Joanne Kyger, had
urged me to try LSD, having tried it himself after either Leary or Al-
pert had passed through Kyoto with the newly discovered drug. Because of all the difficulties I have briefly described, I was afraid something awful would happen to me after Snyder told me that I would see
all my demons if I took LSD. But I said no, even though I was desperate and *feared* that LSD might tear the potential poet in me apart.

A month after having rejected Gary's offer, I spent the better part of a night drinking sake with some strangers in downtown Kyoto bars, and dreamed that night of Snyder in a kind of steamshovel contraption being lowered right over a felt-covered gambling table where he picked up gold coins with his buns (it was Halloween, and the night before, Barbara Eshleman had given her junior high school English students an apple-bobbing party). I awoke with a potent hangover, and early in the afternoon motorcycled to a bar dormitory where I was to meet a male friend who managed a hostess bar. The dormitory Mama-san informed me that my friend was not in, but invited me in anyway for cookies and tea. She sat me down before a TV set and left the room. There was a teenage adventure movie on, in which, during a track meet, a fat boy tried to climb a pole, and failed, to the glee of his peers. While watching this scene, I suddenly thought of Robert Kelly (who weighed 400 pounds in those days), and was moved to tears over what I took to be Kelly's difficulties as a man and as a writer. I left the dormitory after an hour or so, feeling so sensitive it was as if my nerves were in the very surface of my skin.

I decided to cycle out to the Snyders for an impromptu visit, and once again found that the person I had come to visit was not home—but Joanne was, and again I was invited in for tea. We sat at the kotatsu for an hour or so, discussing Jung and a few of his hard-to-grasp terms. I left near dusk, and started home. Cycling down Junikendoori, a wide commercial avenue, I suddenly began to hallucinate: the motorcycle became an ox, its handlebars ox horns; a lumberyard turned into a manger in which I saw wise men kneeling by the infant Jesus. At first I tried to hold on and will myself home, but by the time I got to Nijo Castle, I was afraid I was going to have an accident, so rather automatically I decided to circumambulate the Castle, and left the cycle in the tourist-bus parking lot. At the point I started around the square moated medieval structure, everything was roaring with transformation, and anything I looked at instantly turned into something else. At one point I saw Kyger's eyeballs in the moat. At the far northwest corner of the Castle, I looked up into the sky and saw a human-sized bright-red spider about 30 feel up in the air, drawing thread out of its spinnerets and weaving itself into a pulsating, quilt-like, luminous dusk sky. The appearance of the red spider was the sublime moment of the experience; it signified to me that I was being offered my poetic totem, and thus confirmed that I was a poet.[2]

I did take LSD in the spring of 1965, and in reflecting on the experience[3] it occurred to me that Joanne Kyger could have put LSD in my tea. I asked her about this in 1977; she gave me an equivocal answer. The red spider confirmation was more than a poem—and less than one too. It gave me crucial support and justified my efforts to keep on trying to write in a "grasping for straws" time, when every day was a maze of conventional dead ends and self-destructive lures.

NOTES

1. *Indiana,* Los Angeles, 1969, p. 28. See also "The Octopus Delivery" in *Coils.*

2. For more on the red spider, see "The House of Okumura VI" in *Coils,* "The Book of Coatlicue" in *El Corno Emplumado* # 14, and previously cited "Placements II" in *The Name Encanyoned River.*

3. In a short essay entitled "Novices," written in 1963 and published in *matter* # 3, Robert Duncan writes: "Three sources from which our imagination draws: the sensory universe about us, the works of man and the dream. Of a fourth, 'hallucination' or 'vision,' I am shy, and have few coordinates. I once in near trance 'saw' a man of fire; again, in a mescaline experiment conducted by the Stanford University pharmacy school, I saw the tree of life, but it was a 'work of man,' a figure in a vast weaving, weaving itself, and/or a living mosaic . . .

"[But Charles Olson, in Buffalo, would not accept my using 'hallucinate'; and now, searching out the word I find it means (*alucinor,* to wander in mind, to talk idly—might this really be *to talk oneself into?*—prate, dream; and back of the Latin, Greek: ἀλύσις, distress, anguish. To be beside oneself with grief, see things in that light) O.E.D.: To be deceived, suffer illusion, entertain false notions, blunder, mistake. Wow! no wonder Charles didn't want it.]"

Yet wandering in mind would seem to be an accurate description of creative fits and starts, "life in the labyrinth," and anyone who has ever had a conversation with Duncan himself has experienced the poet's associational weaving/wandering. Frye, in distinguishing Blake as a visionary (in contrast to a mystic or madman), gave that word status, but one wonders: is the tree full of angels glimpsed by the young Blake of a different order of seeing than Duncan's man of fire? In our Protestant society, visions induced by hallucinogens tend to be suspect, but even a cursory glance at world mythology and shamanic activity will show the novice that in a pagan or primitive context the mushroom is viewed as an aid in seeing, an intensifier of visionary potential. Olson himself experimented with hallucinogens, and "Maximus, from Dogtown—II" appears to be written under their sway.

My first LSD experience in the spring of 1965 was an extraordinary experience (its hallucinogenic core is worked into "Origin," *Coils,* pp. 94–95); subsequent experiences with the drug were less rewarding.

CHAPTER 12

The poet's resistance to psychoanalysis is a resistance to discovering his unconscious motives for writing poetry—as if discovering a severing—a witch with a long nose intruding into the play-house window, discovering what the children are "really" doing there. The fear that more information is the end of information is Blake's enemy, "doubt which is self-contradiction," and it hamstrings the novice through developing a reluctance to investigate Psyche—to investigate *anything*.

But I want to cut across what I believe here, and let a poet who rejected analysis and who went ahead to write magnificent poetry after doing so, speak:

Rainer Maria Rilke to Lou Andreas-Salomé, 1912:

> I rather shun this getting cleared out and, with my nature, could hardly expect anything good of it. Something like a disinfected soul results from it, a monstrosity, alive, corrected in red like the page of a school notebook.[1]

> I do feel myself infinitely strongly bound to the once begun, to all the joy and all the misery it entails, so that, strictly speaking, I can wish for no sort of change, no interference from without, no relief, except that inherent in enduring and final achievement. . . . It seems to me certain that if one were to drive out my devils, my angels too would get a little (let us say), a very little fright and—you do feel it—that is what I may not risk at any cost.[2]

Rilke would agree with Auden about allowing no books of criticism in a College for Bards, and, like Rimbaud, is concerned with the monstrous, but from a different angle: Rimbaud intends to *infect* himself to undermine the starched domesticity of Charlesville and make contact with the chthonic powers of poetry. Rilke fears the *disinfected* soul that might result from analysis, as if it could empty him back to the military-school classroom where he was at the mercy of a master's formulaic revisions. By offering his devils (hardly daemons here; more likely neurotic habits) to a Freudian analyst, he fears that he will be removing an essential alchemical component from the compost he needs to nurture his angels, or flowering. For disinfected Rimbaud, ensouling is a reinfecting; on the other hand, Rilke, probably more abused and disoriented by education than Rimbaud, now seeks to protect what he has been able to save of himself. Infection and disinfection coil like snakes about the caduceus of a healing that for the poet is never clearly one or the other.

In 1922, having weathered this critical period of his life without succumbing to analysis, Rilke wrote to another correspondent:

> I believe that as soon as an artist has found the living center of his activity, nothing is so important for him as to remain in it and never go further away from it (for it is also the center of his personality, his world) than up to the inside wall of what he is quietly and steadily giving forth; his place is *never*, not even for an instant, alongside the observer and judge. . . . Most artists today use up their strength in this going back and forth, and not only do they expend themselves in it, they get themselves hopelessly entangled and lose a part of their essential innocence in the sin of having surprised their work from outside, tasted of it, shared in the enjoyment of it! The infinitely grand and moving thing about Cézanne . . . is that during almost forty years he remained uninterruptedly with his work, in the innermost center of it—, and I hope someday to show how the incredible freshness and purity of his pictures is due to this obstination: their surface is really like the flesh of fruit just broken open—, while most painters already stand facing their own pictures enjoying and relishing them, violating them in the very process of the work as onlookers and recipients. . . . (I hope, as I say, someday convincingly to point out this to me absolutely definitive attitude of Cézanne's; it might act as advice and warning for anyone seriously determined to be an artist.)[1]

Artaud:

> I don't want to eat my poem, I want to give my heart to my poem.[4]

For Rilke, the labyrinth of the creative process is a walled monastery, out of which fans the heretical world of analysis, worldly fame, hubris, enjoyment, and relishing. While the present is not walled off from the past, inspiration is to be protected from its correctives, as if it takes its orders from a source that regards forays into its inversions, opposites, and caricatures, as blasphemous (elsewhere Rilke praises Cézanne for not losing an afternoon of painting even to attend his only daughter's wedding).

Rilke's words are profound and brave, and speak from an ability to sustain himself in a solitude that most American artists would find pathological (so gregarious are we, or, in alchemical terms, such "leaky vessels"). However, I see a long-standing problem in removing the poet from a realm that includes correction, self-observation, and judgment. As a European poet born in the nineteenth century, who made good use of some of the last aristocratic patronage, Rilke participates in a removed, high Romantic image which regards the poet as spontaneous and visionary, a receptacle through which a primordial frenzy speaks itself. In a "classic" statement of this viewpoint, Jung, in 1922 (the same year Rilke wrote his mature masterpieces), declared: "as long as we are caught up in the process of creation, we neither see nor understand; indeed we ought not to understand, for nothing is more injurious to immediate experience than cognition."[5]

But there is a shadowy side to this viewpoint: if the poet does not "see" or "understand" while writing, such seeing and understanding will have to be done for him. As one with "special access to the beyond, he is from a societal viewpoint put in the same category with the child, the insane, and the primitive and, at one time, women,"[6] and thus ultimately in need of correction or criticism. He is only to be trusted at the point his writing is rationally framed, canonized, and thus sheared of the fangs that made him special in the first place. Living poets, from this viewpoint, are better off dead, when the irrational and disturbing aspects of their writing have been drained off. A second shadow is this: those who do the draining and evaluating cannot be creative, because spontaneity and self-involvement would weaken critical judgment. For several hundred years, poets and critics have been snapping at each other across a narrow but deep river. The living presence of the poet vexes the critic, who is unsure of what to do with him as he has no historical perspective on him. The poet, on the other hand, not only finds it disgusting that someone outside his "divine frenzy" should be allowed to judge him (and in effect decide whether he is to be read or not by future generations), but suspects that the critic is a "closet" poet who does not have the guts to lay himself bare.

In 1984, I recorded several hours of conversation with the Archetypal Psychologist James Hillman, whose thoughtful and creative books I have been reading for the past decade. We wanted to start to build a bridge across the river I have briefly described, feeling that poetry and psychology can make use of both banks. Neither of us believe in what Hillman refers to as "a certain court model, which splits consciousness from unconsciousness, reason from unreason, creation from criticism." His response to the Jung passage quoted here is as follows:

> I wouldn't agree with that. I would say that when you're in the midst of the process of—I don't want to use the word "creation" either, it tends to get inflated—but in the midst of writing, or speaking a poem, or whatever, let's just say writing, there is a seeing going on in the hand and in the heart, and in the eye, which is not the kind of seeing Jung is talking about which is detached outside seeing, but the fingers have an eye on them. E-Y-E. An eye that knows to put this word and not that word and to cross that out suddenly and to jump to the next thing. That's all seeing. It's not blind. That's a romantic sense that there's natural creativity and then there's detached scientific observation.

In regard to his own practice of analysis, Hillman commented:

> I think most of these alternatives come into the analytical room, especially the one of being a scientific detached judge/critic/observer. Certainly that is a favorite stance one takes in being an analyst. But it is not the only story at all. There's also the talking from that place Rilke is talking about, when you're absolutely inside the image, or inside the emotion or complex that's in the room with the two of you, maybe it's come out of a dream, maybe it has just come out of sitting there and what is said is very free. And now: *is* it blind? . . . are we where Jung said you don't know what you're saying and you don't see what you're doing? I don't think that's the case. I think it's very much like I said. Your fingers have eyes in them. And when you're reacting emotionally and imaginatively to the dream, you are doing the same thing as Rilke is talking about. There is a poesis. You are making a whole new construction, which is not an interpretation. It's a new construction that's closer to what you do when you translate . . . but let's get rid of that word "interpretation," and maybe even "translation." For the moment, that isn't what I want to do with this dream that is coming. I don't want to *interpret* the dream. I want to talk to the dream, talk about the dream, restate the dream, imagine from the dream, but I don't mean a free-floating fantasy. And I sure don't mean a bunch of subjective reactions and feelings and associations: "This makes me think of . . ." You are there, I believe, to *respond* to the dream, and that forces you to stick pretty close to it, much as you have to with a poem that you are translating. The dream is your master, let's say. It provides the limits, the discipline. What you say to it is in service of the dream. Yet, all along the response comes from the imagination.[7]

Robert Kelly:

The Subjective

is not the opposite of the rigorous.
It is the most rigorous, the most difficult.

The *precise subjective* is what philosophers are too
lazy & too generalizing to labor, scientists too
frightened to search out.

The Objective is p.r. for the Generalization.

Objective Order, so-called, is mental artifact,
    consensus, "collective consciousness,"
    "lethargy of custom (STC"

The 'objective' is a consolation prize for those
    who've lost the real.[8]

NOTES

1. *Letters of Rainer Maria Rilke*, 1910–1926, NYC, 1969, p. 44.
2. *Letters of Rilke*, p. 51.
3. *Letters of Rilke, pp.* 273–274.
4. *Artaud Anthology*, p. 101.
5. "On the Relation of Analytical Psychology to Poetry," *The Portable Jung*, NYC, 1972, pp. 301–322.
6. "Part One of a Discussion on Psychology and Poetry," *Sulfur* # 16, p. 58.
7. "Psychology and Poetry," pp. 58, 72–73. At other points in our discussion, Hillman unpacks such loaded terms as "divine frenzy" and "primordial," terms whose ultimate effects are as negative as they are charismatic.
8. "On Discourse," *Io* # 20 (Biopoesis), p. 18.

CHAPTER 13

Paul Christensen introducing the first installment of the Edward Dahl-berg/Charles Olson Correspondence, in *Sulfur* #1:

> In August, 1936, Charles Olson knocked on the door of a boarding house in the town of Rockport, a mile beyond East Gloucester, to in-quire if an Edward Dahlberg were home. The message was sent upstairs, but Dahlberg was keeping to his room to avoid hearing his fellow board-ers saw away at their instruments in their weekly home concert in the parlor below. He sent back the message that he was busy. Olson misun-derstood and proceeded to wait at the front door until after midnight. Dahlberg was again reminded of his caller at the door, and in a fit of pity and embarrassment rushed down to greet the stranger. He was surprised to find a stalk of a man rising six feet seven inches, a twenty-six-year-old man with huge eyes and bushy eyebrows, enormous hands, with shy, in-tense, determined gestures. Dahlberg let him in and the two fell into a conversation about Shakespeare in which they forgot the time. Some hours later, Dahlberg let him out again and realized privately to himself he had met someone who had a chance at greatness. In the instant, Dahlberg became a father to this hulk of potential, this handsome, schol-arly, awkward figure who was the image of his own youth.[1]

The first time I heard the word "apprenticeship": Kyoto, 1963, a li-thographer friend, Will Petersen, introduced me to a sixty-year-old bonsai gardener who was described as the "apprentice" to someone. I later asked Will how old the "master" was. In his late 70s, he said. And then explained: this man will be going off on his own soon and have perhaps 10 years to develop what he has learned.

Elderly Stevens:

> The poem is the cry of its occasion,
> Part of the *res* itself and not about it.[2]

Not, in other words, the cry of the poet himself, a perspective Stevens adopted from the very beginning. For many other poets, the first ten years of writing seem to essentially be one long cry. There is something compelling and honest about being direct in this regard (e.g., *Howl*), or, as in the case of the first poem in Jerome Rothenberg's first book, allowing the cry but also putting it into context that offers resonance beyond a self-pitying ego:

A Little Boy Lost

They took me from the white sun and they
left me in the black sun, left
me to sleep among long rows of overcoats:
I was a city boy lost in the country, a
wound in my hand was all I knew about willows
Can you understand, do you hear the wide
sound of the wind against the cow's
side, and the crickets that run down my
sleeve, crickets full of the night, with
bodies like little black suns? try as I will
there is only this cry in my heart, this cry:
They took me from the white sun, and they
left me in the black sun, and I
have no way of turning now, no door.[3]

Allen Ginsberg came to the door of his NYC 10th Street flat and told me he would talk with me if I would buy him a hamburger. I did, downstairs in the luncheonette, and he talked nonstop for an hour about Shelley and Mayakofsky. Then he told me to go meet Herbert Huncke and tell him Allen had sent me. I knocked, and was met by a gentle face from the pit who invited me in to a living room in which several people were silently camped out on battered furniture. "We're cooking a poem, man," Huncke said, "com'ere." He led me into the kitchen and opened the oven door. There it was, a typed poem on a sheet of paper turning brown around the edges in a 350° oven. Huncke closed the door and shuffled back into the living room, me following. Still no one said anything. After hanging around for a few minutes, I decided I was definitely not hungry, and slipped out.

Louis Zukofsky took me over to his Brooklyn Willow Street front window and asked me what I saw. I said something about the Statue of Liberty being out there. Zukofsky paused for a moment, and then said: "the statue is in the water." A memorable but dumb remark I decided years later.

Cid Corman was preparing to edit the "second series" of *origin* magazine when I knocked on his boardinghouse door in San Francisco, 1960. We had already exchanged a few letters, and one, Corman's response to a group of student poems I had submitted to *origin*, had made me break into tears while I was reading it. In bolt-from-the-blue fashion, it said: get serious about poetry or forget it. When I met Cid, he was brooding about Ginsberg, Burroughs, and the Beats, whom he felt were "sick." The new *origin* series, to be anchored by the serialization of Zukofsky's "A," was to provide an "open" alternative. Eight years later, Corman wrote an "open letter" nominating Allen Ginsberg and Muhammad Ali for President and Vice-President of the United States, which I published in my magazine, *Caterpillar.*

Corman would respond immediately (his letters seemed to come back approximately an hour after you had mailed yours to him) to anything I said, and while his responses were aggressively pedagogical (some of which was undoubtedly an echo of the pounding he had taken from Olson), he was astute and awesomely dedicated, so when I moved to Kyoto about a year after Cid had, I started seeing him on a regular basis. He would leave his room in the afternoon, browse in the Maruzen bookstore or visit art galleries, eat downtown, and with books, letters, notebooks, etc., "retire" to the Muse coffee shop until about 11 PM. If you wanted to see Cid, you called on him at his "office" there. Over the next two years, I dropped in once or twice a week, and learned the rudiments of translation and magazine editing. We did a little translating together, and Cid went over the first few drafts of my Vallejo translations. I watched him on a weekly basis assemble issues of *origin*, and would often walk all the way home from the Muse (about an hour) just to digest, slowly, in the night air, passing through temple grounds and narrow fenced alleys, what Cid had said.

At first in Kyoto I tried to imitate the kind of poetry Corman was publishing in *origin*, but doing so was like compressing my body into my eyes, and my eyes into a few, almost factual lines. After 5 hours of evading most of what was on my mind, I would end up with something that gave no indication of *my* situation, or the energy I had put into those 5 hours. At a certain point, I began to feel that Corman was watching me every minute when I was writing (and sometimes when I was not writing: before doing something I found myself asking myself, what would Cid think of this?). Indeed, he was an unyielding advocate of what he himself practiced, but I had set him like a Nevermore-Alter-Ego-Raven on my shoulder, and once I realized that, I was able to start exploring the kind of poetry I wanted to write—which went against Cid and *origin*. In fact, it was much closer to the "sick" poetry of Ginsberg, in that it began to unpack my impacted past and confront my unresolved identity via some of the "unmentionable" areas that I touched on before in *Novices*. My apprenticeship, by the beginning of 1964, consisted of:

1. Visits to Corman at the Muse, and a correspondence with a wide range of poets, including Jack Hirschman, Thomas Merton, Jerry Rothenberg, W. S. Merwin, Robert Kelly, Paul Blackburn, and Mary Ellen Solt.
2. Working on my own poems every morning, then after lunch motorcycling downtown to the Yorunomado coffee shop where I translated Vallejo until suppertime.[4]
3. After supper, I would walk down the hill to a neighborhood coffee shop and read for several hours.
4. Besides short poems, I was increasingly caught up in an interminable, meandering long poem, "The Tsuruginomiya Regeneration," which was frustrated by my attempts to investigate the Pandorabox of materials that I had opened in the past five years and, at the same time, to prove to myself that I had successfully changed my life.

Of course I did not stick by this schedule every day; at times the impossibility of making things flow as a poet, translator, or reader became so frustrating, I would wander around Kyoto looking for places to take hold—things, or incidents, in which I could perceive something and get beyond a literal description. When occasionally reading, observing, and thinking did coalesce, I would find myself propelled forward and up against a new wall, that was often menacing and bizarre:

Paused on the Shichijo Bridge,

　　　the day misty,
lovely, grisly . . . the Kamogawa fades, shallows forever,
winding out through Kyoto's southern shacks . . .

　　　below, in the littered mud,
a man stabs around in cans and sewage,
in his ragged khaki overcoat and army puttees
I was taken forward to a blind spot

　　　(he pulled himself up
a rope ladder hung over the stone embankment

and with limp burlap sack slung over his shoulder
disappeared down an alley
home?   to the faces?
                          What *do*
I express when I write?
   Knives?   or Sunlight?
           And "everything
that lives is holy" raced through my mind.

      Walking home,
paused under the orange gates of Sanjusangendo, in
under the dripping eaves, cosy,
I noticed a stand of barbwire
looped over stakes I had stepped
inside of

      and then it came to me)

      I would kill for you[5]

At the moment of this realization, "you" was my wife Barbara, and after writing these lines I mainly felt that I had contained the sensations of those thirty minutes on the bridge. Years later, I realized that the stakes I had stepped inside of were the stakes of a commitment to poetry, which Psyche warned me was as severe as taking or protecting life.

Snyder once told me that I was spending too much time on Vallejo and not enough time on Eshleman. I responded that by working on Vallejo I was working on Eshleman—and I think I was right, but I also think Gary's challenge was meaningful.

Unfortunately, each novice has to determine, "without having the full information needed for his choice," how to constellate his own field, knowing that an immense amount will be left out. In my own case: would I have been better off studying Pound than Vallejo? Or doing zazen at Daitokuji instead of reading *The Masks of God*, or Frye's *Fearful Symmetry* on which I spent a full year? How could I have possibly launched into a long poem (roughly 400 pages), without a thorough study of epic poetry and subsequently tracking the evolution of the "serial poem," from Whitman, say, to Spicer? Like many other modern poets, I have made intuitive moves, trying to honor obsessions, and staying away from areas that did not compel me. I have taken the risk that by following my own energies I would in the long run create a more genuine, and hopefully enduring, constellation of nodal emphases, than I would by respecting Anglo-American canons and studying them to the exclusion of peripheral and even inconsequential materials. If something has felt like an energy deposit, a metaphoric vault glinting with possible ore, I have swung over to it, forgetting about what I *should* be doing.

At the end of "People," Robert Creeley writes of:

> the
>
> one
> multiphasic
> direction,
>
> the going,
> the coming,
> the lives.
>
> *I*
> fails in
> the forms
>
> of them, I
> want
> to go home.[6]

Under all of our outward reaching, our attempts to contact what we are not, to elephant-trunk the brush into our maws, there is this countercurrent, this back-pulling creature, so astonishingly evoked by Ferenczi, seeking home, and what really is home—for a poet? what really is home for one involved with a labyrinth that turns in as it turns out, and for whom center is mainly divergence, that inner/outer arabesque, both van Gogh and Reich presented as a cosmic and human core? *I want to go home*—but is not home for the poet a being in and with a "multiphasic" configuration, an abode in imagination, and how different is it from the cradle, how different is the mental sensation of a poem going at full tilt from the boiled eggs my mother would bring to me in the middle of the night when at ten years old I would awake and cry and cry until she would cook something and attend me?

"My house is not my house," Lorca wept, so we could say that our home is not our home, and is the home that is not a home something like the Zen *Mumonkan*, the gate that is not a gate, the "gateless gate"? I have this continuing deep intuition that as I curve out, throwing my crab claw imagination out and out for the prey of material, there is another claw curving back under me that flows outward as the grasper for material swings back in with its "catch." My feelings about this are primarily anchored to one experience.

Soon after I started trying to write poetry, in 1957, I met a slightly older couple, George and Dolly Stewart, who lived in Indianapolis, at a party in Bloomington, and made friends with them. I began to visit them on a regular basis, driving up from Bloomington, and staying with them over the weekend, without letting my parents, twenty minutes north of the Stewarts, know that I was in town. Both George and Dolly were painters, and in their sensual, bohemian apartment, permeated with the aroma of pigments, I felt deeply at home—even on their living-room couch I slept a deep, deep nourishing sleep. I left Indiana in 1961 for the Far East, lost contact with the Stewarts, and when I returned, in 1964, they were no longer in Indianapolis.

Near the end of my mother's life in 1969, while visiting her and my father before they sold the family home and moved into a nursing home, I suddenly became curious as to where I had spent my second and third year. I knew the location of the place to which I had been brought home from the Methodist Hospital, and the location of the rental where we had lived during my fourth and fifth years before moving to 4705 Boulevard Place, our one and only house and home. My mother's health and memory were failing, and she agreed: if we were going to find the place, it was now or never.

We drove to a neighborhood south of us that had changed considerably over the past decade, circling around block after block, with my mother commenting how strange everything looked. She said she only recalled that it was a large second-floor apartment facing Delaware Street. At a certain point, she said: stop—I think that's it. She was staring at a large nondescript house, which had been broken up into first and second floor apartments. It meant nothing to me, but since we were there, I thought, well, make something out of this, at least go up and walk around it. My mother preferred to sit in the car, so I walked up to the house and moseyed around it. At the southeast corner, there was a public side door. I opened it and looked up the staircase—and then decided to climb, feeling, as I ascended, a strange yet pleasant buoyancy. I thought: my god, she's really found it—and then—I nearly dropped in my tracks, for as my head came up to the level of the landing, I found myself staring at George's and Dolly's door. I looked again: the diagonal crack in the interior panel had been painted over but it was still there.

My distressed mother could have been mistaken in regard to finding the house we lived in when I was two—but she did bring me to the place to which I had been magnetized, my chrysalis, as it were, at the point I broke free of college life in Bloomington and sought a new place in poetry. And if this house was indeed the house we moved to in 1936 (and why not give her the benefit of the doubt—her lifelong strength had resided in mothering intuitions), then she had effected a kind of *hierosgamos*, or "sacred marriage," taking my point of poetic discovery (Bloomington) in one hand, and the place where she had taught me the rudiments of speech in the other, introducing me to their fusion in that home within home I had unconsciously chosen in which to incubate myself at the point that I desired that nebulous regeneration that still drips like blood through the sidewalks of clouds.

> O ripe husk within ripe husk,
>   way by which we would bury ourselves in
>   the active tomb of
>   our earliest attempt
>   at speech.

NOTES

1. The complete correspondence between Olson and Dahlberg (published in *Sulfurs* # 1–3) is a moving example of the near-impossibility of apprentice and master recasting their roles in an eye-to-eye relationship at the point the apprentice becomes the equal of his teacher. In the eyes of the master, the apprentice never quite comes up to him, reciprocity from his viewpoint representing a serious diminution of his size. In the eyes of the apprentice-become-equal, the master's values have been surveyed and found wanting (their gaps are space, in effect, for his growth), thus his earlier size was a mirage. Entangled in this whole matter of course are the spectres of natural father and son (or mother and daughter). Olson in 1953, speaking to students at Black Mountain College as he reflects on Cro-Magnon man:

> What I want to pose to you now is: what is your experience of your size? do you, or not, move among the herd of men with the sense of yourself as not yet filling out your size? do you, thus, have the feeling of being smaller, both than yrself and than how others appear to you? The problem is best measured in terms of that illusion of the parents. And that question, are we ever fathers or mothers to ourselves? Actually, I take it, we aren't—that our omnipotence is only always in the eyes of the children of us, not in ourselves except as—because we once were—our parents had that dimension. I have this hunch: that the reason why grandfathers and grandmothers were up until recently lent an authority was that, in fact, only in that third generation do we acquire some of that dimension the first generation seems to have in the eyes of the second—and of course, there is cause of a subtler order than the biological: that by grand time any of us ought, if we have managed our lives, to have filled out more of those outlines of our

possibility we are strained toward. But the living question stays, am I right that most of our time we take ourselves to be smaller than others, to be smallness in face of the world?

(*Olson* # 10, pp. 31–32)

Vallejo in 1937 Paris:

> The accent dangles from my shoe;
> I hear it perfectly
> succumb, shine, fold in the shape of amber
> and hang, colorific, evil shade.
> My size thus exceeds me,
> judges observe me from a tree,
> they observe me with their backs walk forward,
> enter my hammer
> stop to look at a girl
> and, before a urinal, raise my shoulders.
>
> For sure no one's at my side,
> I could care less, I need no one;
> for sure they've told me to be off;
> I feel it clearly.
>
> The cruelest size is that of praying!
> Humiliation, splendor, deep forest!
> Size now exceeds me, elastic fog,
> rapidity hastily and from and joined.
> Imperturbable! Imperturbable! They ring
> at once, later, fatidic phones.
> It's the accent; it's him.

(*Conductors of the Pit*, p. 24)

2. Wallace Stevens, *The Collected Poems*, NYC, 1957, p. 473.

3. Jerome Rothenberg, *White Sun Black Sun*, NYC, 1960.

4. The psychological crux of translation as it pertains to apprenticeship is addressed by Eliot Weinberger: "The dissolution of the translator's ego is essential if the foreign poet is to enter the language—a bad translation is the insistent voice of the translator" (*Works on Paper*, NYC, 1986, p. 132). I have not expounded on my apprentice relationship to Vallejo's European poetry here, as it is amply discussed elsewhere, mainly in the Introduction to *The Posthumous Poetry*, and in three of my own poems: "The Book of Yorunomado," "At the Tomb of Vallejo," and "The Name Encanyoned River."

5. From "The Book of Yorunomado," *The Name Encanyoned River*, p. 23.

6. *The Collected Poems of Robert Creeley*, Berkeley, 1982, pp. 484–495.

Appendix

In September 1957, the seventy-four-year-old William Carlos Williams was interviewed by John Wingate (standing in for Mike Wallace) on the national CBS television program "Nitebeat." As Williams' biographer Paul Mariani writes, "Wingate's questions were provocative, teasing, even entrapping, as the portion of the transcript that appeared in the New York *Post* for Friday, October 18—and which Williams used in *Paterson V*—will show at a glance. Even the caption, 'Mike Wallace Asks William Carlos Williams Is Poetry A Dead Duck,' suggests the kind of high comedy and cavalier dismissal with which the American poet is normally greeted in his own country."

Paterson V appeared in 1958, and sometime between then and the fall of 1959, Cid Corman wrote a "double-take" of the interview, which I published in the first issue of the first magazine I edited, *Folio*, Winter 1960, at Indiana University. The piece has never been reprinted, and I offer it here as a response-to-the-philistines that is still trenchant. It accurately reflects Corman's view that poetry is to be *heard* (sounded) and that its reception and practice engage all of one's life (in contrast to its use in our society for the most part as an occasion to advance personal prestige).

(Double-Take: Another Response
(vide, Paterson V, *Mike Wallace interview)*

Q. Mr. Corman, can you tell me, simply, what poetry is?

A. No, simply.

Q. Can you tell me, then, ah, complexly or in any way?

A. It is an expression of life.

Q. That's rather vague, isn't it?

A. No, it simply doesn't evade vagueness.

Q. Can't you give me a practical definition?

A. If poetry could be defined, it couldn't exist.

Q. But how do you *know* a poem when you see one?

A. I don't. I listen.

Q. And when you listen?

A. I hear life expressed and in that expression realized; and I am moved and renewed by the experience.

Q. All right. Look at this part of a poem by e. e. cummings, another great American poet:

> etc etc etc

Is this poetry?

A. Aren't you begging the question by loading it?

Q. What do you mean?

A. Instead of flattering me by necessarily specious arguments of "greatness," which are certainly irrelevant, or not flattering either to Mr. Cummings or myself by your implied sarcasm, your question might in fairness have simply gone:

> Here is some writing by E. E. Cummings, who is a poet of some repute. Do you think it is poetry?

Q. Excuse me, then. Would you care to answer the question in your improved version?

A. No, I can't respond to part of a poem as if it were an entire poem. That would be like handing me your brains, if it were possible, or some other less noble part, and saying, Now what do you think of me, in view of my brains, or whatever, as a man? I frankly wouldn't think anything of you. How could I?

Q. But can you *understand* this piece of writing?

A. Yes. Insofar as a fragment can be understood in isolation. I see that Cummings has playfully broken his words upon a typewriter in describing or trying to get at the way a child may sense or treat a cat. At least, he implies the childlike in spelling out the word "c-a-t" and gives a kind of gentle humor in his reorganization of simple words.

Q. Can such devices be considered poetic?

A. Why not? If they are expressive of life; that is, if they realize life in particular moment.

Q. Don't you think they are rather too clever and too eccentric?

A. Perhaps they draw too much attention to the printed page and the effect gained may be relatively trivial. But even in so small a fragment there is gaiety and joy, which can't be denied. And Cummings deserves no less than our support and sympathetic attention for trying to extend the possibilities of expression, since that is tantamount to giving more possibility to our lives.

Q. But do you think people can understand such writing?

A. They can, if they care to.

Q. But shouldn't a word mean something at once when you see it?

A. It should mean whatever it is, when you *hear* it. There are difficulties in poetry, as there are in life. And you will have as much "success" in understanding one as the other to the extent that you confront those difficulties patiently and with all the powers of life at your command.

Q. Isn't that asking rather a lot in reading a poem?

A. I'm not asking anything. You are. If you care to read (to hear) poetry at all, you must give yourself to it—completely, just as it is given to you. If you go to poetry, you have a responsibility to it equal to its own.

What follows are two brief reading lists, and a final salute to all of us from Paul Blackburn (1926–1971). The first list is made up of works that I studied as a novice that taught me something about life and poetry, and that haunt me still. The second list is an up-to-date assembly of books that bear upon poetry as I understand it, an assembly that is intended to create a kind of resource indication upon which future poetry might draw.

Bashō's *Back Roads to Far Towns* (Tr. by Corman and Kamaike); Allen Ginsberg's *Howl* (also the Original Draft Facsimile of *Howl*, the annotations to which include Jack Kerouac's "Belief and Technique of Modern Prose"); Franz Kafka's "The Bucket Rider"; Djuna Barnes' *Nightwood*; Vincent van Gogh's letters; William Blake's 1802 letter to Thomas Butts, "Enion's lament" from *The Four Zoas*, and *The Arlington Court Regeneration* painting; Samuel Taylor Coleridge's "Ne Plus Ultra"; Paul Blackburn's "Crank It Up for All of Us, But Let Me Heaven Go"; Basil Bunting's "Chomei at Toyama"; Hugh MacDiarmid's "On a Raised Beach"; Black Elk Speaks; Aimé Césaire's "Lynch" (Tr. by Emile Snyder, in *Hip Pocket Poets* #2); Diane Wakoski's "Slicing Oranges for Jeremiah"; Robert Kelly's "The Exchanges"; Jerome Rothenberg's "The Seven Hells of Jikoku Zoshi"; William Carlos Williams' "The pure products of America go crazy"; Louis Zukofsky's *A*, sections 9 and 11; Henry Miller's "Reunion in Brooklyn"; Wilhelm Reich's *The Function of the Orgasm* and *The Mass Psychology of Fascism;* Vladimir Mayakovsky's "And Yet" (Tr. by Jack Hirschman & Victor Erlich, the version in *Hip Pocket Poets* #1); Gary Snyder's "The Market"; Pablo Neruda's "Walking Around" and "Caballero Solo"; García Lorca's essay on "the Duende," and his "Oda a Walt Whitman"; Hart Crane's "Lachrymae Christi" and "Havana Rose"; César Vallejo's "Hay días, me viene, una gana . . ."; René Char's *Hypnos Waking;* Max Beckmann's *The Departure;* Hieronymus Bosch's *The Garden of Earthly Delights;* Chaim Soutine's paintings of hanging fowl; Bud Powell's "Un Poco Loco"; Lennie Tristano's version of "I surrender dear"; Charlie Parker's "Koko"; Shakespeare's *Hamlet;* the following letters by Rainer Maria Rilke, in vol. II of the Norton *Selected Letters:* #194, 209, 211, and 218— also his "An Experience" and "Archaic Torso of Apollo"; Dylan Thomas's "Fern Hill"; Walt Whitman's 1855 original version of *Leaves of Grass;* Justino Fernandez's *Coatlicue;* Colin Wilson's *The Outsider;* Northrop Frye's *Fearful Symmetry;* Joseph Campbell's tetralogy, *The Masks of God;* the *I Ching* (Wilhelm/Baynes translation); *The Bhagavad-gita* (Tr. by S. Radhakrishnan); Jean Genet's *Miracle of the Rose.*

S. Giedion's *The Eternal Present: The Beginnings of Art.*
Georges Bataille's *Lascaux* (in concert with Annette Laming's *Lascaux,* and Leroi-Gourhan's *Treasures of Prehistoric Art).*
R. B. Onian's *The Origins of European Thought.*
Weston LaBarre's *The Ghost Dance.*
Mikhail Bakhtin's *Rabelais and His World.*
Barbara Walker's *The Woman's Encyclopedia of Myths and Secrets.*
Sandor Ferenczi's *Thalassa.*
N. O. Brown's *Love's Body.*
Charles Olson's *Call Me Ishmael* and *The Maximus Poems.*
Conductors of the Pit: Major Works by Rimbaud, Vallejo, Césaire, Artaud and Holan.
James Hillman's *Re-Visioning Psychology.*
Louis Zukofsky's *A Test of Poetry.*
Robert Duncan's *Fictive Certainties* (plus "Rites of Participation" and "The Homosexual in Society").
Andrea Dworkin's *Pornography.*
Shuttle & Redgrove's *The Wise Wound.*

Rothenberg & Quasha's *America A Prophecy.*
Laura Riding's *The Telling.*
Sjöö and Mor's *The Great Cosmic Mother.*
Wolfgang Giegerich's *The Psychoanalysis of the Atomic Bomb*
 (unpublished as of this date in English).
Carlos Castaneda's *The Teachings of Don Juan.*
Hans Peter Duerr's *Dreamtime.*
Robicsek & Hales' *The Maya Book of the Dead.*
Gary Snyder's *Earth House Hold.*
Susan Howe's *My Emily Dickinson.*
Eliot Weinberger's *Works on Paper.*
Charles Bernstein's *Content's Dream.*
John Clarke's *From Feathers to Iron.*
Donald Ault's *Narrative Unbound.*

The Art

to write poems, say,
is not a personal achievement
that bewilderment

On the way to work
two white butterflies
& clover along the walks

to ask   .
to want that much of it   .

[1989]

II

The Gull Wall

In the autumn of 1960, after I had spent a summer in Mexico writing what I felt were my first real poems, Paul Blackburn and I had lunch at a place in New York City he refers to in his own poetry as "the bakery." At the end of lunch I showed him some of my poems, and after reading "A Very Old Woman" he looked up at me with a big grin on his face and with some superlative exclamation blew me a kiss. By doing so at just the right time he confirmed the fact that I had, on my own, at least got up on my feet. A few years ago, reading one of Robin Blaser's poems, I came across the lines: "the poet's kiss / given—caught *like a love- / adept* on my lips." He was speaking of an actual kiss, and it made me think of what Blackburn gave me, which was a covenant given by an already-confirmed poet to another nonconfirmed one. By confirming me when he did I felt Paul had given me in an ancient and noble way a "charge," the Poet's Kiss, which would only be realized when in some original way it was returned. In 1964, in my poem "Niemonjima," I worked one of Paul's central images, the gull, and transformed it into the Gull-robe:

> And it was only the robe that drove him on,
> a vision of the inland sea, which is called the Gull-robe,
> gorgeous, of white feathers emblazoned with stars & moons,
> the lovely garment every loved woman wears, of midnight-
> blue & silks, in which a light streams for all who ride
> away into the darkness carrying the torches of imaginative
> love, the softness & precision of loved desire.

A slightly different form of this essay appeared in *Sixpack*, #7/8, the "Paul Blackburn Issue," and in *Boundary* 2. In its present form it appeared in *The Gull Wall* (Black Sparrow Press, Los Angeles, 1975) and in my collection of essays, *Antiphonal Swing* (McPherson & Co., Kingston, N.Y., 1989).

A great deal of the meaning Paul Blackburn has for me, his life as well as his poetry, is involved with the role he played in my becoming a poet, and this is especially touching to me because during those years he was beginning to lose grip on his own life and writing. From 1962 to 1964 my first wife, Barbara, and I lived in Kyoto, Japan. I had published my first book of poems before moving there and the poems in it were written while I was either a student, on vacation in Mexico, or teaching. Upon moving to Kyoto, I found myself for the first time cut loose from any job or study routine to depend on; I was suddenly on my own, I had 24 hours to face and fill, and for most of these two years I was tied up in the frustrations from my past that I thought I had evaded by becoming a poet. I was reaching the point when I would either accept my own life as my material, or reject my life, and continue to imitate other poets. This is the point at which what is previously amorphous in a young poet's work begins to appear either original or "academic"—where he begins to doubt the meaningfulness of his first influences. Since I chose the first alternative, I began to feel lost, a feeling which lasted for a number of years.

Originality at that time meant little more than taking my own life to task; the writing that resulted seemed to mean less than what I would have written had I continued to imitate others. I understand something about this now, I understand that apprenticework, in the sense that I am speaking of it, has a great deal to do with letting the held-back dam of one's past break through one's mouth with all its roil, its stones and silt, and that this act itself, taking years perhaps, is only the first stage of approaching an art of poetry for, as the dam gives way the novice must continually create *out of* what is struggling through him as well as keep the past itself in motion. It is the "creating out of" that is felt as a terrible friction, almost blockage to the longed-for flow, especially if the destruction of the dam is sudden.

During those years in Kyoto I would sit for hours before the typewriter, sometimes just staring at the first line I had written trying to figure out how to make it yield poetry, or at other times typing the line out over and over, varying it, repeating it, trying to dislodge it from my own commonsense world of the past which I was still holding on to, not only because I was scared of losing all moorings, but because I was working with the past, I was to a certain extent stuck with the way my mind in the past had functioned. Paul and I wrote each other about every two weeks during those years and every six months or so exchanged tapes. Our correspondence was not strictly about poetry—it was basically about what we were seeing and doing and feeling. It was real sustenance for me because a friendship was being created and I was finding out that not only did I need to find my identity but that my identity was manifold.

In late October 1963, Paul sent me a new tape, which I took over to a man who had a tape recorder. I remember sitting in an empty tatami room by a large window which looked out onto a backyard filled with junk. It was cold gray out and had begun to snow. Paul's voice, filled with images of brick walls and nearly deserted streets, of men huddling by little trash fires in gutters, his peculiar vision of New York City which integrates the literary life with the viewpoint of someone on the Bowery, began to worm into my feeling for my life as it never had before. I was just opening up to seeing a world inclusive of outcasts that Paul identified with.

For I too had been watching outcast leather workers in Kyoto who seemed to live in the street as well as the migratory construction workers who were building a highway down in the cut below where I lived. They worked all night long, keeping an oil-drum fire going, and I was very moved watching them standing around their fire with their yellow helmets and dark blue wool puttees. At that moment there was no distance between Paul's poems and the junk-filled backyard, the cold in my hands, and the endless repetition I felt watching the tape slowly turn. But it was also a specific repetition, it was not just life repeating itself, but repetition becoming a state of mind through Paul's poetry and his voicing of it—he read some *Rituals* that day, which made me think for the first time, what is a ritual, is it any more than repetition, doing something the way my father had done it, and if so, where is the warmth in that? Something about the way Paul was looking at things found a place in me, but it was a place I was trying to destroy by making poetry. What a dense web of ambivalence was being woven between the two of us that late snowy afternoon—I was being bound into the act of a voice which seemed to consume my defenses against poetry. At the end of the tape it was nearly dark and the snow had turned the junk into little castle-like hills—there was only a faint streak of rose-colored sun left in the light. At this point Paul read a poem whose title I do not remember, I remember only two images in the piece: the first was a vision of a group of primitive men standing around in a circle jacking off into the flukes of a dying fire, and the second came moments later: Paul cried out, "O Leviticus, Oil for the Lamps!"

All the negation in my own life was suddenly present, but it was present to me, a gift—Paul spoke of my negation so that I no longer had to wear it but could begin to work with it as an object. The circle of primitive men became a circle of young Indiana men, pledges to the Phi Delta Theta social fraternity at Indiana University in 1953: I was one of them, and we had been shouted down from the dormitory late one night, ordered to strip, and then bend over holding hands making a circle around the double fireplace which hissed and crackled while "the actives" played *Slaughter on 10th Avenue* at full volume (the fraternity was located at the corner of Jordan and 10th Street), and beat us bloody with long wood paddles. In 1963 I was faced in the act of finding poetry with this impotence in my own makeup—what anguish must have been buried in me that I would have allowed myself to be so abused. There must have been something, some ceremony perhaps, which never took place during my puberty, I thought, which, had it taken place, would have released me from boyhood into manhood—but what could that mean in my present life? I had been reading about an Australian sub-incision ceremony which climaxed a puberty initiation, where the boy was held down spread-eagled over the back of a kneeling man and his urethra split with a sharp rock. Would it have been better had something in my boyhood been bled out of me? It was not simply my manhood that I sought—manhood was too easily just the world of grown-ups. I sought the persimmon tree in the Okumura backyard, I wanted to be in contact with it. Blackburn got through to me that there was something which I experienced as being inside me that had to get out for the contact to exist. He made me aware of this not as one who had succeeded in getting whatever it was out, but as one who had failed and whose cry was uttered as a result of having failed.

It was dark when I left where I was and started back to the house of Okumura. At the point I passed the Senryuji Gate, which led in to the Ancient Imperial Burial Grounds, there was a long flight of wide stone steps which led into Imagumano, my neighborhood. I started to descend and immediately recalled an accident I had seen a couple of years before, the legs of a Japanese schoolgirl extending out from under the rear axle of a bus. When I witnessed this I had a desire to roll the bus off her. Now the axle became a turnstile and as I approached the bottom of the steps I imagined that I was heading into death, but the death I was heading into was so singular it immediately became absurd—I was suddenly aware that I could not resolve Paul's misery nor could I resolve the death of the schoolgirl, and that my attempts to do so before were ridiculous. I had been living my life as if it were a life that could be solved from day to day, first I would do this, then get out of it, then that, get out of it, etc., and as long as I had done that I lived with an awful anxiety but pretended there was no fear in my life. But no, that girl's death impinged upon me and it impinged in the living body of Paul Blackburn, and I could not keep Blackburn's sense of life away from me, I was not singular, what I was was not what I had identified myself to be—I reached the end of the steps, I got down to the turnstile I had felt I was descending to, my crib with only *one* being inside, and I was free of its singularity, wonderfully free of the absurdity of my life and within it.

The gull is more than a central image in Blackburn's poetry: it is the presence of the creation itself, the confirmation that Blackburn allows himself—when a gull or a flock appears in a poem there is hope as well as all that the phrase "the creation" suggests—I would almost say that the gull is the presence of God in Blackburn's body of writing, but that would be making a connection he only alluded to in the opening section of what for several years (1963 to summer 1967) he considered to be his masterwork, *The Selection of Heaven*, a 25-page poem he was unable to complete:

GOD,   that it did happen,
that loose now, that
early confirmation
        of birds, the texture set in
        words,   1945,

A Staten Island beach in early October
here in more than flesh and brick,
9th Street,   March 1963. . . .

This grey   .   soft .   overcast   .   not-quite-rainy day,
that I can
swim my mind in it, swim it in overcast, the sun
tries, and there they are, the birds, my gulls
circle over a street to the North.

At about the same time that he wrote these lines in March 1963, Paul enclosed a photo of a gull standing on a rock in a letter to me, and wrote under the picture: *Dear Clay, Never look a gull in the eye, love Paul.* That admonition really puzzled me, because even then I knew that among all other things Paul Blackburn loved to look and watch—some of his finest poems have a basic fulcrum of Paul sitting someplace, like on a street bench or in a park, and watching what is going on around him, presumably writing the poem in a notebook while it is occurring before his eyes. Anyway, I didn't then pick up the literary connection to the line which comes from the poem called *The Purse-seine*, written in 1960:

> we cannot look one another in the eye,
> > that frightens, easier to face
> the carapace of monster crabs along the beach   .   The empty
> shell of death was always easier to gaze upon
> than to look into the eyes of the beautiful killer   .   Never
> > look a gull in the eye.

The "we" includes the woman the poet is with, and thus by implication both she and the gull are held for a moment in the phrase "the beautiful killer." I think that, deeply, for Paul Blackburn woman *was* the beautiful killer, and that since he insisted on always searching for and being with a woman, his failure to overcome that feeling explains much of his failure to develop as a poet and to live longer as a man.

But before I enter into these problems I want to make a few assertions so that the problems themselves can be seen in the proper context. Blackburn is one of the half-dozen finest American poets of his generation. The body of writing that he left us and the generations to come is much larger and much more impressive than what is now publicly and thus as his *image* available. He wrote first-rate poetry at several periods in his life and his finest poetry in the fifties when he lived in Spain, and this work carries on into the early sixties when he lived in New York City. His gifts were various: he had an acute ear and eye that together enabled him to lay a poem out on the page in an utterly unique way—a Blackburn poem is recognizable about four feet away, one can spot it by its shape, the way the lines extend and break, run for full stanzas or bunch in neat units at any place on the page, often in short-lined quatrains. His ability to stop the poem the moment the poem itself stops is uncanny (e.g., *Hot Afternoons Have Been in West 15th Street*). In Blackburn's poetry one always feels that the quatrain has not quite yet been abandoned, it appears, floats out, fragments, dissolves, is felt in two- and three-line units or is *sensed* at times through inner rhyming: one will occasionally *hear* quatrains when on the page none are visible. In other words, the verse never becomes free, gets free of that traditional cohesive—I would even say *communal*—urge, while at the same time it is open enough to accommodate emotional glide. (I almost said "drive" but Blackburn is generally not a driving poet—he more naturally enjoys gliding, veering and banking, or suddenly dropping to a fused position—for just a moment—like his gulls). In many ways, he is the Buddhist path between Robert Creeley and Charles Olson.

As for his content, his best poems warm the reader with a sense of a generous, compassionate and patient humanity, wry and foolish at times, bleak and helpless at others. While there are few revelations of being in Blackburn's poetry, he does get, given the situation he is addressing, a great deal of what it felt like into the composition he is conceiving; he does not approach the poem (as does Gary Snyder for example) having thought its subject through—his poems most often begin with an impulse, a partial perception or sounding, and pick their way out from there. His strongest and most successful poetry is contingent upon a kind of distance that he creates when he is alone, i.e., unobserved somewhere, not directly involved in the action he is watching, e.g., observing Paul Carroll being tossed a white sunburned body by breakers at Bañalbufar (*Affinities II*) or watching common people fill and leave stone benches at dusk on a busy street in Barcelona in the lovely *Plaza Reál with Palmtrees*. While his writing is free of dogma, there is an implied stance suggesting a way of being. One feels this most in his attitude toward women and sex—toward Romance. The source for this, in a literary sense, is the early-medieval Troubadour tradition, which he knew and suffered thoroughly. He spent more than twenty years translating this poetry, and when it is published in book form I believe it will not only be definitive but will never again be equaled in the American language.

One reason that Paul Blackburn translated the Troubadours is that Ezra Pound complained that here was a great body of poetry to be brought to bear on American poetry which no one had really even attempted. Pound's attitude certainly must have been Blackburn's original incentive. However, such an incentive needed a powerful fuel to sustain this project over two decades, and the fact that Blackburn never completed the *Troubadour* translation, or I should say, the fact that he completed it again and again, keeping it alive, revising and adjusting it, suggests that it kept an obsession in him alive, kept it churning. Central to this obsession is the idealization of woman as expressed by the Troubadours—a view in which woman is a grand icy queen of heaven the poet sings for, a queen who will never be lived with, *period*, an untouchable in a much higher social station than the poet himself, who may reward him with her hand to kiss or with a benevolent glance (there are several tremendous burlesques of this maddening situation in the Troubadour poetry Blackburn translated, notably Guillem Comte de Poitou's *Farai un vers pos mi sonelh*, but these pieces hardly dent the idealization). I can imagine how in twelfth-century Europe such an attitude might have had a great deal to do with the evolution of consciousness, adoration of spring and burgeoning being more and more associated with human love, and of course regardless of what it meant to the lives of those concerned, it produced a genuine body of art.

To consider why such an attitude was attractive to Paul Blackburn is complicated. I don't think he himself knew—for like nearly all men of his age he was sexually cracked in a number of directions and the parts never fit together. On one hand, he was a very warm and sensual man who loved cats and food and wine in a way much more European-Catholic than American-Puritanic, and in this sense he lacked typical American hangups regarding hygiene and order; he was messy (his desk was always covered with strata of unfinished letters, translations and poems) but not dirty, or I should say I always had a good natural feeling about the world in his presence. On the other hand, I had the feeling that for Paul sensuality and sexuality did not flow together—I always had the impression that he allowed the woman he lived with to rot on the vine. He had serious problems about his identity regarding men and woman, and he expressed this conflict in a rare self-confrontational passage in *The Selection of Heaven:*

> Tell me what else this shoulder might serve for
> please, I want to live beyond that
> please, the drive back   300   miles
> please, no other life, please,
> please there IS that
> difference, say it
> might have been a man but
> now, no care, who
> could care? it was that dif-
> (small dif-)
> erence be-
> tween the man who filled was
> more a child   .   You can
> turn your back
> or I can turn my back—

                           it is a child
unborn, it is our being
all our being
man and wife, or else the rest
of life is Jack the
life is back, is fact, is black, is
rope enuf, is no rope, is the ripper
        is the ripper
        is the ripper
is the child, un-
born perhaps,
                    and sucking.

An idealization of woman in our time has roots in a man never having gotten enough of his mother and consequently never finding/al-
lowing a woman to equal/surpass her image. I know that Paul's mother
left his father when he was quite young and, with Paul, lived with another woman for most of the rest of her life. Paul's mother was the poet
Frances Frost and while he wrote very little about her I know that she
was very powerfully in him (he once sent me a photo of himself at five
years old clutching the handle of a Mickey Mouse cane; his mother was
standing behind him, dressed in black, with both of her hands placed
firmly on Paul's shoulders—her eyes were extraordinarily intense and
looked straight through you). In his poetry, at least, his primal affection
is for his maternal grandfather, about whom he wrote a great graveside
poem that is the sixteenth selection of *The Selection of Heaven.* He had a
disastrous first marriage; after fighting for years he and Freddie broke
up, and to get a divorce in New York then Paul had to pay her a ton of
money, which he did not have. It required him to work for four years as
an editor in publishing houses as well as an eight-hour-a-day professional translator. If my sense of him is accurate, by the time he married
a second time, shortly after the beginning of *The Selection of Heaven,* he
was losing grip on his life and numb to really living with whom he did
live with. When Sara left him the summer of 1967 he was utterly shattered, and in drunk despair made a few attempts to hurt, or possibly
kill, himself. The fall of 1967 he returned to Europe, having finally received a Guggenheim Fellowship, where he met his third wife, Joan,
who was much younger than he and from a similar Irish-Catholic-
American background; Paul lived with her and their son Carlos until he
died in the autumn of 1971. I think they were deeply happy together,
and I am certain that having a son meant a great deal to Paul—but he

met Joan too late, he was too far into a downward spin, his body was too run down from years of steady drinking and smoking. He died of cancer of the esophagus, and my impression was that the life-negative root I felt in him as early as 1963 was as much involved with this as anything else.

Most people who are artists, though, are not so because they have solved great human problems or even the daily minutiae, but because of the particular way they feel these problems and minutiae are unsolvable in their own lives. It is not even a matter of simply feeling deeply, for there are many, many people who feel deeply and suffer the world thoroughly who never have anything to do with art. No, it takes a particular set of imbalances, incredible stresses in some directions with unusual absences in others, faults, burning explosive deposits and areas of glacial motion that create the energy stresses that volcano under an art. It is not possible to say what is THE artistic conflict (or for that matter, the artistic glory) because each artist is a product of his upbringing, a crucible of his times, as well as a creator of his own vision. True, I can say that a thorough reading of Paul Blackburn's lesser poems reveals him as a man haunted by sex-in-the-head who viewed women as sexual-relief possibilities, but as soon as I point this out I am also aware that his so-called failures are part of the reason he is compelling, and fragments such as got through to me and burned me against my own stem on the 1963 tape he sent me in Kyoto may be the very things that count. Perhaps it is fair to say that he did not explore his obsessions far enough, that he was defeated by the very vulnerability that allowed him to let in and assimilate his world. When I look at photos of Paul taken in the early fifties he looks amazingly compact and focused, and in spite of what happened to him this plumbline was present until the end. He was a very noncompetitive man living in the fifties and sixties in the most competitive art center in the world—he absorbed too much—many people took advantage of his meager defenses, his own generation of poets lacked respect for him—it may be that he was simply too frail to withstand the world he chose to live in, yet when I say that I must also recognize at the very base of what I know of his being a kind of meaninglessness, a failure to know what he was about, to compete, in other words, through asserting his ideas and making them felt in those he was in contact with. It is easy to be sentimental here—surely many people watched Paul Blackburn lug his fifty-pound tape recorder up 2nd Avenue to the St. Mark's Church to record poetry readings once or twice a week for seven or eight years, and many, not just a few, but many poets alive today are beholden to him for a basic artistic kindness, for readings yes, and for advice, but more humanly for a kind of comradeship that very few poets are willing to give. HE WAS AN ANGEL working for no profit or big reputation gain to keep alive a community of poetry in New York City—he stayed with the poets instead of the critics and publishers and he paid for it. In fact, those who let him down the most were often those he felt the closest to. I remember the formation of the Poetry Project at St. Mark's Church around 1967 when suddenly money became available mainly because a poetry program had been built up through Paul's unpaid efforts. The Church, by which I mean the minister and some local poets, decided to establish paid readings as well as a paid director, a poet who would be paid $15,000 a year for doing officially what Paul had done before informally. It was obvious to a lot of people that Paul was the natural choice for the position, but it was not given to him. I recount this episode mainly for its aftermath: Paul continued to serve, continued to tape readings, to read and help arrange readings. I think he continued because in a dogged and pathetic way he was like the old employee replaced by the machine who insists on continuing his work even if in a mock role. Paul lacked the anger to tell the whole gang to go fuck themselves and take his energy and intelligence elsewhere. This kind of mole-insistence is very interesting, and the more I think about it the more it reveals about Paul. When one paid him a visit, often, after being cordially met at the door one was turned into a listener for what Paul wanted to play among recent tapes or what he felt the visitor should hear. At times it felt as if he was teaching something, like helping one to get over a prejudice about someone else's poetry—as for me, I never really knew what was up—certainly there must have been a reason to listen to so-and-so for an hour before being able to have a conversation—or was that just something Paul put *me* through?

One thing I have had to struggle with in writing this is that I must not explain his meaninglessness, must not give it a mythic quality, for when I think of his death I think of an absence that was never explained in his life. It is possible to say any life is meaningless or meaningful, of course, depending upon the good or ill will with which one approaches that life—but I speak of extruding particularities with Blackburn—the anecdotes he enjoyed telling that became more and more without conclusion or point as he grew older and less in control. I have imagined

his relationship to his gull as one of retreating into the gull's head to sit
and be by himself, for it was contact with others that was much of his
trouble, contact—to not have to stay in contact, to avert his eyes, to tell
the story or put on the tape to derail for a moment the other so Paul
would not have to feel he had to make sense of his own life—I see him
enter the gull's head and pick up little things in his hands to look at and
puzzle over, like childhood toys he had almost forgotten—there he is
safe, no one can betray or not betray him in this place—then he becomes anxious after a while and crawls back through the gull's eye into
the presence of others.

                      I went over to Sparky's pen
where the little turds were steaming with joy, I picked them up
and placed them on the out-stretched Gull-robe. After I had a pile
I began to mold them into a gull shape, then I wrapped it in
the robe and dug a hole, burying the Corpse of Gull-robe
    by my childhood place of secret joy.
      As I completed my task a figure loomed at garage edge,
          Weren't you supposed to clean the eaves trough this
afternoon, it said,
        I smiled, ok,
      a ladder was in my hands
I was 9 feet off the ground, Clayton Senior was standing under me,
      the despair in his face, checking me out for evil,
concerned if I was doing a cud job, was I swallowing my cud, was
I doing a cud or was I spitting out the influence, was I swallowing
the cudfluence or was I manufacturing my own salts?
      As he stared at me I transferred myself to 12 years old
and through this transference maintained the vector of his stare
through the eaves trough into the interior of the white garage. Here
is the place I understood Blackburn is to transform himself. I kneaded
the energy from Clayton's eyes, made out the white garage interior,
in the rear was Sparky's inside pen, so she'd be warm in winter,
above the pen the shelf where storm windows were stacked,
building out from this shelf was a false garage ceiling Clayton
had constructed, to pile boards and garden tools on—the ridgepole
and false ceiling made a hazardous little house at its peak
four feet high, an attic of sorts, enormous
wonder of my puberty body up there on a hot summer day
interlocked with urine

Attis
saw, here I now crouched, unzipped,
a vine instiched with tiny skulls spilled out
plums, persimmons, grapefruit, I transferred
outside the white garage again and got more energy from Clayton's
eyes
pumpkins, pears, an outbranch of apples,
the strengthened false ceiling now abounded in vegetation,
I transferred to a wall, picked off the grass stained hedge shears,
began to sever the fruits from my vine, hanging them on pegs and tool
nails,
transferred down to Sparky's pen, scooped up her puppies
drawing the birth-glisten from their blind bodies
I built tensile webs; now the walls went into transformation, spider
guardians began to scuttle
in and out of the vegetal wall, this circulation developed for a week,
the following Saturday I opened the right-hand garage door onto a
jungle! A place Clayton had never seen—I left the cavern and started
forth,
Blackburn's presence was now everywhere, about a mile from the cavern
I could see the blue Mediterranean waters, out on the beach in solitude
a figure was seated on a little wood chair at a table writing,
as I approached it turned and watched me, its beak closed, its eyes
beady, unmoving, at the base of its feathered neck were human
shoulders,
from the freckles I knew, yes, and from its short muscular build—
Can you speak, I said
the creature nodded yes then shook its beak no,

it sat at Blackburn's kitchen table on one
of his kitchen chairs,
I walked over to see what he had written,

*In a way, it's hard to know that I know you anymore. Deep, Okay,
yes, forever, etc. But you've learned & grown & changed so much in
the last couple years it IS hard to know. Things do get thru in poems
to & from both of us, I guess, that are not discussed in letters. Then
long time when I do not feel like letters or any other contact, that
problem. And the whole problem of experience, the sharing of it,
giving it to someone, or wholly.*

I've returned the Gull-robe, I said,
   and fashioned a place for you, for when it gets cold out here,
would you like to see it?
                    The Gullpaul stood up and began to walk
   back with me, along the path he took my hand,
and we walked hand in hand to the Cavern of Self

I have to leave you here, I said—
as you gave me your life
that moment in Kyoto 1963
when I was nearly dead with despair,
so I have created
a place for you wrought
from the most intense moment of my puberty—
this is not how I thought it would end,
but the weight of the sadness of death is
in me, even facing you here—
I had thought to put a bar in along the right-hand wall
but that meant comfort, and the place I leave you
is shelter yet terrible, is formed of my spirit
which you helped form, yet dark with Clayton's eyes
transformed into spider guardians,
Use this place, or abandon it,

     he entered it, his back lost in the echoing struggle

                    [1973–1974]

Remarks to a Poetry Workshop

Many creative writing students put too much of their energy into defending what they write, forming a resistance to change which occurs while attempting to write in a way that depends on change as its primary characteristic.

Rimbaud tells us that I is another. He means by this that the I one brings initially to writing poetry is at best a chrysalis for incubating an imago, an imaginatively mature, or monstrous I whose life is in the poem. To achieve this second I one must *translate* the first I, moving it from the language of experience and memory to the language of imagination and inspiration.

The poet Rilke has declared that no one should engage in such a "translation" unless he would be willing to acknowledge that he would have to die if it were denied him to write. After making this severe statement, Rilke somewhat softened the matter, adding: "above all: ask yourself in the stillest hour of the night: *must* I write?"

Rilke is extreme on this point because he knows that a half-hearted response to such a calling leads nowhere. Some students may feel that I am too hard on them, too, critical of what they write. My response is that I am trying to instill in them a sense of just how hard they must become on themselves to be able to translate their given I into a creative I.

However, I would be willing to depart from Rilke's command and say that a limited commitment has its uses, and that working on poems can make one a better reader, a better seer, maybe a better lover.

In both cases, it is hard to advance without at first imitating or translating poems of those who seem to be beacons of the art.

This piece was originally written to be Xeroxed and handed out to students in a senior-level creative writing workshop at Eastern Michigan University. It was subsequently published in the February 1994 issue of AWP Chronicle.

Then one must learn to corner oneself, in the process of being hard on oneself, and to eliminate the two intertwined enemies of the young poet.

The first is obscurity and the second, obscurity's opposite, obviousness. Like two facing banks of a roily river, these two enemies beckon, as if offering refuge from the undertow.

Obscurity is tempting because it releases the writer from the burden of making what he is writing meaningful. One's being obscure is an attempt to shift the burden to the reader, to make him feel that failure to find significance in the poem is his fault, that there is something paradoxically significant about obscurity. In the same way that obscurity frames the obvious, obviousness frames obscurity. What is obvious about obscurity is its failure to articulate a mid-ground, a place that the reader has to reach for (it is not obvious), *and* a place that contains a reward (significance) for those willing to reach. In the words of Havelock Ellis:

> If art is expression, mere clarity is nothing. The extreme clarity of an artist may be due not to his marvelous power of illuminating the abysses of his soul, but merely to the fact that there are no abysses to illuminate. . . . The impression we receive on first entering the presence of any supreme work of art is obscurity. But it is an obscurity like that of a Catalonian cathedral which slowly grows more luminous as one gazes, until the solid structure beneath is revealed.

Such poems as Yeats's "Byzantium," Hart Crane's "Lachrymae Christi," Dickinson's "My life had stood a loaded gun," Rilke's "Duino Elegies," or César Vallejo's "Trilce I," argue that if the reader is willing to go 50% of the way, the poem will match that 50%. At the point of fusion, a child that is half poem, half reader-apprehension, is born.

When Rilke writes in the sonnet "Archaic Torso of Apollo," that "there is no place / that does not see you. You must change your life."—he seems to suggest that one must either transform oneself or be seen through. There *is* no unseeing refuge—one stands revealed at every point. This god torso, itself fragmentary, refuses to allow Rilke to cozy up to it. The torso insists that he change his life in order to perceive it, that he match its change (from a block of marble) with his own. Rilke's stirring lines are darkly echoed, some forty years later, by Paul Celan's:

> Once, when death was mobbed,
> you took refuge in me.

—a two line poem that bears in a haiku-like instant the European Holocaust and perhaps Celan's anguish over having to turn his heart into habitation, to admit a dear one, and to cherish all that this person was, including of course her death.

Only when one has cornered oneself can a center be found, a way of being in the poem that accepts one's gestures *and* nourishes one in return. So I lean on you to help you lean on yourself. I push you back so that in being pushed you may feel what in you is pushable. I resist you to help you feel what you yourself resist in the act of working on a poem.

You may handle this pressure in several ways. You may feel that my role is mainly to confirm what you write so that you will not feel that any deep changes must take place. This attitude evades the principle of the workshop, which, as I see it, should be a place where constructions are examined, taken apart, maybe destroyed, maybe reassembled, occasionally perfected.

You can also listen to me and reflect on what I say, scrutinizing my comments: are they useful? Disprove them out loud to yourself if they are not. Where do they lead? If anywhere, make a list of possibilities. What do they make you feel about what you felt when you were working on the poem? Have you actually written what was on your mind or have you "poeticized" it?

You may also swallow my suggestions whole hog, which is probably not much better than totally rejecting them.

When I rewrite one of your lines, rewrite my rewrite.

There is no way the reader can know what is on your mind unless you articulate it. A good poem, in this sense, is one that fills and reveals its own contextual space. It allows the reader to enter, and to think with or against it—at the same time that it protects its own integrity.

Often an unexperienced writer is baffled by what is on his mind. He writes about something that happened, drawn to it, moth-like, and before he can imagine it, or dream it, or ponder it in trance, he is consumed by it. The experience sits there on the page, thumbing its nose at both writer and reader, sealed about itself.

To corner oneself, to face the opacity, not go over or around or under it, but through it. Van Gogh:

> What is drawing? How does one learn it? It is working through an invisible iron wall that seems to stand between what one *feels* and what one *can do*. How is one to get through that wall—since pounding against it is of

no use? One must undermine the wall and drill through it slowly and patiently, in my opinion.

To stare for an hour at a line on a sheet in the typewriter, to realize its limitations (Who does it sound like? Has it been uttered before?). To ask such questions with a book by an admired poet open by one's side. To talk to oneself while Wallace Stevens is listening in.

Ideally, you don't need a workshop—or, I should say, you can start and run your own, with and of yourself. But as an American, you may understandably find the solitude of a Rilke or a Cézanne nearly pathological—we are so gregarious, such leaky vessels.

That is when you meet me, or someone like me, unlike most of your professors someone who practices what is at stake rather than standing outside of it and writing about it. Those of us who are writers who also teach are like pigs at a pork-judging contest. We are living examples— not always satisfactory ones—of what is under inspection. We are also burdened, as scholars are not, by our desire to be, as writers, equal to that which we are teaching. And while we may bring a gut level of creative experience to the workshop, we are to varying degrees the victims of our own tested views.

I don't think I ever leave my poetry. I may walk across campus to be with you and your attempts at poetry, but in some way I am always working with the last unfinished thing, when I cook, when I dream— even in dreamless sleep, material is seeping into the unfillable abyss called my life. As I resist accepting your writing as it is, wanting it to be more, wanting you to want more of it, a similar process—more weathered and distant from birth than yours—is turning like a cement mixer in me, folding and refolding the weight and the murk of the *to be*. If we can understand how these processes overlap, and draw off each other as well as support each other, perhaps our time together will not be wasted.

[1993]

The Lorca Working

After Lorca is a puzzling mixture of Spicer's translations of Federico García Lorca's poems and original poems by Spicer himself. Thirty-four poems, all in all, which are interspersed with six "letters" which discuss Spicer's evolving sense of poetry and function like a kind of chorus behind and between the poems. The first thing to do, in seeing what *After Lorca* is about, is to decide which poems are translations and which are not, and to also see what Spicer has done as a translator and how the translations function in regard to his own poems in the book. So I am going to proceed poem by poem through *After Lorca* from a translational viewpoint. In the case of poems which are translations, I will point out the page number in the 1968 Aguilar *Obras Completas*. (Spicer, Robin Blaser tells us, used the 1955 edition, which I have been unable to locate; I assume the texts are the same in the 1968 edition and that only the page numbering differs.) Because there is some evidence that Spicer used other translations of Lorca poems while he was making his own, I will also note if a particular Lorca poem had been translated and was in print previous to 1957. While Spicer's translations are never imitative of others, existing translations may have spurred him to make certain interpretations in order not to appear to be imitating Honig, Merwin, or Belitt, etc. The other translations I have been able to find are: *New Directions Annual* #8 (1944, about 40 pages of Lorca translations by Edwin Honig), *Selected Poems of Garcia Lorca* (New York: New Directions, 1955, versions by 18 different translators), and *Poet in New York* (New York: Grove Press, 1955, translated by Ben Belitt). Paul Blackburn did some Lorca translations in the early '50s which were to appear in *Selected Poems* (which were blocked from publication by

This essay was written for the Fall 1977 Jack Spicer issue of *Boundary 2*.

Lorca's brother because he thought they were inaccurate and inventive), but to my knowledge none of these versions appeared in print until I ran 14 pages of them in *Caterpillar* #5 in 1968. The Bellit translation of *Poet in New York* is not of much concern in this context, as Spicer translated only one poem from that book, Lorca's "Ode to Walt Whitman." I have a hunch that the appearance in 1955 of not only the Aguilar *Obras Completas* but also the New Directions and Grove Press volumes had something to do with Spicer's Lorca working. Since there are only a couple of Spicer poems dated 1956, and since *After Lorca* is the only work dated 1957, it seems fair to assume that he became involved with Lorca in 1955 and completed this involvement two years later. Perhaps I should mention that the books I list above were not the only collections of Lorca translations in print in the early and mid '50s; however only the ones I list contain poems translated by Spicer.

Poem #1: "Juan Ramón Jiménez"
(Aguilar Obras Completas, *p. 384).*

A typical Spicer translation: the greater percentage of the poem is accurately, if uninventively, translated, with patches of mistranslation, some of which appear to be meaningful, some of which appear to be arbitrary. Perhaps the best thing to do here is to set Spicer's version against my own consistently literal version of Lorca's poem:

Spicer version:	*Literal version:*
In the white endlessness	In the white infinite,
Snow, seaweed, and salt	snow, spikenard and saltmine,
He lost his imagination.	he lost his fantasy.
The color white. He walks	The color white, walks,
Upon a soundless carpet made	on a silent carpet
Of pigeon feathers.	of dove/pigeon feathers.
Without eyes or thumbs	Without eyes or gesture
He suffers a dream not moving	unmoving he suffers a dream.
But the bones quiver.	But he trembles inside.
In the white endlessness	In the white infinite,
How pure and big a wound	what a pure and large wound
His imagination left.	his fantasy left!
Snow, seaweed, and salt. Now	In the white infinite.
In the white endlessness.	Snow. Spikenard. Saltmine.

The arbitrary mistranslations are easy enough to pick up: the meaningful ones may be more difficult to see. On the basis of what Spicer wrote in the third "letter" in the book, I assume he opened *After Lorca* with this poem because he wanted to signal his attempt to become "utterly independent of images. The imagination pictures the real. I would like to point to the real, disclose it, to make a poem that has no sound in it but the pointing of a single finger." The mix of the two Zen koans aside, that statement indicates that in the Jiménez translation the poet has "lost his imagination" in favor of another way of working; thus Spicer's replacement of "fantasy" with "imagination" makes a certain amount of sense, i.e., what is left, once the imagination has been lost, is snow, seaweed, and salt, the pointed-to "real" things. I say "a certain amount of sense" because in the same "letter" Spicer also expressed a continuing affinity with imagination ("the truer imagination of a dream . . ."), and also because his use of key words such as "real" and "imagination" is never made clear and often seems paradoxical and simplistic. One also might assume that "thumbs" and "bones" replace "gesture" and "inside" because they are objects (again, see the third "letter"); however, at the same time, "thumbs" is very odd and utterly mistranslates the original Spanish rather than slightly reshaping it. I can see no point at all in rendering "nardo" and "salina" as "seaweed" and "salt." Surely Spicer knew what the words actually meant, and as I puzzle over the matter, the only thing that comes to my mind to explain it is the idea of "dictation" which later in his life Spicer developed to justify his poetry as coming from the outside as opposed to the inside (see *Caterpillar* #12, p. 176). The matter of "dictation" is complicated, and to really deal with it here would make me lose my focus on the translating in *After Lorca*. Suffice it to say that whether the word "seaweed" comes from the outside or the inside it appears to be an arbitrary mistranslation and, if anything, is less interesting than the correct equivalent, "spikenard."

Poem #2, "Ballad of the Little Girl Who Invented the Universe" (Aguilar, p. 571; New Directions Annual, p. 372).

Lorca's title is literally "Casida of the Dream in the Free Air." Spicer consistently, and for no apparent reason, mistranslates the words "casida" and "gacela" (words for Arabic verse forms which Lorca keeps in his Spanish and which do not mean "ballad"). Note that Spicer begins each line with a capital and only occasionally acknowledges Lorca's commas and periods; since this kind of punctuation is consistently followed in virtually all of his own poetry and is thus part of the image of a Spicer poem, the Lorca "translations" look more Spiceresque than they would had Spicer followed Lorca's punctuation. Poem #2 has more arbitrary mistranslating than #1. Lorca's last line reads: "in the bull the skeleton of the little girl," which Spicer renders as: "The skeleton of a little girl turning." There appears to be no reason for taking the bull out and making the little girl turn.

Poem #3: "Ballad of the Seven Passages"

The first Spicer poem. Most of the nontranslations can be visually identified; they are irregularly shaped in contrast to Lorca's tendency to write in regular stanzas. In this case not only the shape but the disconnected command-like content feels like Spicer, although the second line, which is repeated four times, "Your heart will never break at what you are hearing," has an edge of Lorca to it—yet running a cliché like "your heart will break at what you are hearing" against itself is pure Spicer.

Poem #4: "Debussy" (Aguilar, p. 385).

Minimal distortion, a few arbitrary mistranslations, and one that is perhaps meaningful. Spicer changes Lorca's "reflections of quiet things" in the sixth line to "Unmoving images." Spicer seems to enjoy mistranslating a word in such a way that the ghost of the correct equivalent is present, e.g., "acequia" (canal) is rendered as "ditch." While "ditch" is hardly even close to "canal" in meaning, their shapes do correspond—and as I write this sentence I become aware of Spicer's statement in the third "letter": "Things do not connect; they correspond."

Poem #5: "Frog"

The second Spicer poem. Most interesting as a kind of mistranslated elaboration of Bashō's famous frog haiku (literally: "Ah, the old pond, a frog leaps, water sound"), another example of Spicer's Zen and haiku fascination at the time. Also "Debussy" was the first, and this is the second, of the many poems in *After Lorca* that have something on or in water.

Poem #6: "Buster Keaton's Ride" (Aguilar, p. 893).

One of Lorca's brief plays translated fairly accurately. Occasional additions and arbitrary changes by Spicer (the last two lines of the piece are literally: "On the horizon of Philadelphia shines the rutilant star of / the police," which Spicer renders as: "The lights of Philadelphia flicker and go out in the faces of / a thousand policemen"). On page 19 (*The Collected Books* [Los Angeles: Black Sparrow Press, 1975]), lines 8, 9, 15, and 16 are entirely Spicer's.

Poem #7: "Ballad of the Shadowy Pigeons" (Aguilar, p. 354; NDA, p. 374; Selected Poems of Garcia Lorca, p. 179).

First indication that Spicer used *Selected Poems* at least some of the time: in line 2, "saw" translates the Spanish "vi" as it appears in the *Selected Poems;* in Aguilar (unless the word was printed differently in the 1955 edition which I have not checked) the word is "van," which would probably be rendered as "go" or in this context "fly." Minimal distortion, a rather awkwardly literal version. Spicer here creates stanzas where there are none in the original.

Poem #8: "Suicide" (Aguilar, p. 406; Selected, p. 53).

This translation is a good example of what happens when Spicer considerably distorts and mistranslates, and worth quoting against a literal version so the reader can see how it differs from the Jiménez poem.

Spicer version:	*Literal version:*
At ten o'clock in the morning	The youth forgot.
The young man could not remember.	It was 10 in the morning.
His heart was stuffed with dead wings	His heart was filling
And linen flowers.	with broken wings and rag flowers.
He is conscious that there is nothing left	He noticed that nothing remained
In his mouth but one word.	in his mouth but a word.

When he removes his coat soft ashes Fall from his arms.	On removing his gloves, there fell, from his hands, a smooth ash.
Through the window he sees a tower He sees a window and a tower.	Through the balcony he saw a tower. He felt himself balcony and tower.
His watch has run down in its case He observes the way it was looking at him.	Surely he saw how the clock fixed in its frame watched him.
He sees his shadow stretched Upon a white silk cushion.	He saw his shadow stretched out and still on the white silk divan.
And the stiff geometric youngster Shatters the mirror with an ax.	And the rigid, geometric young man shattered the mirror with an ax.
The mirror submerges everything In a great spurt of shadow.	On its shattering, a huge jet of shadow inundated his chimerical bedroom.

Poem #9: "Bacchus" (Aguilar, p. 384).

Typical Spicer version, more or less like the Jiménez piece. The trunk of Lorca's poem visible with most of its branches intact although bent in slightly different ways.

Poem #10: "A Diamond"

The third Spicer poem (there is a Lorca poem with the same title on p. 208 in the 1968 Aguilar edition, but Spicer's poem bears no relation whatsoever to it). First mention of "diamond," which becomes a key word in Spicer's later poetry (it will appear in an important section, #9, of *Billy the Kid*, and later, in *Magazine Verse*, transformed into the fixed course on which poetry is played). The poem mostly announces theme material; e.g., the seagull on the pier, noticed here, becomes the central image in the opening poem of *A Book of Music*.

Poem #11: "The Little Halfwit" (Aguilar, p. 404; Selected, p. 51).

Typical version, with one especially awkwardly rendered stanza (the third, which is perhaps set that way to suggest Spicer talking back to the text (or a "dictating" voice).

Poem #12: "Verlaine" (Aguilar, p. 383).

Typical version. Spicer seemed attracted to Lorca's poems that used artist's names as their titles (though Spicer might have been attracted to this piece for its water and shadow imagery). Where Lorca writes: "The song / which I shall never say," Spicer writes: "A song / Which I shall never sing"—which loses the former's tension.

Poem #13: "The Ballad of the Dead Woodcutter"

Given the title and the regular couplets, it looks like a Lorca poem, but it is the fourth Spicer poem playing at being a Lorca poem.

Poem #14: "The Ballad of Weeping" (Aguilar, p. 569; NDA, p. 370; Selected, p. 171).

Typical version, perhaps a bit more awkward than usual. "There might be room for . . ." in line 7 is Spicer's addition. The force of Lorca's thrice-repeated "inmenso" (immense) is lost in Spicer's "big." Thinking back to the ditch/canal change (Poem #4), it strikes me that perhaps Spicer thought words like "ditch" and "big" were less literary, more spoken, than "canal" and "immense."

Poem #15: "Alba"

The fifth Spicer poem, and another piece in which, like Poem #11, there is a sense of two arguing voices, here the speaker of the first 4 lines being answered by another speaker in the last 4. Up to this point, Spicer's own poems in *After Lorca* have been short and tentative, and don't make much of an impression. None of them, for example, are up to the originality of "Song for Bird and Myself" or "Poem to the Reader of the Poem" (both of which are dated 1956 by Robin Blaser), nor do any of them have the thought and weight of the first four *Imaginary Elegies* (dated 1950–55). The feeling is one of Spicer just barely keeping his own hand in, between the Lorca renderings, if for no other reason than to keep the reader guessing.

Poem #16: "Song of the Poor" (Aguilar, p. 380; Selected, p. 41).

(Lorca's poem is entitled "Es Verdad"—"It Is True"; Spicer's reti-
tling makes no sense at all.) This translation is a mess. Spicer has kept
Lorca's opening and closing couplet in Spanish, has butchered the second and third stanza and added his own fourth stanza, which is so dumb
it almost functions as a parody of Lorca's poem. Interestingly, though,
this failure comes right before the toughest and most engaging poem
and translation in the whole book.

*Poem #17: "Ode for Walt Whitman" (Aguilar, p. 522; Selected, p. 125;
Poet in New York, p. 119).*

While at points Spicer considerably distorts this complex and very
tricky Lorca poem, after all is said and done, his is by far the best version to date (and I take into consideration the recent Steve Fredman
version, in his stiffly literal translation of the complete Lorca book, *Poet
in New York*, in *Fog Horn*, No. 1, 1975). A quick comparison between
certain Spicer renderings and their literal equivalents will open up not
only Spicer's tonal emphasis but the whole dramatic struggle in Lorca's
original poem.

Spicer version:	*Literal version:*
wet-dreamed anemones . . .	stained anemones . . .
prick pierced through by . . .	sex transfixed by . . .
tight-cocked beauty . . .	virile beauty . . .
toilets . . .	sewers . . .
taxi-drivers . . .	chauffeurs . . .
cocksuckers . . .	fairies . . .
burning virgin beard . . .	chaste and luminous beard . . .
bars and night-clubs . . .	cars and terraces . . .
drippings of sucked-off death . . .	drops of filthy death . . .
opening their flies in parks . . .	open the plazas . . .

[Note: Robert Duncan's discussion of this poem in his Preface to the
recent Sand Dollar edition of *Caesar's Gate* is worthwhile reading at this
point.]

In the original poem, Lorca is split, in the agony of the difficulty of expressing freely his sexuality, between a repugnance and hate for those who do, and an idealization of manly love, as if what Whitman prophesied was somehow "above" the practice of homosexuality (yet ironically Lorca argues in his poem that it is the actual practice that keeps his "higher" vision of Whitman before his eyes). By toughening the language (and bringing the class structure down a notch), Spicer has drawn out Lorca's implied bile. At times this works, at times it doesn't. "Wet-dreamed anemones" is so distorted and forced that it speaks only of Spicer's own obsession with his wet dreams. On the other hand, "prick pierced through" seems to me perfectly acceptable for "el sexo atravesado. . . ." Rendering "maricas" as "cocksuckers" makes for a real dilemma: relatively speaking, "marica" is inoffensive and rather mild (deriving from *maria* so that one hears something like "little Mary" or perhaps "sister boy"—at most "fairy"); "cocksucker," on the other hand, was dynamite in 1957, and my hunch is that that is why Spicer used it (Lorca could have written *mamapollo*, which means "cocksucker"). Thus Spicer carries forward at a more extreme pitch Lorca's ambivalent and fascistic leaning in this poem, brushing aside the veil that still lingers in the word "fairy" to a confrontation with what the "fairy" actually does— which can be taken once again as his concern for "real objects," for "the lemon to be a lemon." As I will elaborate later, this push for the "real" or the "actual" in Spicer is constantly frustrated by his equally strong desire for diamond-hard purity, free of personal emotions.

The Belitt version of this poem is worth looking at in comparison to Spicer's because in turning the image of Whitman into something like an old lamplighter it attempts to phase out the very elements that Spicer intensifies.

The second indication that Spicer used *Selected Poems* is found in this poem: on page 29, in *Collected Books*, in line 23, the Spanish "soñaban" is rendered as "counting on," which makes no sense at all until one notices that in *Selected Poems*, page 128, the Spanish word is not "soñaban" but "señalan." The latter also appears in the Grove Press edition, page 120. "Counting on" is an adequate translation of it.

Poem #18: "Aquatic Park"

The sixth Spicer poem. Spicer watching boys in the park, with an interesting turn on "sprawling" in the penultimate stanza. There is an increase of poems in which living as well as dead boys appear after the "Whitman" ode. Spicer dedicates this piece to himself, and while it is rather slight, it has a rather mysterious quality to it, coming on the heels of the gigantic "Ode."

Poem #19: "Forest" (Agular, p. 410).

Accurately translated, virtually no mistranslation. The boys in "Aquatic Park" blend into the "brown child" (clearly feminine in Lorca's original). At this point it is worthwhile noting that the third "letter," which falls here, in spite of its verbal slipperiness, is the most engaging of all the six "letters" in the book (and the piece Spicer chose as a statement on his poetics for the *New American Poetry* anthology). The amount of tension and effort involved in the translation of the "Ode" appears to give a special focus to the half dozen pieces that follow it—the best translating, the most interesting "letter," and the single strongest Spicer poem (#23). As if suddenly, for a little while, Spicer had become "faithful" to Lorca.

Poem #20: "Narcissus" (Aguilar, p. 411).

The first, and best, of two Lorca poems with the same title. Spicer appears to meaningfully mistranslate the first stanza, altering Lorca's "Narcissus. / Your fragrance. / And the depth of the river," to: "Poor Narcissus / Your dim fragrance / And the dim heart of the river." Other than this intentionally deprecative view of Narcissus, the poems is accurately translated.

Poem #21: "He Died at Sunrise" (Aguilar, p. 396).

With the exception of the third stanza, with two mistranslations, the poem is accurately rendered. Chosen probably for its image of the lemon, which is tied in with rejected love.

Poem #22: "Ballad of the Terrible Presence" (Aguilar, p. 558; NDA, p. 362; Selected, p. 158).

Similar to Poem #8 in the extent of its distortion. However, Spicer's mistranslations here are for the most part very interesting: e.g., Lorca's "broken arches" become "wornout rainbows" in Spicer's version. By rendering Lorca's "don't show me your fresh waist" as "don't show me that cool flesh," Spicer links the piece to the poem before it as well as to the "Whitman" ode.

Poem #23: "Ballad of Sleeping Somewhere Else"

Like #13, this one looks like a translation, but is actually the seventh and most successful Spicer poem. The high point in the book in regard to what Spicer has mixed of Lorca into his own work. While it feels like a sexual love lament, the sudden appearance of "Child, you are too tall for this bed" near the end of the poem gives it an eerie, obscure texture. Spicer's failure to connect with another (which seems his choice as often as not), which is perhaps his most constant theme in all of his poetry and undoubtedly has much to do with his belief that "things do not connect," is beautifully assimilated here, mainly through his drawing on Lorca's affinity with the nature world. A couplet such as "The windows sag on the wall / I feel cold glass in the blankets" seems to be written by one poet called Garcia Spicer.

Poem #24: "Narcissus" (Aguilar, p. 386).

Adequately translated. Interesting as a poem mainly for the continued presence of the "child" (Lorca's "niño," which Spicer usually renders as "boy"), which, as Narcissus, becomes Spicer before the water.

Poem #24: "Ballad of the Dead Boy" (Aguilar, p. 560; NDA, p. 364; Selected, p. 161).

A number of arbitrary mistranslations; Spicer's placement of it, following #24, gives it a heightened quality, as if the child in "Narcissus" changes into the boy here who dies every afternoon, who thus becomes real and irreal, dissolving/being reborn, the face of Lorca perhaps as it passes in and out of the working. What for Lorca is "an archangel of cold" becomes for Spicer "an archangel, cold." Once again the translation fleshes out the original.

Poem #26: "Song for September" (Aguilar, p. 249; Selected, p. 7).

Believe it or not, this is a very early Lorca poem, literally "Ballad of the Little Square," and the difference in titles is a fair indication of the difference between Lorca's poem and Spicer's version. The most distorted translation in the book; at least 80% of the lines appear to be arbitrary mistranslations and the shape of the original poem is completely altered.

Poem #27: "Buster Keaton Rides Again: A Sequel"

The eighth Spicer poem, a takeoff on #6, well done, a free-for-all, which reminds me more of "The Unvert Manifesto" than anything else in *After Lorca.*

Poem #28: "The Ballad of Escape" (Aguilar, p. 565; NDA, p. 368; Selected, p. 167).

It is fascinating how the asexual "As I lose myself in the heart of certain children" (Spender/Gili version, *Selected Poems*) becomes vividly sexual when Spicer takes the "boy" option for Lorca's "niños": "Like I lose myself in the hearts of some boys." The change transforms the poem, linking it to the real/irreal Narcissus. Everything, except the last two lines, is accurately translated. Lorca ends it with: "Unaware of the water, I go seeking / a death full of light to consume me." Spicer: "Along the vastness of water I wander searching / An end to the lives that have tried to complete me."

Poem #29 "Venus" (Aguilar, p. 385).

With a couple of exceptions, accurately translated. "The dead girl / in the winding shell of the bed" evokes dead Eurydice (who as such appears several times in Spicer's early poetry), a covering image for the absence of women, other than as shades or whores, in Spicer's poetry.

Poem #30: "Friday, the 13th"

The ninth Spicer poem, linking up the fateful day with "dictation." The poem is similar to several in *Admonitions*, the book following *After*

Lorca. At about this point in the book I feel Spicer losing interest in the Lorca working—the focus maintained from Poem #17 through Poem #23 has been lost.

Poem #31: "Song of Two Windows" (Aguilar, p. 368).

For the most part a Spicer imitation of a Lorca ballad—yet since about one quarter of the poem is a translation of Lorca's "Nocturnos de la Ventana," I suppose it should be considered a translation. By stanza: the first is all Spicer, as is the second (which echoes "Venus," Poem #29); the third stanza is more or less section 2 of the Lorca poem and Spicer's fourth stanza in prose is more or less Lorca's section 3; the fifth stanza is about half Lorca half Spicer, in alternating lines, and the sixth is mostly Lorca. The poem is mostly interesting as an idea, and as an actual poem is not very interesting—perhaps the "unfaithfulness" of the piece has more to do with Spicer's loss of interest in Lorca.

Poem #32: The Moon and Lady Death" (Aguilar, p. 264).

Similar to the poem before in the way that the lines are mixed. The piece opens with several Lorca lines, adequately rendered, then departs from the original in the last three lines of the first stanza; the second stanza keeps a sense of the Lorca original but every line is mistranslated and several lines have been pulled in from a later stanza of the original poem; third stanza like the first; fourth stanza all Spicer except for the last two lines. At this point Lorca disappears (other than being told goodbye in the sixth "letter" one poem later).

Poem #33: "Afternoon"

The tenth Spicer poem. The Lorcaesque refrain, "13 empty boats / And a seagull," becomes increasingly meaningless each time it is repeated, and at the same time becomes more and more an object as the narrative around it disintegrates.

Poem #34: "Radar"

The eleventh Spicer poem, and the last piece in the book. Intentionally vague, the poem scans the horizon as if trying to pick up something—and for a moment in the beginning of the final stanza two people in bed appear (Spicer and Lorca?), yet they are divided, untouching, and disappear immediately with a splash (Narcissus falling into his reflection?), and the plop itself disappears into a vague land- and seascape repeated from the beginning of the poem.

I read the Bashō frog haiku as a poem essentially about meaning; that is, something leaps forth and something else responds. Thus, it is as if Lorca leapt into Spicer's narcissistic gazing, breaking it up into small shadows. The force of the plunge occurs in Poem #17, the "Whitman" ode, the ripples seem to hold for a moment (through Poem #23), then subside until at the end only a flicker of the two men remains. What appeared to be a connection (Spicer and Lorca) turns out to be Lorca corresponding through Spicer gazing at his reflection. Psychologically, Spicer has found a stay from his own frustration and anger. As a poet, he has moved from the early Yeats-inspired poem with its grammatically controlled sentences to the kind of poem he will write for the next couple of years, in which each line appears to have a chance to be faithful or not to the line before it.

Perhaps the quickest way to suggest the difference the Lorca working made in Spicer's poetry is to take a poem he wrote before *After Lorca* and one a year later, both on the same subject, and set them side by side:

"Orpheus in Hell" (around 1950)	*"Orfeo" (1958)*
When he first brought his music into hell	Sharp as an arrow Orpheus
He was absurdly confident. Even over the noise of the shapeless fire.	Points his music downward. Hell is there
And the juke-box groaning of the damned	At the bottom of the seacliff.
Some of them would hear him. In the upper world.	Heal Nothing by this music.
He had forced the stones to listen.	Eurydice
It wasn't quite the same. And the people he remembered	Is a frigate bird or a rock or some seaweed.
Weren't quite the same either. He began looking at faces	Hail nothing The infernal
Wondering if all of hell was without music. He tried an old song but pain	Is a slippering wetness out at the horizon.
Was screaming on the jukebox and the bright fire	Hell is this: The lack of anything but the
Was pelting away the face and he heard a	eternal to look at

voice saying, "Orpheus."

— — — — — — — He was at the entrance
again
And a little three-headed dog was barking at
him.
Later he would remember those dead voices
And call them Eurydice.

The expansiveness of salt
The lack of any bed but one's
Music to sleep in.

It is interesting to think of the "Orfeo" poem as a kind of translation of "Orpheus in Hell." One could say that an aspect of poetic development is the ability to improve one's translations of one's experience, so that at times the effect will be that of translating an earlier poem into a sharper, more forceful version of itself. At this point the reader might want to look at the first poem in the "Poems 1946–56" section in *Caterpillar* #12; which, along with a few others reprinted in the Jack Spicer issue of *Manroot* (#10), make up his early poetry. That first poem, "The dancing ape is whirling round the beds," is controlled by The English Department: once a sentence is entered, it becomes a straitjacket that insists on being completed in terms of an object that is faithful to the original subject, and on a larger scale this lock takes place in the poem as a whole. By the time Spicer wrote "Orpheus in Hell," on a linguistic level at least he had gotten his poetry out of the English department's hands. His voice is relaxed enough to be able to explore its material— the poem has a conversational feel to it. It is not quite sure where it wants to go and runs the risk of disappearing into itself; such hesitation becomes part of the drama of the piece, i.e., Orpheus hears his own voice called and is snapped back to the upper world again, at the entrance to hell. When one compares this poem to "Orfeo," it seems to be an explanation in search of a poem, for the latter piece is "on" from beginning to end, taut, and listening to itself (the way "hell" gives way to "heal" and "heal" to "hail"); visually it is as if "Orpheus in Hell" was the block out of which "Orfeo" was chipped.

Of course it is impossible to say exactly what writing *After Lorca* had to do with this. However, in looking at the taut, chiseled quality in many of the poems written in 1958, I am reminded that as a translator myself I have felt from time to time that translating has a contractive effect on my own poetry—not so much now, since I have been doing it off and on for 18 years, but when I was looking for my own way to be in poetry, back in the early '60s, I went through a period in which translating time spent on Neruda and Vallejo seemed to result in smaller and tighter poems when I turned back to my own work, the danger being that such tightness eliminated exploratory movement, and I would often end up with a small dry thing too elliptic to show the thought process that I had actually put into it. I don't want to make too much out of it, but I feel that Spicer's Lorca involvement resulted in his writing a harder poem afterward, harder in the sense of its texture and harder in terms of its intellectual penetrability too. As poems in *Admonitions* and *A Book of Music* go, "Orfeo" is very accessible; more typical in this regard, are poems like "When they number their blocks they mean business," and "People who don't like the smell of faggot vomit" in *Admonitions* in which two voices seem to be at work, one interrupting the other, in a kind of brusque argument with it, so that the poem never really straightens out and resolves but remains like a clutch of hands around a baseball bat, the stem visible but the surface knobby and twisted. Later in his life, Spicer brings in the matter of dictation to talk about his method of composition and if what he says makes sense to one (it does not, really, to me), I suppose it is possible to think of the various "voices" as dictations that are only partially, if at all, aware of what other dictations are saying. However, in 1958 the shifting field of command and argument that informs the process of composition appears more like an afterglow from the Lorca working than it does as dictation. I doubt if Spicer knew Spanish very well, so that there was considerable resistance felt in translating, *as if it were coming from the Spanish text itself.* As if Lorca were resisting being translated. And given Spicer's own concern to find a way to work that utterly avoided echoing Yeats and being trapped in Freshman Composition all his life, there was much resistance on his part too, for he was also constantly in the position of wanting to crush what he called "the big lie of the personal" which infernally kept jabbing into his writing. It is too bad that Robin Blaser does not give us at least one completely frank and detailed description of how Spicer lived in his essay in *The Collected Books* (such as, say, Ross Russell opens his fine book on Charlie Parker, *Bird Lives!*, with). For I suspect that the way Spicer drank is hardly "the comfortable explanation" for his death that Robin states it is. In addition to the qualities I have discussed above, there is also a dull metallic feel to quite a bit of his writing that appears to me to be the darker side of drunk writing—the more useful side being the chance ability to make irrational things correspond in distortion. Since it appears to be a medical fact, at least, that Spicer drank himself to death, I think it is just to consider the role alcohol played in his poetic composition. But to do so, one would need more information than is presently in print.

So at this point, the function of *After Lorca* seems to have been that it intensified and perhaps contracted his resistance—and here I am thinking of resistance as an actual agent in composition, that the act of writing a poem for Jack Spicer could be seen as moving very slowly through a multidimensional solid called resistance out of which the poem is chipped. I put it this way because I want to emphasize the *sculptural* quality that the poems after *After Lorca* start to take on (although it is also there in the two very strong pieces he wrote in 1956, especially in "A Poem to the Reader of the Poem"). If Spicer had been more open to the sensual side of Lorca, I doubt if the poetry of 1958 and 1959 would have shaped up as quickly as it did—but he was not, nor was he really interested in making poems out of "real objects," as he argues in that third "letter." One only needs to watch him chew up Williams' red wheelbarrow in *A Red Wheelbarrow* to know that he was primarily interested in making his own kind of meaning, opaque and abstract. In this sense, *After Lorca* is a kind of farewell to allowing any kind of sensual pleasure to get into the poem. Perhaps this is some of what Spicer meant when he managed to say to Blaser at the end of his life, "My vocabulary did this to me." For these unique dehydrated iron creatures we think of as his poems were achieved by resisting, once the Lorca working had run its course, Lorca's incredibly lush sensibility.

The seeds of *Billy the Kid* are in "Psychoanalysis: an Elegy." There he had written:

> I think that I would like to write a poem that is slow as a
>   summer
> As slow getting started
> As 4th of July somewhere around the middle of the
>   second stanza. . . .

In this early poem (late '40s, I would guess), he is mostly pondering aspects of California that he would like to take over and make use of in his poetry. He feels trapped by the extent to which the potential poem is still attached to his California background, and he keeps going over and over what he is thinking, wondering

>   how many times this poem
> Will be repeated. How many summers
> Will torture California
> Until the damned maps burn
> Until the mad cartographer
> Falls to the ground and possesses
> The sweet thick earth from which he has been hiding.

A decade later, he was out of the trap. *Billy the Kid* begins:

> The radio that told me about the death of Billy the Kid
> (And the day, a hot summer day, with birds in the sky)
>   Let us fake out a frontier—a poem somebody could hide in with a
> sheriff's posse after him—a thousand miles of it if it is necessary for him to
> go a thousand miles—

The summer and the roads previously the property of his past, and thus only available in psychoanalytic description, have become portable, collapsible, and can be translated as a stage-set for Spicer's meditation on Billy the Kid. Much of his drive toward "the serial poem" was to release himself from the situation in which the poem, viewed as a "discrete" performance, was really no more meaningful than a joke. By engaging early, middle, and quite late Lorca poems, Spicer was able to experience the created time in another's lifework. Looking at *After Lorca* from a kind of bird's-eye view, I see Spicer slowly turning Lorca over, like apple bites, in his mouth, and also tasting the core, Lorca's most self-conflictive single poem, thus his most resistant, the "Ode to Walt Whitman." The thing that seemed to tease Spicer's imagination the most about what he chose to present of Lorca was the dilation between "niño" and "muchacho" and "joven" which for a brief period of time allowed Spicer to have his own longing and to have it bumpered at the same time, distanced by Lorca's shadow and light. The gift of Spicer's lingering over these real/irreal narcissistic shades is his allegiance to "the kid" whose death is configured on the stage built with Spicer's own California background.

Not only did Spicer learn of Billy the Kid's death via the radio and the day but also through, I presume, one of Jess Collin's collages (section II). This is where Spicer's lemon might actually have a believable place, as a rind, or piece in the process, as a collage is a kind of serial poem. So the process itself informs. Billy is more distant than Lorca and both below and above Spicer—which Lorca was not (Lorca was above him, which is one reason for Spicer converting the chauffeurs into taxi drivers in the "Whitman" ode). I assume the radio comes in immediately in homage to Cocteau's Orpheus hunched before the car radio in the film, that is, in homage to dictation. So the three elements that come together immediately are dictation and serial process, staged by the poet's freed background. If one were sitting in Spicer's seat, that would be like being dealt a flush—the only thing is, he has to play the hand.

Billy the Kid is Spicer's "Ode on a Grecian Urn." Billy is doomed, dead, yet living—he is immortal in the time of the poem because Spicer is suddenly touched to allow Eurydice to rise from the dead as Lady of Guadalupe (who then becomes Our Lady), and bless the poem while Billy shoots her heels off. The poem ends too quickly, possibly because Spicer is unable to linger in history or invent a sensual field through which he could draw more life and death from Billy. Yet the poem is genuinely haunting because Spicer has briefly realized his "real." And the real, here, is more a *balance* than anything else—as if poets write their most memorable poems when the fundamental things that they think about, and that have brought them to poetry in the first place, assemble as a kind of "combined object," a mental galaxy in which the separate powers and demons group together, happy for a moment, and make a new shape.

As soon as Our Lady appears, Spicer distances his heart and watches it break into small shadows. Section IX is the climax of the work:

So the heart breaks
Into small shadows
Almost so random
They are meaningless
Like a diamond
Has at the center of it a diamond
Or a rock
Rock.
Being afraid
Love asks its bare question—
I can no more remember
What brought me here
Than bone answers bone in the arm
Or shadow sees shadow—
Deathward we ride in the boat
Like someone canoeing
In a small lake
Where at either end

There are nothing but pine-branches—
Deathward we ride in the boat
Broken-hearted or broken-bodied
The choice is real. The diamond. I
Ask it.

This is Spicer's farewell to love, and under it is the more personal "A dead starfish on a beach" from *Admonitions*. It is as if Spicer, having lost a potentially living love, rises embracing Billy the Kid, who now lives briefly in Spicer's imagination, being dead, as Spicer briefly realizes just how dead he is, being alive—the two are equal, and so the poem finds its way into the canceling out parallels, "diamond . . . diamond," "rock . . . rock," "bone . . . bone," and "shadow . . . shadow." Spicer has not only given up on love, but he has lost touch with his origin too ("I can no more remember / What brought me here . . ."), which is the price he pays for the poem.

[March 15, 1977]

Companion Spider

In Kyoto, October 1962, I had become aware that I needed some sign—like Rilke's touching the crotch of a seaside tree and passing through to what he called "the other side of nature," or Ginsberg, after masturbating, in Harlem, hearing Blake's voice proclaiming "Ah! Sunflower"[1]—to justify writing poetry. While I can't say that I was literally on my knees, begging for a vision, I had reached a point in which nerve and blind desire *had* to be backed up by, in Blake's words, "divine aid."

It all began with a gorgeous red, green and yellow spider centered in her web attached to the persimmon tree in the Okumura backyard. I got used to taking a chair and a little table out under the web where I'd read *The Masks of God* and struggle to digest and translate César Vallejo's *Poemas humanos*. After several weeks of "spider sitting," the weather turned chill, with rain and gusting wind. When I went out one afternoon, the web was wrecked, the spider gone. Something went through me that I can only describe as the sensation of the loss of one deeply loved. I cried, and for several days felt nauseous and absurd. A week or so later, I was picked up by some sake drinkers in our local sushi bar—something that happened only this one time in my three years in Japan. The following day, I decided to motorcycle out to northwest Kyoto and visit Gary Snyder. Gary was not home, so I had tea with Joanne Kyger and, late in the afternoon, started the half-hour drive back home. I had been pleasantly hungover all day, sensory field narrowed, a lot of tendrils into areas that, in my case at least, are ordinarily available

This essay was written for "The Recovery of the Public World: A Conference and Festival in Honour of the Poetry and Poetics of Robin Blaser," held in Vancouver, 1995. It first appeared in the *AWP Chronicle* (May/Summer 1996) and was reprinted in *The Recovery of the Public World*, a collection of texts and talks from the conference, published by Talonbooks, Vancouver, 1999.

but not encloistered. Saintly sensitivities, little bowls of holiness—that is the sensation—if you can just pick out the right pebbles they will lead to a "see through."

Riding south on Junikendoori, I noticed that the motorcycle handlebars had become ox horns and that I was riding on an ox. A lumber company turned into a manger of baby Jesus with kneeling Wise Men. I forced myself to stay aware that I was in moving traffic, and looking for a place to turn off spotted Nijo Castle with its big tourist bus parking lot. Getting off my ox-cycle, I felt commanded to circumambulate the square Castle and its moat. I saw what appeared to be Kyger's eyeballs in the moat water. At the northwest corner, I felt commanded to look up: some forty feet above my head was the spider, completely bright red, the size of a human adult, flexing her legs as if attached to and testing her web. After maybe thirty seconds the image began to fade. I immediately felt that I had been given a totemic gift and that it would direct my relation to poetry. Out of my own body, I was to create a matrix strong enough in which to live and hunt.

I completed my circumambulation of the Castle, and very slowly cycled down Junikendoori to a coffee house in which, for what seemed to be ages, I stared at my book of Robert Herrick poems in a mass of glowing blue light. I finally got home at around midnight and after sleeping soundly woke up refreshed. Everything I tried to write about what had happened at Nijo Castle seemed superficial, so I went on to other things.

For all of 1963 I worked on Vallejo translations every afternoon in the Yorunomado coffee house in downtown Kyoto. I had convinced myself that getting these 104 poems into decent English was to be my apprenticeship to poetry. Because of what seemed to be insurmountable difficulties, I began to fantasize that I was in a life-and-death struggle with the spectre of Vallejo. I was trying to wrest his language away from him as if it were his food while he ferociously tried to thwart my thievery.

In the winter of 1964, I began to work on the first poem of my own that fully engaged and tested me. I called it, after Blake's short prophetic books, "The Book of Yorunomado,"[2] in honor of the coffee house, my Vallejo workshop. The poem had a double focus: a coming to terms with my first wife's abortion the year before, and an attempt to imagine my Jacob/angel struggle with Vallejo's labyrinthine texts. I tried to pair what was never born, as an infant, with what I was unable to bring forth of myself into the American English via Vallejo. The only thing I was able to wrest away from this Peruvian was a stone, and with stone in hand I found myself in a different time and place frame. I was in a large, pebbled courtyard in a medieval Japanese palace complex. The spectre of Vallejo, now dressed as an overlord, commanded me from his regal porch to commit harakiri, as a dishonored samurai. So I did, slicing into my Indiana guts. An eerie ecstasy ran through me as I envisioned the destruction of my given life, as if I was ripping my mother and father out of me. In the poem's final passage, "a dark red flower" appeared, opening and closing, "moving with heaven's untiring power." At the time, I made no conscious connection between the color of the flower and the spider. While I had been defeated by Vallejo at the time, I *had* written a poem I could live with.

The way the spider and the Vallejo experiences intertwined has, over the years, led me to some notions concerning muse and mentor. Initially, they play oppositional roles (for the mature poet they are in harmony). The muse is emanational (making poetry possible), while the mentor is spectral (contesting the novice's right to speak in poetry). Harold Bloom's sense of influence, welded to anxiety, is thus spectral. Neither muse nor mentor is sheerly what it appears to be; rather, they are more like the Siamese twin aspects of a single force that would inspire us at the same time it would enable us to be critically aware of what we are writing. Vicente Huidobro has a deft phrase for this. He writes: "Invent new worlds and back up what you say."[3] While the muse is traditionally feminine (for both men and woman), and mentor (possibly as a historical development of the great mother/son-lover complex) masculine, the gendering of these forces is troubling, to say the least. This problem has the smell of what Weston LaBarre called an "archosis," "a massive and fundamental misapprehension of reality, often of incalculable antiquity."[4] In a tiny poem written for but not included in the second *Maximus* volume, Charles Olson wrote[5:]

the IMMENSE ERROR
of *genderizing*
the 'Great Mother'

                    inCALCULABLE
damage

So I do not want to equate red spider with muse or Vallejo with mentor. I would like to keep them in an open dimension, though specifically in and under that persimmon tree web where they were in such close proximity. The orbed web with a female spider at center is a compelling metaphor for the labyrinth. The male spider, with semen-loaded paps, must make his way to the center without signaling via the wrong vibrations that he is prey, inseminate the much larger female, and then skedaddle before she seizes and devours him.

In the Cretan labyrinth a hybrid man-bull, the Minotaur, lies in wait at the center for those who attempt to pass through. In one version of the myth, Theseus with a thread from Ariadne (whose name relates to Arachne, the weaver turned into a spider by Athena) kills the Minotaur, exits the labyrinth, and with others transmutes its turns into a weaving dance. The alchemist Fulcanelli writes: "The picture of the labyrinth is thus offered to us as emblematic of the whole labour of the Work, with its two major difficulties, one the path which must be taken to reach the center—where the bitter combat of the two natures takes place—the other the way the artist must follow in order to emerge. It is there that the *thread of Ariadne* becomes necessary for him, if he is not to wander among the winding paths of the task, unable to extricate himself."[6]

Fulcanelli turns the web-become-labyrinth into a transformational arena. This triple overlay may offer some useful leads in understanding self and other. Jung offers considerable information on his view of the self in *Psychology and Alchemy*. He calls the self the union of opposites *par excellence*, the opposition between light and good on one hand and darkness and evil on the other. He proposes that the self is absolutely paradoxical, representing in every aspect thesis and antithesis and, at the same time, synthesis. It is the totality of the psyche, embracing the conscious and the unconscious. It is the *lapis invisibilitatus*, a borderline concept, and ultimately indeterminate.

The red spider pierced my heart as an extraordinary gift. Did it bestow a self? Working through Jung, I would have to say no. It confronted me with an extreme otherness that has taken years to process, and its presence, and absence, must have bled into "the bitter combat of the two natures" that I engaged in with the obdurate *Poemas humanos*. Fulcanelli tells us a bit more about this "bitter combat," describing it as a battle between an alchemical Eagle and Lion who tear at each other until, the eagle having lost its wings and the lion its head, a single body (referred to as *animated mercury*) is formed. As a hybrid, the Minotaur consists of a grotesque synthesis prefigured by mating spiders. Both conjunctions emit a lethal aura.

Making his way between biology and classical myth here may be the ur-poet, the shaman, who at the center of his or her initiation undergoes symbolic torture, dismemberment, and rebirth. While the animal-masked dancing shaman originates with prehistoric hunting peoples, in the 20th century there are intriguing parallels between the career of a shaman and the life and work of Antonin Artaud. Both share a nervous crisis, a painfully isolated initiation, symbolic death—in Artaud's case, a ninety-minute coma after electroshock—and rebirth, a new name and new language, chanting, gesturing, drumming, and detailed accounts of their spirit world adventures with allies and demons. The material here is much more complex (and utterly unintentional on Artaud's part) than those associations that cropped up in the understandably disputed "white shamanism" of the 1970s.

Shamanism aside, it is possible to make use of Fulcanelli's mutilated, single body to understand something that happens in literary translation. A new body is arrived at through strife and destruction. Loss is registered by what can never be brought over from the original, as well as in the second language's limitations and inability to overcome such loss.

For the shaman as well as for Jung's initiate seeking the integration Jung called "individuation," the combat of the self, or selves, is registered either as charisma or as a dream record. While charisma or dream journals may effect the way we respond to a particular poet, the proof of the pudding for the poet is in the ability to translate self-combat into a poem. Centers begin to abound and overlap. Both Jung and Robin Blaser have emphasized indeterminacy in their work. In a copy of *Image-Nations 1–12*, Robin had written me: "this is my most incomplete and best loved work—in my view, the indeterminate is my subject and open—."[7] I checked the word the other night in my Webster's *International Dictionary* and found "see INFLORESCENCE." Under "inflorescence," I found eleven illustrations of the budding and unfolding of blossoms. Like spider webs, inflorescence is both centripetal and centrifugal.

Caught up in the propulsive maze of the now well-known process, "form is but an extension of content," the poet, everywhichway in conflict, may very well seek out an otherness to curb the action. Curbs are circumferences. For Blake, "Reason is the bound or outward circumference of Energy." For Emily Dickinson, circumference for a butterfly is purposeless but in resurrection full. A year before his suicide, Hart

Crane was given profound advice about labyrinth and circumference by the bacteriologist Hans Zinsser.[8]

Other is a heartless word; these days we sometimes set "significant" before it to romanticize its neutrality. The other is what Theseus sees in the Minotaur. For Blaser, other is multifoliate. He identifies it as ourselves, the unthought of, a translation of oneself, the chiasmatic (via Merleau-Ponty), the anonymous, and: silence. Such definitions in transit wind out from "that odd Fork in Being's Road" (Dickinson),[9] or, "the Place of Twisted Water (Aztec), transpersonal yin-yang-like symbols for the center which is, alas, actually diffused throughout the entire labyrinth. For example: any creative project worth its salt lacks an aerial view. It is always "Groundwork: In the Dark," for decisions must be made about one's route without the overview needed to spot the resolution or exit. As Anton Ehrenzweig noted: "This dilemma belongs to the essence of creativity."[10]

"Companion" appears to come from "com" (together) and "panis" (bread), the one with whom one shares bread. Blaser associates the word not only with "refreshment," but with "opposites": "those opposites, who are companions." In *The Holy Forest*, might they be the two treed men at the beginning of the work who become "the great companions," Pindar and Duncan, as the work moves toward resolution? Blaser also writes that "the world of 20th century poetry involves a huge companionship," and in the same essay (on Olson and Whitehead), he states that "great poetry is always after the word—it is a spiritual chase . . . never simply subjective or personal." "La Chasse spirituelle," according to Verlaine, was Rimbaud's single greatest poem—irretrievably lost! (Such a comment resounds as an unscheduled moment in Robin's ongoing series, "The History of Laughter.")

Blaser's lifework imagines a world in which the human is not demonically separated from the other, a heroic task, and one over which the W. H. Auden of "The Poet and the City" (1962) broods.[11] For Auden, the poet's vocation is now much more difficult than in the past because of an encirclement of losses: "the loss of belief in the eternity of the physical universe; the loss of belief in the significance and reality of sensory phenomena; the loss of belief in a norm of human nature which will always require the same kind of man-fabricated world to be at home in; and, the disappearance of the Public Realm as the sphere of revelatory personal deeds."[12] In *The Human Condition*, Hannah Arendt comments: "The public realm . . . was reserved for individuality; it was the only place where men could show who they really and inexchangeably were."[13] Both Auden and Arendt are here concerned with the classic Greeks. Auden continues: "Today, the significance of the terms private and public has been reversed; public life is the necessary impersonal life, the place where a man fulfills his social function, and it is in his private life that he is free to be his personal self. In consequence the arts, literature in particular, have lost their traditional principal subject, the man of action, the doer of public deeds."

In Auden's, Arendt's, or Blaser's sense of it (in Blaser's case I refer to his essay "The Recovery of the Public World"), there is no evidence that twentieth-century poets have recovered a public world that has been unavailable to them for hundreds of years, much more unavailable in the twentieth century than in the nineteenth. T. S. Eliot's audience of 14,000 people that filled the University of Minnesota's football stadium in 1956 to hear the Nobel Laureate lecture on "The Frontiers of Criticism" is such an anomaly that it should make us groan. However, it is just too easy to trot forth a litany of the senses in which the phrase can be contested. I do want to make a couple of points about our distancing in this regard before suggesting a way in which the phrase can be true and support all of our coming together here in Vancouver, 1995.

Politically, the contemporary poet is undermined because, unlike Yeats or Whitman, say, he is not intimately related to figures of power (he is mainly aware of them via the sensory deprivation tank of media filtration). Whitman, for example, saw Lincoln up close, often, in 1861, could describe him in "doughnut complexion" detail, and felt that he was a comrade. Thus the "Lilacs" elegy reflects a public *and* a personal loss.

In regard to nature, which regardless of the "death of Pan" has been a sempiternal theme of poetry, ecologically, the contemporary poet is witness to its disappearance (or its confinement in expanded versions of the zoo). Money is what is behind such destruction, and money and spirit are turning into each other now more than ever, credit and credo, as billions and billions of dollars circulate constantly every day above our heads in "heaven" via telecommunication satellites. Luther thought a black, excremental Devil was the God of this world. Can you imagine what he would make of the exploitation of rain forests and the now lurid precipitate of money, not simply shit, but the pollution of the planet?

However, there is another perspective possible concerning the recovery of the public world. Such works as *The Maximus Poems, Passages,* and *The Holy Forest*—to name but three recent American examples—have drawn into their nets an immense amount of historical, philosophical, esoteric, popular, primitive, and psychological materials, many of which had previously not been made part of poetry's responsibilities. The "huge companionship" of which Blaser speaks involves, in the twentieth century, in Robert Duncan's words, "all things coming into their comparisons." There is, in fact, an adjective-defying interplay between destruction and recovery in this century, which may be its most heartbreaking hallmark. As if a response to Auschwitz, in 1947 Artaud wrote *To have done with the judgement of god.* While one may argue that Artaud's poem is but a drop of manna in a sea of blood, it is still a heroic attack on eternal damnation, the great blight of Christianity that even Dante supported.

Under the circumstances, in our century many artists have done the utmost that could be expected of them. Is there now too much grief for thought to handle? About that, I am unsure. But it is still possible for a novice to bring his or her given life into confrontation with a created life, for a blindly desiring beginner stuffed with categories (each of which claims a wholeness) to connect with the force of a lore that liquefies boundaries and opens out into a world.

Robin Blaser, in two prophetic passages from *The Holy Forest*, articulates what I take to be the antiphonal tension, regarding community, of our times. From "Salut":

> there is nothing here but an intense
> interior monologue with moments of colour, forms
> flowing toward beloved plants   the cost has
> been high   when all the world is loved by the
> daimon of mediocrity,   you, unpriestly, among
> hierarchs on fire   burned mouth

> must know why you strike

and from "sapphire-blue moon":

> we still dream behind us of a perfected
> humanity   a religion of cities   and
> take the thought east   the twentieth-
> century project, delving centuries of
> mind and heart for a new relation among
> things,
>   overwhelmed
>   to dream again

of *laissez-faire*   going fair   along paths
through the gardened wreckage and consequences
the State and the Nation agog with redemption   religions smoke on the hills, sacrificial as
                              always

Is not this "intense, interior monologue" and a "dream behind us of a perfected humanity" the sensation of so many twentieth-century poets as we hover, from Auden to Artaud, over the abyss monologue and dream expose?

The companion may be the least damaged of the poet's loves. In the French cave known as Pech-Merle, decorated at around 15,000 BCE, in a hidden corner, is a male figure (identified as such by a dangling penis), with a bird-like head, whose body is traversed by long, thread-like lines.[14] The body is slack, as if strung upon the lines passing through it. Caressing the figure's head is what appears to be the tip of one leg of a schematically drawn spider. Might the traversing lines be magic projectiles, as in shamanic dismemberment? I take this bird-headed figure to be an initiate depicted at a crucial stage of his transformation. And the caressing spider? The companion of all who have ventured into the maze of a searching for that confrontation that would generate a self strong enough to love, strong enough to not judge, and strong enough to disintegrate.[15]

NOTES

1. For the Rilke, see "An Experience," in *Selected Prose* (New Directions, 1960); for the Ginsberg, "A Blake Experience," *On the Poetry of Allen Ginsberg* (University of Michigan Press, 1984).

2. Three differing versions of this poem have been published in *Poetry* (Chicago), July 1965; *Indiana* (Black Sparrow Press, 1969); and *The Name Encanyoned River* (Black Sparrow Press, 1986).

3. From Huidobro's poem, "Arte Poética." There is a fuller consideration of the line's significance in "Still-life, with Huidebro," *Under World Arrest* (Black Sparrow Press, 1994).

4. From *Muelos*, Columbia University Press, 1984, cited by Robin Blaser on p. 365 of *The Holy Forest* (Coach House Press, 1993).

5. *Olson* #9, University of Connecticut Library, 1978.

6. *Le Mystère des Cathédrales* (Neville Spearman, 1971), pp. 48 and 91.

7. The ancient Welsh poem, the *Kat Godeu*, proclaims in its opening line: "Before I was free, I was multiform," and then goes ahead for hundreds of lines to list the facets of the human and natural universe that had made up this multiformity, or indeterminacy. We are caught up in the paradox of seeking to be and know ourselves while participating in a round dance that makes up a world. When we call the

dancer to our left or to our right "companion," perhaps we send the shiver of a loving humanitas out as an encircling chord. In "Fousang" (from *The Holy Forest*), Blaser writes:

> the living creatures stomp on the earth,
> tell it, repeat, enter the shine
> of
>   how old we are
> back to back the larks sing, back
> to back the creatures sing, back
> to back, the beginning and the
> end of it—out of it, the
> light-patches of a crazy-quilt
> arrange, derange, a range
> of the movement—lifted, so that
> at one moment end and beginning meet
> full of laughter.

Blaser then translates "the beast" into "a violet, golden, sweet, the violet companion."

8. This advice is quoted in Chapter 9 of *Novices*.

9. *The Complete Poems of Emily Dickinson* (Little, Brown, 1960), #615, dated 1862. The "Our" suggests a pilgrimage that is suddenly confronted with "the bitter conflict of the two natures," for Dickinson, death and eternity. The speaker is paralyzed (yet speechful) before this "center." Her circumference is Argus-eyed with gods, evoking Rilke's "There is no place that does not see you." Dickinson does not attempt to release the paralysis, which is to the poem's benefit, since the double bind of blocked center and judgmental circumference is, as an enactment, completely sufficient.

> Our journey had advanced—
> Our feet were almost come
> to that odd Fork in Being's Road—
> Eternity—by Term—
>
> Our pace took sudden awe—
> Our feet—reluctant—led—
> Before—were Cities—but Between—
> The Forest of the Dead—
>
> Retreat—was out of Hope—
> Behind—a Sealed Route—
> Eternity's White Flag—Before—
> And God—at every Gate—

10. *The Hidden Order of Art*, University of California Press, 1971, pp. 35–37. I have briefly summarized Ehrenzweig here. The pertinent passage is quoted in full in Chapter 7 of *Novices*.

11. The center itself is not merely a mating, grappling, or paralyzing place, but the reservoir of the *anima mundi*, the center of the Tibetan world wheel, the mandala, the Fountain of Youth, the face of the Sun God Tonatiuh at the center of the Aztec Calendar Stone, Sumer in Olson's vision of civilization's "One Center" from 3378 to 1200 BCE, and even the earth itself seen midway between light and dark-

ness. In Paris, it would be Notre Dame, with *arrondissements* winding out centrifugally within the bounding *périphérique*. In Cairo, today it appears to be the Al-Ahram building, a glossy steel-glass-and-marble office tower in which executives communicate with secretaries by closed-circuit television, fifty yards away from which "begins a labyrinth of narrow lanes where millions of Egyptians live in seedy shacks and dark warrens above and below ground, often without water, sewers, or electricity" (*New York Review of Books*, April 6, 1995, p. 32). Or, as Eliot Weinberger writes (*Artes de México* #21, p. 86), in Oaxaca, Mexico, it is the zócalo, "a place for doing nothing, sitting at the center of the universe. . . . Sitting in the zócalo, one's eyes are invariably drawn to the center of the center, to the ornate and Ruritanian bandshell. It is the late European contribution to this concept of a sacred place: that at the absolute center is not a cosmic tree or sacred mountain or pillar of stone—ladders between heaven and earth—but rather an enclosure of empty space. The English word *bandshell* captures it perfectly: *band*, the source of music; *shell*, a bounded hollow, a seashell you hold to your ear."

12. Reprinted in *Poetry and Politics* (Morrow, 1985).

13. *The Human Condition*, University of Chicago Press, 1958, p. 41.

14. I know of two photographs of this image. One is in Giedion's *The Eternal Present: The Beginnings of Art* (Bollingen, 1957, p. 467). The other is in Leroi-Gourhan's *Treasures of Prehistoric Art* (Abrams, 1967, p. 420). There is a poor reproduction of the Giedion photo in Hadingham's *Secrets of the Ice Age* (Walker, 1979). I am the only one who identifies the image by the line-traversed figure as a spider. Giedion calls it "a large and curious symbol"; Leroi-Gourhan describes it as "a brace-shaped sign"; Hadingham calls it "an abstract sign." None of these scholars sees it as part of a compound image involving the lines, or threads, traversing the human figure's body.

15. The conversion of the other into a companion, sounded by Blake's "Everything that lives is Holy," is one of the grand human themes, in daily life as well as in art. Eugenio Montale's poem, "L'Anguilla," in Cid Corman's translation, provides an extraordinary example of such a transformation. "Pirenean" in the poem refers to the famous fountain associated with Pegasus. Corman's version first appeared in *origin*, second series, April 1963.

> The eel, the siren
> of the cold seas that leaves the Baltic
> to reach our seas,
> our estuaries and rivers
> that travels upstream deep, under the spate
>   opposing,
> from branch to branch and then
> from hair to hair, attenuated,
> always more within, always more in the heart
> of flint, filtering
> through gullies of slime until one day
> a light struck off chestnuts
> ignites its flicker in pools of standing water,
> in the channels that go down
> from the terraces of the Appenine to the
>   Romagna;
> the eel, torch, lash,
> arrow of Eros in earth

that only our gulches or desiccate
Pirenean streams lead back
to paradises of fecundation;
the green spirit that seeks
life there where only
heat and desolation gnaw,
the spark that says
everything begins when everything seems
burnt out black, buried stump;
the brief iris, twin
of her whom your eyes enchase
and you make shine intact amidst the sons
of man, immersed in your mud, can you
not believe her a sister?

III

At the Locks of the Void:
Cotranslating Aimé Césaire

I first discovered Aimé Césaire in the second issue of Jack Hirshman's tiny *Hip Pocket Poems*, 1960. Césaire's prose poem, "Lynch 1," since edited out of the 1948 *Soleil cou coupé* (*Solar Throat Slashed*), was translated by Emile Snyder, a French transplant who was an early translator of Césaire. The poem sank into me like a depth charge. Emile's translation was adequate, but a close scrutiny of it and the original text revealed that he simplified a few of the poem's erudite words and tropes, so I retranslated it in 1995 during the O. J. Simpson trial. Here it is:

Lynch 1

Why does the spring grab me by the throat? what does it want of me? so what even if it does not have enough spears and military flags! I jeer at you spring for flaunting your blind eye and your bad breath. Your stupration your infamous kisses. Your peacock tail makes tables turn with patches of jungle (fanfares of saps in motion) but my liver is more acidic and my venefice stronger than your malefice. The lynch it's 6 PM in the mud of the bayou it's a black handkerchief fluttering at the top of the pirate ship mast it's the strangulation point of a fingernail up to the carmine of an interjection it's the pampa it's the queen's ballet it's the sagacity of science it's the unforgettable copulation. O lynch salt mercury and antimony! The lynch is the blue smile of a dragon enemy of angels the lynch is an orchid too lovely to bear fruit the lynch is an entry into matter the lynch is the hand of the wind bloodying a forest whose trees are galls brandishing in their hand the smoking torch of their castrated phallus, the lynch is a hand sprinkled with the dust of precious stones, the lynch is a release of hummingbirds, the lynch is a lapse, the lynch is a trumpet blast a broken gramophone record a cyclone's tail its train lifted

Written for the 1998 Lecture Series at La Maison Française of Columbia University, and read there on November 11. The lecture was first published in *New American Writing*, summer 2000. It was reprinted in *Pores* #1, 2001, a web magazine edited by William Rowe, published by Birkbeck College, University of London.

by the pink beaks of predatory birds. The lynch is a gorgeous shock of hair that fear flings into my face the lynch is a temple crumbled and gripped by the roots of a virgin forest. O lynch lovable companion beautiful squirted eye huge mouth mute save when an impulse spreads there the delirium of glanders weave well, lightning bolt, on your loom a continent bursting into islands an oracle contortedly slithering like a scolopendra a moon settling in the breach the sulfur peacock ascending in the summary loophole of my assassinated hearing.

In its "logic of metaphor" chain reaction, its linking of social terror with the violence of sudden natural growth, and its sacrifice of a male hero for the sake of sowing the seeds of renewal, "Lynch 1" is a typical and very strong Césaire poem of the late 1940s. For years I didn't know what to make of it, yet its strangeness was mesmerizing. It seemed to imply that for the speaker to suddenly inhale deeply, to offer himself to the wild, was to induct the snapping of a lynched neck. Erotic aspects of the poem came to mind in the 1970s when I saw the Japanese film *Realm of the Senses*, in which the sex-addicted male lead makes his partner choke him to wring the last quiver out of his orgasm. At that time I started to read Césaire at large bilingually and determined that he was a poet of extraordinary importance, and that he had not been translated as well as he might be (at that point only around one-third of his poetry had been translated at all). I decided, as I had with César Vallejo in the 1970s, that the best way to read Césaire would be to translate him, since the antiphonal traffic of translation, for me, opens up a greater assimilative space than monolingual reading. I will have more to say about this later.

In 1977 I received a California Arts Council "Artists in the Community" grant that involved my teaching poetry for a school year in the predominantly African-American Manual Arts High School in south-central Los Angeles. I got the idea of translating Césaire's "Notebook of a Return to the Native Land" while teaching at Manual Arts and presenting the translation to my students at the end of the year. As soon as I began to seriously work on the poem, I realized that I was in over my head, and that to do a thorough job I would have to work with a cotranslator. I teamed up with Annette Smith, a professor of French in the Humanities Division at the California Institute of Technology and, to make a long story short, working 20 or so hours a week, we translated all of Césaire's 1976 *Complete Poetry* between 1977 and 1982. Our work was published in 1983 by the University of California Press as *Aimé Césaire: The Collected Poetry*. We had planned to call the book "the complete poetry," but in 1982 Césaire surprised us with a new collection, *moi, laminaire (i, liminaria)*, which we subsequently translated along with Césaire's early poetic oratorio, *Et le chiens se taisaient (And the Dogs Were Silent)*. This collection was published in 1990 by the University Press of Virginia as *Aimé Césaire: Lyric and Dramatic Poetry 1946–1982*.

Our working method was as follows: we would both read a poem and take notes on it. Then Annette would dictate a version of it to me which I would take home and type up, questioning this and that in an attempt to isolate specific translation problems in the second draft. In most cases, Annette would have spotted difficulties that I was not aware of. Our work on the third draft was mainly an attempt to theoretically solve these problems, leaving us with the challenge of how to actually translate them. We worked together as much as possible, in tandem, as it were, constantly questioning each other's information and solutions. By doing so, we avoided the often disastrous results that occur when the person responsible for the original language hands or mails a literal version to the person responsible for the second language and he finishes it on his own. In our case, I met with Césaire in Paris twice on my own and once, when we had our questions down to a dozen, with Annette. At the point that a final draft was possible, I holed up for two weeks in the stacks of the Cal Tech Library with a typewriter and piles of reference materials.

As a cotranslator, I have been extremely fortunate to have had two great cotranslators to work with, Annette and, with Vallejo's posthumously published poetry, José Rubia Barcia. Besides being very alert and responsible, Annette and José were both rigorously honest, which means in this context, among other things, being able to express ignorance, which leaves a problem open, rather than sealing it into a guess.

While the syntactical difficulties involved in translating Césaire are formidable, to properly discuss them we would all have to sit down at a table, as Annette and I did, and examine original texts against their translational possibilities. Here I would like to draw upon some of the material from our "Translators' Notes" in our Introduction to *The Collected Poetry*. Annette was primarily responsible for this material (in a spirit that balanced my primary responsibility for the final American version of the text).

Syntactical difficulties aside, the lexicological ones were even more taxing. Large numbers of rare and technical words constantly kept us bent over various encyclopedias, dictionaries of several languages (including

African and Créole), botanical indexes, atlases, and history texts. Once
we were fortunate enough to identify the object, we then had to decide
to what extent the esoteric tone of the poetry should be respected in the
American. Dispatching the reader to the reference shelf at every turn in
order to find out that the object of his chase was nothing more than a
morning glory (convovulus) or a Paraguayan peccary ("patyura") hardly
encouraged sustained reading. A delicate balance had to be maintained
between a rigorously puristic stand and a systematic vulgarization. The
case of plant names was especially complex, as we had to be careful to
highlight Césaire's concrete and political interest in Caribbean flora.
The following comments by Césaire himself (from a 1960 interview)
reinforced our concerns in these regards: "I am an Antillean. I want a
poetry that is concrete, very Antillean, Martinican. I must name Martinican things, must call them by their names. The cañafistula mentioned in 'Spirals' is a tree; it is also called the drumstick tree. It has
large yellow leaves and its fruit are those purplish bluish black pods,
used here also as a purgative. The balisier resembles a plantain, but it
has a red heart, a red florescence at its center that is really shaped like a
heart. The cecropias are shaped like silvery hands, yes, like the interior
of a black's hand. All of these astonishing words are absolutely necessary, they are never gratuitous. . . ."

Neologisms constituted another pitfall. Some were relatively easy to
handle because their components were obvious. "Négritude," "nigro-
mance," "strom," and "mokatine" were clear by association with "infin-
itude," "néromancie," "maelstrom," and "nougâtine" (a rich French al-
mond candy). But coining equivalents for "rhizulent," "effrade," and
"desencastration" (which we translated respectively as "rhizulate,"
"frightation," and "disencasement," in the last case giving up on the
castration aspect), required a solid sense of semantics. Only Césaire
himself was in a position to reveal, in a conversation with me in a Paris
café, that "verrition," which preceding translators had interpreted as
"flick" and "swirl," had been coined on a Latin verb "verri" meaning
"to sweep," "to scrape a surface," and ultimately "to scan." Our rendi-
tion ("veerition") attempted to preserve the turning motion (set against
its oxymoronic modifier "motionless") as well as the Latin sound of the
original—thus restituting the long-lost meaning of an important passage (the last few lines of "Notebook of a Return to the Native Land.").

As a final example, the problems involved in translating the word
"nègre" go to the heart of Césaire's poetics. Put as simply as possible,

the lexical background is as follows: before the Second World War the French had three words to designate individuals or things belonging to the black race. The most euphemistic was "Noir" (noun or adjective). The most derogatory was "négro." In between, on a sort of neutral and objective ground, was the word "nègre," used both as a noun or as an adjective (as in "l'art nègre"). For the general public, "noir" and "nègre" may well have been interchangeable, but the very civilized and very complexed Antilleans considered themselves as "Noirs," the "nègres" being on that distant continent, Africa. And it is in this light that one must read Césaire's use of the word "nègre" and its derivatives "négritude," "négrillon" and "négraille": he was making up a family of words based on what he considered to be the most insulting way to refer to a black. The paradox, of course, was that this implicit reckoning with the blacks' ignominy, this process of self-irony and self-denigration, was the necessary step on the path to a new self-image and spiritual rebirth. It was therefore important to translate "nègre" as "nigger" and its derivatives as derivatives or compounds of "nègre" and "nigger" ("negritude," "nigger scum," "little nigger," etc.).

Césaire's "Notebook of a Return to the Native Land," as allusively dense as "The Wasteland," and as transcendental as "The Duino Elegies," is one of the truly great poems of the twentieth century. With its 1055 lines that constantly shift back and forth between poetry and prose poetry, it is more of an extended lyric than an epic. After the initial burst, it moves into a brooding, static overview of the psychic and geographical topology of Martinique, generally in strophes that evoke Lautréamont's *Maldoror.* A second movement begins with the speaker's urge to go away; suddenly the supine present is sucked into a whirlpool of abuses and horrors suffered by blacks throughout their colonized and present history. The non-narrrative "fixed/exploding" juxtapositions in this movement reveal Césaire's commitment to surrealism even though thematic development is always implied. The second movement reaches its nadir in a passage where the speaker discovers himself mocking an utterly degraded old black man on a streetcar. The final, rushing, third movement is ignited by the line: "But what strange pride suddenly illuminates me?" In a series of dialectical plays between the emergence of a future hero giving new life to the world and images from the slaves' "middle passage" of the past, the "sprawled flat" passivity of the first movement is transformed into a standing insurrection that finally wheels up into the stars. The incredible burden of the poem is that of a parthenogenesis in which Césaire must conceive and give birth to himself while exorcising his introjected and collective white image of the black.

Here is the initial burst, which contains, in telegraphic shifts, many of Césaire's lifelong themes:

> Beat it, I said to him, you cop, you lousy pig, beat it, I detest the flunkies of order and the cockchafers of hope. Beat it, evil grigri, you bedbug of a petty monk. Then I turned toward paradises lost for him and his kin, calmer than the face of a woman telling lies, and there, rocked by the flux of a never exhausted thought I nourished the wind, I unlaced the monsters and heard rise, from the other side of a disaster, a river of turtle-doves and savanna clover which I carry forever in my depths height-deep as the twentieth floor of the most arrogant houses and as a guard against the putrefying force of crepuscular surroundings, surveyed night and day by a cursed venereal sun.

Three sentences: two swift commands to the police and priests, followed by a third made up of ten hairpin-curving clauses containing Césaire's basic contraries: on one hand, he commits himself to a sacred, whirling, primordial paradise of language, open to his subconscious depths and destructive of "the reality principle," or as he himself puts it, "the vitelline membrane that separates me from myself." On the other hand, his quest for authenticity will also include confronting the colonial brutality in his own overpopulated and defeated Martinique where, as Michel Leiris once pointed out, "no one can claim to be indigenous, since the Indians who were the first inhabitants were wiped out by immigrants from Europe a little over three centuries ago and since the white settlers made use of Africa to furnish its manpower."

This is a vision of Eden that also includes its night side, a dyad that is incredibly difficult to maintain, because a vision of paradisal wholeness and existent human suffering in the present negate each other. A significant part of the energy in Césaire's language is generated by his attempt to transform the language of the slave masters of yesterday and the colonial administrators of his own day into a kind of *surfrançais*, as in *sur*real, a supercharged French that in its own fashion is as transformational as surrealism attempted to be of bourgeois, patriarchal, French mentality.

In terms of Césaire's career as a poet (which extends from the late 1930s to the early 1990s), the first half of my earlier set of contraries—

a whirling paradise of language—dominates the 1940s. Much of the writing in the 1946 *Les armes miraculeuses (The Miraculous Weapons)* has a hallucinatory concentration to it, as if Césaire has taken Rimbaud's il-luminated vistas to a new plane. Here are the first two pages of the seven-page "Les pur-sang" ("The Thoroughbreds"):

And behold through my ear woven with crunchings
and with rockets the hundred whinnying
thoroughbreds of the sun syncopate harsh uglinesses
amidst the stagnation.

Ah! I scent the hell of delights
and through nidorous mists mimicking flaxen
hair—bushy breathing of beardless
old men—the thousandfold ferocious tepidity
of howling madness and death.
But how how not bless
unlike anything dreamt by my logics
hard against the grain cracking their licy piles
and their saburra and more pathetic
than the fruit-bearing flower
the lucid chap of unreasons?

And I hear the water mounting
the new the untouched the timeless water
toward the renewed air.

Did I say air?

A discharge of cadmium with gigantic weals
expalmate in ceruse white wicks
of anguish.

Essence of a landscape.

Carved out of light itself fulgurating nopals
burgeoning dawns unparalleled whitescence
deep-rooted stalagmites carriers of day

O blazing lactescences hyaline meadows
snowy gleanings

toward streams of docile neroli incorruptible
hedges ripen with distant mica
their long incandescence.
The eyelids of breakers shut—Prelude—
yuccas tinkle audibly
in a lavender of tepid rainbows
owlettes peck at bronzings.

Who
riffles
and raffles
the uproar, beyond the muddled heart of this
third day?

Who gets lost and rips and drowns
in the reddened waves of the Siloam?
Rafale.
The lights flinch. The noises rhizulate
the rhizule
smokes
silence.

The sky yawns from black absence

behold—
nameless wanderings
the suns the rains the galaxies
fused in fraternal magma
pass by toward the safe necropolises of the sunset
and the earth, the morgue of storms forgotten,
which stitches rips in its rolling
lost, patient, arisen
savagely hardening the invisible faluns
blew out

and the sea makes a necklace of silence for the earth
the sea inhaling the sacrificial peace
where our death rattles entangle, motionless with
strange pearls and abyssal mute
maturations

the earth makes a bulge of silence for the sea
in the silence

behold the earth alone,
without its trembling nor tremoring
without the lashing of roots
nor the perforations of insects

empty
empty as on the day before day . . .

In 1978, I tried to explain to Florence Loeb, the daughter of the famous Parisian art dealer, the desire for the prodigious in Césaire's
poetry and some of the circumstances under which it takes root. She

listened to me and then said something I will never forget: "Césaire uses words like the nouveaux riches spend their money." She meant, of course, that this prodigal son of France, educated and acculturated by France, should cease his showing off, racing his language like roman candles over her head, and return to the fold (to the sheepfold, I might add, to a disappearance among the millions for whom to have French culture is supposed to be more than enough). To this aristocratic woman, Aimé Césaire's imaginative wealth looked like tinsel. I carried this sinister cartoon of his power around with me for a couple of years. One morning what I wanted to say was a response to Césaire himself:

For Aimé Césaire

Spend language, then, as the nouveaux riches spend money
invest the air with breath newly gained each moment
hoard only in the poem, be the reader-miser, a new kind of snake
coiled in the coin-flown beggar palm, be political, give it all away
one's merkin, be naked to the Africa of the image mine in which
biology is a tug-of-war with deboned language in a tug-of-war with
Auschwitz in a tug-of-war with the immense demand now to meet
    the complex
actual day across the face of which Idi Amin is raining—
the poem cannot wipe off the blood
but blood cannot wipe out the poem
black caterpillar
in its mourning leaves, in cortege through the trunk of the highway of
history in a hug-of-war with our inclusion in
the shrapnel-elite garden of Eden.

Césaire's spontaneous, dream-like surges of language that dominate the 1940s seem to be posited on a belief in the possibility of a fundamental change in the Martinican situation as well as in human society at large. I should mention here that Césaire backed up his poetic ideology with a parallel full-time career of political action: at the end of 1945, he was elected mayor of Martinique's capital, Fort-de-France, and, as a member of the French Communist Party, became one of the deputies to the Constituent Assembly from Martinique. He was responsible for the bill in the French parliament that transformed the so-called "créole" colonies—Martinique, Guadeloupe, French Guyana, and Réunion—

into constituent departments of France with full right of citizenship for all their inhabitants, an act for which he has been bitterly criticized by more radical Caribbean thinkers who insist on independence, and for whom departmental status represents a serious compromise.

In the 1950s, and since, Césaire's language of paradise has been increasingly freighted with political consternation, based on the limitations and complications in any genuine change. *Ferrements (Ferraments)*, published in 1960, is permeated with fantastic evocations of black bondage through history. It is as if every line in this collection is the "Flying Dutchman" of a slave ship, each word the ghost of branded flesh. We are told a relentless tale of abduction, pillage, and dumping, of vomiting broken teeth, of ants polishing skeletons, of chunks of raw flesh, of spitting in the face, of trophy heads, of crucifixion. The transition point between *Ferraments* and the much earlier *Miraculous Weapons* is Césaire's shortest collection, *Corps perdu (Lost Body)*, ten poems, published in 1950 and illustrated with thirty-two engravings by Picasso (in 1986 George Braziller published a facsimile edition of this book with Annette's and my introduction and translation). In *Lost Body* Césaire seems to have realized that in certain ways the black would remain in exile from himself and, in effect, not enter the house called *negritude* that Césaire had been building for him.

In "Word," the opening poem of *Lost Body*, the speaker commands the "word" (which initially suggests The Word, or Logos) to keep vibrating within him. At the moment that its waves lasso and rope him to a voodoo center-stake where a shamanic sacrifice ensues, it is also revealed that the "word" is "nigger"—and by implication, the curare on the arrow tips—as the quiver of social stigmata associated with "the word 'nigger'" is emptied into him.

When Annette and I visited Aimé Césaire in his apartment in Paris in 1982, after we had received responses to our final batch of questions, we asked him if he would read us a poem. From some five hundred pages of published work, he chose the title poem of *Lost Body*. Here is the poem in our translation:

Lost Body

  I who Krakatoa
I who everything better than a monsoon
I who open chest
I who Laelaps
I who beat better than a cloaca

I who outside the musical scale
I who Zambezi or frantic or rhombos or cannibal
I would like to be more and more humble and more lowly
always more serious without vertigo or vestige
to the point of losing myself falling
into the live semolina of a well-opened earth
Outside in lieu of atmosphere there'd be a beautiful haze
no dirt in it
each drop of water forming a sun there
whose name the same for all things
would be DELICIOUS TOTAL ENCOUNTER
so that one would no longer know what goes by
—a star or a hope
or a petal from the flamboyant tree
or an underwater retreat
raced across by the flaming torches of aurelian-jellyfish
Then I imagine life would flood my whole being
better still I would feel it touching me or biting me
lying down I would see the finally free odors come to me
like merciful hands
finding their way
to sway their long hair in me
longer than this past that I cannot reach
Things stand back make room among you
room for my repose carrying in waves
my frightful crest of anchor-like roots
looking for a place to take hold
things I probe I probe
me the street-porter I am root-porter
and I bear down and I force and I arcane
　I omphale
Ah who leads me back toward the harpoons
　I am very weak
I hiss yes I hiss very ancient things
as serpents do as do cavernous things
I whoa lie down wind
and against my unstable and fresh muzzle
against my eroded face
press your cold face of ravaged laughter
The wind alas I will continue to hear it
nigger nigger nigger from the depths
of the timeless sky
a little less loud than today
but still too loud
and this crazed howling of dogs and horses
which it thrusts at our forever fugitive heels

but I in turn in the air
shall rise a scream so violent
that I shall splatter the whole sky
and with my branches torn to shreds
and with the insolent jet of my wounded and solemn shaft

I shall command the islands to be

For a moment, Césaire's body of work buckles with the dilemma that true humanity might only be discovered in madness or apocalypse. The severity of this moment is registered by the wrenching ending where the black, although torn apart by the white devil's hounds, destroys the sky and re-creates primal islands in one paroxysmic gesture. Such an ending recalls Hart Crane's poem "Lachrymae Christi," in which a Nazarene/Dionysus who is crucified, torn asunder, and burned at the stake is beseeched to reappear whole. Both poems confront the reader with a radical vision of creativity that is bound up with an assimilation of such destructiveness as to render it, in the moment, sublime and absurd.

Earlier I contrasted translating with monolingual reading. As the translator scuttles back and forth between the original and the rendering, or in this case engages in dialogue with a cotranslator, a kind of "assimilative space" does open up, in which "influence" may be less contrived and literary than when drawing upon masters in one's own language. Before considering why this may be so, I want to propose a key difference between a poet translating a poet and a scholar translating a poet.

While both engage the myth of Prometheus, seeking to steal some fire from one of the gods to bestow on readers, the poet is also involved in a subplot that may, as it were, chain him to a wall. That is, besides making an offering to the reader, the poet-translator is also making an offering to himself—he is stealing fire for his own furnaces at the risk of being overwhelmed—stalemated—by the power he has inducted into his own workings.

But influence through translation is different than influence through reading masters in one's own tongue. If I am being influenced by Ezra Pound, say, his American is coming directly into my own. You read my poem and think of Pound. In the case of translation, I am cocreating an American version out of—in the case of Césaire—a French text, and if Césaire is to enter my own poetry he must do so via what I have already, as a translator, turned him into. This is, in the long run, very close to being influenced by myself or by *a self I have created to mine*. Antonin Artaud once wrote: "I want to initiate myself off of myself—not off the dead initiations of others."

When I speak of creating an American version out of a French text, I don't want to imply that I think of myself as writing my own poem in the act of cotranslating Césaire—or to put it more vividly, à la Kafka's "In the Penal Colony," writing my own sentence in the back of a victimized text. I do not believe in so-called "free translations," Lowellian "Imitations," or Tarn's "transformations." I see the poet-translator in the service of the original, not attempting to improve on it or to outwit it. He must, alone or with a coworker, research all archaic, rare, and technical words, and translate them (in contrast to guessing at them or explaining them). As I see it, the basic challenge is to do two incompatible things at once: an accurate translation *and* one that is up to the performance level of the original.

All translations are, in varying degrees, spectres or emanations. Spectral translations haunt us with the loss of the original; before them, facing the translator's inabilities or hubris, we feel that the original has been sucked into a smaller, less effective size. Like ghosts, such translations painfully remind us to what an extent the dead are absent. Emanational translations, on the other hand, are what can be made of the original poet's vision; while they are seldom larger than their prototypes, good ones hold their own against the prototype and they bring it across as an injection of fresh poetic character into the literature of the second language.

The emanation and spectre distinction is originally William Blake's, but I am lifting it out of his bisexual vortex and applying it to the influence one poet may have upon another. As someone who has been translating almost since I began to write poetry, I have probably been much more influenced by César Vallejo, Aimé Césaire, and Antonin Artaud than I have by any English or American poets. Taking into consideration the curious matter of self-influence that seems to be one of the mixed blessings of poetic translation, I would say that their combined and most potent gift has been one of permission—of giving me permission to say anything that would spur on my quest for authenticity and for constructing an alternative world in language. Here I would also keep in mind Vicente Huidobro's sterling injunction: "Invent new worlds and back up what you say."

Surely influence in the form of the gift I have described is emanational and not the spectral blockage Harold Bloom equates with the whole matter of influence in his wrong but useful study, *The Anxiety of Influence*. Poets who have somehow managed to speak, if only in part, in an original way, convey a permission to do the same to some of those who assimilate their work. Poets who primarily represent a dilution of others' energies—I am tempted to say "academic poets" here, but such is true for "anti-academic" or street or experimental poets as well— tend to project a spectral influence. Uninspired and conventional writing is much more the result of the writer's timidity, evasiveness, and willingness to be easily shaken loose from what he has sunk his teeth into than it is of the innovators he has read.

I worked on Césaire when I was beyond my apprenticeship to poetry and thus his effect is less initiational, much less crucial to my being a poet, than is Vallejo's. However, I got seriously involved with Césaire at the same time that I was starting a long period of field and library research on what I have come to call "Paleolithic Imagination & the Construction of the Underworld." Césaire's dyadic emphasis on both the deep past ("I am before Adam I do not come under the same lion") and the often unbearable present encouraged me, on my own terms, to try to do the same.

The most direct use I have made of Césaire's poetry is in my poem from the late 1980s called "The Sprouting Skull," a fantasia based in part on the four lines that end Césaire's poem "Lay of Errantry." In 1995, struggling to find a way to write about the Brown and Goldman murders and the trial and acquittal of O. J. Simpson in a way that would not simply restate what readers and TV observers already knew, Césaire's description of three fabulous beasts in another poem edited out of *Solar Throat Slashed* gave me the idea of creating my own fabulous beast images for Simpson, Brown, and Goldman at the moment the murders occurred. Once these images were in place, I was able to finish the poem, "Gretna Green."

The use of Césaire's work in such pieces is a kind of bonus based more on familiarity with his writing than on being porous to its character. Aspects of Césaire's solemnity, ferocity and tenderness, startling imaginal shifts, and word coinage have become mixed into the strata of my subconscious. Occasionally I will look at a poem after I have written it and sense that while there is no visible presence of an influence there is a lot of Césaire weather in the climate of its construction. I would like to end this presentation with one such poem, "Short

Story," written in 1992. I'm pretty confident that the last two lines would not have been written without the assimilated companionship of Aimé Césaire.

Short Story

Begin with this: the world has no origin.
We encircle the moment, lovers
who, encircling each other, steep in
          the fantasy
now we know the meaning of life.

Wordsworth's *recollection:* wreck election,
the coddling of ruins, as if the oldest man
      thinking of the earliest thing
offers imagination its greatest bounty.

A poem is a snake sloughing off the momentary,
crawling out of now (the encasement of
          its condition)
into layered, mattered, time.
Now is the tear and ear of terra's torn era.
For the serpentine, merely a writhe
          in appetite.

We posit Origin in order to posit end,

and if your drinking water is sewage,
to do so is understandable.

When the water is pure, Lilith's anatomy
is glimpsable in each drop.

But the water is never pure.

Before time, there appears to have been
a glass of pure water.

Therefore, we speculate, after time,
there will be another.

Life, a halo surrounding emptiness.

Continue with this: not body vs. soul,
but the inherent doubleness of any situation.
Thus in fusion there is also abyss.

Conclusion: I am suspended between origin and now,
or between origin and a bit before now.
Unknotting myself from both ends,
I drop through the funnel the y in abyss offers.

Nothing satisfies. And,
my suffering is nothing. Two postage stamps
glued, back to back,
abysscadabra.

What is missing? A poetry so full of claws
as to tear the reader's face off.
Too much? Look what men do to women.
Why should art be less?

Poetry's horrible responsibility
in language to be the world.

A Tribute to Américo Ferrari

It is a pleasure to offer an homage to the scholar, translator, and professor Américo Ferrari, on the occasion of his retirement from the University of Geneva. Those of you involved in the School of Translation and Interpretation are certainly aware that in many instances two heads are better than one when it comes to translating a difficult text. In my experience, it is not uncommon for a poet to work with a scholar in the process of translating poetry. American poets are often, as am I, self-taught in the languages from which they translate. While we may have an ability to approach the performance level of the original in our own language, we may lack the vocabulary range in a foreign language, as well as a firm background in the literary and historical matrices out of which the poet to be translated comes.

Américo Ferrari is the leading scholar in the world on the poetry of César Vallejo. Suffice it to say here that he has cotranslated Vallejo into French, written a number of superb essays on the poet, and master-minded the definitive *César Vallejo / Obra Poética* (Colleción Archivos, 1988). I discovered Vallejo in the early 1960s. Over the past thirty years as a poet as well as a translator I have carefully studied his poetry, and published a translation of his European poetry in 1968 as well as a re-translation of the same poetry in 1978. In 1988, I decided to translate Vallejo's most difficult book, *Trilce* (1922), making use of Ferrari's edition and his annotations to *Trilce*.

I originally decided to team up with Julio Ortega, a Peruvian writer and editor whom I had known since 1965, currently a professor at Brown University. Our plan was to do a cotranslation, as a poet/scholar team. After working out several drafts of the translation, it became

This piece was written for a special issue ("Mélanges en l'honneur d'Américo Ferrari") of *Cabiers de l'Ecole de Traduction et d'Interprétation*, Université de Genève, 1996.

apparent that Ortega and I had different ideas of what a *Trilce* translation in English should be—and we also had different amounts of time
to put into such a translation, so we ended our association. Ferrari can
tell you of the perils involved in a reading of *Trilce*, let alone a translation of the book. It is more like a new planet than a book of poetry. One
is convinced that it makes, if not common, uncommon sense—that its
density and bizarre associations do not boil down to nonsense, but,
rather, register an imaginative synthesis that is still a bit beyond the
reach of most earthlings. Such a situation for a translator is daunting,
for responsible translating presumes a constant level of understanding
of the original text.

Once on my own, on planet *Trilce*, I discovered that in most cases,
drawing on a battalion of dictionaries, the glossaries of Ferrari (1988),
Meo Zilio (1967), and Larrea (1978), along with what had been written
about the book, I could find my way. However, "in most cases" means
that in some cases I had to make translating decisions without any solid
ground on which to stand. At this point I determined that the only person in the world who could, and did, help me was Américo Ferrari.
This may seem like an overstatement, but it is not. Ferrari was the only
person I dared count on to be rigorously honest with me, to access
sources—often a time-consuming task—that I did not know existed,
and to then try to think through "*Trilce* knots" that for all we knew no
one had ever thought through before.

My first letter to Ferrari, in March 1990, contained thirty-seven
questions, all of which he answered completely or at least partially.
That exchange is much too long to be printed here. There were several
more exchanges of varying lengths, and the last, in November and December 1991, consisted of eight questions and eight responses. I think
the clearest illustration of Ferrari's mettle, in this regard, is to share this
exchange with you, offering first my question (asked in English) and
Ferrari's response (made in Spanish). The roman numerals refer to
poems in *Trilce* which are roman numeraled but otherwise untitled.

1. VI: 4th line from the end: *Capulí de obrería.* Is this phrase in any way
   idiomatic, or, as I fear, is it utterly invented by Vallejo? It appears to
   suggest "a sterling piece of work," and I am tempted to translate it
   that way. Literally it means, in English, "a cape gooseberry of work-
   manship" (since I think we can eliminate the religious denotation as
   being irrelevant here). Does *capulí* mean anything special to a Peruvian? Is it used in idiomatic expressions? Are there Peruvian expres-

sions that end in *de obrería?* I think the literal meaning is clumsy and inappropriate.

1. VI: *Capulí de obrería. Capulí* es en el Perú una planta que da una flor y un fruto, una especie de baya, como la fresa o la cereza, muy apreciada sobre todo en la sierra; puede tener a veces, aplicado a las mujeres, la connotación de belleza delicada y *morena;* "color capulí" es equivalente de color moreno o *trigueño* (cf. v. 14). Te adjunto una fotocopia sacada del *Diccionario de peruanismos* (1970) [Biblioteca de cultura peruana, vol. 10, Paris, Desclée de Brouwer, 1938] de Juan de Arona, nombre de pluma des escritor Pedro Paz Soldán y Unanue, donde explica cómo el capulí era uno de los frutos escogidos por su belleza para hacer unos ramilletes especiales llamados *misturas.* En cuanto a *obrería* no creo que designe otra cosa que el trabajo de su "obrera" Otilia que le lavaba y planchaba la ropa: por consiguiente, *capulí de obrería* = flor de obrería, en el sentido corriente en español, dechado, modelo, lo mejor de, pero con connotación del color de la tez de la obrera, color capulí or trigueño (color de trigo maduro, moreno y dorado).

2. IX: line 10: *Pelo por pelo* looks simple, but appears to be rare. Apparently it means "pelo a pelo" = sin adehala o añadidura en los trueques o cambios de una cosa por otra. I am tempted to translate it *tit for tat* since such means 1) equal exchange, this for that, plus 2) implies a blow, and since there are number of *golpes* in this poem, *tit for tat* seems appropriate. The only problem is that *pelo* may have a literal meaning, since *belfos* (thick lips) probably refers to vagina, and thus the *pelos* are pubic hairs. Thus: *hair by hair* might be more appropriate.

2. IX: *pelo por pelo.* Efectivamente, el poema entero tiene significado sexual. Lo más normal en el contexto y al lado de *belfos* = labios, es entender "pelo por pelo" como los pelos del pubis. Estamos a la entrada de la vulva.

3. XXVIII: line 20. *El yantar.* Old-fashioned word for eating, I know, but the question is: is it in any sense in fashion now, in Perú, as slang for eating? Like, in English, *chowing down?* If it is archaic, and utterly out of usage, it could be translated as *viandry,* an old-fashioned word for food (the word comes up in LXX, and there I translate it as *purveyance,* the food and supplies provided kings as in medieval times they passed through villages of their empire). Have you any sense of how it might have sounded to a northern Peruvian in 1918?

3. XXVIII: *El yantar.* La comida con connotación arcaica, no argótica. Es probable que se dijera todavía en la época de Vallejo en su lugar natal, la sierra norte del Perú. Las montañas andinas conservan muchas antiguas palabras castellanas. Vale cualquier término inglés algo arcaico que signifique *comida o comer.*

4. XXXVIII: line 13—*si él no dase por ninguno de sus costados*. I have translated it as: "if it doesn't surrender any of its sides" (= if it does not yield through any of its sides). I also think it could possibly be rendered as: "if it does not show any of its sides," but that seems too simple.

4. XXXVIII: *no dase por ninguno de sus costados*. Pienso que hay que entenderlo en relación con el verso 14: *espera ser sorbido de golpe:* ninguno de sus costados se entrega aisladamente: hay que sorberlo todo de un solo golpe: *surrender* es por consiguiente, me parece, la traducción más exacta.

5. LXIV: line 15, *de mucho en mucho*. Idiomatic in any sense, or utterly invented by Vallejo? I render it literally at this point as "from much in much."

5. LXIV: *de mucho en mucho*. Probablemente calco sintáctico interno de *de tiempo en tiempo* (idea de tiempo) o *de trecho en trecho* (idea de espacio) = con intervalos de mucho tiempo o de mucho espacio: pienso que su traducción: "from much in much" da una equivalencia suficientemente general y por consiguiente adecuada.

6. LXXI: last two lines. My understanding is that in Perú a *pulpería* is a kind of general store, which, unlike North American stores, sells alcohol. So someone could go to a *pulpería* for a drink, as well as to buy foodstuffs. The *copa de agua* in the line above, suggests that instead of a glass of wine or brandy that in this *pulpería* the speaker is having only water, but that he is drinking water in a place where others would drink alcohol. I have rendered these lines as:
   Rejoice, orphan: down your shot of water
   from the general store on any corner.
(to *down a shot* is generally to drink whiskey quickly—here this keys in that alcohol is part of the image if not part of the drink. If I write "drink your glass of water" in "a general store" the American reader would not know that alcohol could have been the beverage).

6. LXXI: Tu interpretación es exacta. En las pulperías se vendían comestibles y bebidas, y los clientes podían tomar un trago de pisco en el mostrador o barra, como en un *bar:* como en el *almacén* de los argentinos. A ninguno de los borrachines que frecuentaban las pulperías se le hubiera ocurrido ir a beber ahí una *copa de agua* (además en el Perú la *copa* se entiende solamenta para tomar vino y licores, nunca agua). Tu traducción "down your shot of water" funde perfectamente la idea de *bar* con la *copa de agua*.

7. LXXII: line 14, *de para nunca*. I take it that the *de* is a carryover from the line before (*de violentarte*), and does not need to be translated. I

also understand *nunca* as the opposite of *siempre*, and have rendered the phrase as *fornever* (in contrast to *forever*).

7. LXXII: De acuerdo. No es necesario traducir *de* en *de para nunca;* la creación *fornever* traduce bien la intención de la expresión creada por Vallejo *para siempre—para nunca.*

8. LXXIV: line 7. *La sien.* I am unsure what *la* refers to. The temple of the speaker? Temples in general (one's temple, say, referring to the temples of the kids involved in the mischief) or even *its temple,* the temple of the mischief.

8. LXXIV: *la sien.* En su edición de *Trilce,* ed. Cátedra, pp. 343–345, Ortega cita las interpretaciones de diversos comentadores. El comentario de Escobar se refiere específicamente a "se rompe la sien" y "rota la sien": es probable en efecto que aquí *sien* implique cavilación fuerte e intensa y dolor de cabeza; muchas veces el dolor de cabeza se siente particularmente en la sien o en las sienes (cf. me duelo tanto la cabeza que parece como si me fueran a *estallar las sienes*). Cf. también el *columnario dolor de cabeza* de T. XLVII. Se refiere por consiguiente a las personas, probablemente los niños o yo mismo, el hablante poética, o quizá incluso las severas madres: en todo caso pienso que "one's temple" traduce en su generalidad y en su ambigüedad el *se rompe* del poema.

In each case, Ferrari's response led me directly or indirectly to a final decision about the word or phrase. In a few cases, he was the only person I communicated with who actually researched the word and discovered its meaning, thus enabling me to translate it rather than guess at it and treat it as an obscure neologism.

One would wish to think that more poet-translators would seek out scholars like Américo Ferrari to help them out rather than just guessing and inevitably coming up with something more obscure in the second language than the word in the first. But the fact is: the Ferraris in the world are rare. More often than not—and all of us have a tendency to indulge in this—informants give an opinion based on memory or sheer guesswork instead of reliable information.

Translating *Trilce* was the mountain I had to climb as a poet-translator, and all in all I am proud of the work that I ended up doing. In helping me out as he did, Ferrari not only came through for Vallejo in English, but verified for me that when I called out for help, there was someone out there who was willing to respond in such a way that our mutual devotion to the poetry of César Vallejo was affirmed and renewed.

REFERENCES

Arona, Juan de (1938): *Diccionario de germanismos* [1870], vol. 10, Paris, Desclée de Brouwer.
Eshleman, Clayton (1992): *César Vallejo. Trilce*, Spanish text established by Julio Ortega, introduction by Américo Ferrari, New York, Marsilio Publishers.
Ferrari, Américo (1988): *César Vallejo. Trilce.*
Ferrari, Américo (1988): "Glosario [Trilce. La poesía de Paris]," *César Vallejo. Obra poética*, Madrid, Colección Archivos, 665–669.
Larrea, Juan (1978): "Vocabulario de las obras poéticas de Vallejo," *César Vallejo, Poesía completa*, commentaries by Juan Larrea, Barcelona, Barral Editores, 781–911.
Ortega, Julio (1991): *César Vallejo. Trilce*, Madrid, Cátedra.
Vallejo, César (1988): *César Vallejo. Obra Poética*, commented edition, Américo Ferrari (coord.), Buenos Aires/Bogotá/Madrid/México, Colección Archivos.
Zilio, Meo (1967): *Neologismos en la poesía de César Vallejo*, Università degli Studi di Firenze, Casa Editrice d'Anna, 5–98.

A Translational Understanding of Trilce #1

Over the years, I have come to believe that while it is possible to do a fine translation of a single poem, or a group of poems, translation that establishes an accurate and compelling image of a foreign poet can only occur through the translator taking on a complete collection, and doing all of it, including the secondary poems that would probably not be included in an anthology. The translator is also responsible for scholarly research, so as to bring to bear upon the translation as much background information as possible. Especially in the case of poems with a deep structure but an opaque surface, such as one finds in César Vallejo's *Trilce*, this research may make the difference between a coherent and an arbitrary translation.

When I began to translate *Trilce* in 1989, I collected all of the previous English and French versions, and typed them up, with all the same lines together. While I was working on *Trilce*, two more translations were published. Here I offer six versions of the opening couplet of #1 in chronological order:

Who's making all that noise, and
disinherits the islands that stay behind
—David Smith, 1973

Who is so shrill and keeps
the remaining islands from their last will.
—Edward Dorn/Gordon Brotherson,
1976

Who is so noisy that he keeps
The islands that remain from testifying
—Reginald Gibbons, 1976

This piece was published in the September 1993 issue of AWP Chronicle.

Qui fait tout ce vacarme, et ne laisse même pas
testamenter les îles demeurantes.
—Gérard de Cortanze, 1983

Who makes so much noise, and doesn't let
the islands that go on lingering make a will.
—prospero saíz, 1990

Who makes so much noise, and disinherits
the islands he keeps leaving behind.
—Rebecca Sieferle, 1992

Also, while studying these other translations, it appeared that none of them had taken into consideration two important information sources: Juan Espejo Asturrizaga's *César Vallejo, Itinerario del Hombre* (1965), and Giovanni Meo Zilio's *Neologismos en las Poesía de César Vallejo* (1967). Espejo Asturrizaga's book, still the only memoir we have of Vallejo's years in Peru (1892–1923), offers some commentary on the relationship between events and poems. Meo Zilio's work (which has been critiqued and extended by André Coyné, Juan Larrea, and Américo Ferrari) analyzes the neologisms in Vallejo's poetry, many of which are so subtle that without Meo Zilio's perceptions they go unnoticed. In discussing my translation of *Trilce* #I, I'd like to stress that without consulting these scholars' work, it is next to impossible for a translator to contextualize the poem and, armed with a viewpoint, do coherent translating.

Espejo Asturrizaga comments that #I is one of eight poems that Vallejo wrote while incarcerated in the Central Trujillo Jail from November 1920 to February 1921 (112 days). He tells us that the inmates were taken outside to use the latrines four times a day, and that instead of allowing the men to take their time, the guards shouted at them, mocking and reviling them, and demanding that they hurry up.

The first two stanzas of a later poem in *Trilce*, #L, indicate that this is not gratuitous but quite pertinent information:

Cerberus four times
a day wields his padlock, opening
closing our breastbones, with winks
we understand perfectly.

With his sad, baggy-assed pants,
boyish in transcendental scruffiness,

standing up, the poor old man is adorable.
He jokes with the prisoners, their fists
jammed into their groins. And even jolly
he gnaws some crust for them: but always
doing his duty.

Cerberus, the three-headed dog that guards the entrance to the
Greek underworld, is here the jail warden. The four times a day that he
"wields his padlock" must refer to the four times a day Espejo claims
the men were taken out to the latrines. The second stanza is probably a
commentary on the activities of the standing warden and the squatting
men. While Cerberus is "baggy-assed" (sloppy but at least dressed), the
men are squatting and straining, their forearms pressed down upon
their thighs, hands doubled up into fists jutting down between their
thighs.[1]

If we now look at the opening couplet from #I, several things immediately become pretty clear that without Espejo and the backup information from #L would be utterly puzzling:

> Quién hace tánta bulla, y ni deja
> testar las islas que van quedando.

> Who's making all that racket, and not even leaving
> testation to the islands beginning to appear.

It seems that the racket-makers are the warden and guards, and that
the "islands" are the inmates' turds. If the latter is so, it determines how
"islas que van quedando" should be rendered in English—not as "islands that remain" but as "islands beginning to appear." The islands are
in the process of being created by the inmates and because of that they
do not refer to geographical formations, which would of course have
been there before the racket occurred.

"Testar" means "to testate," or "to make a last will." By turning it
into a noun I am able to keep it in place, flush left, thus maintaining the
tension and development of the couplet.

It is also important to keep "deja" (leaving) and "quedanda" (appearing) in place, as they interlock dialectically and make a point in doing
so: leavings are beginning to appear. A poet-creator is beginning to assemble his book, or the unique world of *Trilce*, out of his own body in a
way that may remind us of the Rig Veda where a primeval being creates
gods out of his mouth, demons out of his abdomen, the atmosphere out
of his navel, etc. On one hand, the scene is primordial (it also makes me

think of the painting "The Third Day of Creation" on the closed wings of Bosch's *The Garden of Earthly Delights*). On the other, an attempt to address, and transform, the absurdity of jail humiliation. Not only will the guards not let the men testify, they won't even let what they produce testify! In a rather childlike way, Vallejo makes the reader a gift of his basic, and base, situation.

The second stanza slants the couplet's action off in a particular direction and complexes it:

> Un poco más de consideración
> en cuanto será tarde, temprano,
> y se aquilatará mejor
> el guano, la simple calabrina tesórea
> que brinda sin querer,
> en el insular corazón,
> salobre alcatraz, a cada hialóidea
> grupada.

> A little more consideration
> as it will be late, early,
> and easier to assay
> the guano, the simple fecapital ponk
> a brackish gannet
> toasts unintentionally,
> in the insular heart, to each hyaloid
> squall.

Guano, the dried excrement of seabirds, found mixed with bones and feathers on certain Peruvian coastal islands, was a widely used fertilizer (of considerable value to the country). Espejo tells us that guano workers visited the mainland ports and cities on their days off, and that Vallejo would have been able to observe them not merely in Trujillo itself, but in the vicinity of the jail.

My encyclopedia informs me that "a Pacific gannet is one of the chief producers of guano of the off-shore islands of Peru." Thus "alcatraz" should not be confused with "albatros" (albatross). Blue-footed booby is another possibility, but given the inappropriate denotions of "booby" it is not a good choice.[2]

While "alcatraz" follows the verb "brinda," it is undoubtedly the subject of the verb (and not the other way around). Since "brinda" is intransitive, it probably means "to toast," rather than to "offer."

In line 4, as an apposition to "guano," "calabrina" is archaic, and means an intolerable, intense stench. If translated simply as stench it reflects "hedor," not "calabrina," meaning that an archaic English word had to be found to match it (ponk). The demand here is to make the poem as difficult in English as it is in Spanish, to offer a *translation*, not an explanational gloss.

The word modifying "calabrina"—"tesórea"—is even more difficult to deal with. Meo Zilio tells us that it is a neologism based on "tesoro" (treasure). He argues that the coined suffix incorporates the latter part of "estercórea" (excrement), influenced by the guano references in the stanza and, we can add, by the activities alluded to in the opening couplet. But how render it in English? The simplest solution is to tack a bizarre suffix onto treasure, such as "treasurey" or "treasoria" or—a bit more interesting "treasurhea" (intending to evoke "diarrhea"). The problem with the latter is that it turns the adjective into a noun (though I suppose one could try to live with "treasurheal"). I don't see any obligation to be literal in such situations. As long as one respects the original, a construction based on another approach is justified. Thus, I compounded "capital" and "fecal" as "fecapital," which also fits nicely, soundwise, p-wise, between "simple" and "ponk."

I hope that the reader can see by this point that inch by inch sense is being made out of the poem as it is translationally worked through. Uncommon sense, to be sure, but not nonreferential "language poetry," as #1 is, given the adopted viewpoint, grounded in very specific and personal experience.

As stanza 2 opens, the speaker appears to be asking those mocking him for a little more consideration. Not only is time passing all too quickly (it must be late in the afternoon, according to stanza 3), but with a bit of understanding it might be possible to analyze what he is doing/producing—to "assay" it. This verb evokes the weighing/analyzing of gold, and this evocation will be reinforced by the play on "treasure" in the next line as well as by the last line of the poem. The coupling of a vile product with gold suggests an alchemical transformation, or a way of looking at the creative process at large. As he continues to meditate, the speaker's ambivalence toward his activity deepens. In spite of jail humiliation, Vallejo may be changing the course of Spanish-language poetry. Yet what he is doing, from the warden's viewpoint, is worth less than what gannets do on the offshore islands—their "product" is worth more, as valuable fertilizer, than his poems. Thus, the speaker is not only mocked by the guards but by the gannets! As they shit into the gusting wind, they toast the human condition. They don't

toast *on* "the insular heart"—they toast *in* it, meaning, I think, that from
the narrow-minded, illiberal viewpoint of the warden and guards, art
and culture are shit. If, as the fruit, or marriage, of the imagination and
the world, writing poetry is the highest human activity—according to
Wallace Stevens—at the wrong moment it can feel like the lowest. We
know that the sacred is often the accursed—a sense of anti–value spins
at the core of great value. Put in its most simple terms, the stanza
argues that under the present circumstances it is very difficult for a person to weigh what he means (thus perhaps more necessary than ever),
with the implications that one is always, to some extent, facing the ass
of nature.

The request that opens stanza two is repeated (as if unheard) in
stanza three:

> Un poco más de consideración,
> y el mantillo líquido, seis de la tarde
> DE LOS MAS SOBERBIOS BEMOLES.

> A little more consideration,
> and liquid muck, six in the evening
> OF THE MOST GRANDIOSE B–FLATS.

The absence of a verb between "and" and "liquid muck" makes the
latter phrase abrupt, even jarring. Even if there were to be a little more
consideration, the only outcome is liquid muck. One is left with one's
own pile of "islands" as the evening comes on, a miserable squatting
creature against a backdrop "OF THE MOST GRANDIOSE
B–FLATS" ("B" must be added to "FLATS" so as not to evoke "apartments"). Well, I hear Beethoven in this line (and almost translated it as
"OF THE MOST BEETHOVEAN FLATS" to get rid of the
otherwise-to-be-added "B"). And I also hear the men farting in the latrines. Stanza 3 constricts and darkens the rich ambivalence of stanza 2,
as if adjusting it to the feelings that continued squatting in the darkening light brings about.

Then, sudden, it is as if the speaker stands up:

> Y la peninsula párase
> por la espalda, abozaleada, impertérrita
> en la línea mortal del equilibrio.

> And the peninsula raises up
> from behind, muzziled, unterrified
> on the fatal balance line.

In Latin America, the verb "parar" (to stop), in the reflexive, often means to raise up, or to stand. I prefer "raises up" here as I want to anthropomorphize the peninsula as little as possible—for, on another level, it is an augmentation of the islands in stanza one. I understand "por la espalda" (from behind) as in such idiomatic expressions as "hablar por las espaldas" (to talk behind someone's back). Since the entire poem has been ass-focused, the raising of the ass in the act of raising up suggests the extent of the speaker's continuing preoccupation with that part of his anatomy.

Meo Zilio suggests that in "abozaleada" (muzziled), Vallejo has substituted an -ear ending for a word with an -ar ending: "abozalada" (muzzled). My slight adjustment evokes "exiled" which, in context, seems not only acceptable but fortuitous.

In the last line, one can choose between "equilibrium" and "balance" for "equilibrio." I much prefer the latter, as it harks back to the act of assaying in the second stanza. Something called an "assay balance" is actually used in the assaying of gold and silver. "The balance line" then relates to the beam of a balance scale, which is a line from which the balance pans are suspended.

And we have been prepared for this last line, as the poem is occupied with the struggle to create an equilibrium against Vallejo's jail circumstances. What the artist leaves as testament is the world he has created, and such a world must go back to the child's first creative act, with excrement sensed as a thing of value: simple fecapital ponk. At the beginning of *Trilce*'s seventy-seven-poem peregrination, the end inherent, the mortality that contours all we do and are. *"You are dead"* Cid Corman writes at the beginning of *OF*—"speak now." If muzzled, be unterrified. As if all imagination expansion is posited on early physical constriction. As if my shit is in sync with my breath. Lips and sphincter, the body a winding cavern working a double peristalsis. All activity, no matter how grand, is underscored by physical leveling. We who even with bountiful consideration never go far beyond the liquid muck.

I find much integrity in such a view, integrity to the actual as opposed to idealized human condition. Some may find #I a very negative poem with which to open a book. From an alchemical viewpoint, there is no philosopher's stone, or gold, without an impure, vilified product at the start to transform. Artaud: "There where it smells of shit, it smells of being." Seventy-two poems later, Vallejo will write:

Absurdity, only you are pure.
Absurdity, only facing you does this excess sweat golden pleasure.

[1993]

NOTES

1. When translating "their fists / jammed into their groins," I had a *déjà vu* feeling, and went back to Rimbaud. In "Les Poètes de Sept Ans" I found the following
lines:

> Passing along the darkness of corridors with mildewed wallpaper
> he would stick out his tongue, his two fists
> in his groin; and he would see specks on his closed eyelids.
> (Tr. Oliver Bernard)

We know that Vallejo read French Symbolist poems in Spanish translation, but
I do not know if "Les Poëtes de Sept Ans" was one of them. Regardless, the way the
fists in the groin overlap is fascinating. Vallejo's phrase not only suggests repressed
fury but masturbation (which is more directly expressed in two other poems in
Trilce, #XIII and #XLI).

2. "Pelican" would also be an accurate translation of "alcatraz," though to my
ear it is less effective than "gannet," which carries the hard "a" sound in the first syllable of "brackish."

Introduction to Watchfiends & Rack Screams

Antonin Artaud is one of the greatest examples in art of imaginative retrieval of a life that was beyond repair. What he ultimately accomplished should bear a torch through the dark nights of all of our souls. Given the new perspectives on his writing and drawing that he created in what may now be considered his second major period—from his regeneration in the Rodez asylum in 1945 to his death outside of Paris in 1948—it seems especially pertinent to introduce a new translation of key works from this period with an essay that attempts to compactly yet fully detail the way his life and work intertwine and reverberate.

Antoine Marie Joseph Artaud, called Antonin (or "little Antoine," to distinguish him from his father), was born on September 4, 1896, in Marseilles, France. His father, a ship chandler, and mother, a Levantine Greek who married her cousin, had nine children, only three of whom survived. Such an excessive mortality rate may have been in part due to congenital problems, which also played a role in Artaud's successive illnesses.

At four years old, he suffered terrible head pains from the onset of meningitis, one side effect of which led him to see double. In desperation (there was then no cure for acute meningitis), his father found and used upon the child a machine that produced static electricity, transmitted by wires attached to the person's head (prefiguring the electroshock treatments Artaud would receive in the Rodez asylum many years later). Whatever the alleged home cure's worth, he recovered, although he remained nervous and irritable throughout his youth.

This introduction appeared in Antonin Artaud's *Watchfiends & Rack Screams: Works from the Final Period,* edited and translated by Clayton Eshleman, with Bernard Bador, Exact Change, Boston, 1995.

Between the ages of six and eight, he stuttered and experienced contractions of his facial nerves and tongue. "All this," he wrote in 1932, was "complicated by corresponding psychic troubles which did not appear *dramatically* until about the age of nineteen."[1]

Antonin was also deeply affected by the death of his seven-month-old sister, Germaine, when he was nine. Because the baby would not obey the commands of her nanny to stop crawling away from her, the nanny slammed Germaine down on her lap with such force that she perforated the baby's intestine, causing an internal hemorrhage from which she died the following day. Germaine haunted Artaud to the extent that much later he would induct her into his set of "daughters of the heart, to be born." Such "daughters," based on family members and friends, represented a repudiation of his own birth and a seeing of himself as the sole progenitor of a new family "tree."

In 1914, right before graduating from high school, Artaud had a nervous breakdown, destroyed his earlier poems, and gave away his library to friends. Extremely agitated, he prayed constantly and determined to become a priest (a religious crisis that would manifest itself again, with greater force, at Rodez). At this point, the family arranged various rest cures that, with the exception of a few breaks (one in which Artaud was briefly inducted into the army), continued for the next five years (again suggesting another early life/later life parallel: during the first World War, Artaud spent most of his time in clinics and thermal spas; for all of the second World War, he was incarcerated in five asylums).

In the year after his 1914 breakdown, Artaud later claimed he had been stabbed in the back by a pimp while walking down the street. The alleged assassin told him, he recounted, that it was not *he* who had perpetrated the attack; rather, at that moment, he had been possessed. In setting forth the first of some alleged half dozen attacks on his life, Artaud was beginning the elaboration of a systematic "attack syndrome," composed of fact and probably fiction, in which evil forces were to ceaselessly obstruct his attempts to fulfill his destiny.

During 1917, suffering acute head pains and stormy, incomprehensible moods, Artaud, reading Baudelaire, Rimbaud, and especially Poe, was moved from clinic to clinic, at considerable expense to the family. He ended up, at the end of 1917, in a Swiss clinic, near Neuchâtel, under the care of Dr. Dardel, who, besides encouraging him to draw and write, also prescribed opium, setting up his lifelong addiction to drugs (and again prefiguring a later parallel: his ambivalent relationship at Rodez with Dr. Ferdière, who also encouraged him to translate and draw, during which he subjected him to electroshock treatments).

After two years in the Swiss clinic, Dr. Dardel proposed that Artaud strike out on his own and go to Paris. It was arranged for him to move in with Dr. and Mme. Toulouse, while the former was coincidentally engaged in a study on artistic genius. While Artaud had yet to begin his career as an actor, his theatrical bent is implicit in a photo from 1920, taken shortly before his departure for Paris. One sees a thin, sharp-featured, flowing-haired young man in coat and tie, head thrown back, eyes closed, wrists crossed over his breast, his long-fingered large hands clenched into fists. The figure seems at once laid out vertically, dead or asleep, and twisted in a paroxysm of inner torment.

Artaud's first set of years in Paris (1920–1936) were the most frenetic of his life. In order to fulfill his desire to become a film actor, he began taking roles in stage theatre to obtain experience. While he achieved some memorable success as a film actor—notably as Marat in Abel Gance's "Napoleon" (1925) and as the monk Massieu in Carl Dreyer's "La passion de Jeanne d'Arc" (1927)—he discovered that he had no interest in commercial filmmaking. However, he continued to act in films up through 1935, out of financial need, ultimately appearing in twenty-two films. Artaud's father died in 1924 (which ended family monetary support) and his mother moved to Paris to be closer to her children. From the mid-1920s on, Artaud was chronically broke (though capable of maintaining what had become a laudanum addiction), and he often moved in with his mother when he could not pay his hotel bills. The combination of poverty and addiction relentlessly undermined his life and work during these years. His theatre projects necessitated funding in order to be realized, and addiction destroyed his relationship with the actress Génica Athanasiou, with whom he had his only sustained love affair. In 1933, attempting to confront his addiction, he wrote:

> If I stop taking drugs, that means death. I mean that only death can cure me of the infernal palliative of drugs, from which only a precisely calculated absence, not too long in duration, allows me to be what I am. . . . I can do nothing with opium, which is certainly the most abominable deception, the most fearsome invention of the void which has ever impregnated human sensibilities. But at any given moment, I can do nothing without this culture of the void inside me.[2]

This "culture of the void" became an increasingly integral part of Artaud's personality. Almost immediately after publication of his first book—*Celestial Backgammon* (1923), an unimpressive collection of stilted, quasi-surreal lyrics—he began to engage the editor of the prestigious literary magazine, *La Nouvelle Revue Français* (henceforth NRF), Jacques Rivière, in a correspondence that when published the following year would put him on the literary map. Rejecting the closed lyric in favor of the fragment, and agonizing over his inability to think (by which he meant: to realize his imaginative energy at large in writing), Artaud ascribed his scatteredness to "a collapse of the soul" that so undermined his physical sense of himself as to make him feel nonexistent. Artaud was saying, in effect, that he refused to settle in writing for anything less than expressing what he most truly felt was happening to him. He worried in his letters to Rivière that someone or something was deliberately invading his thought process and robbing him of what he was attempting to express. This "higher and evil will attacking the mass of feeling" is the progenitor of Artaud's later elaboration of fiends and doubles pillaging not only his thought but his bodily fluids.

Much of Artaud's Rivière correspondence would have fit right in with his second and third books, *The Umbilicus of Limbo* and *Nerve-Scales* (both 1925). Composed of fragments, a play, theatre manifestos, denouncements of literature ("All writing is pigshit"), reworked letters, and descriptions of paintings, these books are generally described as prose poems. While such a description is superficially acceptable, it fails to indicate the diversity of the literary genres involved, which would, in the 1940s, be braided into single pieces of writing: letters, for example, that at the same time were poems, chants, manifestos, and essays. In these books of 1925, Artaud relentlessly complains of feeling paralyzed, abyssal, absurd; he is without works, a language or a mind that he can respect. He seems to refuse to bypass or attempt to transcend this negativity because he feels that within its turbulence is a power that if transformed will put him at one with himself:

> . . . thinking means something more to me than not being completely dead. It means being in touch with oneself at every moment; it means not ceasing for a single moment to feel oneself in one's inmost being, in the unformulated mass of one's life, in the substance of one's reality; it means not feeling in oneself an enormous hole, a crucial absence; it means always feeling one's thought equal to one's thought, however inadequate the form one is able to give it.[3]

While Artaud's differences with official Surrealism are fundamental, his two-year (1924–1926) involvement with it is understandable. The Surrealist contempt for bourgeois values, and its fascination with ritual, the subconscious, dreams, and trances, excited the ambivalent poles in Artaud that despised society and affirmed the possibility of drawing upon what Gary Snyder has called "the Great Subculture," that rich vein of African, Eastern, and esoteric Western materials, some of which, via Surrealism, were making their way into the poetic consciousness of the 1920s.

Artaud briefly ran the Surrealist Research Center, which had previously been open for the public to come in and record their dreams (Artaud closed the center to the public and unsuccessfully tried to use it for disciplined Surrealist research). He also contributed to the first two issues of the official Surrealist magazine, *La Révolution surréaliste*, and edited and wrote most of the third issue. At the same time he continued to act in commercial films, and with the former (expelled) Surrealist poet Roger Vitrac and the writer Robert Aron attempted to launch the Alfred Jarry Theatre. Both of these activities brought him into conflict with the inflexible Surrealists, who despised commercial filmmaking and disputed Artaud's association with Vitrac. The Surrealists—chiefly André Breton—also suspected that all theatre was bourgeois and profit oriented, and were on the verge of an alignment with the French Communist Party, an alignment that Artaud, who maintained all revolution must be physical (as opposed to political), could not abide. At the end of 1926, Artaud and Phillipe Soupault—Breton's former coauthor of *The Magnetic Fields*—were officially expelled.

Susan Sontag articulates Artaud's temperamental differences with the Surrealists:

> The Surrealist, he thought, was someone who "despairs of attaining his own mind." He meant himself, of course. Despair is entirely absent from the mainstream of Surrealist attitudes. The Surrealists heralded the benefits that would accrue from unlocking the gates of reason, and ignored the abominations. Artaud, as extravagantly heavyhearted as the Surrealists were optimistic, could, at most, apprehensively concede legitimacy to the irrational. While the Surrealists proposed exquisite games with consciousness which no one could lose, Artaud was engaged in a mortal struggle to "restore" himself. Breton sanctioned the irrational as a useful route to a new mental continent. For Artaud, bereft of the hope that he was traveling anywhere, it was the terrain of his martyrdom.[4]

To this one must add that constitutionally Artaud was a combination of director and loner who could only briefly and provisionally work with a group. Much of his failure to make any kind of theatre he could respect work was determined by his isolation and poverty. Success demanded extensive collaboration and real funds. While the Alfred Jarry Theatre put on four productions between 1926 and 1929—Dadaesque skits and plays with no sets, stressing hallucinations and rude confrontations—they were interrupted and heckled by the Surrealists, reviews were mixed at best, and each production was a financial loss. While Artaud continued to act in films sheerly for money, he did not act on stage again until 1935, when his adaptation of *The Cenci* was performed, with disastrous results, seventeen times. All in all, he directed six plays and performed in twenty-two.

Artaud's most important work, as a Surrealist, is his film scenario, *The Seashell and the Clergyman*, filmed by Germaine Dulac in 1927, without Artaud's participation. As the first of the Surrealist films—followed by Buñuel's *The Andalusian Dog* and *The Age of Gold*—it centers on the metamorphic image of a seashell, exploring via abrupt cuts and juxtapositions the claustrophobic atmosphere of repressed sexual desire generated by a clergyman and an idealized woman. The anti-narrative structure is realistically dreamlike in its jolting, illogical sequences. Artaud actually wrote fifteen film scenarios,[5] of which, along with *The Seashell*, *The Butcher's Revolt* is the most extraordinary. In the latter work, bits of sound are percussively imposed out of sync with the visual action.

The failure of the Alfred Jarry Theatre to become an ongoing venture ended Artaud's first attempt to effect French theatre. However, his visit to the Balinese Dance Theatre in Paris (1931) revitalized and transformed his ideas about what a theatre might be. The Balinese emphasis on precise, subtle, and ritualistic gestures (creating the atmosphere, as he put it, "of an exorcism which made the audience's demons flow") was to affect Artaud for the rest of his life. It also began to fill in his void with rich fantasy material. As he put it in his essay, "On the Balinese Theatre":

> This perpetual play of mirrors which goes from a color to a gesture and from a cry to a movement, is constantly leading us over paths that are steep and difficult for the mind, and plunging us into that state of uncertainty and ineffable anguish which is the domain of poetry.
> From these strange gestures of hands that flutter like insects in a green evening, there emanates a kind of horrible obsession, a kind of in-

exhaustible mental ratiocination, like a mind desperately trying to find its way in the maze of its unconscious.

And it is much less matters of feeling than of intelligence that this theatre makes palpable for us and surrounds us with concrete signs.[6]

Drawing also upon Lucas van Leyden's painting "The Daughters of Lot" (calamity, incest, metaphysicality) and two Marx Brothers films (hilarity and anarchy), Artaud began to lay the groundwork for a theatre that would function as a total art form. Dialogue, psychology, all sense of entertainment (escape from life) were refused; even the playwright was jettisoned, with the director becoming the "unique Creator." The theatre was to be on the scale of, and up to, life itself—thus the title of Artaud's now famous and influential collection of essays and manifestos: *The Theatre and Its Double* (1938).

The concept of the "double" here is complex. It is not only life itself, but specifically the plague (to which Artaud compared his theatre-to-be, sensing in both forces creative upheaval and renewal). Effective acting also involves the double: the actor is to become "an eternal ghost radiating affective powers." The double redoubles, so to speak, throughout Artaud's life and work, and ultimately becomes a kind of surrogate for Artaud himself as "Artaud the Mômo," the carnally obsessed reviler homunculus who rises out of the ashes of electroshock at Rodez.

To the "double," as a crucial Artaud word, one must add "cruelty." Artaud's concept of a "theatre of cruelty" did not mean a physical assault on actors or audience, but rather the steely rigor and dramatic intensity with which a "spectacle" would be carried out. While no theatre of Cruelty performance, on a grand scale, ever occurred, by 1933 Artaud had conceived of a potential presentation: the Conquest of Mexico—a cataclysmic historical event crammed into a time and space frame that could rivet an audience with its annhilatory grandeur. Such could obviously not take place on the traditional stage. Stephen Barber details the kind of spectacle Artaud envisioned:

> Artaud's innovations were aimed at every aspect of the theatre space, the actor's work and the spectator. He wanted to create new musical instruments to reinforce the aural dimension of his spectacle. These instruments would produce strange vibrations and extremely loud noise. The lighting would be like "arrows of fire." The entire spatial volume of the performance would be explored; the barrier between the stage and the spectator would be obliterated, in order to facilitate a "direct communication" between the spectator and the spectacle. The spectator's viewing position would be reversed; the action would take place around the edges

of the building, and the spectators would be placed in the center, on re-volving chairs. A central space was to be reserved only for the most im-portant points of convergence in the spectacle's action. The building (rather than a theatre) in which the performance would take place would be bare, undecorated. The actors, in spectacularly exaggerated costumes, would have to carry all the spectator's attention. For Artaud, the actor would function as the skilled instrument of the director's intention, thus able to articulate intricate physical states. At the same time, Artaud was willing to allow the introduction of an unstable element of chance, whereby the actor's power of gestural metamorphosis could transform him back from an instrument to an individual. In all, Artaud's concepts amounted to an attack on the spectator as well as on the stability of the theatre as an institution. His audience was still an unknown quantity. The Theatre of Cruelty would necessarily generate its own audience: "First, the theatre must exist."[7]

Artaud's first manifesto for the Theatre of Cruelty appeared in the NRF in 1932 and was predictably met with hostility and noncompre-hension. Not only was Artaud attacking the traditional spectator and the stability of the theatre, he was also replacing language with gestures and cries, a thrust that struck at the heart of classical French theatre. Such implied that all social discourse was suspect as an authentic com-munication.

The following year, in April, Artaud delivered his essay/lecture, "The Theatre and the Plague," at the Sorbonne. By now the need to break down (or "liquefy") boundaries had begun to affect Artaud's pres-entation of himself. After beginning the lecture as planned, he aban-doned his text and began to act out the plague. Anaïs Nin, in the audi-ence, has described what happened:

Then, imperceptively almost, he let go of the thread we were following and began to act out dying by plague. No one quite knew when it began. . . . His face was contorted with anguish, one could see the perspiration dampening his hair. His eyes dilated, his muscles became cramped, his fingers struggled to retain their flexibility. He made one feel the parched and burning throat, the pains, the fever, the fire in the guts. He was in agony. He was screaming. He was delirious. He was enacting his own death, his own crucifixion. At first people gasped. And then they began to laugh. Everyone was laughing! They hissed. Then one by one, they began to leave. . . . Artaud went on, until the last gasp. And stayed on the floor. Then when the hall had emptied of all but his small group of friends, he walked straight up to me and kissed my hand. He asked me to go to a café with him. . . . . He spat out his anger. "They always want to hear *about*; they want to hear an objective conference on 'The Theatre and the Plague,' and I want to give them the experience itself, the plague itself, so they will be terrified, and awaken. I want to awaken them. They do not realize *they are dead.*"[8]

Besides acting to make money, Artaud occasionally took on writing projects that while not strictly commercial would probably not have engaged him had he not needed money. In 1933, he was commissioned by the publisher Denoël to write a biography of the third century adolescent Roman emperor Heliogabalus. The decadence, anarchy, and catastrophe that permeated the life and times of Heliogabalus played into Artaud's widening obsessions, stimulated by Hitler coming into power[9] and the threatening atmosphere. "Poetry is the grinding of a multiplicity which throws out flames," Artaud wrote in *Heliogabalus*, associating the emperor with poetry as well as with himself. One useful result of research on the book was the amount of material on the occult, mysticism, and primitive mythology that he dug up, some of which was fed into the evolving concept of the Theatre of Cruelty, and some of which not only stimulated Artaud's Mexican journey but surfaced in the mid-1940s as visions and practices he would attack. Artaud dictated the final version of *Heliogabalus*, initiating a procedure used in the completion of many of his key, late works. During this period, he lived in wretched poverty (unable to afford new clothes), with several failed attempts at drug detoxification. Psychologically, he wavered between deep depressions and exaltations over the spectacles he would direct.

Artaud's last attempt to launch his own theatre was his production of *The Cenci* in May 1935. He had adapted Shelley's five-act tragedy of 1819, and incorporated material from the 1837 Stendhal translation of extracts from the archives in the Cenci palace. An atheist and sodomist, Count Cenci raped his daughter, and was subsequently murdered, in real life, by the Castellan of Petrella, who in Shelley's tragedy became a pair of professional killers. Artaud, in turn, made them mutes, and in his adaptation, it is unclear who murders the Count. Artaud associated incest with cosmic cruelty, and he initially saw *The Cenci* as the first demonstration of the Theatre of Cruelty. He soon became aware that the adaptation was a fixed text and made use of the conventional theatrical mannerisms that it was the Theatre of Cruelty's job to demolish.

Like Heliogabalus, Count Cenci was a spectacular monster with whom one part of Artaud identified. And his insistence on playing the Count suggests that he was already predicting his own destruction. It also suggests that he believed that he would be destroyed as someone he was not, as if the real Artaud was still an indestructible unknown. Theatrically speaking, these double murders (murdered doubles)— Heliogabalus hacked apart by the guards in his palace latrines, Count Cenci murdered with nails driven into his throat and one eye—terminate Artaud's relationship to French society as actor, director, and playwright. While he will briefly return to Paris after eleven months in Mexico, his true, or transformed, return will not take place until 1946, when he will return with an internalized "one man band" show of the Theatre of Cruelty.

With the failure of *The Cenci*, due to insufficient funding and ticket sales, Artaud was finished as a person capable of raising money for avant-garde theatre. For many in his situation, the options would have been to make a conventional move or to self-destruct through increased drug intake and malnutrition. Instead, Artaud decided to leave France and explore Mexico, a decision based on his fantasy that in Mexico he would not only discover a still viable revolutionary situation (one that would welcome his ideas), but indigenous ritual that would enable him once and for all to penetrate the dead crust of European society and engage the origin of culture. No longer capable of tolerating collaborators, he was also playing with sloughing off his European skin— as tattered as it might be, it still proclaimed his identity—and seeking to merge with "the Red Earth," "the constant irrigation of the nervous system" that he believed "flowed beneath the Mexico of the Spanish Conquest, making the blood of the old Indian race boil."

Artaud spent the latter half of 1935 trying to raise money for his Mexican trip and writing lectures to give in Mexico City.[10] He also completed the material for *The Theatre and Its Double* (which would appear in 1938 when he was in the second of his five asylums). Before leaving Paris in January, 1936, he again attempted a detoxification, which he could not go through with.[11] He also became infatuated with a young Belgian, Cécile Schramme, to whom he would become engaged after his return from Mexico.

While passing through Havana on his way to Veracruz, Artaud attended a voodoo ceremony and was given a small sword embedded with fishhooks by a sorcerer. Once in Mexico City, he gave a series of well-received lectures condemning Marxism, proposing a revolution based on fire, magic, and anatomical transformation, as well as praising his own

attempts to "rediscover the secret life of theatre just as Rimbaud managed to discover the secret life of poetry." As usual, his enthusiasm
quickly became absolute: Mexico was *the* place in the world where dor-
mant forces could be aroused, one of the two "nodal points of world
culture" (Tibet being the second, but its culture, according to Artaud,
was for the dead). In the spring of 1936, he arranged for a journey to
visit an Indian community, choosing the Tarahumaras in central northern Mexico because he had heard that they were completely uncontam-
inated by colonial Spanish culture.

At the end of August, with a government grant, he made the 750-
mile train trip to Chihuahua, and then traveled on horseback for a week
across the Sierra Madre into Tarahumara country. Artaud's particular
attraction to the Tarahumaras involved their ritual use of peyote, which
he guessed might do more than merely decrease his pain (apparently
the main function of the opium and heroin addiction). He immediately
attributed superhuman powers to peyote, believing it to be at the core
of Tarahumara resistance to colonialism and the Indians' ability to survive for hundreds of years in a barren wilderness. He threw the last of
his heroin away upon entering the Sierra Madre, and for the next week
suffered from withdrawal and dysentery. He was blown away by the Tarahumara landscape, which appeared saturated with hybrid forms. In a
mountain, he saw "a naked man leaning out of a large window, his head
nothing but a huge hole in which the sun and moon appeared by turns."
In rocks: "an animal's head carrying in its jaws its effigy which it de-
voured." He came upon "drowned men, half eaten away by stone, and
on rocks, above them, other men who were struggling to keep them
down. Elsewhere, an enormous statue of Death held an infant in its
hand." Such visions, taking place in the "sobriety" of heroin withdrawal, appear to be the most specific sightings that Artaud took away
from Mexico.

At the Tarahumara village of Norogachic (six thousand meters above
sea level), he was housed with the local schoolteacher, who, also being
the region's government representative, was opposed to native ritual, including the use of peyote. Luckily for Artaud, a tribesman had recently
died, and in order to protect the dead man's double, the schoolteacher
consented to a peyote ceremony. Artaud had to wait twenty-eight days
for it, and according to his essay, "The Peyote Dance," by the time the
ceremony was performed, he was utterly exhausted, and feeling the old,
terrible emptiness he had complained about in Paris a decade earlier.

While he was moved by the all-night ceremony, he also felt that its essence was eluding him. The peyote itself mainly made him drowsy. He decided that the significance of the ritual was contained in the rasping sticks carried by certain sorcerers. "The Peyote Dance" ends with Artaud preparing himself for a crucifixion which he associated with a conflagration "that would soon be universal." Given the approaching European destruction, Artaud's prophecy seems prescient, yet we must keep in mind that he had written, as early as 1925, that: "There is something which is higher than all human activity . . . this crucifixion in which the soul destroys itself without end." To find himself being crucified at the end of a Tarahumara peyote ceremony indicates the extent to which Artaud was still registering his angst in Catholic terms. This semiconscious Catholic captivity continued to spread below his life, as it were, and suddenly poured up through him during an identity crisis in Rodez. In 1943, he would state not only that the Tarahumaras were really worshipping Jesus Christ, but that Christ had bestowed peyote upon the Tarahumaras.

Arriving back in France in November, Artaud reconnected with Cécile Schramme, and after a temporarily successful detoxification in April 1936 made the second of his three international trips of this period: to Brussels, with his fiancée, to meet her wealthy parents. While the relationship was doomed from the start (Cécile was also an addict, and her promiscuity infuriated the increasingly, vehemently antisexual Artaud), the Brussels trip was a typical disaster: at the Maison d'Art, Artaud departed from his prepared lecture, "performed," and after he had scandalized the audience (which included the Schramme family), the engagement was terminated.[12]

Back in Paris, Artaud continued to waver toward disintegration. He decided that his name had to disappear, and insisted that his account of his Tarahumara adventure be printed anonymously in the NRF. In another work of this period, *The New Revelations of Being*, he signed the work simply (or not so simply) as "The Revealed One." This move into prophetic anonymity also involved him in Tarot card interpretation, and the increasing detecting of magical signs and omens everywhere. At this time he was given a cane that was supposed to have belonged to St. Patrick. Artaud believed that the cane had "200 million fibers in it, and that it [was] encrusted with magic signs, representing moral forces." In Tarot symbolism, sticks represent fire. Artaud had a metal tip welded to the cane's end, so that it would emit sparks as it struck the sidewalk. While he was beginning to orchestrate apocalyptic destruction in his writing with sword and cane, in his daily life he provoked Anaïs Nin to jot down in her diary: "The Dome at nine in the morning. Antonin Artaud passes by. He is waving his magic Mexican cane and shouting."[13]

In *The New Revelations*, Artaud predicted the end of the world on November 7, 1937. Illogical as it may appear, he also decided that it was time to "wake the Irish up by making them recognize the Cane of St. Patrick." He arrived in Cobh on the 14th of August, crossed Ireland to Galway on the western coast, visited Inishmore (the largest of the Aran Islands), returned to Galway, and ended up in Dublin in early September. His activities in Ireland must be pieced together via the postcards and letters he sent to such friends as Breton and Jean Paulhan, the editor of the NRF. While still in France he had identified with Christ as a sorcerer-magician who fought desert demons with a cane; by the time he arrived in Dublin he had begun to speak with the voice of God. He informed Breton that the anti-Christ hung out at the Deux Magots café, and that Jacqueline, Breton's wife, would be the wife of his identity-to-be. He also predicted that England would sink into the sea, and began to cast spells on people he wanted to destroy. The spells were small pieces of paper, filled with curses and colored ink spots, then burned with a cigarette in order to wound the body of the recipient.

Down to pocket money almost from the time he reached Cobh, he managed to run out on hotel bills until, in the later part of September, he was put out on the street in Dublin, and instead of looking for a new hotel, sought refuge at the Jesuit College, which turned him down. A few days later, he was arrested for vagrancy and put in Mountjoy Prison for a week. When the French Ambassador's representative asked him his name, and place and date of birth, he declared that he was Antonéo Arlaud or Arlanopoulos, born in Smyrna in 1904. Deported to France as an "undesirable," he attacked ship workmen who came into his cabin (he apparently freaked out when he saw their monkeywrenches), and was put in a straitjacket. When the boat docked at Le Havre, he was taken to the General Hospital. It was September 30, five weeks before his prediction of the world's end. For all identifiable purposes, Antonin Artaud did not exist.

Artaud spent the next eight years and eight months in five insane asylums. One of his acquaintances, Jacques Prevert, said that what he went through was worse than internment in a concentration camp.

At Le Havre, he was held for seventeen days in a straitjacket, his feet strapped to the bed. Hallucinating cats and black men everywhere, he refused to eat or take medicine out of fear of being poisoned. He heard armies of his friends, led by Breton, try to set him free. He also heard an actress he knew being hacked to death in the next cell.

On October 16 he was transferred to Quatre–Mares, near Rouen. There he was officially institutionalized. He described himself as a Greek, and Christian Orthodox, who was being persecuted for religious beliefs. He gave his profession as a caricaturist. He appears to have written no letters while in Quatre–Mares, and since he had falsified his identity his mother did not locate him until the end of December. He did not recognize her. After five and a half months, she succeeded in having him transferred to Sainte-Anne, a hospital in Paris.

While in Sainte-Anne, he was determined to be chronically and incurably insane and held in solitary confinement. Jacques Lacan, then in charge of diagnosis at Sainte-Anne, told Roger Blin, the only friend to visit him there, that Artaud was "fixed," and although he would live to eighty he would never write another line (Artaud later referred to Lacan as a "filthy, vile bastard"). After eleven months, with still no precise diagnoses made, Artaud was moved to the much larger Ville-Evrard east of Paris.

At Ville-Evrard, where he was to remain four years, his hair was cropped and he was given an inmate uniform to wear. Because he was now diagnosed as exhibiting a syndrome of paranoid delirium and incurable, there was no attempt at any treatment. He was also said to be graphorrheic (subject to continual and incoherent writing). In a willynilly way, he was moved from ward to ward (maniacs' ward, epileptics' ward, cripples' ward, undesirables' ward) seventeen times. The onset of the war was accompanied by severe food shortages—cabbage soup being the primary "starvation ration."

Reluctantly at first, he began to see family and friends. Once back in contact with his mother, who was now nearly seventy, he wrote her long, pathetic letters begging for an amazing range of provisions. Euphrasie Artaud was initially only allowed to visit her son twice a week, but in order to bring him food on a regular basis, she obtained permission for a third weekly visit. She would often just stand and watch Artaud, shattered. She must have loved him deeply.

The young interns in charge of Artaud noted their amazement at the ferocious energy with which he would fight the demons that he claimed surrounded him day and night. They also noted that he was utterly harmless to other patients. One of these interns, Leon Fouks, fascinated by Artaud's recounted and mimed stories, asked him to write out a biography. Among its details are the following: he was still Antonéo Arlaud, now born of a Turkish mother. Before he was two, he had suffered meningitis. He was orphaned at seven. After his trip to Mexico, he had discovered that he was St. Patrick as well as God the Father, and he had gone to Ireland to find a cane with which to combat the "Initiates." The doctors at Ville-Evrard and his friends in Paris were all infested with Doubles who were Initiates. Because "they" participated in orgies and sexual spells against him, he was compelled to ceaselessly fight them. Antonéo Arlaud himself had been invaded by Doubles, among whom were Astral, Flat-nosed Pliers, Those Born of Sweat, and the Incarnation of Evil, Cigul. They often dictated letters in his hand, and continually spied on him, attempting to steal his thoughts before he could make them conscious.

The last complaint evokes the 1923 Rivière correspondence in which Artaud protested against someone or something invading his thought process and robbing him of what he was attempting to express. What had changed was that what had been in 1923 an abstraction (or void, as Artaud would have said) had become a drama, with plot and roles, a variation on the theatre of Cruelty, conceived and performed by and in the mind and body of Artaud/Arlaud. In retrospect, it would appear that the beginning of Artaud's regeneration took place in Ville-Evrard. Although his thought was still being robbed, he was beginning to identify the robbers as fantasy formations. In this sense, he was beginning to apprehend them, since he was filling in the void with their names and strategies.

While in Ville-Evrard, Artaud wrote letters, new spells, and the biographical sketch for Fouks. He does not appear to have initiated any creative writing projects. There were several more stages for him to pass through before his surge of creative activity at the beginning of 1945. One of these stages occurred in August 1939, when he dropped Arlaud and announced that he was Antonin Nalpas. Nalpas was his mother's maiden name.

Concerned that her son would not survive Ville-Evrard—he is described in 1942 as having become so emaciated that he looked like a walking skeleton—Euphrasie asked an old Surrealist friend, Robert Desnos, to find a way to have him moved to a more humane institution.

Desnos had a friend, a Dr. Gaston Ferdière, who was head psychiatrist at the asylum in Rodez in deep southwestern France, in a zone unoccupied by the Germans. Life was more stable there than in the Paris area. Ferdière, who had met Desnos through the Surrealist movement, thought of himself as a Surrealist poet with anarchic tendencies and he was proud of that. Critics had called his poetry "cretinous" and "the product of a moronic mind." He agreed to accept Artaud and after considerable red tape brought about the transfer on February 10, 1943. At this time, Artaud's total possessions consisted of:

1 passport
1 paper knife
1 file

Gaston Ferdière's initial response to Artaud, filled with mixed feelings, appeared in 1958, as part of his article "I Treated Antonin Artaud":

> On the very morning of his appearance at the hospital, after waiting for the arrival of the ambulance bringing him from the station, I held my arms open. He threw himself into them, making out that it was a reunion with the dearest of friends, that we had known each other for 15 or 20 years. He mentioned a dozen common friends whose names I did not know, reeling off a long string of specious memories which I was careful not to contradict. I told him immediately of my plan to give him his liberty, restore him to Parisian life, to the world of arts and letters, and I took him straight away to lunch at my home. My wife made an admirable effort, welcoming him with open arms, allowing herself to be kissed by this repulsive-looking creature. It is embarrassing for a housewife to have a guest who gulps noisily at his food, mashes it up on the tablecloth, belches regularly and, before the meal is over, kneels down to psalmodize. I was soon able to calm him down by giving him back a little inlaid sword which I had just found listed in his inventory. You can buy them at any of the markets in Toledo.[14]

During the initial months of his three-year-and-three-month confinement at Rodez, Antonin Nalpas also claimed to be Saint Hippolyte and a pure angel sent to replace the fallen angel, Antonin Artaud. Ferdière said that it was impossible to discuss any point with him and described his condition as "a poorly organized delirium." For his part, "Nalpas" claimed that he was attacked especially at night by demons whose goal was to steal his semen and excrement. According to Bettina L. Knapp:

He would begin telescoping his syllables, indulge in verbal gyrations, make strange noises, change his intonation and the vocal range of which he was a master; speak first in a sonorous, then monotonous, and finally in an insipid register; whereupon he would break out in mellow and full tones. . . . At other times, hours were spent in articulating words forcefully, injecting each syllable with a kind of metallic ringing sound; treating words as something concrete, actual beings possessing potential magic forces. For the non-initiated, or those unable to understand Artaud, these syllable-words seemed to blossom forth helter-skelter; for Artaud, however, they created a tapestry of verbal images and rhythms.[15]

Such information suggests that as early as 1943 Artaud had begun to experiment with the "syllable-words" that were to be set, in stanza-like sound blocks, into letters and poems, occasionally in 1943 and 1944, and then regularly from 1945 on. From the viewpoint of the late work, Artaud simply moved his workshop to Rodez in 1943. The crux, of course, is that the creative significance of such "syllable-words" is contingent upon the fact that Artaud had the truly extraordinary capacity to gradually organize and ultimately give form to the chaotic subconscious invasions through which the "clinically insane" are incapacitated.

By the spring of 1943, "Nalpas" had again become obsessed with God and was taking communion several times a week (at one point he is said to have swallowed 152 hosts). He would sometimes pray with, and at others insult, the asylum chaplain. His humming and gesturing increasingly vexed Ferdière. According to Stephen Barber: "[Ferdière's] position was that Artaud was 'violently anti-social, dangerous for public order and peoples' security.' He believed that Artaud could never be cured, but that he might be returned to a more creative and socially useful life. For all these reasons, Ferdière took the decision in June 1943 to give Artaud a series of electroshock treatments."[16]

Ferdière would later claim that it was because of such treatments that Artaud returned to his literary work and became capable of living in society again. Because such claims have been hotly contested by a number of people, it is useful to examine the relationship of Ferdière's attempts at getting Artaud involved in art therapy and the five series of electroshocks he prescribed.

After the first series (three shocks), Ferdière tried some translation therapy on Artaud, giving him the chapter from *Through the Looking Glass* in which Alice meets Humpty-Dumpty to work with. Artaud translated this (and later came to detest Lewis Carroll), along with poems by Poe, Southwell, and Keats.

In early October, Artaud, on his own, wrote a long poetic text, much of which was made up of the language he was inventing.

At the end of October, Ferdière prescribed a second series of twelve electroshocks.

After the second series, Artaud wrote a critical account of a story he had read, and worked out a new text on his Tarahumara adventure. All this writing, including the poem with invented language, was intercepted by Ferdière and his staff when Artaud tried to put it in the mail. Artaud appears not to have been told of this interception.

In the fall of 1943, Ferdière tried out some photography therapy, requesting photographs from Artaud with which to illustrate a nursery rhyme that Ferdière found interesting.

At the beginning of 1944, Ferdière provided Artaud with some charcoal sticks and crayons. Artaud made a few drawings (including one of his Havana dagger) that Ferdière did not care for, and the project ended.

In May 1944, a third series of twelve electroshocks was administered (by one of Ferdière's assistants, never by Ferdière himself).

In August, a fourth series of twelve shocks.

In December, a fifth series of twelve shocks. All in all, Artaud received fifty-one electroshocks during this eighteen-month period.

From the first series on, the treatment injured and terrified Artaud. In June 1943, his ninth dorsal vertebra was fractured, forcing him to remain in bed for two months, constantly dosed with pain killers. During a subsequent series, Artaud stated that he was in a coma for ninety minutes (three to four times longer than the typical coma following electroshock), and that before he came to, Ferdière had ordered that his body be dispatched to the mortuary. In 1944, Artaud suffered the first of a number of serious intestinal hemorrhages (Barber suggests that they may have been the result of Artaud's near-starvation in Ville-Evrard, and the first indications of his intestinal cancer, which went undiagnosed until the winter of 1948, when it was inoperable). Throughout 1944, Artaud wrote long letters to Ferdière and Dr. Latrémolière (who administered and kept a record of the treatments), beseeching them, on what seems to be a quite reasonable basis, to halt the treatment.[17] While Artaud's fantasy life ranged, almost at will, through all of his activities during this period, the facts are that his vertebra was fractured and that he was genuinely terrified of the treatment. Whether or not the hemorrhaging is related is unclear. Also, by the end of 1944, his remaining teeth had fallen out.

Responding to mounting attacks on him, at first by Artaud and then by Artaud's friends, Ferdière in 1958 gave his version of what had taken place in treating Artaud. In brief, he claimed that electroshock was utterly painless and that Artaud had only received between six and nine shocks (in contrast to the documented fifty-one). He also revised and oversimplified the relationship between shocks and art therapy, saying that Artaud had received a few shocks and then "asked to read again" (which according to Ferdière led directly to his translating and writing and return to Paris).[18] It also might be pointed out that considerable disingenuousness is involved in telling an inmate that you plan to give him his liberty while being under the impression that he is incurably insane and a menace to society.

While the electroshocks and art therapy were going on, Artaud continued to work on himself. Right before the second series of shocks, constantly praying and dressing as a marine officer in donated clothing, Antonin Nalpas—to some extent pressured by Ferdière—became Antonin Artaud again. Such a "return" did not release him from his religious fervor for another year and a half. Apparently to be Artaud again was not in itself sufficient to clear out the religiosity central to his upbringing. In the fall of 1945, Artaud decided that his rejection of Christianity had taken place on Passion Sunday of that year, and he wrote to Roger Blin: "I threw the communion, the eucharist, god and his christ out of the window. . . . I decided to be myself—that is to say quite simply Antonin Artaud, an irreligious unbeliever by nature and by soul, who has never hated anything more than God and his religions, whether they are based on Christ, Jehovah or Brahma, not forgetting the nature rituals of the lamas."[19]

On the basis of such an assertion, one might think for a moment that Artaud had become "normal." But in the same letter he also insists that his asylum release is being obstructed by the oceans of spells put on Paris, the earth, and Rodez itself, and that he continues to await two young women, his daughters Cécile Schramme and Catherine Chile. Artaud's behavior, in fact, continued to fluctuate wildly throughout his years in Rodez regardless of his relationship to his creativity at a given moment. As late as the spring of 1946, when he knew he was shortly to be released, he was still blowing his nose in newspapers, spitting everywhere, sneezing like an enraged cat, and growling and hissing through his meals.[20] What is crucial to note here is that as this bizarre behavior continued, increasing amounts of his fantasy energy were being articulated, especially in a number of letters to the Parisian publisher Henri Parisot in the fall of 1945.[21]

It is unclear why Ferdière did not resume Artaud's electroshocks in 1945. Artaud later claimed that he threatened to strangle Ferdière if the shocks continued, but there is no way to verify this, or, for that matter, if it did happen, whether it had any effect on Ferdière. Perhaps the closest thing we have to an answer is that at the beginning of 1945 Artaud began to draw on his own, and with such an all-absorbing intensity, that it may have appeared to Ferdière that there had been a crucial shift in Artaud's focus from unacceptable misbehavior to a concentration on a creative project. If such a conjecture makes sense, it would of course give Ferdière a self-congratulatory reason for ending his torture: here, from his possible viewpoint, was living proof that electroshock worked!

According to Barber, the seventeen-month period over which Artaud was expressing himself via drawing was the crucial bridge to the literary works of the final period. What Artaud confronted in working on large sheets of paper with pencils, crayons, and chalk was his own destruction. In flurries of dismemberment and reconstitution, images of splinters, cancers, torn bodies, penises, insects, spikes, and internal organs were projected and realigned. Significantly, at this time, Artaud was befriended by a new doctor, Jean Dequeker, who had just come to work at Rodez, who in contrast to the others supported Artaud's routines of sounds and gestures. Dequeker later set down the following record of watching Artaud work on a self-portrait at this time:

> I was present for several days at the drilling of such an image, at the savage hammering of a form which was not his own. On a large sheet of white paper, he had drawn the abstract contours of a face, and within this barely sketched material—where he had planted black marks of future apparitions—and without a reflecting mirror, I saw him create his double, as though in a crucible, at the cost of unspeakable torture and cruelty. He worked with rage, shattering pencil after pencil, suffering the internal throes of his own exorcism. At the heart of the most inflamed screams and poems which had ever emerged from his tortured spleen, he struck and cursed a nation of stubborn worms—then suddenly, he seized reality, and his face appeared. This was the terrible lucidity of the creation of Antonin Artaud by himself—the terrible mark of all the enslaved horizons—launched as an act of defiance against the poor means and the mediocre techniques of painters of reality. Through the creative rage with which he exploded bolts of reality and all the latches of the surreal, I saw him blindly dig out the eyes of his image.[22]

Artaud also began to write in notebooks, which he filled one after the other, and which over the next year and a half came to some two thousand pages. Drawing and writing began to overlap, with words and phrases spilling into and around visual images. At the same time, he began to transfer his humming and chanting into written sound blocks, which he inserted into letters and entries. One is tempted to say that in a period of roughly six months Artaud taught himself how to draw and write again. But to leave it that way would seem to me to undermine and reduce what was taking place. The Artaud manifested in the winter and spring of 1945 carried on its train, like a glacial movement, active detritus that had been accumulating not only for years but probably back into the memory wisps of childhood and infancy (the redo of his family genealogy overturns his natural birth). The achievement was less a relearning how to do than a breakthrough enabling a cratered psyche to rise into view, still smelling of its multiple deaths (indeed, with its multiple suicide deflections), and proud of its contours, affirmationally ghastly in its power to at once protect and organize its loathed and beloved cores. Central to this display was Artaud's creation of the "daughters of his heart, to be born." By reaccepting the paternal family name, he was not merely reaccepting his father, since Antoine had previously been at first dented (as Arlaud) and then rejected when Antonin adopted Nalpas as his family name. The rejection here of Nalpas too suggests that both mother and father had been internalized, or composted, as it were, to make way for Artaud's creation of himself as one capable of parthenogenesis. Iconically speaking, if Artaud had now achieved his own self-combustion, the daughters were his charred circumference.

By the fall of 1945, with the war over, Artaud began to be visited not only by old friends from Paris, such as Jean Dubuffet and his wife, but by new, young friends, writers and actors such as Arthur Adamov, Marthe Robert, Henri Thomas, and Colette Thomas, who had recently discovered his work. Such support was immensely invigorating to the reengaged Artaud. Ferdière was now willing to release him on two conditions: financial support had to be guaranteed, and a satisfactory nursing home had to be found. Adamov collected manuscripts and paintings for a benefit auction from such writers and artists as Char, Joyce, Stein, Césaire, Sartre, Bellmer, Chagall, Picasso, and Giacometti. He also arranged for Artaud to move into a clinic at Ivry-sur-Seine, twenty minutes southeast of Paris. While the actual benefit only took place after Artaud's release, Ferdière was reassured, and signed the papers.

A photo taken of Artaud on a bench in the asylum grounds sitting next to Ferdière right before his release shows him in much of his complexity at this time. At fifty, he looks nearly seventy; the area around his mouth is puckered from tooth loss; he is dressed in a thick, ill-fitting suit donated by French Mutual Aid. Yet he appears amazingly compact and focused, a little dandyish even, with a vivid and interiorized gleam in his eyes. Ferdière's final diagnosis: "Displays a chronic, very longstanding delirium; for several months, there has been the absence of violent reactions, his conduct is much more coherent, takes care of his appearance . . . it seems that an attempt at readaptation is now possible."

On the evening of May 25, 1946, Ferdière accompanied Artaud on the night train to Paris, where they were met by some of Artaud's young friends in the Gare d'Austerlitz at dawn.

On his arrival at the Ivry clinic, Dr. Delmas—who turned out to be genuinely friendly to Artaud—said to him: "Mr. Artaud, you are at home; here are your keys." Soon aware of Artaud's routines of sounds and gestures, Delmas installed a large block of wood in Artaud's room, which Artaud would pound with a poker (which he had twisted into the shape of a snake). Several months after his arrival, Artaud discovered a spacious, abandoned eighteenth-century hunting lodge deep in the clinic's wooded grounds. In spite of its having no running water, electricity, or central heating, he insisted on moving in, under the impression that Gérard de Nerval had once lived there. Delmas arranged for water and fire logs to be brought in daily. Artaud was delighted with the place. For the first time in his life he had an ideal—large and isolated—workshop.

After the ferocious discharge of energy in Rodez, and with no need to worry about support (the benefit auction was hugely successful), Artaud flowed creatively without letup for what would be the remaining twenty-two months of his life. He worked even more relentlessly than he had in the final year and a half at Rodez, scribbling and drawing wherever he found himself, in the metro, in cafés, in bed, while eating, etc. He generally traveled into Paris during the day and maintained contact with his young friends, who found him awesome, bizarre, charming, funny, and avuncular. New editions of his books had appeared in

1944 and 1945; his writing was suddenly, as never before, in demand and much discussed. He was also back on laudanum, and when that became almost impossible to obtain he shifted to chloral hydrate, one side effect of which was to plunge the patient into sleep, to the extent that Artaud would sometimes collapse in the street. There is a photo from this period showing him sitting on a bus bench, holding a pencil up vertically against his back, like an apotropaic Gorgon eye. At times, walking down the street, he would thrust a knife violently into tree trunks.

One of the young friends that Artaud prevailed upon to procure laudanum was the poet Jacques Prevel, who was wretchedly poor and tubercular. Prevel kept a journal of his meetings with Artaud. One day when they were together in Artaud's new quarters in the Ivry woods, Artaud insisted that Prevel join him in screaming. Prevel apparently froze. According to Prevel's journal entry, Artaud then said:

> "You will not leave this room alive if you do not answer me."
> And he stuck his knife straight into the table. So I started to shout with him. It relieved me, since I had been hearing him doing it for two hours and I felt the need to do it myself.
> "You have done something very remarkable," he told me immediately afterwards. "If we had been on stage, we would have been a great success."[23]

Artaud's final performances were either solo events or small-group recitals with young artists he was close to and had coached for the occasion. At the end of 1946, his friends encouraged him to present himself publicly, as if to fully register his return. Artaud was offered the Théâtre du Vieux-Colombier for the evening of January 13, 1947; he proposed a program entitled "The Story Lived by Artaud-Mômo," and prepared to read from the five-section poem "Artaud the Mômo," as well as some additional prose concerning the imposition of death by society on the human body. By now Artaud had conceived a fantasy of what had happened to him during electroshock: borrowing the concept of Bardo from the Tibetan Book of the Dead—the forty-day period between death and either rebirth or Nirvana—he determined that electroshock created a kind of Bardo state in which parasitic beings, mysteriously associated with human organs, had unrestricted access to the one in electroshock coma. Artaud stated that he had seen these beings when he was in his ninety-minute coma and thus, from his point of view, dead. Beyond his control, he had been forced back into life, as if into a rebirth, so that these fiends could live off him.

Nine hundred people crammed into the Vieux-Colombier for what turned out to be, depending on the viewpoint, a freak show or a hair-raisingly moving manifestation. Artaud stayed with his prepared text for the first hour, took a break (during which André Gide embraced him), and then returned to read his lecture on the imposition of death. He became flustered, dropped his papers, and winged it for the next two hours, sobbing and screaming between gashes of silence about the hell he had been through for the past decade.

In spite of serious disagreements, he had tried to keep in contact with Breton over the years. While the two men were the same age, Breton had a tendency to treat Artaud as a kind of black sheep younger brother. Breton now attacked Artaud for having made a fool of himself, and told him that he was still a theatrical performer. At the same time, he invited Artaud to participate in an International Exhibition of Surrealism. As if proof of his finally gained genuine independence, Artaud tore apart Breton's put-down, and, refusing to participate in the Exhibition, painfully and with certainty ended their relationship.[24]

At the end of the same month, there was a major exhibition of van Gogh paintings at the Orangerie. Probably in an attempt to incite an explosive response, Pierre Loeb—the art dealer who would give Artaud his own drawings show later the same year—showed him an article on van Gogh by a psychiatrist who spoke of the painter in terms similar to those used by Ferdière to explain Artaud. Artaud did respond, writing "Van Gogh / Suicided by Society," a forty-page poem-like essay, in several days. Filled with deft evocations of van Gogh paintings and grinding comparisons of the two artists' betrayals by psychiatry, the work argued for madness as an honorable choice in a society devoid of human honor. Artaud also made his clearest statement about the origin of art and what he valued in an artist:

> No one has ever written, painted, sculpted, modeled, built, or invented except literally to get out of hell.
> And I prefer, to get out of hell, the landscapes of this quiet convulsionary to the teeming compositions of Brueghel the Elder or Hieronymus Bosch, who are, in comparison with him, only artists, whereas van Gogh is only a poor dunce determined not to deceive himself.[25]

Artaud's own drawings had undergone modulations since leaving Rodez. While he still wrote and drew antiphonally in notebooks, his large drawings now mainly focused on the human face—self-portraits, and the faces of his friends. Many of these works evoke the "X-ray technique" associated with Australian aboriginal bark paintings, in which an interior life is imagined as part of a creature's surface. Magnetized to the human face, Artaud took his vision of the human body in his writing out into the unthinkable: a true body, one that had overcome "the glamour that organs cast on man to bind themselves more closely to him,"[26] would become organless, all bone and nerve, "A walking tree of will." By eliminating organs, Artaud also eliminated sexuality and, implicitly, the possibility of doubles, demons, and parasitic invasions. This transfigured body is oddly similar to N. O. Brown's "unrepressed man," free of guilt and anxiety, as well as "oral, anal, and genital fantasies of return to the maternal womb."[27] Both Artaud and Brown end up here in a Christian fantasy: a resurrected body, free of filth and death.

Underlying Artaud's rewriting/reconstructing of the body is a head-on collision between de Sade and Savonarola. On one hand, Artaud identified with Heliogabalus, Count Cenci, and Ambrosio (who rapes his sister and kills his mother in Artaud's adaptation of Lewis's *The Monk*). On the other hand, he insisted that all forms of sexuality should be abstained from (in a kind of "official Surrealist" way he would "expel" friends who had affairs or became pregnant) and absolutely believed that the practice of sex was vampiric and drained his body of the powers he needed to live. Freedom, if such a word is cogent at any point in Artaud's system, would thus be contingent upon total libertinism and total asceticism. Such a contradiction is somewhat understandable, in terms of Artaud alone, when we take into consideration the onslaught against his body and the fantasy structures he erected to be able to express his experience. It should also be borne in mind that Artaud's best friends were women as well as men—several of his women friends loved him dearly. Underlying his ambivalence toward the other is a similar ambivalence autoerotically speaking. While he vituperated against masturbation, the creation of the "Mômo" in the poem with that title is implicitly masturbational, as if the double were issuing from the speaker's own body. Such recalls the ancient Egyptian theology in which Atum says: "I copulated in my hand, I joined myself to my shadow and spurted out of my own mouth. I spewed forth as Shu and spat forth as Tefnut."[28]

In November 1947, Artaud received an invitation from Fernand Pouey, a director at Radiodiffusion Française, to prepare a program for a new series called *La voix des poètes*. He was to be allowed complete freedom in regard to his choice of texts, and he could choose the readers. He also had at his disposal a xylophone, drums, kettle drums, and gongs. He quickly assembled the radio poem *To have done with the judgment of god* (a title with massive vibration, coming as it did at the end of the Second World War), reworking material on the peyote ritual and writing several new sections preoccupied with the hopeless vulnerability of the given human body and the necessity to reconstruct it. With only one reading, and no rehearsals, the five-section text was recorded with three actors and Artaud himself (reading the first and final sections). On February 1, the day before the program was to be broadcast, Wladimir Porché, Pouey's boss, listened to it, found it obscene, and banned it. While Pouey assembled a jury of cultural figures who unanimously supported the broadcast, Porché refused to lift the interdiction. The taped part of the text, along with newspaper articles the controversy inspired, was published in April 1948, shortly after Artaud's death.

Artaud regarded *To have done* as "a grinding-over of the Theatre of Cruelty," and its rejection hurt him deeply. He believed that what the poem addressed was universal, and he wanted working people to hear it, under the impression that the pain and oppression it engaged was theirs, and that they would understand it.

A few days later, a doctor who had examined Artaud informed a close friend that he had a long-standing and inoperable intestinal cancer. Although Artaud himself was not informed, he seemed to be aware of the situation. While he now declared that he had said everything that he had to say, he kept on writing until the last days of his life. His final fragment reads:

> And they have pushed me over
> into death,
> where I ceaselessly eat
> cock
> anus
> and caca
> at all my meals,
> all those of THE CROSS.[29]

Artaud's body was discovered by the Ivry gardener who brought him his breakfast on the morning of March 4. Artaud was seated at the foot of the bed, holding his shoe. Because he had been taking unregulated amounts of chloral hydrate, there was the possibility of suicide. This eliminated a Catholic burial service. Artaud's remains today are at the Saint Pierre cemetery in Marseilles, not far from where he was born, under a large stone cross. The sole inscription reads: "Family of Antonin Artaud."

While Artaud cannot be called a shaman, there is a shamanic resemblance binding his life and work. This presence contributes significantly to the way his image strikes us. While there is nothing in Artaud's materials, to my knowledge, that would indicate that he consciously made use of shamanic lore or stance, this lack makes the resemblance more pertinent. "Resemblance" is too vague: yet vagueness is of the essence here. When I hold up Artaud's image, I see shamanic elements in it, like a black rootwork suspended, coagulated yet unstable, in liquid.

Shamanic quest, initiation, and practice often involve the following[30]: a spiritual crisis as a youth during which the novice appears crazed or dead. Such a crisis can lead to a vision quest, which can be prolonged and excruciating. To gain access to invisible powers, the novice must undergo a transformation involving suffering, symbolic death, and resurrection. Sometimes both crisis and transformation are initiated by forces over which the novice has no control: lightning or epileptic seizure. In other cases, psychotomimetic plants are ingested as "bridges" to the supernatural world. In the trance state of initiational torture the novice's body is "dismembered," sometimes "cooked," and replaced by a "new body," with quartz crystals instead of intestines. Such crystals are associated with lightning. One definition of a shaman is that he is one whose body is "stuffed with solidified light." The novice also learns a new language, which he will intone to invoke spirit allies (or dispel spirit enemies), and he often takes on a new name.

Once a shaman, his (or her) work is to maintain the spiritual equilibrium of his community, keeping open communication between the three cosmic zones: earth, sky, and underworld. He facilitates this via the *axis mundi*, or World Tree, located at the center.[31] The World Tree appears in many guises: ladder, bridge, vine, stairs, etc. The long and dangerous excursions to sky or underworld—to retrieve lost souls or to accompany the recently dead—involve rhythmic chanting and drumming. The shaman's drum, thought of as his horse, carries him to the center and also helps him drive away demons. Besides his drum, his paraphernalia include a staff marked with ancestral figures. During trance, he may speak in tongues, babble, or prophesy in a falsetto

voice. He is sometimes androgynous and often prey to paranoid erot-
omania. He spits and gestures to discharge illnesses and spells attacking his body.

I have already pointed to the parallels between shamanism and the
life and work of Artaud. The pattern, in a somewhat crazy-quilt way, is
there, from teenage crisis, complaints throughout the 1920s of being
nonexistent, a vision quest to the Tarahumaras (several decades before
Carlos Castaneda popularized such journeys), use of a magic dagger
and cane, the loss of self-identity, and the possession by doubles and demons. To all of this we must add Artaud's subjection to a particularly
pernicious kind of twentieth-century lightning, electroshock, during
one seizure of which he was thought to have died. "Dismembered" in
Bardo comas by battalions of hungry ghosts, he returned,
semi–invented, with a new language composed of incantation and brilliant, if paranoid, argument, suggesting a lower and a higher register or
a kind of vertical, vocal writing. He bore, out of his heart, a new prog-
eny of warrior-daughters who became his assaulted messengers and
saviors. He used the block of wood that Dr. Delmas placed in his room
like a drum. He also had a "bridge," which he wrote was located
between his anus and his sex, and it was upon that bridge that he was
murdered by God, who pounced on him in order to sack his poetry.
Spitting, a falsetto voice (in his part of the recording of *To have done with
the judgment of god*), and sexual consternation were also present. His envisioned organless body was an unsolvable problem because the lightning that destroyed "the old Artaud" (burying him in his own toothless
gum) did not provide new quartz organs, or chunks of solidified light.

What is devastatingly missing in this shaman scenario is a community. On this level, Artaud is a Kafka man, put through a profound and
transfiguring ritual while finding out, stage by stage, that it no longer
counts. The Theatre of Cruelty he pours himself into is ultimately
truly cruel because the ceremony itself—what I would call the imaginative design of Artaud's madness—means nothing to anyone but Artaud.
Artaud is a shaman in a nightmare in which all the supporting input
from a community that appreciates the shaman's death and transformation as an aspect of its own wholeness is, instead, handed over to mock-
ers who revile the novice at each stage of his initiation. One might object here that Artaud was closely attended by a small but cultic group of
friends in his last years, and that since his death his aura has continued
to spread. Japanese Butoh looks like something he planned.

Such, however, is peanuts relative to the price of the loss of a func-
tional community. Artaud ends up as an adored pariah, having literally
failed in all his projects and performances. Robert Duncan wrote perceptively in the late 1950s that "we can entertain what [Artaud] suffered."[32] At first, I heard "we can be entertained by what Artaud suffered," which may strike a deeper and more unnerving chord than
Duncan's actual words. Certainly, Artaud enables us to entertain—reflect on—a level of suffering and fantasy response to that suffering that
has been traditionally repressed in the art of poetry. That in itself is a
unique achievement, as unique as van Gogh's writhing olive trees. But
one fears that relative to the infernal combustion of the work, the
reader today is at such a remove as to put Artaud at the center of the
bullring and himself in the bleachers. The burden of this introduction
is to illustrate the terrible congruity of Artaud's life and work in such a
way that any entertainment point of view is undermined. And to also
argue that at moments the fumes emanating from Artaud's pit separate
to reveal, in the depths, those regal and leprous lineaments of shamanic
transformation that are the heart of poetry.

Dead now for nearly fifty years, Artaud's power to fascinate, even mes-
merize, has not abated. His position in international modernism is
fixed, and while some casual readers still dismiss him as a psychotic
masquerading as a visionary, my feelings are that within the next
decade, as the full range of his writings and drawings becomes available,
such dismissals will taper off. Here we should keep in mind that Americans know virtually nothing about the drawings (a major portion of
which will be shown at MOMA [the Museum of Modern Art] in New
York City in 1996), and that our knowledge of his writing, at least in
translation, at this point is still confined to less than half of his published work.

Americans know Artaud for the most part through two anthologies.
Jack Hirschman's *Artaud Anthology* (1965) was translated mainly from
magazines and limited editions at a time in which only the first two
Gallimard volumes of the *Complete Works* were available. Helen
Weaver's *Antonin Artaud / Selected Writings* (1976), in many ways an advance over the earlier anthology, drew on volumes I–XIII of the *Complete Works*, and while it contains some of the key post-Rodez poems, it
is weighted in such a way that Artaud's significance is posited as a writer

of prose poems, theatre essays and manifestos, and letters. In effect, the Weaver anthology proposes that Artaud's importance lies in pre-Rodez work.

With Stephen Barber's critical biography *Blows and Bombs* (1993), and the continuing publication by Gallimard of volume after volume of Rodez and post-Rodez writing, the shape of Artaud's body of work has radically altered. As Barber writes:

> The last phase of Artaud's work, in particular, has suffered from a certain marginalization. It is the work of a man newly released from nine years in five successive asylums, and has sometimes been dismissed summarily. But this last phase is far from a psychosis-induced linguistic stalling. More than any other phase of Artaud's work, that from the period after his release from Rodez conveys a magnificent lucidity and lust for life. Utterly stubborn in its torrent of invective and denunciation, it is immensely versatile in terms of its imagery of the body, and in its linguistic experiments.

Barber has also written extensively on Artaud's drawings, and his *A New Anatomy: The Drawings of Antonin Artaud* will be published in 1996.

This is not to downplay the significance of such 1930s works as *The Theatre and Its Double;* rather, it is to propose that Artaud has two major periods, with the shorter second period (1945–1948) containing more material than the entire first period (1923–1938). In the fall of 1994, Gallimard brought out Volume XXVI, and there are still more to come. There are now two major projects facing future Artaud translators: the 300-page *Suppôts et suppliciations* (Volume XIV presented in two books), which Artaud considered to be his summational work—and the *Cahiers de Rodez* (Volumes XV–XXI), over 2000 pages, worked at daily throughout Artaud's recovery period in Rodez. There are also four volumes of notebook material from Artaud's last two years in Paris.

This present translation attempts to do several things: to present very carefully worked (over twenty years) versions of what at this point appear to be Artaud's major poems and to present some of these translations (for the first time) bilingually, enabling the reader with some French to do an "on-site" inspection of the work. By adding to these poems two seminal letters, a short essay on his drawings, and a prose poem and some dictations from *Suppôts et suppliciations*, we hope to be offering an accurate image of Artaud in his hybrid manifestations. As the one responsible for the final versions, my aim is to be absolutely accurate, on one hand, and, on the other, to attempt to match Artaud's challenging language performance whenever possible. Artaud is a translator's dream—and nightmare. One is always scrambling for new solutions that when found seem to add something unique to American English. Occasionally, the combination of puns and coined words are such that one ends up not simply throwing in the towel but eating it: something semitranslated in the text and then commented on in the Notes that follow.

In our exploded and massively wallpapered age, I have found that in Artaud the ancient, black springs of poetry are graspable, like a writhing piece of star gristle. Antonin Artaud is the stamina of poetry to enact in a machine-gunned hearth the ember of song.

NOTES

1. I am extremely indebted to Stephen Barber's *Blows and Bombs* (Faber and Faber, 1993), Thomas Maeder's *Antonin Artaud* (Plon, 1978), and Helen Weaver's *Antonin Artaud / Selected Writings*, with a fine introduction by Susan Sontag, and notes by Sontag and Don Eric Levine (Farrar, Straus, and Giroux, 1976) for much of the material in this Introduction. To varying degrees, I have also made use of Ronald Hayman's *Artaud and After* (Oxford, 1977), Bettina L. Knapp's *Antonin Artaud / Man of Vision* (Avon, 1971), Naomi Greene's *Antonin Artaud: Poet Without Words* (Simon & Schuster, 1970), Martin Esslin's *Antonin Artaud* (Calder, 1976), and Charles Marowitz's *Artaud at Rodez* (Boyars, 1977).

2. Barber, p. 64.
3. Weaver, p. 70,
4. Weaver, from the Sontag introduction, pp. xxvi–xxvii.
5. Several of these scenarios are translated in *Tulane Drama Review* #33 (fall 1966).
6. Weaver, p. 223.
7. Barber, pp. 54–55.
8. Hayman, pp. 89–90. Lest the reader get the impression that Nin's view of Artaud was shared by everyone at the time, here are Jean-Louis Barrault's impressions of Artaud in 1932:

He had an extraordinary forehead that he always thrust in front of him as if to light his path. From this magnificent brow sheaves of hair sprouted. His piercing blue eyes sank into their sockets as if in that way they could scrutinize further. The eyes of a rapacious bird—an eagle. His thin pinched nose quivered incessantly. His mouth, like the whole of Artaud, preyed upon itself. His spine was bent like a bow. His lean arms with their long hands, like two twisted forked trunks, seemed to be trying to plough up his belly. His voice, rising up from his innermost caverns, bounded toward his head with such rare force that it was dashed against the sounding board of his forehead. It was both sonorous and hollow, strong yet immediately muted. He was essentially an aristocrat. Artaud was a prince. (Hayman, pp. 81–82.

9. Artaud claims to have met Hitler in Berlin in 1932 (see Barber, pp. 50–51). In 1943, he dedicated a copy of *The New Revelations of Being* to Hitler (see *Artaud Anthology*, City Lights, 1965, p. 105). See also *Invisible City Magazine* #6, 1972, in which Hirschman offers additional material on this dedication. In 1946, in a piece called "The Theatre and Anatomy" (tr. by Hirschman in the issue of *Invisible City*), Artaud wrote:

> For since 1918 who—and this isn't for the theatre—has tossed you a depth-charge "in all the lower depths of accident and chance" if not Hitler, that impure Moldavian of the race of innate monkeys.
> Who appears in the scene with a belly full of red tomatoes, polished with dirt like a parsley [sic] of garlic, who with bites of rotating saws has drilled himself into the human anatomy because room was let to him in all the scenes of a theatre that was born dead.
> Who declared the theatre of cruelty utopian and went ahead sawing vertebrates into barbwired mise en scènes.

10. Artaud's Mexican lectures and writings are collected in *Messages révolutionnaires* (Gallimard, 1971). Weaver has translated some of this material in *The Peyote Dance* (Farrar, Straus, and Giroux, 1976) and *Selected Writings*.

11. Barber mentions that in 1935 Artaud was taking a dose of forty grames of opium once every sixty hours (generally absorbing it in the form of laudanum—a solution of opium in alcohol). From what I can tell, this is slightly less than DeQuincey's average dose. Molly Lefebure, in her *Samuel Taylor Coleridge: A Bondage of Opium* (Stein & Day, 1974), comments that both Coleridge and DeQuincey took what "would now be fatal doses of laudanum, because it contained so much less morphine then than now, when the quantity has become standardized." It is impossible to say, without more specific information, what the effect of laudanum (and heroin) had on Artaud's imagination. Like Coleridge and DeQuincey, he became addicted when he was young, and drugs were not used experimentally (contrary to the case of Michaux and mescaline). While Cocteau's commentary on opium addiction is of interest (*Opium*, Librarie Stock, 1930), it sheds less light on Artaud's life and work than does DeQuincey's (see J. M. Scott's *The White Poppy*, Funk & Wagnalls, 1969, pp. 53–56). For example: "I seemed every night to descend—not metaphorically but literally to descend—into chasms and sunless abysses, deaths below depths. . . . the state of gloom which attended these gorgeous spectacles cannot be approached by words. . . . In the early stages of the malady, the splendors of my dreams were indeed chiefly architectural; and I beheld such pomp of cities and palaces as never yet was beheld by the waking eye, unless in the clouds." For Artaud, might there have been visions of a theatrical abyss? Glimpses of his cosmically expanding Theatre of Cruelty?

12. "Artaud's lecture was to transform itself into another of the outrageous, invective events that stretch from his lecture on the plague at the Sorbonne in 1933 to his final performance at the Vieux-Colombier in 1947. Artaud immediately announced that he had abandoned his prepared text. He then spoke about his journey to Mexico, his voice and gestures becoming increasingly hostile and violent. He also dealt with the effects of masturbation on the behavior of Jesuit priests, thereby causing a large part of his scandalized audience to leave the hall. . . . At the close of the lecture, Artaud screamed and told the remnants of his audience: 'In revealing all of this to you, I have perhaps *killed* myself!'"

13. Esslin, p. 49. Nin understandably mistook the "Irish cane" for something Artaud had brought back from Mexico.

14. Hayman, p. 124. Marowitz also translates this passage, with slightly different emphases, p. 109.

15. Knapp, p. 180. Knapp is quoting from J. H. Armand-Laroche's *Artaud et son double*, Pierre Franlac, 1964, p. 58. I have not seen Armand-Laroche's book, but according to Barber, who has, Armand-Laroche had access to Artaud's clinical records at Rodez, and his use of them appears to be accurate.

16. Barber, p. 106.

17. Weaver translates three of these letters, pp. 423–432.

18. Marowitz, p. 73. Anyone interested in learning more about Ferdière's recollection of his relationship with Artaud in Rodez should look at both of the pieces in Marowitz, the second of which is semi-hysterical and extremely defensive. See also Barber's commentary, especially pp. 8–9.

19. Hayman, p. 129.

20. Maeder, p. 254. Artaud's behavior described here did not take place at Rodez, but at Espalion, a village 30 km from Rodez, where Ferdière installed Artaud in a hotel to see how he would do in a nonrestrictive environment. He spent a week there in the company of André de Richaud, an alcoholic writer who was also in Rodez. Artaud's behavior provoked the hotel proprietor to write to Ferdière demanding Artaud's removal.

21. Six of these extraordinary letters to Parisot are translated by Weaver, pp. 441–465.

22. Barber, pp. 114–115.

23. Barber, p. 128. Artaud was not without humor, and I have tried to bring out his playfulness, ringed with bile as it may be, in various passages in this translation (e.g., the passage beginning "And now / all of you, beings" in *Here Lies*). Speaking with Marowitz, Arthur Adamov commented:

> "In spite of all his illness, [Artaud] always had an extraordinary sense of humor; one of the people with whom you laughed most." He then tells a few anecdotes, of which this is one: "One day I remember, at the home of Marthe Robert who was a great friend, we were having a discussion and Artaud began to exasperate us by insisting that there were lamas in Tibet who were willing his death. I don't know why, but we were very irritable that evening. We couldn't really believe that he was mad and so we said, 'Listen, Artaud, there may well be people who want you dead, but don't tell us they're in Tibet! Don't go on any more about Tibet.' And then he was very angry and left in a huff. After he'd gone I said to Marthe Robert, 'We've really been stupid. We shouldn't have contradicted him like that. You see how angry we made him.' Two days later, on rue Jacob, I came across Artaud, who suddenly burst out laughing and said, 'You remember that other evening at Marthe Robert's house? There's never been such a good talk this side of a Dostoyevsky novel.' (Marowitz, p. 83)

24. Artaud's part of this exchange of letters was published in *L'Ephémère* #8, 1969, Paris.

25. Weaver, p. 497.

26. See David Maclagan's article, "A Language of Flesh and Blood," *Link Magazine*, spring 1969, p. 10.

27. N. O. Brown, *Life Against Death*, Vintage Books, 1959, pp. 291–292. See Naomi R. Goldenberg's commentary on this passage, in *Returning Words to Flesh*, Beacon, 1990, Ch. 2.

28. Erich Neumann, *The Origins and History of Consciousness*, Pantheon, 1964, p. 19.

29. Barber, pp. 161–162.

30. Material on shamanism here comes from Mircea Eliade's *Shamanism / Archaic Techniques of Ecstasy* (Princeton, 1974) and Weston LaBarre's *The Ghost Dance* (Delta, 1972). For additional material, see "Hallucinogens and the Shamanistic Origins of Religion" by LaBarre in *Flesh of the Gods*, ed. P. T. Furst (Allen and Unwin, 1972). Maclagan also brings up parallels between the career of a shaman and Artaud's own life in the Link article. In *Technicians of Ecstasy* (Bramble Books, 1993), Mark Levy dismisses such a connection.

31. For a gripping, visionary response to the destruction of the World Tree, see Charles Olson's "Hotel Steinplatz, Berlin, December 25 (1966)" in *The Maximus Poems* (University of California Press, 1983).

32. *Derivations*, Fulcrum Press, 1968, pp. 89–90. The entire passage reads:

A man's fortune starts when his fortune is told. To demand a new threshold of excitement and to work there: eventually to be unsatisfied, or shaken or destroyd in excitement? this is when no composition appears. Artaud is torn apart by actual excitations which are intolerable to his imagination and to his material. Neither his desire nor the object of his desire can endure his excitement. The writing he has left is evidence of the area of endurance. And Artaud's "charge" is higher, in an entirely other category, than the charge at which I work. Yet I am concernd. His art—in which we have intimations of what we call "insanity"—makes articulate what without this communication we would not be prepared to feel. We can entertain what he suffered.

This passage originally appeared in *Letters*, 1958.

Artaud's True Family, Glimpsed at Pompidou

I walked into the Artaud drawings exhibition, September 1994. Facing
me, taking up all of one wall, was a stenciled presentation of

"Ten years that the language is gone,
that there has entered in its place
this atmospheric thunder,
                    this lightning,
facing the aristocratic pressuration of beings,
of all the noble beings
                    of the butt,
cunt, of the prick,
of the lingouette,
of the plalouette
                    plaloulette
                    pactoulette,
of the tegumentary trance,
of the pellicle,
racial nobles of the corporeal erotic,
against me, simply virgin of the body,
ten years that I once again blew up the Middle Ages,
with its nobles, its judges, its lookout,
                    its priests above all,
                    its churches,
                    its cathedrals,
                    its vicars,
                    its white wafers.
How?
With an anti-logical,
                    anti-philosophical,
                    anti–intellectual,
                    anti-*dialectical*

This piece was published in Volume 45, Number 1, 1999, of *Chicago Review*.

blow of the tongue
with my black pencil pressed down
and that's it.

Which means that I the madman and the momo,
kept 9 years in a lunatic asylum for exorcistical and magical passes and because I supposedly imagined that I'd found a magic and that it was
crazy,
one must believe it was true,
since not a single day during my 3-year internment at Rodez, Aveyron, did
the Dr. Ferdière fail at 10:30 AM, the visiting hour, to come and tell me:
Mr. Artaud, as much as you may wish, Society cannot accept, and I am here
the representative of Society.
If I was mad in my magical passes, what did it then matter to Society which
could not feel attacked or injured and had only to despise and neglect
me.
But the Dr. Ferdière presenting himself as a defender of that Society and
entrusted to defend it must have recognized my so-called magical so-
called passes since he was opposing me with Society,
I therefore say that the dismissed language is a lightning bolt that I was
bringing forth now in the human fact of breathing, which my pencil
strokes on paper sanction.
And since a certain day in October 1939 I have not written anymore without drawing anymore either.
But what I draw
are no longer subjects from Art transposed from imagination to paper, they
are not affective figures,
they are gestures, a verb, a grammar, an arithmetic, a whole Kabala, and
one that shits to the other, one that shits on the other,
no drawing done on paper is a drawing, the reintegration of a strayed sensibility,
it is a machine which has breath,
it was first a machine which at the same time has breath.
It is a search for a lost world
and one that no human tongue integrates
and the image of which on paper is even no more than a
tracing, a sort of diminished
copy.
For the real work is in the clouds.

Words, no,
arid patches of a breath which gives its full
but there where only the Last Judgment will be able to decide between
values,
the evidences,
as far as the text is concerned,
in the moulted blood of what tide
will I be able to make heard

the corrosive structure,
there where the drawing
point by point
is only the restitution of a drilling,
of the advance of a drill in the underworld of the sempiternal latent body.
But what a logomachy, no?
Couldn't you light up your lantern a bit more, Mr. Artaud.
My lantern?
I say
that look ten years with my breath
I've been breathing hard forms,
        compact,
        opaque,
        unbridled,
        without archings
in the limbo of my body not made
and which finds itself hence made
and that I find every time the 10,000 beings to criticize me,
to obturate the attempt of the edge of a pierced infinite.

Such are in any case the drawings with which I constellate all my notebooks.

In any case
the whore,
oh the whore,
it's not from this side of the world,
it's not in this gesture of the world,
it's not in a gesture of this very world
that I say
that I want and can indicate what I think,
and they will see it,
they will feel it,
they will take notice of it
through my clumsy drawings,
but so wily,
and so adroit,
which say SHIT to this very world.

What are they?
What do they mean?

The innate totem of man.

Gris-gris to come back to man.

All breaths in the hollow, sunken
        pesti-fering
        arcature
of my true teeth.

Not one which is not a breath thrown with all the strength
of my lungs,
with all the sieve
of my respiration,

not one which does not respond to a real physiological activity,
which is not,
not its figurative translation
but something like an efficacious sieve,
on the *materialized* paper.

I am, it seems, a *writer.*
But am I writing?
I make sentences.
Without subject, verb, attribute or complement.
I have learned words,
they taught me things.
In my turn I teach them a manner of new behavior.
May the pommel of your tuve patten
entrumene you a red ani bivilt,
at the lumestin of the utrin cadastre.
This means maybe that the woman's uterus turns red, when Van Gogh the
mad protester of man dabbles with finding their march for the heavenly
bodies of a too superb destiny.
And it means that it is time for a writer to close shop, and to leave the written letter for the letter.
                    April 1947"

Across from the stenciled wall was a small glass case with opened first
editions and some letters

"Anyway, Antonin Artaud,
I am now no longer able to live
a single moment without feeling
in the depths of my being that you
are there
        Paule   30 June
                    1947"

To the right of this case was a 1992 photo of Paule Thévenin, who met
Artaud in 1946. She spent over 40 years deciphering, editing, and an-
notating thousands of pages of his journals and notebooks. Thévenin
was dying of cancer when this photo was taken. She is cradling her
neck with her right hand, weary on a couch, wearing black Chinese
slippers, her eyes still alert, suspicious, her left hand draped across her
lap. She had just been denied permission by Artaud's nephew, Serge

Malusséna, to reproduce two Artaud drawings in her book, *Ce désespéré qui vous parle*

I then wandered into other room displaying Artaud's drawings done in Rodez, along with portraits of his friends, done at Ivry-sur-Seine, after his release from Rodez. In these portraits there is ant shrapnel, exorcism as excoriation, an abrading of the face to reveal its abraxas, its cemeterial grue, its fecal infinity. In these portraits of his friends, I felt Artaud had assembled his true family (people in their twenties who had discovered his work while he was in Rodez, who then befriended him during the last two years of his life)

I looked at the portrait of Colette Thomas (August, 1947), at her semi-erased lips, her face swastikaed with shadow, bits of cuneiform milling in her forehead, her hair turning white and falling out in sooty clumps, her soft wondering eyes—the right eye appearing to weep a derrick. To the left of her head, Artaud had written: *paunctru nopi*
                          ler diaripa

        ler   *d*   *airipa*
          or re chti   *ba*

The writing in these portraits is the head's excrescence, its aura's dressed out insides, its apotropaic rags—but who is speaking? The portrait, or Artaud?

Jany de Ruy (2 July 1947), the girlfriend of Jacques Prevel who adored Artaud and supplied him with drugs. Jany de Ruy is depicted as infested with demons, an eye is ablaze in her neck, an imp in hunches grinning by her left ear. Below the portrait, Artaud wrote:

I am still too young to have wrinkles,
I beget these children from poor wrinkles,
I send them to do battle in my body—Only
I lack energy and that anyone can see,
I am still terribly romantic like this drawing
which in fact depicts me all too well,
I am weak, a weakness—
~~shit on me~~

To the left of de Ruy's blue shawl-like aura, Artaud has written: *who today will say what?* It is the postwar Paris question—Henri Pichette (21 November 1947) pistons up into a void, tack-like sailboats race his shredding neck, his eyes are gris-gris, his face is responsible for its own demolition and without title to completion, face swept by derricks, cranes, the metallurgy of material encasement

The actor Roger Blin's tousled scalp lifts up as if in revolt against his stuttering, while his nose, cheeks, and jaw set like cement—unlike most of Artaud's subjects he has no torn neck, he is intact

No one is dressed up here, or combed. Jacques Prevel's hair looks like it's never been washed, it twists around into greasy rat tails as if seeking escape from Prevel's hunchhead which is in the process of dividing, the right skullside bulging up and away from the left. Prevel's head looks like a mammoth in profile, part of his head a mammoth's head, the other part its sloping back. At the foot of his forehead, Prevel's eyes and nose are a winding, sardonic knot over braced valentine lips—"I see you as a man pestered by a certain kind of fly" Artaud told him

Around Paule Thévenin's portrait—like pieces of a broken frame—Artaud wrote:

> I posted   my   daughter   as   a   sentinel
> she is   faithful   for Ophelia   got   up late

—the portrait is called *Paule with ferrets* (the irons used for trying melted glass); this is Artaud's annealing of Thévenin to withstand the inquisition she would face as his "gate guardian" and scholar. Here he takes a blowtorch to Thévenin's soul to reshape it as if it were molten glass. *Paule with ferrets* is also a love song. By portraying Thévenin at 24 *and* 70, as very pretty *and* very battered, he plasticizes her shadowings, imbuing them with a shiver of eternity

Goodbye, Paule Thévenin,
you have made a gift to all poets:
editing with love,
love as an editorial act,
dedication to the soul of Antonin Artaud whose life,
ruins,
is now,
because of you,
a mountain to be climbed.

[1997]

IV

A Note on the Death of Paul Celan

While living in Sherman Oaks, California, in the spring of 1970, I had the following dream: a man that I recognized as Paul Celan walked to the bank of the Seine in Paris and stepped up onto a stone which I also recognized as the "Vallejo stone." Celan stood there for a moment—then leapt into the river.

When I mentioned my dream to someone a week or so later, I was informed that the poet had just drowned in the Seine, an apparent suicide.

The "Vallejo stone" refers to a poem that César Vallejo wrote while living in Paris in the mid-1930s. Like many of the poems that Vallejo wrote during these years, "Parado en una piedra" records his acute sensitivity to human suffering. This particular poem strikes me as a stay against suicide. In the early 1930s, Vallejo still believed that a Communist-inspired world revolution would occur, but this belief was beginning to founder, overwhelmed by the suffering he found everywhere daily.

Vallejo's untitled poem opens with the following two stanzas:

> Idle on a stone,
> unemployed,
> scroungy, horrifying,
> at the bank of the Seine, it comes and goes.
> Conscience then sprouts from the river,
> with petiole and outlines of the greedy tree;
> from the river the city rises and falls, made of
> embraced wolves.
>
> The idle one sees it coming and going,
> monumental, carrying his fasts in his concave
> head,

A slightly different version of this note appeared in Studies in 20th Century Literature, Volume Eight, Number One, fall 1983. A French translation by Jean-Baptiste Para appeared in *rehauts* 7, Spring 2001, Paris.

on his chest his purest lice
and below
his little sound, that of his pelvis,
silent between two big decisions,
and below,
further down,
a paperscrap, a nail, a match . . .

Bottom thoughts. The generational body, out of work, ends in the trash in the Seine's slime.

I think of this "Vallejo stone" as a locus of exile where lamentation is tested. It brings to mind a passage from Rilke's 10th *Duino Elegy* that evokes the crisis of lamentation for the twentieth century. A young woman, identified as a Lament, responds to a young man's questions, saying:

> We were a great clan, once, we Laments. Our fathers
> worked the mines in that mountain range. Sometimes
> you'll find a polished lump of ancient sorrow among men,
> or petrified rage from the slag of some old volcano.
> Yes, that came from there. We used to be rich.

Attempting to read my dream in the penumbra of Vallejo's and Celan's lives and poetries, I see that Vallejo, still weighted with some of the riches of lamentation, could address the misery of humankind from his stone, and then walk away from the Seine to write other poems.

For Celan, both of whose parents were murdered in Nazi death camps, lamentation was not entirely empty but was so distorted by the absurdity of praising anything that its so-called riches had been undermined. I suspect that at a certain point he could no longer even feel sorry for himself.

From *Sprachgitter* (1959) onward, the movements of words and lines in Celan's poetry have a strong, twisting, downward propulsion, like strands of a rope that is, at the same time, tightening with increasing weight *and* self-destructing through torsion into cast free strands. As if the direction is vertically commanded by a central suck, a whirlpool. Language as spars, rapidly milling. For example (in Cid Corman's translation from "The Syllable Ache," a poem in *Die Niemandrose*, 1964):

> Forgotten grabbed
> at To-be-forgotten, earthparts, heartparts
> swam,

sank and swam. Columbus,
the time-
less in eye, the mother-
flower,
murdered masts and sails. All fares forth,
free,
discovering,
the compass-flower fades, point
by leafpoint to height and to day, in blacklight
of wildrudderstreaks. In coffins,
in urns, canopic jars
awoke the little children
Jasper, Agate, Amethyst—peoples,
stock and kin, a blind

Let there be

is knotted in
the serpentheaded free-
ropes—:

By modifying "Let there be" with "blind," freedom and license twist into each other, and for a moment Aleister Crowley's "Do What Thou Wilt" shows its lust-deformed face. By putting it that way I attempt to indicate to what an extent Celan's poetry contains a pronouncement of creation emptied of meaning. When "Do What Thou Wilt" becomes, as it does for Crowley, the only law, there is no meaningful creation. The god-spark is exterminated, one is no one, one says one's prayer to ashes.

On another level, Celan's contraries were "I" and "Thou," and in his mature poetry they grow unbearably close, closer than contraries can to function; one could say they devour each other, the living become the dead, the dead the living, and out of such devastation a grand but dreadful vista opens. Celan's voice is finally consumed in a "we" that is the living and the dead scratching a message on stone to "no one." Under the stress of such an anti–vision, nothing is forgotten: memories of the death camps and insignificant slights have hundreds of doors opening on each other. It is a condition in which there cannot be poetry *and* in which there can only be poetry.

In regarding Paul Celan today, I meditate on the stamina of his wound. He neither allowed it to flow at full vent, nor did he brilliantly cicatrize it at the right hour. He worked it as a muscle as long as there was any strength left in it—he knelt at its altar alone, and thus did not set other energies in motion that might have given him reasons to continue to live at the point that the wound ceased to ache.

Then there was only numbness. And a great poetic testimony in which Paul Celan and annihilated millions can be sensed as a single "we" that you and I can try to pronounce.

[Los Angeles, 1975]

Two Introductions: Gary Snyder and Michael Palmer

Gary Snyder

Since 1956, when he read his poems about the Native American trickster Coyote at a reading in San Francisco during which Allen Ginsberg read Part One of *Howl*, Gary Snyder has been developing a selfless, sensual, landscape-attuned poetry of change and becoming that in the light of our current awareness of planetary potential and doom has become a clearing in American consciousness. It presents itself as ruggedly and thoroughly as monumental Chinese Sung Dynasty landscape painting in a context of interconnectedness involving lore, research, meditation, and a range of living and mythical companions. In "the cold companionable streams" of Snyder's poetry, there is a deep faith in the capacity of the earth to injure and to restore.

Rivers and Mountains Without End is Snyder's sixteenth book, 138 pages of text, thirty-nine poems in four sections or movements.

This work was struck, some forty years ago, off a Sung Dynasty scroll painting. Snyder's opening poem, the key to the book, describes the painting as, scene by scene, it unfurls to the left. He comments: "At the end of the painting the scroll continues with seals and poems. It tells a further tale." *Rivers and Mountains Without End*, then, is the twentieth-century addition to the painting. In its own interlocking, unfolding segments, it draws upon ecological awareness and nature's architecture to such an extent that I want to coin a term for what is happening, to suggest that *Rivers and Mountains Without End* is an *ecotecture*, a habitat-structure. It redirects Whitman's "adhesive love" from solely

I introduced Gary Snyder's reading from *Mountains and Rivers without End* at the University of Michigan, November 16, 1996. The Michael Palmer introduction took place at Eastern Michigan University, February 4, 2000.

human comradeship to a comradely display that includes artemisia and white mountain sheep. Thus I feel that this work is not really an epic, as the dust jacket states, in the tradition of Pound and Williams. Snyder himself thinks of it as a sort of sutra. A string of kayaks comes to mind. Functionally speaking, this book is a rock with centrifugal eddies that can be set at the center of Snyder's life work.

What appears to be the leanness in the work is actually Snyder's precise observation, which obviates explanation. At its most intense, his observational power evokes prayer and praise.

Snyder adheres to the Buddhistic principle of emptiness; there is no self, everything we see and are is empty. Thus the absence of the sensitive or tormented psychological subject in this poetry.

In the spirit of Sung landscape painting, as well as in the later Cézanne, one thing is as important as another, each part is as important as the whole. Thus the nodes of illumination strung throughout the writing. Snyder's world is redolent with common wealth—his elixir of enlightenment is buttermilk.

Finally, all is metaphoric, or let's say any truth is in the synapse between the parts of a metaphor. For example: two kilograms soybeans equals a boxwood geisha comb. Four thousand years of writing equals the life of a bristlecone pine. Our love is mixed with rocks and streams.

To overturn two thousand years of Christian dominion over "unChristian" nature—"over all the earth and over every creeping thing that creepeth upon the earth," including women and human slaves—the scale of values has to be massively rebalanced. *Mountains and Rivers Without End* is the first major Western poem to sweepingly foreground the natural world from a Buddhist perspective and, without cynicism, to present civilization on a sharply diminished scale.

Or as Furong Daokai, as quoted by Dōgen, puts it:

The green mountains are always walking;
a stone woman gives birth to a child at night.

Michael Palmer

Palmer writes: "I was born in Passaic in a small box flying over Dresden one night, lovely figurines. Things mushroomed after that. . . . As a child I slept beneath the bed, fists balled. . . . I grew to four feet then three. I drove a nail through the page and awoke smiling. This was my first smile." Observationally speaking, Palmer was born in New York City and has lived in San Francisco since 1969. He has worked extensively with contemporary dance for more than twenty years and has collaborated with numerous visual artists and composers. The most recent of his ten collections of poems is *The Promises of Glass.* He has also published a number of translations from the French, and has cotranslated and edited Russian and Brazilian poetry. Since 1982 he has been a contributing editor to *Sulfur* magazine, which I edit here at Eastern Michigan University.

Relative to traditional and conventional poetry, Palmer might be said to practice a counterpoetics, based on resistance to meaning in the simplest sense but not resistant to signification in a larger sense. More precisely, his writing resists preinscribed meaning, and predictable gestures of narrative and emotion. He thinks of the poem as a profound exploration that can renew form and answer to his specific needs.

In Palmer's poetry the ephemerality of human focus is constantly tested. Each of his poems might open with the following road sign: "Perpetual Earthquake Country." While individual lines often seem to carry customary information, in juxtaposition they scramble anticipated narrative and become in-process records of the mind's tilting attentions, its fugal looseness, its overlapping edges, ripples, blanks. Fragments of conversation move through Palmer stanzas, intersected by observations and reflections. While B may follow A, it will turn out to be part of C, which may seamlessly turn into D, which will turn out to belong to E. There is a constant sense of collage, with found and invented phrases cut and spliced so as to create hybrid assemblies.

The painter Willem de Kooning once described himself as a "slipping glimpser." One could apply this fascinating self-definition to Palmer's method of setting up a proposal that immediately slides or inverts only to return again, in the same poem, with different emphasis and framing.

Robert Duncan's well-known statement that in our time all things have come into their comparisons might be altered to: in our time all things have come into a shredded milling. Images now can mean anything; disposability has so infested perpetuity that to say "Ivory Tower" is to simultaneously evoke a poached elephant tusk. What a writer like Palmer is inside of today is an inside out whose new inside makes the ravaged nature of the world at once abstract and intimate to his skin.

"A and Not A are the same," Palmer writes, and elsewhere he refers to "The A of Not A." Which is to say that in poetry a thing can be at the same time A and Not A. It can be both raining and not raining—and not only snowing in the tropics but snowing sand in the arctic tropics. Such poetic logic (in contrast to classical logic) was memorably expressed by John Keats as "Negative Capability, that is when man is capable of being in uncertainties, Mysteries, doubts, without any irritable reaching after fact and reason." Figurative wonder is of course based on literal wonder; the extraordinary event compels the mind to match it in its own way. When I mentioned the word "arctic" a moment ago, I thought of a passage in Wade Davis' "Hunters of the Northern Ice" chapter in his book *Shadows in the Sun*. Davis writes: "There is a well-known account of an old man who refused to move into a settlement. Over the objections of his family, he made plans to stay on the ice. To stop him, they took away all his tools. So in the midst of a winter gale, he stepped out of their igloo, defecated and honed the feces into a frozen blade, which he sharpened with a spray of saliva. With the knife he killed a dog. Using its rib cage as a sled and its hide to harness another dog, he disappeared into the darkness."

This is also a wonderful parable of the artistic project at large. Out of A, Not A is made, and out of Not A, A is made. In his A Not A poem, his A Not A vehicle, the poet, in this case Michael Palmer, flashes through inflection, nuance, pun and nonsense, the shadows of denotational language.

Padgett the Collaborator

Over the past thirty years, Ron Padgett has created a unique body of poetry, prose poems, translations, and essays. By the late 1960s, Padgett had begun to assimilate strategies from a combination of earlier French and American poets—in particular, the manic prose poems of Max Jacob, the Cubist precision of Pierre Reverdy, the café conversation lines of Guillaume Apollinaire, as well as the feisty, urban immediacy of Frank O'Hara, and the veering into-themselves-disappearing narratives of Kenneth Koch (with whom Padgett studied at Columbia University).

For many years now, along with several other New York City–based poets of his generation, Padgett has been referred to as a "second-generation New York School poet." While such a labeling was not inappropriate in the 1970s, at this point it is inaccurate. I suspect that it is mainly based on Padgett's first book (*Great Balls of Fire*, 1969; reprinted in 1990), in which the French and O'Hara/Koch influence is the strongest. However, by the late 1970s, in such collections as *Toujours l'amour* and *Triangles in the Afternoon*, Padgett became Padgett. With his 1992 translation of Blaise Cendrars' *Complete Poems* and his own *New & Selected Poems*, it is clear that he is a major figure in contemporary American letters.

Literary influence aside, Padgett's writing is amply grounded in popular culture. No one in American poetry, for example, has made more use of the comic strip and animated cartoon than Padgett. He accounts for the amount of memorabilia in his poetry in the following way: "I ascribe it to having grown up in a prospering, consumerist America in the 1940s and 1950s with parents who had just edged upward from poverty

This piece first appeared in *Chicago Review*, spring 1997.

into the middle class and who very much enjoyed the entertainments and objects they could thus afford. My mother loved popular music and movies. She and I went to hundreds of movies together, movies of all kinds, and she was very nice about taking me to cartoon festivals. Also, both she and my father provided an endless supply of comic books, my favorite reading matter. I read very little children's literature as a child. Aside from the fact that my parents were bootleggers, my upbringing was quite 'normal': toys, baseball, movies, cars, with their attendant vocabularies (such as, respectively: Slinky, frozen rope, You're dern tootin', overdrive)."

Padgett's poetry ripples with immediacy—it is a poetry of primary colors, as it were, calling to mind the thing-grounded work of W. C. Williams. Relative to Williams, Padgett is more garrulous and much more humorous. His lines are peppered with off-stage remarks, exclamations ("By gum," Bgawk," "Yipes," Yaba-dabba-doooo"), and sudden soliloquacious excursions that just as quickly swerve into something else, or go up in smoke. In one poem, George Frederick Handel is set on fire; in another, Papa Bear's coffee cup explodes; in another, Mr. Bushwanger's glasses fall to the floor and burst into flame. This Spike Jones atmosphere is modulated by an austere, existential probing, and a keen sense of the liquid boundary between being and not being at all.

Let me ground these initial remarks by quoting and responding to a complete poem. Here is "Ode to Poland" (from *Triangles in the Afternoon*, 1979):

Ode to Poland

It is embarrassingly true
that you don't begin to die
until you begin to live,
embarrassing because it is a truism
uttered by big fat idiots.
I am a thin person, myself,

seeing the golden sunlight
of sunset radiant against red bricks
that appear quite ordinary too,
lifting me out of my shoes and into some real
or imaginary sense of the Eternal

as I turn into the New First Avenue Bakery
where the girl is saying, "At home
our manners have to be perfect.

I have to set the table just so,"
the light on the buildings set just so

and Intellect extending its puny arms
toward some greatness of cognition—
only to have the proverbial bully
of Mystery kick sand in its face.

Back home I pound on the table,
knocking a lamp into the air sideways.

Straight lines appear in the air
around the lamp as it falls.
These are they.

There is no fat in these six stanzas; each new one swivels off the one
before it, moving the poem through a grid of at once timeless and chronological events. The "swiveling" is a technique that Padgett employs like
a master, pushing into new material almost seamlessly as aspects of prior
material are also brought forward, weighting the poem while not losing
its ongoing inquiry. Such phrases as "big fat idiots" and "lifting me out of
my shoes" evoke the comic-strip world, as does the central, oblique
metaphor: the Charles Atlas weight-lifting display ads that appeared for
years in comic books. A lily-white "97 pound weakling" appears on a
beach blanket with a beauty he is courting only to have sand kicked in his
face by a brawny bully, leading him to lose the girl until, after having
purchased and used Atlas's "dynamic tension," he has become the ideal
"He-man." The "weakling" is elicited at the end of Padgett's first stanza
and then held in reserve until the fourth stanza when he fills out
Padgett's frustration over not being able to carry perception beyond
protocol into "some greatness of cognition." With no bully to punch out
(or proper girl to defend), Padgett takes his frustration out on the table,
knocking over a lamp whose fall is, as in comic strips, reinforced with
motion lines. The baffled, often ridiculously inept Pole of the "Polish
joke" is here saluted as a figure to be found in all of us. Like certain
poems by Kenneth Rexroth, "Ode to Poland" is erudite and available
poetry that anyone who knows how to read can grasp.

There are even more accessible Padgett poems than "Ode to Poland," and because of the way they immediately give themselves to the
reader, they may lead some to think of Padgett as a poet of "light
verse." As an image of his poetry at large, such a view would be false—
in fact, there is a fascinating range of transparency/opaqueness that I
would like to comment on, using the cornucopia as a metaphor.

The fruits spilling out of the mouth of the horn are such poems as "To Woody Woodpecker" and "Chocolate Milk," quick odes, whose briefness and utter availability is in proportion to their subjects. A bit inside the horn are such pieces as "Sweet Pea," a love poem woven of flower names, and "Wilson '57," written as if one were, in a somewhat goofy and nostalgic mood, turning the pages of one's junior high school yearbook and recalling, with haiku brevity, the signature aspects of one's classmates, or one's relations with them. As we move deeper into the horn—meaning that we, as readers, have to do correspondingly more work—we find such poems as "Ode to Poland" and "High Heels," in which double takes and shifts—single line changes of context which act as hinges to swing the poem off into a new direction—occur.

About halfway down the horn (the point at which in a cave light ceases to penetrate), we find the poems that I believe will identify Padgett's art. In this group I'd name "The Music Lesson," "Famous Flames," "Ode to Stupidity," "Tom and Jerry Graduate from High School," "Second Why," and the masterpiece "Cufflinks" (a poem that should be in any anthology mapping the 1970s). These poems are constructed on the basis of associational shifts (puns, correspondences, off-the-wall notions), which layer and densify the writing in a way that defies calling it either serious *or* humorous. It is emphatically both. Some of these poems, on their own terms, come to a logical conclusion. Others shift once again, as if into a new poem but one that becomes the current poem's last line.

We now move toward the core (or apex) of our metaphoric horn, with such poems as "The Statue of a Libertine," "Tone Arm," "The Ems Dispatch," and "To Francis Sauf Que," all poems written in the 1960s which experiment with non-sequitur juxtapositions that render significant parts of them opaque. On their behalf, it should be said that they show the "too much" that must be engaged for a writer to discover the "enough."

Ron Padgett is one of the finest living translators of twentieth-century poetry, but before offering an example of his translating, I would like to situate him in a context that includes translation: collaboration. For Padgett, translating a poem by Apollinaire is a form of collaboration that also includes writing poems in tandem with Berrigan and Tom Clark, and doing books with such visual artists as Brainard, George

Schneeman, Jim Dine, and Alex Katz. In Padgett's own poems, one can see how this complex sense of collaboration has generated interior dialogues and a sense of many figures involved in the construction of a single poem.

The poet and translator Bill Zavatsky published two of Padgett's best collections of poetry (*Toujours l'amour* and *Triangles in the Afternoon*) under the SUN imprint. He knows Padgett's work as well as anyone, so I asked him for his opinion of Padgett's collaborative efforts. Zavatsky responded: "In his extensive work with children as a teacher of poetry writing, the collaboration was central to Ron's approach. It loosens up writers of any age, gets them laughing, it makes poetry joy. The Surrealist passion for capturing the child's taste for comedy and the outrageous includes the kinds of dizzying wordplay and sudden shifts of tone that one finds in *Bean Spasms*, cowritten by Padgett and Berrigan in the mid-1960s." Zavatsky also cotranslated *The Poems of A. O. Barnabooth* by Valery Larbaud (1977) with Padgett, an activity that draws several strands of collaboration together. Zavatsky recalls: "I see us somewhere in the early '70s hovering over ham and egg sandwiches and malteds at a long-gone luncheonette on Broadway near 96th Street. We are munching and laughing maniacally, trying to get at Valery Larbaud, thrilled by some new meaning or beauty that we have found in his lines, wowed by a translational *coup* that one of us, it didn't matter *which* one, had fished up. We weren't two young men working together, we were one, lost—and thrilled to be—in the words of a great poet. If that isn't the essence of Surrealism, I don't know what is."

What is still fascinating about the writing in *Bean Spasms* is to try to figure out where one poet leaves off and another comes in. In the following passage, I sense Berrigan trying to corner Padgett ("How could you stand Pat coming in . . ."), who deftly changes the subject in a way that will become a key strategy in his own poems in the following decades:

What holiday is this, Clarence? Why it's the fasching season
When Lords and Ladies play 'Roll Out the Barrel' or lay abed
Because they don't have to know the right ping-pong table size
To stop climbing up a ladder toward a certain grey fat
Hee-haw there kid! How could you stand Pat
Coming in while your hand was under the dressmaker's machine?
Danger in them thar hills, said Boy, finger, and nostril
Too much room here said the fat
Miniature of Mao Tse-tung, as you dropped a tear on the crockery
Rubbing me the wrong way near the Manhattan Bridge.

So now we're zipping up a one-way street
Only, who turned on the cameras, you charming Boy?
Here is the glum Bengali of the dangling hairs, at his
Cub Scout meeting; remember the time he kissed you and broke his tooth?
Yes, he was with the alcoholic young lady in white
Who disappeared through the rectangle with the dangling thing!
Followed at a distance of one half inch by seven men and a posse.
What excitement when your hairy pants were not a hit!

By the late 1970s, Padgett's own poetry had become more focused and covered more ground in less space than this. But the ghost of such a collaboration is always present. In "Déjà Vu" (1979), notice how image particles come forth and are then cross-stitched throughout a brief but realized piece of work:

Déjà Vu

I'm back in the saddle again,
splitting every situation into three equal parts
and hearing the voice of Aunt Jemima
emerge from the Delphic Oracle.
It's pancake time in Greece, huge
flapjacks draped over the countryside:
shadows of moving clouds,
blotches of ideas projected down
from the great old Mr. Everything,
he who at this very moment checks his watch
and looks down at me.

To the world of collaboration, we must also add deliberate mistranslations, which Padgett appears to have done while he was writing collaborative poems with Berrigan and Clark. The following is from "Some Bombs" *(Great Balls of Fire)*:

El Paso invents the bush of gout
The tru
Kill gout
The pen drool key bat dances the maize on is come a cur
The isle has dice monuments where Lon foods rat er milly hair
"Ew!" to hear kill coon

These lines are mistranslations of the following lines by Pierre Reverdy:

Elle passe devant la bouche d'égout
Le trou
Quel degoût
La pendule qui bât sans la maison est comme un coeur

Il y a des moments où l'on voudrait être meilleur
Ou tuer quelqu'un

In the same period, in a different part of Manhattan, with much different goals in mind, Louis Zukofsky was "reading" the lips of Catullus, watching his wife's lips as she read Catullus to him. He heard an American English that in no sense did he feel was a mistranslation.

Padgett's intentions here, banked off the sound of the French, but clearly also mishearing it, seem aimed at breaking up conventional narration and modification to arrive at what might be called a disruptive syntax, out of which spill "dice monuments" and "milly hairs," new combinations that owe some of their background to Gertrude Stein's mistranslations in a work like "Yet Dish," André Breton's "exploding/fixed" Surrealist image, Jackson Mac Low's chance operations, and the "hydrogen jukebox" atmosphere of Ginsberg's "Howl."

In response to my question as to what he considered to be the value of literary collaboration, Padgett answered: "For me the value was—I don't do much of it anymore—various. First of all, it was very exciting and sometimes a lot of fun. Second, it showed me ways to write while being simultaneously in control and out of control of the piece at hand. It also showed me new ways in which two heads can be better than one, that a poem can have more than one voice in it and still not fly apart, that when it's going well the two voices actually create a third voice, maybe even a fourth or fifth. I liked the sense of multiplicity, possibility, depth, and range that collaboration suggested, all of which one might also have when writing solo."

Aside from his collaborative translation work with Zavatsky, Padgett has worked alone on his translations of Apollinaire and Cendrars. A sense of his expertise can be gleaned by looking at the first fourteen lines of his translation of Apollinaire's "Zone" (to be found in Koch and Kate Farrell's anthology, *Sleeping on the Wing*). First the French, followed by what Padgett does with it:

Zone

A la fin tu es las de ce monde ancien

Bergère ô tour Eiffel le troupeau des ponts bêle ce matin

Tu en as assez de vivre dans l'antiquité greque et romaine

Ici même les automobiles ont l'air d'être anciennes
La religion seule est restée toute neuve la religion
Est restée simple comme les hangars de Port-Aviation

Seul en Europe tu n'es pas antique ô Christianisme
L'Européen le plus moderne c'est vous Pape Pie X
Et toi que les fenêtres observent la honte te retient
D'entrer dans une église et de t'y confesser ce matin
Tu lis les prospectus les catalogues les affiches qui chantent tout haut
Voilà la poésie ce matin et pour la prose il y a les journaux
Il y a les livraisons à 25 centimes pleines d'aventures policières
Portraits des grand hommes et mille titres divers

You're tired of this old world at last

The flock of bridges is bleating this morning O shepherdess Eiffel Tower

You've had enough of living in the Greek and Roman past

Even the cars look ancient here
Only religion has stayed new religion
Has stayed simple like the hangars at Port-Aviation

O Christianity you alone in Europe are not ancient
The most modern European is you Pope Pius X
And you whom the windows observe shame forbids this morning
Your going into a church and confessing
You read the handbills the catalogs the posters that really sing
That's poetry and there are newspapers if you want prose this morning
There are dime serials filled with detective stories
Portraits of great men and a thousand other categories

Anyone with some French will probably have noticed that the lines of "Zone" are slant-rhymed couplets. That they are also conversational creates a special problem for a translator: how be accurate and approximate not only the slant rhymes but the tone? Most translators of "Zone" (Dudley Fitts, Roger Shattuck, Charlotte Mandel, and recently Donald Revell) do not deal with the rhyme at all. To my knowledge, only Samuel Beckett in his version has recreated the rhyme, but his version pays dearly for this, creaking with the awkward phrasing that maintaining rhyme can bring about.

Padgett's handling of the four words referring to the past in the opening lines is particularly adroit. His rhyming has a Yeatsian ease to it. His language, with one minor exception, is idiomatic and it registers Apollinaire's details without distortion.

Earlier I mentioned Padgett's extensive use of the comic strip and the animated cartoon in his poetry. The "straight lines that appear in the air" in "Ode to Poland" are but one example of the permutations of comic-strip visuality that affects not only the tone but the descriptive language of a Padgett poem; e.g., human beings turn into "exclamation points," trees "are toothpicks," "ecstatic natives" are "inexpensive green cardboard," Woody Woodpecker is surrounded by "speed lines in the air," and "a great yellow bolt of lightning strikes" through "a great green rent in the sky" (on p. 98 of *Toujours l'amour*, a comic-strip slash of lightning has been drawn in). With these examples in mind, I'd like to ask the reader to look back to the poem I quoted called "Déjà Vu." Nearly all of it can be read as conditioned by comic-strip imagery.

To this descriptive atmosphere must be added the parade of comic-strip and animated cartoon characters who appear in lines and titles, and the extent to which such color the entire atmosphere of a poem in which they appear. One must also take into consideration the comic-strip collaborations with Brainard and Schneeman included in poetry collections, as well as Padgett's professed "self-image": that of a "minor." This is not to imply that the authorial sensibility in Padgett's poetry is that of an adolescent, but rather to suggest that the tools he uses to express adolescent and adult views of the world come from what for most Americans born in the 1930s and 1940s is the main source of visual artistry up through adolescence. This is not true for most poets starting out today. But for those of us brought up in these periods—especially in the midwest in contrast to the more European east coast—the comic book and the Saturday Matinee (often consisting solely of animated cartoons) were our introduction to the creative life.

I'd say that most American poets upon discovering poetry (which in its traditional garb is utterly remote from popular American culture) feel a need to abandon comic books and become so "serious" that in many instances the reader learns nothing about the poet's adolescent years and their formative largesse. Padgett is certainly not alone in his insistence that his adolescent loves count in his poetry, but much more than most he has refused to downgrade their hold on him and to dismiss the extent to which they offered him the rudiments of imagination.

In response to my query, as to how reading "the funnies" affected his poetics, Ron wrote: "Having learned to read by looking at comic books, I'd guess that any whole sense of the connection between reading and writing originates from those wonderful pages filled with bright colors and with odd and interesting characters (talking animals, men wearing fantastic costumes as they fly through the sky, timid ghosts, kings who never talk, etc.). At an early age I must have come to feel that reading should pull the reader into a beautiful little world, a world with a structure, because every cartoon or comic strip, whether eight pages or only four little panels long, had a beginning, middle, and an end. Some were better than others, but all of them, despite their sometimes bizarre events and characters, were orderly. My best poems, despite their sometimes bizarre moments, do, I hope, create a sense of order. The other thing that strikes me about comic strips and cartoons is their extraordinary clarity of line. I don't admire cartoonists like Ernie Bushmiller (creator of *Nancy*) because they have become legendary pop icons, but because they were such good clear draftsmen and designers. I think that clarity made me receptive, later, to notions such as *le mot juste*."

For Ron Padgett, "the exact word" is a result of a long collaborative adventure that is the fruit of mistranslation, collaborative poems, accurate translations, teaching, editing, and writing a poetry that draws on all of these elements. Padgett's staying power and hilarity are at their peak in the 371-line "Cufflinks," a poem that begins with a meditation on the "Fall" of the frankfurter and ends with a photo-finish horse race narrated by the poet as a sportscaster. In between, in a grand zigzag of spatial and temporal episodes, there are appearances by Donald Duck, Mrs. Asturo-Torres, Helen Kafka, Rodney Harlem, Ralph Waldo Beverly (a stagehand), Heraclitus, a Dagwood sandwich, and a brief interview with Picasso. One third of the way through this "grand galop," the narrator bursts forth, center stage, proclaiming:

> The first thing I think of in the morning is
> "Good God, another day! Incredible!"
> And I dive whistling a merry tune into my clothes
> and burst onto the street with a radiant smile
> and an irrepressible air of joy and exultant optimism.
> Passersby mumble into their English muffins,
> "Doesn't he know about modern man's existential dilemma?
> Doesn't he realize the rocks are falling?" They turn
> away and step into massive piles of dog dood.
> Now they are really pissed off. Some leap right
> out of their shoes and run down the street in their stockings.
> The shoes scrape themselves off and plod onward
> toward work. The elevator is filled with empty shoes.
> All over the busy metropolis
> the shoes are trodding, trodding,
> they are leaving the offices and stores,

the tiny pink ones in kindergartens
and the clodhoppers at construction sites,
the terrifying white numbers stream from the hospitals,
the scuffed pumps from the thrift shop, plate-glass windows
kicked out by shoes escaping from the shoe store, all
heading along waves of force . . .

In his introduction to his cotranslation of Valery Larbaud's poetry, Padgett passes along Larbaud's description of the poet he had dreamed of being: "whimsical, sensitive to racial differences, peoples, countries . . . international . . . humorous . . . a funny Walt Whitman of joyous irresponsibility . . . at once the successor of Laforgue, Rimbaud, and Walt Whitman."

Such strikes me as a perfect bank-shot description of Ron Padgett himself.

Spider Sibyls

From the late 1970s through the early 1980s, Michel Nedjar created some of the most unique and unforgettable "things" of the latter half of this century. These "things" are referred to as dolls, but since they are unlike any dolls I have ever seen, I prefer to approach them with the spirit in which Rainer Maria Rilke spoke of "things," as strange, mystical entities, in his second lecture on Rodin.

Working essentially with detritus—dirty torn rags, abandoned trampled clothes—Nedjar first ties and stitches, then bathes in a vat of dye what when lifted to view are creatures that, on one hand, appear to be as old as humanity's oldest image making and, on the other, seem to be the enfleshed souls of those gassed and burned in the European Annihilation. In these works, Nedjar, in effect, fuses the earliest decorated rock shelters of Europe with Auschwitz—a Cro-Magnon gouging a vagina into a cave wall with a sharpened rock echoed in time by a concentration-camp victim scratching his or her name on a cell wall with a nail.

While Nedjar's dolls are not directly beholden to any artist's work, they are not only the children of prehistory brought up against recent history but reflect an extreme point in permutations on the theme of the doll—a word, I should add, whose roots are obscured in etymological conjecture. Sensing that "fetish" and "idol" are bound into its global significance, I also spot the pun on i-dol, an I doll, realizing that Nedjar's creatures could more accurately, if somewhat obscurely, be called no-dols—or, pushing the pun perhaps beyond the breaking point, id-owls, creatures whose ids are inhuman.

The admittance of the inhuman sets up another line of imaginal con-

This essay was written for a catalogue of the dolls and paintings of Michel Nedjar, *les ongles en Deuil*, produced by Galerie Susanne Zander, in Köln, Germany, 1996.

jecture: if the doll is a sentinel of mother nature, then revelations concerning its soul are bound to evoke creatures of nonhuman kingdoms.

Before addressing this matter, I would like to briefly trace a few twentieth-century doll permutations.

In 1914, Rilke wrote an essay called "Some Reflections on Dolls," based on the wax, Expressionist dolls of Lotte Pritzel. Commenting on Pritzel's work, Max von Boehn writes: "One hardly dares to use the word 'doll' for these creatures, since this word so easily leads one astray. These figures possess a psychological strength, in marked contrast to their butterfly forms. 'They come to life,' as H. Rupé says, 'like improvisations of the unconscious.' . . . The artist has baptized her fantasies with the names of Simonetta, Omphale, Ganymed, Bajadere, Chichette, the Unveiled, Hamlet, Adoration, and so forth."

Such names may call up for readers of poetry the strange cast of figures in Gérard de Nerval's *Chimeras*. That aside, Rilke's essay itself does not appear to address Pritzel's dolls directly but uses them to reflect on those "things" that prepare us, as children, for our relationship with the world. The most precious of things, Rilke proposes, are the thinly painted, sawdust-filled dolls we play with, drag about, and finally abandon. As often with Rilke, a complex ambivalence moves through his evocations: "At a time when everyone was still intent on giving us a quick and reassuring answer," he writes, "the dolls were the first to inflict on us that tremendous silence (larger than life) which was later to come to us out of space, whenever we approached the frontiers of our existence at any point. It was facing the doll, as it stared at us, that we experienced for the first time that emptiness of feeling, that heart-pause, in which we should perish did not the whole, gently persisting Nature then lift us across abysses like some lifeless thing." A curious turn! For in becoming "some lifeless thing," do we not become doll-like—suggesting that the doll may be the first messenger of our own mortality.

A decade after Rilke wrote his doll essay, Hans Bellmer also met Lotte Pritzel. He discovered in her dolls not a trip back to childhood but an erotic nest: Omphale as a blonde in black stockings and lace, also Chichette as a provocative adolescent in silks and satins wielding a riding whip. Pritzel's figures suggested to Bellmer the possibility of an adolescent girl-sized doll that he could construct himself. His revision of the doll is radical: the fetus-sized idol or toy is expanded to a sexually saturated symbol of polymorphous desire.

Bellmer's first doll (1933) had a hollow wood framework with jointed legs and one jointed arm. Significantly, the stomach contained a panorama with six partitions in which diverse materials—like a hand-kerchief soiled with a girl's spittle—represented "the thoughts and dreams of a young girl." As Peter Webb describes it in his monograph on Bellmer, to make the panorama revolve, the viewer pressed a button on the doll's left nipple and then peeked through a peephole in the navel (a situation which of course evokes Marcel Duchamp's later Etant Donnés). The doll was placed in various positions and arrangements of its parts and then photographed. Implicit in such presentations was the notion that the doll was no longer confined to naturalistic representation, that games could be played with her by moving her about in various combinations.

Bellmer's first doll was to some extent a stick figure; his second (1935), constructed of paper and glue, was formed to sensuously depict the mannequin-like body of a young woman. The panoramic center of the first doll was now transformed into a stomach sphere to which multiple pelvises, torsos, breasts, legs, arms, and a head could be attached. In becoming an anagram, or a galaxy, this doll had broken through "the human form divine," and with several legs and vaginas radiating out from her navel began to suggest nonhuman forms of life.

In displacements and arrangements packed with sadistic and masochistic sensation, the new doll was not only photographed in rooms, doorways, against shadowy staircases and on beds, but out in the woods in positions that implied rape or crucifixion. In one position, as Herbert Lust has written, "the top genitality seemed to invite sexuality from the sky while the bottom genitality invited sex from the earth," a combination eerily evoking a spider in its tree-strung orb.

In several of Bellmer's final engravings (1969), the panoramic center become stomach sphere has been transformed into the head of a vulval, fanged spider, surrounded by revolving lissome, feminine legs, poised to attack and devour.

Nedjar has acknowledged the spider as the primary familiar in his life and art. His associations with it mainly relate to tying, sewing, and weaving (as well as the braiding of images in the films he has made, one of which is called "A quoi rêve l'araignée" / "Of What Does the Spider Dream?"—a question that could be a koan). My tracking of doll reflections and permutations in Pritzer, Rilke, and Bellmer is not to imply that they have directly influenced the kind of doll Nedjar began to construct in 1978 (a year he calls "the fall of the angel"), but that on an aesthetic level, Bellmer especially in severely revising the naturalistic doll created a kind of psychic space into which a grounded Nedjar could enter and then spin, as it were, his own variations on an archetype already dissected and opened out. It should be added that another space-clearing force for Nedjar is his considerable familiarity with an international range of folkloric and magic dolls, which he collected on his travels during the 1970s in Morocco, Afghanistan, India, Guatemala, and Mexico.

On a historic level, the European Annihilation, which Nedjar became aware of as a teenager, having lost some of his family (excluding his mother and his rag-picker grandmother) during the roundup of Jews in Paris during the Occupation, seems to be crucially involved in his choice of materials—outcast stuff no longer acceptable for human use—as well as the gaping, spectral images the rags are knotted into.

I am only familiar with what I take to be a small percentage of Nedjar's dolls. The ones I have seen, or scrutinized in photos, consist of heads, or rhizome-like head combinations, and figures whose slack bodies often pustulate with heads erupting in their crotches. The most powerful of these pieces have not lost their rag rawness. The semblance of heads and boneless, muscleless bodies, vivid and ghastly, remains subordinated to the rotting tuggings and warps of *schmates*. In some, heads seem webbed together about a single head in a way that reminded me of a recent horror out of Rwanda: a Mr. Murumba who was spending his days masked, pulling bodies from Lake Victoria, was quoted in *The New York Times:* "One time, I found a woman," he said. "She had five children tied to her. One on each arm. One on each leg. One on her back. She had no wounds."

The face of another Nedjar doll looks like the area of the groin from which a leg has been torn off. Another that is vaguely heart-shaped is composed of two soft skulls siamesed over a stump trailing vein-like threads. Another looks like the ghost of a Mexican jaguar mask with a smashed, phallic nose stitched between huge, pit-like eye orifices, all of which feels amphibious. There is nothing I know of in Post WWII European art to which such visions can be compared.

The closest relatives of these "monuments" are the naked, white-dusted, tongue-lolling Butoh dancers, who began to writhe in the 1960s on stages which we are told looked like flea markets (Nedjar worked in one for years in Paris), wearing rags and bizarre combinations of Japanese dresses or Western and Japanese costumes. To read Richard Rhodes' *The Making of the Atomic Bomb* is to be confronted with horrors—people as black bundles stuck to bridges, people whose skin hung from them like rags, men without feet walking on their ankles, children who looked like boiled octopuses—that one feels have, on a European plane, pushed through Nedjar's mind and hands to find themselves arrested as pupa-like explosions, trapped between total absence and the almost human. They seem to squirm between the cracks in the cave wall upon which images, in the deep past, were first attempted.

The Butoh dancer Tanaka Min comes very close in sensibility to Nedjar. I saw Tanaka perform in Paris in 1979. Naked, hairless, his entire body dusted with a fine, tan powder, his penis wrapped in what appeared to be a cloth condom, he danced for over an hour mainly spread out on the stage, groundedness and inertia becoming positive elements in a dance of the dead. From statements he has made about his art:

"I was dancing so slowly it was almost invisible."

"To be naked was for me a way to dress myself up."

"To evacuate one's own body, to step in obscure regions of matter . . ."

"The body surface that envelops the flesh is like a wrapping paper; and what is important is the pattern printed on it. The patterns of society are inevitably printed on the body surface as it rolls around on the Earth. The dance permeates the body surface and reaches the flesh. My body is turned into a receptacle."

"The dancers are insects under a tree watching the moon. The wooden frames are used for drying rice straw, or for hanging *daikon*, and they have different names in different districts. I like them when they have been weathered after being left out for a long time. Then they look like bones. The figures wrapped in paper are presents to the world. They are covered with the names of many cities throughout the world. There are many dancers in the group from all over the world. I am sending them back."

"I am an avant-garde who crawls the Earth, a corpse trying desperately to become life in the circle of life and death."

Our bodies, constricted and draped in cloth, exude and slowly wear the cloth out. We destroy our clothes, treating them somewhat like children treat dolls, shuffling around in them, playthings of the body, to finally discard them, as Rilke sees dolls cast away, tossed like snake skins into some corner, used and filled with us.

Since Nedjar's own spider associations involve tying and braiding, we might think of his art as spider work, and of his dolls as prey that he has seized and bound. He is in fact fond of referring to a doll as a "Chair d'âme," or as the flesh of a soul. His bound prey is alive for him, alive with the past life discharged into what are now rags, formed rags. His task then is to bind the rags into shapes that expose the extent to which a soul can be expressed.

Historically, such becomes a revelation of the attempt in the 1930s and '40s to put an end once and for all to the people we can imagine could very well have worn these or similar clothes. On this level, Nedjar's art is one of memory, of testimony, of not forgetting—of insisting that the vast piles of concentration-camp clothing, already rags, can be understood, with a deft transformational adjustment, as the flesh of souls.

If Nedjar's activity is spider-like in one way, it is counterspider in another. Far from becoming Michel Nedjar's meals, these enfleshed souls are now being given a kind of eternal life. It is impossible here not to think of the Cumean Sibyl from Petronius's *Satyricon*, blessed with eternal life by Apollo but doomed to perpetual old age. A perpetuity we might say Nedjar's creations must suffer, forever battered and old. Unlike the Cumean Sibyl, however, these dolls, were they to be asked, "What do you want?" would not reply: "I want to die." Surely they would simply watch our eyes imploring them for our own eternal youth.

[1995]

V

The Gospel According to Norton

"When you write mystery stories, you have to know something; to be a poet, you don't have to know anything."
                                                    —Richard Hugo (NAMP, 1121)

Once upon a time, there was a great, great poet named Yeats [55].[1]

Yeats was so great, in fact, that he "dominates this century's verse as Wordsworth dominated that of the last." Indeed, a year before this century even began, with *The Wind Among the Reeds*, Yeats "set the method for the modern movement." Drawing upon the discoveries of Romanticism—"diversified expression of the self," "the primacy of the imagination,"—as well as upon French Symbolism—"truth in mental operations rather than in the outside world"—Yeats became the poetic overlord of the twentieth century. Furthermore, he inserted his own symbology, as well as his mortal body, into his second, or mature, phase, and dwelling "boldly upon lust and rage, mire and fury, he envisaged more passionately the state of completeness to which incompleteness may attain."

In the shadow of what might be called French-Symbolism-become-Yeatsean-Symbology, several other great but clearly (and unexplainedly) lesser poets were picking around the ruins, trying to make sense out of the new (though from a Yeatsean viewpoint, finished) century. Both Pound [31] and Eliot [28] "wrote about the modern world as a group of fragments." Pound believed in "'direct treatment of the thing,'" and in this way he was an ally of Williams [34] and his "no ideas but in things." Since "the general framework within which modern poets have written is one in which the reality of the objective world is

This essay first appeared in *American Poetry Review*, September/October 1990.

fundamentally called into question," the reader is to understand that Pound, Eliot, and Williams were unable to achieve the completeness achieved by Yeats. Eliot's "sifting and fusion ended in a surprisingly orthodox religious view." Pound ceases to be of much interest after being found mentally incompetent to stand trial for treason after WW II, and in spite of his attempt in the *Cantos* to find a pattern, "the total impression may rather be one of shifting, intersecting forms, coming into being and then retreating on the page." Williams, who "agreed with the poets Verlaine and Rimbaud in opposing 'literature' as a phenomenon created by the 'establishment,'" felt that the poem should be "allowed to take its own shape." "He sees most writing as having taken a wrong turn and regards his own efforts, even if stumbling, as at least in the right direction." The few British poets "who followed the lead of Eliot and Pound made relatively little impact on their readers." Exceptions are Sitwell [5], MacDiarmid [4], Jones [10], and Bunting [6]—but they are all of minor importance and worth only a handful of pages. "For in England as in America, the influence of strongly programmatic poetry" (Pound, Eliot, Williams, or anyone with a new poetics) "was balanced by much more traditional modes of verse."

Thus not only was 1922 "the year of *The Waste Land* and of Joyce's [8] *Ulysses* . . . it was also the year when a group of teachers and students at Vanderbilt University brought out a literary magazine called *The Fugitive*." Up to this point, all the poets have been introduced under the Yeatsean canopy called "Symbolism." We are now in a period described as "Elegant and Inelegant Variations," presumably on Yeats and his lessers. While Lawrence [22] "centered his own verse in the passions of tortoises and elephants," and Frost [24] "converted his self-disgust and loneliness into verses of Horatian dignity," such Georgians as de la Mare [3], Graves [10], Sasson [5], and Edward Thomas [5] "wished to preserve rural England in traditional prosody." In this regard, they were compatible with *The Fugitives* (Ransom [11], Tate [11], and Warren [11]), "who hoped to keep for the South some of its traditional values." *Fugitive* ramifications are Empson's [5] *Seven Types of Ambiguity* (1930), Ransom's *The New Criticism* (1941), and Warren and Brook's *Understanding Poetry* (1938), the latter of which "had a vast influence on the teaching of verse at American colleges in the forties, fifties, and early sixties; the influence was even greater on the many imitative textbooks it spawned." "In England during the late twenties and early thirties, the most important young poets were W. H. Auden [22], Stephen

Spender [7], Louise MacNiece [11], and C. Day Lewis [4]," who, "eager to express radical political attitudes, preferred to do so through older verse techniques."

The sun continues to set. We are now in that period called "Poetry from 1945 to 1975," which is introduced as follows: "During and immediately after the Second World War, most poets living in the United States came to write in a way that poets of the twenties and critics of the thirties had prepared for them." I believe we are to understand here that *The Fugitives* and the Auden group were the overwhelming influence on post WW II American poetry. In reaction to Dylan Thomas's [9] "apocalyptic mode," "a loose association of university poets who called themselves, badly, 'The Movement'"—Amis [6], and Larkin [14]—favored wit "over prophecy and extravagance, urban and suburban realities over the urbane." "For some years after the war the esthetic of the New Criticism helped to shape most new American verse." "The qualities it enshrined, such as metaphysical wit, an irony too complex to permit strong commitments, and a technique which often calls attention to its own dexterity, are characteristic elements of what its detractors called an academic style." Effected were: Jarrell [10], Eberhart [6], Shapiro [5], Roethke [11], Lowell [16], Berryman [6], Bishop [14], Wilbur [13] Nemerov [7], Miles [6], Simpson [6], Hecht [8], and Hollander [7]. In reaction, under the "subversive influence" of Williams and Pound, we find Ammons [14], Ginsberg [14], and Creeley [6]; the latter was also "one of the poets who gathered around Charles Olson [7] at Black Mountain College, an experimental and unaccredited school in North Carolina." The Beats—Ginsberg and Ferlinghetti [5]—who "tended to dismiss the Black Mountain poets as too much at ease with authority figures," "found a congenial milieu in San Francisco, where a poetic renaissance had already been fomented within 'the alternative society.'" It included Rexroth [4], Duncan [7], and Snyder [10]. "This kind of poetry came to be known as 'confessional.'" There was also the New York school—O'Hara [6], Ashbery [12], and Koch [14]—these poets "practiced a calculated effrontery and discontinuity of perception." A "new surrealism" (Surrealism being defined as "a mode which exploits as material the distortion imposed upon reality by the unconscious") is found in the poetry of Bly [5], Wright [13], Merwin [8], Strand [5], and Wakoski [11]. By 1959, "it seemed at first that Lowell might himself be becoming a Beat, but in fact his verse is more controlled than it appears." "Other poets who wrote in this intensely autobiographical vein"—Snodgrass [9], Roethke, Berryman, Plath [10], and Rich [17]—"either played against conventional form or wrote free verse in a peculiarly unrelaxed way. These poets are generally melancholy." Black poets of this period are Brooks [13], Baraka [6], and Lorde [8].

We have now reached the present—"Poetry Since 1975"—a decade with no new poetics, experimentation, or American poets of more than modest significance. The late David Kalstone[2] identifies this period (which, quoted, becomes the Norton definition) as one of "personal absences." He means that the main events of this period are: "the deaths of Bishop, Lowell, Wright and Hugo"; "the comparative silence of others"; and the fact that only "four of the more prominent post-1945 writers"—Ashbery, Ammons, Merrill [18], and Rich—"have continued to develop." In summary, "the major poetic innovations and consolidations earlier in the century are now simply history." The closest to anything new is a kind of "regionalism . . . a vigorous use of vivid experience in a particular place: what Richard Hugo [9] called a 'triggering town.'" Other than Carolyn Forché [7], who "places herself and us, strongly, in El Salvador," all of these "regionalists" are Black, Chicana, Chicano, or Native American poets: "Gary Soto [10] in the San Joaquin Valley, Rita Dove [10] in Akron, Ohio, and Cathy Song [10] in small Hawaii towns." Younger women poets "do not always seem impelled to take gender as their central subject." Some, like Cathy Song or Rosanna Warren [4], "make poems out of visual art"; others—Rich, Lorde, Marilyn Hacker [6], and, "in 'Kalaoch,'" Forché—"write about women's love for women." "With all this diversity, it would be hard, if not impossible, to point to poetic trends." "The personal is a prominent subject." "A significant mode is that of the dramatic monologue." "Many recent poets are writing longer poems or poetic sequences, such as Stanley Kunitz's [6] "The Wellfleet Whale," William Everson's [10] "The Poet is Dead," James Dickey's [9] "Falling," and Frank Bidart's [8] "Golden State."[3] The commentary ends with several paragraphs on contemporary Canadian, English, and Irish poets. Al Purdy [5], born in 1918, is identified as Canada's "foremost countercultural spokesman." James Fenton [9] is identified as "having explored the Cambodian wars in terms of a battlefield dinner party." About the leading Ulster poet we are told: "Seamus Heaney [19] has said that the Irish poet cannot hate the English, because without them he would not have their language, his chief resource as a poet."

In the above condensation/pastiche of the Introduction to the *Norton Anthology of Modern Poetry* (second edition, 1988; henceforth, NAMP), I have attempted to raise the primary features into a stark topology. It is worth doing so, because at 1,865 pages (fifty-five lines to the page), given Norton's distributional effectiveness along with the classroom tendency to rely on a single big anthology to be used all semester long, the NAMP, over the next decade, may very well reach more classes than all the individual collections by twentieth-century English language poets combined. Before considering omissions and misrepresentations, I'd like to make a few observations based not only on the 10,000-word Introduction, but on the contents.

In his thoughtful essay on American Poetry Anthologies,[4] Alan Golding, considering the 1975 Norton *Anthology of Poetry*, writes: "they never discuss what governs their choices. Distinctions between 'major poets' and 'their interesting contemporaries' are assumed to be clear and not open to question." Golding also points out that "you can't read a Charles Olson poem in the same way that you read a Richard Wilbur poem. But the structure and purpose of the teaching anthology limit these new ways of reading, perpetuating old ways of reading the new poetry." Both of these objections still hold true for the NAMP, and the limitations they address are a good deal more formidable than they might appear.

Other than the generalization (quoted in the first part of my essay) concerning the fundamental questioning of the objective world, "modern poetry" is not defined, let alone pondered, in the NAMP. If one considers the Objectivists (omitted en masse), Williams, much of Pound, Rexroth, Bunting, Bishop, Snyder, etc., the generalization falls apart. The terms "Modernist" or "Post-Modernist" do not even occur in the Introduction; instead we have such phrases as "modern verse," "the modern movement," which, under the vague precursor categories of Romanticism and Symbolism, are used to include such clearly Victorian figures as Carroll, Bridges, Wilde, Housman, and Kipling, as well as the Georgians, *The Fugitives*, the New Criticism, and ultimately the writing of young writing workshop apprentices who we are told have no relationship to the past, whatever it is. In the NAMP context, "modern" means little more than the poetry written in English over the last one hundred years. This means that anything that appeals to the editors' taste can come in.[5] It means that the book is shipwrecked from the start, because there is no working definition from generation to generation to distinguish the sheep from the goats. And since there is none, and since "teachability" (more on this later) anchors the editors' taste, "traditional verse" (not even "poetry") becomes the book's common denominator. Certainly Whitman, Dickinson, and Hopkins are there, at the beginning, but they are islands in a sea made up of rhymed "verse," much of which is doggerel.

By the 1930s, in order to advance their taste for traditional verse, the editors use the New Criticism, or classroom-oriented professor-poetry, to provide a criterion for mainstream poetry up through the 1980s. The new is continually set up as a reaction to the traditional (with token page allotments to innovative figures who are used to promote a fake "diversity"). There is no glint of awareness that such poets as Olson and Duncan were not reacting to Hardy or Tate, but were building on, advancing in their own ways, the work of such emanational figures as Williams and Pound. A sense of "making it new" is never allowed a foothold as an ongoing transformational force in poetry, and because of this the NAMP emits black light. I have forced myself to read it twice over the past year and a half; never before have I had such difficulty in continuing to read a book. The message is that from Yeats onward, the energy in modern poetry is entropic; while there are occasional disturbances (*The Wasteland, The Cantos,* etc.), the calm we should depend on consists of story-like verse in which a first-person speaker describes an event from the past. If there is any essential change between 1900 and now, it is that flat, conversational workshop poetry has replaced rhymed verse.

Omissions: all of the Objectivists (in the introduction to the six-page Bunting section, Zukofsky is mentioned as one of Bunting's "associates"). All of the figures who kept avant-garde possibilities open between 1914 and 1945, e.g., Arensberg, Brown, Duchamp, Freytag-Loringhoven, Hartley, Loy, Crosby, Fearing, Henri Ford, Gillespie, Jolas, Lowenfels, Cage, Mac Low, Patchen, and Riding.[6] While Post-Modernism is mentioned once, it is not discussed, and there is no indication that such poets as Olson, Ginsberg, Snyder, and Rothenberg represent a turning away from the Anglo-American tradition (toward Third- and Fourth-World cultures, primitives, and the East) that goes beyond the Modernist preoccupation with the Other. Deep Image, Ethnopoetics, Concrete and Visual Poetry, Performance Poetry, and

Language Poetry are not mentioned (meaning that none of their practitioners are included or mentioned either). Such a list of omissions only begins to indicate the NAMP's distortion of twentieth-century American poetic action,[7] and while I dislike making lists of omitted, important poets, I have to do so here to illustrate not just how the Objectivists and the Language Poets have been erased, but how many other innovative directions have had their principle figures omitted, and how movements in part acknowledged by the NAMP editors ("the Black Mountain poets," "the Sun Francisco poets") have been undermined and diminished through the refusal to include most of the poets who gave such movements their solidity.

Zukofsky	Lamantia	Wieners
Oppen	McClure	Tarn
Reznikoff	Whalen	Padgett
Rakosi	Corman	Coolidge
Riding	Corso	Sobin
Loy	Guest	Sanders
Bronk	Bukowski	Simic
Blackburn	Schuyler	Taggart
Eigner	J. Williams	Bromige
Dorn	E. Williams	Cortez
Kerouac	L. Anderson	Ortiz
Niedecker	Berrigan	Reed
Cage	Rothenberg	Henderson
Mac Low	Kelly	Cruz
Spicer	Antin	Irby
Blaser	Lansing	F. Howe
Palmer	Silliman	S. Howe
C. K. Williams	Hejinian	R. Johnson
Bernstein	Perelman	Kleinzahler
Schwerner	DuPlessis	Grahn

Thirty years ago, it was customary to make a simplistic, dualistic distinction between academic, or closed, poetry and experimental, or open, poetry. In his 1960 acceptance speech for the National Book Award, Lowell appropriated Claude Levi-Strauss's distinction between the raw and the cooked. One wonders how Lowell saw himself. For the author of *Life Studies*, raw poetry was "huge blood-dripping gobbets of unseasoned experience dished up for midnight listeners," while cooked was "a poetry that can only be studied." Even for the early sixties, Lowell's distinction is suspect, if not outright sloppy. *Howl* might have some blood in it, but the experience was hardly unseasoned; is Oppen cooked or raw? Spicer? Corman? Implicit in the old distinction is the idea that the experimental is thoughtless, and inappropriate for study. Thus, a false distinction, loaded as usual against the new.

In the NAMP section introduction to Wilbur, this distinction is referred to with the following elaboration: "Wilbur's poetry is elaborately cooked, or, to elevate the metaphor, he is Apollonian while Lowell is Dionysian: that is, he centers his work in the achievement of illuminated, controlled moments rather than in sudden immersions in chaos and despair." Again, a fake distinction (even for Lowell: all of *Life Studies* is "illuminated, controlled moments" regardless of Lowell's neuroticism). The new twist here is that "chaos and despair" have now been added to the experimental's burden of unseasoned experience, or thoughtlessness and its failure to reward study. It is as if we are now watching anything that is confrontational, up front about experience (meaning some of it is bound to be negative, or despairing, given the world we all live in) sink out of sight, with the outright lie that such poetry does not reward study. Anyone aware of post–WW II poetry knows that certain avant-garde poetries, based on international research, are more ideological than academic mainstream writing (writing found in *The New Yorker*, *APR*, *Poetry* (Chicago), the Knopf series, the last 200 pages of NAMP, etc.). From all this I conclude that the contemporary equivalent of *The Waste Land* of "Canto VII" would not stand a chance of getting into the NAMP (or virtually any other teaching-oriented anthology). I take Hugo's remark that I have used as an epigram to this essay very seriously: if one expects to be anthologized (and taught, etc.), one's poetry should know very little—it should not be emotionally confrontational, seriously critical of government and society, or imaginatively dense. While one may find mid-career Ivor Winter's too logical and dry, it is, in comparison to the last several hundred pages of the NAMP, extraordinarily thoughtful, and "difficult." In 1960, it would have been considered "academic." Today, textbook-anthology-wise, while it would not be thought of as raw or experimental, it would be dismissed, and were its intensity to be performed without regular rhythms, stanzas, and rhymes, it would be judged chaotic, and in effect be judged, and treated, like the poetry of William Bronk, Robert Kelly, or Ron Silliman.

Not only is the idea of the new and the old perverted in the NAMP, but the seemingly clear distinction between the omitted and the included has several subtexts. The NAMP is able to perpetuate old ways of reading new poetry not only by setting up the new as an unsatisfactory reaction against the old, but also by leaving out key new texts that, were they to be present, would make it much more difficult for the new to be misread. To this we must also add the number of pages allotted to each author, which, more often than not, is used to imply that uncanonized authors of the new are worth less attention than more traditional and teachable poets. To examine this in detail would extend this essay beyond what seems appropriate here. What follows are some examples, which could be multiplied fourfold in terms of the book at large.

Whitman's [23] "Song of Myself," which understandably opens the book, lacks stanzas 15 through 45, or over half of a masterpiece that would have taken up all of 24 pages had the entire 1855 version been printed.

The Dickinson [8] section, includes several trivial poems, but omits a number of major works, including my candidate for the single finest nineteenth-century lyric, "My Life had stood—a Loaded Gun."

The four pages of Stein make her look like an oddball instead of a writer whose language and composition still test the limits of poetry.

The Stevens [23] section has all the early "teachable" poems we have seen in anthologies for years. It includes 21 lines from *Transport to Summer*, and 18 lines from *Auroras of Autumn*, his two greatest collections.

Both Bunting and MacDiarmid are utterly falsified. Bunting's section lacks the extraordinary "Chomei at Toyama," and MacDiarmid's gives no indication whatsoever that he is the author of "On a Raised Beach" and "In Memoriam James Joyce."

Keeping in mind that Olson's more traditional contemporaries (Auden and Lowell) are presented with their major works, it seems grossly unfair that the small Olson section omits "The Kingfishers" (the Post-Modernist equivalent to *The Waste Land*), "In Cold Hell," "The chain of memory is resurrection," and selections from the last three-quarters of *The Maximus Poems*.

In the table of contents, Ginsberg's *Howl* is listed as "Howl." One presumes this means the complete *Howl*. Turning to the Ginsberg section, we find that *Howl* Parts II and III are not there. Part II is arguably the finest two pages in all of Ginsberg. One wonders if the phrase "Cocksucker in Moloch!" kept it out of the NAMP.

The Duncan section is a disaster. Its seven pages include several early lyrics, a 10-line poem from *Bending the Bow*, and three of the slightest pieces from *Groundwork I*. Missing: "Poem Beginning with a Line by Pindar," "My Mother would be a Falconress," "Uprising" (the greatest of the anti–Vietnam War poems), and everything from "The Tribunals" and "The Regulators," the two major sequences in *Groundwork*.

Looking at the NAMP from the viewpoint of page allotment, one encounters one bizarre juxtaposition after another. Is it possible that Rita Dove is more than twice as significant as Hugh MacDiarmid? Do Hopkins [16] and Richard Howard [16] really deserve the same number of pages? Is it possible that Gary Soto is more significant than Emily Dickinson? Lorna Dee Cervantes [6], the author of a single book (1981), is offered the same amount of pages as Bunting. Gavin Ewart [7], an English author of sexist doggerel, receives more than twice the pages alloted to Samuel Beckett [3].

One might inquire of John Benedict, the Senior Norton Editor whose presence is often felt in the NAMP (he appears in footnotes as the recipient of author query responses), why the late Ellmann and O'Clair were contracted to edit such a book. The superficial answer seems to be that both men coedited the 1973 Norton *Anthology of Modern Poetry* and the 1976 Norton *Modern Poems: An Introduction to Poetry*. O'Clair appears to have been a Victorian scholar who never published a single book or article of his own (according to *Contemporary Authors*, Vol. 77–80). The only clue in the NAMP as to why O'Clair was involved in such projects is the following sentence in the Preface: "In making selections of all poets and poems, the editors were guided by the responses of the many teachers who have used the earlier edition, as well as by Robert O'Clair's unerring sense of how well a poem works in the classroom."[8] Other than offering a rather meager explanation for O'Clair's right to codetermine what millions of college students are to read in the name of poetry, the statement implies that the entire organization of the NAMP is primarily determined by what O'Clair and other teachers consider to be easy to teach, and secondarily determined by what the editors believe is the most masterful writing. Does this explain the omission of such poets as Zukofsky and Mac Low? In a publicity brochure for the Third Edition of *The Norton Anthology of American Literature* (1989), the slightest revised Olson section is identified as "an accessible offering of *The Maximus Poems*."

As for Ellmann, most readers will know that he is an emminent scholar of Irish Literature, with several acclaimed books on Yeats and Joyce, and in his last period, a biography of Wilde. The uncomfortable question is: could Ellmann, in the 1980s, ill, living at Oxford, working on Wilde, have kept up with contemporary poetry?

Going back to the Preface, we also read: "We have provided liberal annotation, translating phrases from foreign languages and explaining allusions when they are not common knowledge, so that every poem can be read without recourse to reference books." The intention here seems to be to save the student from his dictionary and ultimately from the library itself. Such "translations" and "explanations" often result in one-word synonyms. In Stevens' "A High-Toned Old Christian Woman," nine words are footnoted: they are nave, citherns, peristyle, masque, bawdiness, palms, flagellants, muzzy, and spheres. I have several problems with this annotation. The movement from poem to reference book takes time; such time is valuable for assimilation and exploration of the unknown word. To glance down at the bottom of the NAMP page takes a second. One look down from "muzzy," spots "3. Confused" and bounces back into the Stevens line. "Muzzy," I propose, has not registered in the way it might had an International Dictionary been opened to the appropriate page. In my Second Edition Webster's, I find: "Dull-spirited; muddled or confused in mind; stupid with drink," and I also note that "muzzy" is connected with "to muzzle:" "Dial. Eng. *a*) To root or grub with the muzzle, or snout; said esp. of pigs. *b*) To muffle, esp. church bells. *c*) To make muzzy. *d*) To handle roughly; maul; thrash." In the next Stevens poem, "The Emperor of Ice-Cream," the phrase "cups concupiscent curds" is footnoted as "Literally, lustful milk solids." All the work has been taken away from the reader; he can say, oh, that is what that mysterious phrase means—and glide on. Such a "translation" erases the difficulty, and releases the reader from the crucial activity of recomposing the metaphor on his own terms (or finding it opaque, or silly, or whatever). On the other hand, it is appropriate to footnote "Bickfords" in "Howl I," and to offer some information on words that are not in International Dictionaries. NAMP's procedure wavers in these respects: at times, fairly common words are footnoted—at other times, very esoteric words receive no annotation. I counted over two dozen typographical errors, and some errors in verifiable information, such as Hart Crane's death year, and the misidentification of the Martinician poet Aimé Césaire as "a Congolese writer."

* * *

Beckett's three pages in the NAMP are filled with his early poetry, of some interest, but only tangential to the vision by which he is recognized. Joyce is also in the book; his eight pages are split between early verse, and the "Anna Livia Plurabelle" passage from *Finnegans Wake*, with footnotage rising like water in a sinking ship. The presence of Beckett and Joyce cause me to question: should they even be in a book that purports to cover "modern poetry," and if so, shouldn't they be represented by their pathbreaking writing? An insight of Hugh Kenner's is useful to bring in here. In his essay "The Making of the Modernist Canon,"[9] he cites F. R. Leavis' *New Bearings in English Poetry* (1931) as the first attempt to canonize Hopkins, Eliot, and Pound, and then points out that Leavis' subsequent dismissal of Eliot and Joyce was based on an ignorance of two things of great scope: 1) the unprecedented interdependence of prose Modernism and verse Modernism, and 2) awareness that the English language, by 1931, had split four ways, leaving English natives in control of but a fraction. Kenner proposes that by 1925, three countries—Ireland, America, England—were conducting substantial national literatures and that by mid-century there was a fourth center, "locatable in books but on no map: International Modernism." For Kenner, the four masterpieces of Modernism are *Ulysses*, *The Waste Land*, the first 30 *Cantos*, and *Waiting for Godot* (two Americans—two Irishmen—no Englishmen). Kenner's "split" illuminates the extent to which the energy of the new had left geographical England. Like Leavis, the NAMP appears to be ignorant of this development (in 1988).

In my view, if one adds Post-Modernism, there is a fifth split-off, as of 1949, the year of "The Kingfishers." Or we could say that International Modernism turns out to have a much wider thrust in time and space than Kenner calculates. Whether one sees Post-Modernism as a distinct "new wave" of Modernism, or the two as facets of International Modernism, one thing is clear: the movement is not confined to the English language alone. If we agree with Kenner regarding the interdependence of prose and verse, then sections of *Ulysses* and *Waiting for Godot* are prime candidates for a text that addresses the "split" English language. If we acknowledge that the domain of International Modernism is a "floating world" of the imagination, then we may salute 1922 not only as the year of Eliot's and Joyce's masterpieces, but also of Vallejo's *Trilce* and Rilke's *The Duino Elegies*. And with these two new additions, we may also agree that any representative International Modernism text would also have to represent the likes of Breton, Césaire, Artaud, Mayakofsky, Mandelstam, Cendrars, Neruda, Paz, Celan, Radnoti, Holan, Lorca, Borges, and Genet. To do so would be to shrink the English-language list to only those writers who have made genuinely innovative contributions to International Modernism. What a grand book—or two books—it could be. All of the above have been by now, at least in part, excellently translated. My guess is that the phenomenon could be displayed in a NAMP-sized book, and were they to spend a year with it, students might well emerge with a revolutionarily complete sense of the diversity and range of twentieth-century writing.

While I believe that such a book might be possible by the end of the century, it still does not seem just around the corner, and until we get to it, there are a couple of lesser but quite meaningful American anthology projects (I am not going to argue here against anthologies per se; while I don't currently use them myself, I know that thousands of professors do, and will continue to; I propose instead that they be offered something more dynamic than the anthologies that are available right now).

1. An expanded and updated version of Don Allen's *The New American Poetry* (1960)[10]—a book that would cover 1960 to 1990. Besides poets whose work began to appear in this period, it might resourcefully contain advances by writers who broke new ground earlier. The fact that no book like this exists now shows to what extent the NAMP and its kin dominate the poetry textbook anthology market.

2. An expanded and updated version of the Leary/Kelly *Controversy of Poets* (1965). It would be very interesting for students to have twenty pages of the best Olson set side by side with twenty pages of the best Lowell, etc., in such a way that the cards were not stacked in favor of one writer against another.

Until such books appear, the anthology atmosphere is grim indeed. For the NAMP, the sun rose and set a long time ago, leaving poets in a kind of changeless Scandinavian winter light. As we sit at our desks, a figure shuffles by our window daily with Kantian regularity. It is the spectre of Philip Larkin, intoning:

Give me your arm, old toad;
Help me down Cemetery Road.

NOTES

1. The bracketed numbers are the number of pages given a specific author in the NAMP *(Norton Anthology of Modern Poetry)*. I include opening and closing pages even though they may not be full pages. Such page allotments clearly represent the NAMP hierarchy (Yeats at 5 is 21 pages more than Williams at 34—with 3 pages, Edwin Honig, Bernard Spencer, and Beckett are the low—the average allotment must be around 10 pages). Contemporary American poets with 10 pages or more are Merrill, Howard, Rich, Everson, Brooks, Wilbur, Levertov, Koch, Ammons, Ginsberg, Ashbery, Wright, Walcott, Wakoski, Harper, Pinsky, Soto, Dove, and Song.

2. Kalstone is quoted here probably because along with Patricia B. Wallace he was coeditor of the "American Poetry Since 1945" section of the 1989 *Norton Anthology of American Literature* (Third Edition, Volume 2). While there is, because of understandable space limitations, less post–WW II American poetry in the NAAL than in the NAMP, someone—Wallace perhaps—has added Niedecker, a couple of late *Maximus* poems, Duncan's "Poem Beginning with a Line by Pindar," Creeley's "The Finger," and Snyder's "The Blue Sky." Although the overview of post–WW II poetry is essentially that of the NAMP, such additions are a start in offering a more realistic picture of the period's innovations. However, on the back of the volume, as part of the blurb material announcing changes and amplifications, we find the following line: "Poets of the 'Objectivist school'—Lorine Niedecker, Robert Duncan, Robert Creeley." When it comes to the avant-garde, it is as if Norton can never get things right.

3. What the Introduction does not tell the reader is that these "long poems" are 138, 190, 175, and 270 lines long, not even "middle length" poems by current long poems standards. This is a typical NAMP maneuver, to identify and at the same time utterly misrepresent a genre. We live in an era that includes Zukofsky's 803-page *A*, Olson's 634-page *The Maximus Poems*, and Kelly's 415-page *The Loom*.

4. "A History of American Poetry Anthologies," in *Canons*, ed. Robert von Hallberg, University of Chicago Press, Chicago, 1984, p. 302.

5. In 1928 Robert Graves and Laura Riding published *A Pamphlet Against Anthologies*, a 200-page book that, while dated, is very well written and filled with pithy observations that are still pertinent. Here is their paragraph on "taste": "The greater the intergrity of the private anthology, particularly when the author is a well-known poet, the more dangerous it is when put on the market: by its publication it appears to be on an act of criticism instead of a mere expression of taste. Taste is the judgment an individual makes of a thing according to its fitness in his private scheme of life. Criticism is the judgment that an individual makes of a thing according to its fitness to itself, its excellence as compared with things like itself, regardless of its application to his private scheme of life. With taste, a poem is good because it is liked; with criticism, it is good because it is good. Now, it is not objectionable for a person who has not sufficient originality to make his own criticism to accept another's; for criticism, unlike taste, which is arbitrary opinion, can be tested. The criticism of one person thus accepted can become another person's taste. But for one person to accept another's taste deprives the former of self-respect. Our charge against anthologies is, then, that they have robbed the poetry-reading public of self-respect."

6. I am indebted to Jerome Rothenberg's *Revolution of the Word* (Seabury Press, New York, 1974—now out of print) for a mapping of American avant-garde poetry between the two world wars. Some of these writers also appear in the Rothen-

berg/Quasha *America a Prophecy* anthology (Random House, New York, 1973 — also out of print), which displays an even larger dimension of poetic activity. The current teaching anthologies offer little or no indication that the poetic spirit is originally, and essentially, bound up with song, dance, and ritual, and that for tribal societies it is communal and central to the life view of all involved.

7. I have focused on American poets in this regard because while NAMP makes gestures to Canadian, Irish, and Australian poetry, the anthology is essentially about American poetry with English poetry presented as a kind of "curtailing angel" around American writing. I should point out, however, that the NAMP gives no indication of any innovative non–American based poetry after Lawrence, Bunting, and MacDiarmid. A more complete "omission list" would have to include such non-American poets as Peter Redgrove, Jeremy Prynne, Allen Fisher, Pierre Joris, Daphne Marlatt, Steve McCaffrey, BP Nichol, Roy Fisher, Ian Hamilton Finlay, Tom Raworth, Edward Brathwaite, and Kofi Awoonor, among others.

8. Hugh Kenner's remarks on the New Criticism in his "The Making of the Modernist Canon" (*Mazes*, North Point Press, San Francisco, 1989, p. 38) contextualize O'Clair's classroom actvities: "It was in 1947, under Marshall McLuhan's informal tutelage, that I first became aware of my own century. Such a lag was perhaps possible only in Canada. By then an American movement called the New Criticism was enjoying its heyday. Like most critical stirrings on this self-improving continent, it was almost wholly a classroom movement. Stressing as it did Wit, Tension, and Irony, it enabled teachers to say classroom things about certain kinds of poems. Donne was a handy poet for its purposes; so was Eliot; so, too, was the post-1916 Yeats. Thus Eliot and the later Yeats became living poets, and a few Americans such as Richard Eberhart, also a few Englishmen, e.g., William Empson. The Pound *of Mauberley* was (barely) part of the canon, 1920 having been Pound's brief moment of being almost like Eliot, tentative and an ironist. But when Pound was working in his normal way, by lapidary *statement*, New Critics could find nothing whatsoever to say about him. Since 'Being-able-to-say about' is a pedagogic criterion, he was largely absent from a canon pedagogues were defining. So was Williams, and wholly. What can Wit, Tension, Irony enable you to say about 'The Red Wheelbarrow'? 'So much depends . . .' says the poem, and seems to *mean* it; for a New Critic that was too naive for words. I can still see Marshall chucking aside a mint copy of *Paterson I*, with the words 'pretty feeble.'"

9. "The Making of the Modernist Canon," pp. 31–34.

10. Allen's anthology was updated, with the help of George Butterick, as *The Post-Moderns* (Grove Press, New York, 1982). Rothenberg argues in a review of the new version (*Sulfur* #6, 1983, pp. 181–90), that it is not successful. Not only are a number of significant individual poets left out, but according to Rothenberg many of the new "alternative poetic strategies . . . ." "Concrete & Visual Poetry, The New Performance Poetry, The 2nd or 3rd Generation New York School, The New Black Poetry, Indian Poetry, Latino Poetry, The 'Language' Poets, and The Poem in Prose: The 'New Sentence' (R. Silliman)" are not included.

ADDENDUM, 2001

In 1994, Norton published *Postmodern American Poetry*, edited by Paul Hoover, with short selections of 104 poets, only a few of which are in the book that is the subject of my 1990 polemic. The *Postmodern* anthology might appear to redeem Norton from some of its chronic refusal, over many years, to acknowledge and include innovative/experimental American poetry in its widely disseminated anthologies that determine what many undergraduate college students will read. However, it seems to me that the *Postmodern* anthology is a token gesture. It is only when Norton brings out a large, general anthology that in a nontoken way includes "postmodern poetry" that my "Gospel" will become irrelevant to contemporary poetics.

Complexities of Witness

In his review of my book *Under World Arrest* (*Small Press*, summer 1995), Michael Duff contests the effectiveness of a poem on the beating of Rodney King (a video that was replayed for weeks, King beaten again and again, in contrast to the almost bodiless Gulf War on TV). He also dislikes some poems he does not name that "excoriate American leaders." I am not particularly bothered by Duff's criticism, since I know that the political poem in America is always in a state of disputed effectiveness. I would like to take his comments as a point of departure to reflect on some of the problems that arise when a poet attempts to, as directly as is possible, address war and violence at large.

Robert Duncan wrote some of the most commanding political poetry of the late 1960s—in particular "Up Rising" (linking Johnson with Hitler and Stalin, as Johnson intensified the American bombing in Vietnam) and his variation on Southwell's "The Burning Babe" (written in 1595), in which Duncan responded to horrifying photos of napalamed Vietnamese girls, which had been suppressed from *Ramparts* but published in my magazine, *Caterpillar.* Yet Duncan's response to a Denise Levertov poem ("Life at War") about the same war was to charge Levertov with projecting a personal and unresolved problem into what many readers felt was a realistic response to the war. "Delicate man," Levertov wrote,

> still turns without surprise, with mere regret to the scheduled breaking open of breasts whose milk runs out over the entrails of still-alive babies, transformation of witnessing eyes to pulp-fragments, implosion of skinned penises into carcass-gulleys.

This essay appeared in Sulfur #37, 1995.

In a letter to Levertov (quoted in her essay "Some Duncan Letters—A Memoir and a Critical Tribute"), Duncan quoted this stanza and commented: "the words in their lines are the clotted mass of some operation . . . having what roots in you I wonder? Striving to find place in a story beyond the immediate."

In the same period, Duncan also attacked James Dickey (in Duncan's essay "Man's Fulfillment in Conflict and Strife," in which he justifies writing "Up Rising" and discusses its background and borrowings). Citing a few lines from Dickey's poem "The Fire-Bombing," Duncan wrote: "'The Fire-Bombing' dwells on [Dickey's] own fantasies, fed by his actual missions over Japan in the Second World War . . . the poet projects an exultant and fearful inner reality . . . exultant in his hostile cravings for destructive power"—as if Duncan, as the author of "My Mother Would Be a Falconress," did not have a "fearful inner reality" of his own!

In both criticisms, Duncan proposed that Levertov and Dickey were mainly revealing something ugly about themselves. Levertov was responding to news reports; Dickey was recounting what Michael Palmer would call a witnessing (which involved the fire-bombing, by Dickey and others, of Japanese villages).

It is hard to say who has more subjective room. Levertov has the whole range of news information, and one could argue that such a range of selectivity allows for a greater subjectivity on her part (through which projections can emerge). Yet anyone following the war in those days with a critical eye toward what our government was doing knew that Levertov was not making up sliced breasts, pulped eyes, and skinned penises. Via the network established by some five hundred New York City artists involved in "Angry Arts," we knew that stuff was going on over there that was more hideous than we could see on TV or find in any mass circulation magazine. I refer the reader here to Douglas Kahn's essay "Body Lags" (*City Lights Review* #5), in which, among other shocking revelations, Kahn writes that the true story of what went on in Vietnam is buried in Vietnam vets' attics in shoeboxes: snapshots of necromutilation.

Let's say Dickey *is* exulting over enemy destruction—is it fair to generalize, as Duncan appears to have done, that such reveals "hostile cravings for destructive power?" Should Dickey have kept his mouth shut about what turned him on and written poems (as did many American poets involved in Word War II) that pretended that no violation of the human had occurred?

Poetry is still regarded by many as a sacred cow domain, or Sunday museum, in which X may be exposed but only certain conditions and in certain ways. Is American poetry then still prisoner of a genteel English tradition that Owen and Lawrence, for example, tried to abolish? Or is there something paddling about in the Puritan depths of the American poet that says: hold off in really saying it as you imagine it to be. From such a perspective, Whitman's guarded openness seems heroic. Are we not called upon today to go at least as far from what is conventionally acceptable as Whitman went from Victorian dissimulation?

No one I know or have read has implied that Mark Danner's book-length exposé of the El Mozote massacre in Salvador revealed anything ugly about Danner. Is this because, in Danner's case, we credit him with an objectivity that, when psyche comes into play, we refuse?

Alas, news reports are as unstable in their own way as psyche is in hers. One can argue that when psyche comes into play, a significant additional aspect of the human becomes involved. Secretly, we know that all are monstrous in psyche. Psyche is an inverse panopticon: as she reveals self, there is no place, in Rilke's words, "that does not see you." Also keep in mind that all so-called "objective reports" come via the bodies and minds of human beings. The media filter system (much more complicated than book publishing) is a political mine field of priorities and agendas. How do we know who is telling the truth? Poetry is interesting in this regard, for *because of* its excessive subjectivity the truth of a given matter can often be detected.

The last focused period for political poetry in America was the late 1960s. While significant political poetry has been written over the past twenty-five years (Baraka, Rothenberg, Rich, Grahn, Duncan, and Cortez immediately come to mind), it has been an isolated response in contrast to the coalescing of collective conscience in the late 1960s. The 1960s were, politically speaking in the arts, a burgeoning; the seeds and early growths are in the late 1940s and the otherwise flat-footed 1950s. Does it take a prolonged war (with significant American loss) to give heft to a politically effective art? Aesthetically speaking, over the past twenty-five years, poetic energy has undergone the division between writing workshop displays of self-sensitivity and an inventive yet nonreferential Language Poetry that declares itself political but refuses to work with event in the poem itself.

In a recent interview with Michael Palmer *(Exact Change Yearbook 1995)*, Peter Gizzi mentions that he understands Palmer's "The Circular

Gates" (1974) "as a poem constructed out of the Vietnamese War."
Palmer agrees, so I went back to the poem. While such phrases as
"Some talk of war" and "Sometimes we are at war" occur here and there
in this fifteen-page poem, Vietnam is not mentioned, nor are there any
images or references in the poem that would link it to a concern with the
Vietnamese War. Palmer's commentary following Gizzi's description of
"The Circular Gates" is interesting and worth our attention:

> It was very much so; I was looking for a means of representation that I
> could feel honest with. In other words, I think one of the problems of an
> overtly political poetry now is something that Octavio Paz has brought
> up, that so much of it has to do with newspaper reports and so little of it
> has to do with witness. We look at the powerful poems of witness of this
> century and they are not about newspaper reports, and they're not about
> proposing one's particular *point de repère*, point of view, position, so much
> as facing something that may even overwhelm the poetic sign in its mul-
> tiplicity of meanings, something often horrible. The American tendency
> is to read our politics out of these distant events and then to write some
> almost self-congratulatory oppositional work. And so what I tried to face
> (speaking of "Seven Poems within a Matrix of War" now) was, what did
> we experience of that thing—which was the overwhelming flood of im-
> ages, the controlled imagery that was poured over us, whether that be
> the exploding suns over Baghdad on the CNN nightly news, or . . .

It would be interesting to have the full Paz statement,[1] for in Palmer's
comments its significance is hard to grasp. Since Paz has become increasingly conservative as he has aged,[2] the chances are that the "something" Palmer is recalling is not in support of abrasive political poetry.

Palmer's distinction between witness and newspaper report (à la Paz)
seems unrealistic to me. Significant poems solely based on direct witness, such as Radnoti's or Owen's, are more rare than one might think.
Vallejo relied mainly on newspaper and radio reports, or word of
mouth, even though he was in Spain at the time (1937) and did visit the
Madrid front, to write *España, aparta de mí este cáliz*. Neruda's huge
Canto general is a mix of witnessing and historical research. Celan's
poetry, the fruit of the death camps, is an utter entanglement of witnessing, memory, hermeticism, literary reference, and attack on the
German language. As Jed Rasula has perceptively noted: "With Celan,
the German language itself becomes the means of its own disembodi-
ment. In his hands, more and more of the language simply goes up in
smoke. . . . A prick from a rose killed Rilke. Celan writes as if an entire
crown of roses were being held in place in his mouth. Beauty is bloody."

I wonder where Palmer would place Duncan's "Up Rising." Since Duncan never visited Vietnam, the poem is not one of direct witnessing. Yet as Duncan has written: "Riding the wave at once of my own high blood pressure—a physical disorder I was ignorant of at the time but to which the poem refers clearly—and of my outrage in the 'high blood pressure' attack of the American government on Vietnam . . . I saw Johnson as the demotic leader, unleashing into action and moved by the secret evil of American karma as Hitler or Stalin had impersonated the evil karma of Germany or Russia." Thus the "Up Rising" of the poem's title is, again in Duncan's words, "multiphasic." It draws on the whole man, and could qualify as one of "the powerful poems of witness of this century."

Palmer proposes that when an unwitnessed political event is engaged directly in a poem the result may be "self-congratulatory oppositional work." Here the problem of self-projection raised by Duncan reading Levertov takes on a new twist: the media blizzard that Palmer later in the interview calls "hallucinatory" produces a poem that is deflected from the political into a space possessed by the non-sequitor information storm of truth and lies. It is as if a new purgatory, a postmodernist DMZ, has insinuated itself between the poet and some event out there. This purgatory is multifaceted: while it is packed with cul-de-sacs, it is also permeated with global information on a scale undreamed of before the Vietnamese War. W. H. Auden, in his essay "The Poet and the City" (1962), a bit dated but still sharp and unnerving, discussed the increasing difficulty in poets using public figures as themes for poetry "because the good or evil they do depends less upon their characters and intentions than upon the quantity of impersonal force at their disposal."

In the so-called "Gulf War" (Chomsky referred to it as a "form of international terrorism"), "impersonal force" was presented as a video game, intercut with information-screened press conferences. It was awful, as awful in its own way as the "war," but somehow many of us figured out what *was* going on, and six months later, via books and magazine articles, I, for one, felt I had enough solid information on which to make a response, goaded by the fact that I was originally, in the months before our invasion, taken in by the media hype of Iraq's awesome military power.

Both Palmer and I look out workroom windows and see healthy trees and hear chirping birds. As white middle-class males, our immediate environment is almost always at odds with much of what pierces it via the information storm. As Americans, especially as white ones, we have permission to say anything in print that we want to say (with the recent qualification that what we say may be ignored because we are white American males). Our lives and the lives of our families will not be imperiled by anything we declare. We are thus permitted to live in a kind of cocoon through which odorless information zips, a significant amount of which implies, and mortifies, us as citizens. We do not depend on newspaper reports: we "witness" via TV, as witnesses twice removed. Unlike Aimé Césaire, say, we do not have the opportunity to speak for those who cannot speak for themselves or write.[3] We primarily speak for, and to, ourselves.

At the same time, no one is shooting at us—yet. Like at least some of our admired predecessors, we are able to daily engage the ancient adventure of not only attempting to "know ourselves" but of working on and contesting a self in poetry. These opportunities must not go unacknowledged. In comparison to writers in such diverse places as China, Algeria, and Yugoslavia, we are left alone, financially sufficient, and our books somehow get published. However—and here I must speak solely for myself—I feel an absolute obligation to pull some of the offended outside I am implicated in through the information purgatory and push it to the fore in my poetry. I really do not care if it offends people even to the extent of leading them to dismiss all that I have done.

Paz's preference for a political poetry of direct witness, taken up by Palmer, is sounded throughout what may be the largest gathering of such poetry ever assembled into a single volume: Carolyn Forché's *Against Forgetting: Twentieth Century Poetry of Witness*, an 800-page anthology with 145 poets. Forché believes that for significant political poetry to occur, the poet must have directly experienced one or more of the following conditions: "exile, state censorship, political persecution, house arrest, torture, imprisonment, military occupation, warfare, and assassination." At the same time, she states that political poetry may involve the "personal" (which she inadequately defines as "lyrics of love and emotional loss") and does *not* have to address the "extreme conditions" she has insisted the political poet must have experienced. She adds that she "was interested in what these poets wrote, regardless of the explicit content."

One implication of these somewhat confusing statements is that poems that would not strike one as political would qualify for inclusion as long as they had been written by someone who had been exiled, say, or had spent time in the army. In contrast, a powerful political poem written by someone who had not met at least one of Forché's personal experience criteria would not be, in effect, significantly political. I also wonder about "assassination." According to Forché, were a poet to be assassinated, his prior poetry would qualify as being political.

At the beginning of each poet's section, Forché offers a brief biographical note that identifies the "experience of extremity" justifying the poet's inclusion. On the basis of these notes I came up with the following figures:

Forty-five of the poets had a "military occupation," which often involved "warfare" (and, I presume, killing).

Forty-eight of the poets were "imprisoned," or "under house arrest," sometimes "tortured," and in six cases "assassinated."

Fourteen of the poets were either briefly or for an extended period of time in "exile." Some of those exiled (St. John Perse is a good example) were self-exiled, lived well in exile, and continued to remain in their country of exile after they could have safely returned home.

This leaves us with thirty-eight poets, some of whom appear to have experienced "state censorship" or "political persecution." The latter category is so broad as to nearly be irrelevant; e.g., in America, nearly every minority writer would fall into this category. Thus Ray A. Young Bear is identified as simply having lived in the Mesquakie Tribal Settlement, having taught at several universities, and as being a singer and the cofounder of a dance troupe. In other cases, the "political persecution" does not strike me, on the basis of the information given, as being "extreme." Wislawa Szymborska's first book "was deemed incomprehensible and overly morbid by the Communist government." Nicanor Parra "refused to leave Chile after the coup that brought Pinochet to power." Adonis is included on the basis of work that is "marked by a strongly nontraditional sense of social commitment." No "experience of extremity" is noted in his or several other cases.

While pondering this group of poets—which make up between one quarter and one third of the book—I realized that with very few exceptions every poet I consider to be impressive could have found his or her way into this group. Forché herself acknowledges in her introduction that "When I began this project, I was hard pressed to find a significant poet who could not be included, who in some important way or another did *not* bear witness to the ravages of our time." Then, needing to constrict this openness to a focus that would justify those who were included, she writes: "I decided to limit the poets in the anthology to those for whom the social had been irrevocably invaded by the political in ways that were sanctioned neither by law nor by the fiction of the social contract." "The social" is a curious phrase to use here; does she mean "their lives"? Clearly, such an invasion means one thing for Otto René Castillo, a Guatemalan poet who was incarcerated, tortured, and burned alive—and something else for Young Bear, Adonis, Parra, or for Sipho Sepamla whose biographical note, in its entirety, reads: "Born in Krugersdorf, South Africa, trained as a teacher. A prizewinning writer of fiction as well as poetry, he is director of the Federated Union of Black Arts in Johannesburg."

In other words, Forché seems to make up rules as she goes along, making many of her inclusions seem arbitrary and primarily based on her taste. Even though aspects of the contributor information indicate that a vague kind of political correctness is involved, many omitted poets could have been included on that same arbitrary basis. While reading the anthology (and without doing any research), I came up with a significant list of omissions, some of which are shocking, and some of which could have been included using Forché's criteria.

Artaud	Duncan	Perelman
Bly	Enzensberger	Rexroth
Braithwaite	Ginsberg	Reznikoff
Cardinal	Gunn	Rich
Cendrars	Grahn	Rothenberg
Césaire	N. Guillen	Sanders
Cortez	Jeffers	Snyder
Csoori	MacDiarmid	U'Tamsi
Depestre	Mac Low	Waldman
Dickey	Pasolini	C. K. Williams
Dorn	Paz	

Granted, everyone will have his list of omissions. However, the absence of Artaud, Césaire, Ginsberg, Pasolini, and Reznikoff is serious enough to throw the authenticity of the anthology into question.

Under one guise of restricting her inclusions to poets who directly experienced violence, generally in war, Forché has acted as if conscientious objection (Rexroth), ecology (Snyder), gay liberation (Gunn, Rich, Grahn) or women's rights (Cortez) are not significant witnessing. Given her emphasis on "extreme conditions" (the word "extreme" is the key word in her introduction), how is it that Artaud, aptly defined by Susan Sontag as "one of the great daring mapmakers of consciousness *in extremis*," is not included?

The answer to such a question has several facets. Forché's section divisions, from *The Armenian Genocide* to the final *Revolutions and the Struggle for Democracy in China*, are all based on wars. All of the included poets must fit into one of these war sections. This means that parts of the world not covered in one of the fifteen war sections are not represented at all. There are no Caribbean, Irish, Scandinavian, Australian, Canadian, Scottish, Central African, or Algerian poets.

Thus if an individual's writing does not connect with a war-oriented section, he or she, from the book's viewpoint, is simply not a significant witness and is outside the so-called "experience of extremity." Alienation, addiction, madness, and subsequent incarceration (the Artaud trajectory) have no slot. Artaud's imprisonment (which spanned the Second World War, involved near-starvation and fifty-one electroshock sessions), unlike Jimmy Santiago Baca's ("arrested for drug possession with intent to sell"), is not valid.

James Fenton, an Englishman who worked as a reporter in Vietnam and Cambodia, is included. He fits into the *War in Korea and Vietnam* section. Ed Dorn, who wrote a long reportage on the Shoshonean Indians, is not included. Had Dorn been conscripted into the U.S. Army (or following the Santiago Baca example, had he been arrested for drug dealing), he would, according to the book's peculiar logic, have qualified. However, he also might not have: Santiago Baca was not only arrested on drug charges but he is an Indian. Arrest coupled with ethnicity gave him entree.

Forché *has* included a number of quite significant poets that few of us would dispute. Some of these poets, however, are very curiously represented. A few examples:

Vallejo's two and a half pages consisted of two poems from his first book (1918), written a decade before he developed a political consciousness in his writing, and one minor piece from his years in Europe. Given what Vallejo could have been represented by—most obviously, his Spanish Civil War poems—the Vallejo section is dumbfoundingly weak.

Parra is presented as anthology-valid because he refused to leave Chile after the coup that brought Pinochet to power (1974). Yet all the included Parra poems were written before 1972, or before, in the book's terms, he had made a significant political commitment.

In Lorca's case, the "assassination" oddity I mentioned earlier comes up. He is mainly represented by poems he wrote in New York City in the late 1920s. Does his political execution make these poems political? Well, they are—but not because he was executed. Allen Ginsberg's poems on New York City are not included, in spite of the fact that *Howl* was banned, that he was thrown out of Cuba and Czechoslovakia for political reasons, and currently his poetry cannot be broadcast in this country between 6 A.M. and 8 P.M. I'd call these matters "State Persecution."

The fact that Galway Kinnell "actively protested the war in Vietnam" (as did several hundred other poets) is used to explain the inclusion of his poem "Vapor Trail Reflected in the Frog Pond" in which there are several references to "Asia." However, Duncan, Sanders, Bly, Mac Low, and Rothenberg, who also actively protested our invasion of Vietnam, are not included.

One might also inquire why none of Denise Levertov's poems on the Vietnamese War (in particular, "Life at War") were included. They are much more powerful than the pieces she wrote during her 1972 visit to Vietnam (three of which are included).

Amiri Baraka's entire section consists of poems he wrote before 1965, when he was Leroi Jones and, relative to the past three decades, politically inactive.

Quasimodo is permitted to write about Auschwitz, which he never directly experienced, while Reznikoff's *Holocaust*, one of the few major American responses to the Holocaust in poetry, and one that consists entirely of testimony from the Nuremberg trials, goes unrepresented (as does Rothenberg's "Khurbn," a long poem based on the poet's visit to the remains of the death camps in the 1980s).

I mentioned earlier that Vallejo received two and a half pages in the anthology. Celan and Radnoti, the most commented-on poets in the Introduction, receive three and four and a half pages, respectively. Yet a versified "war" short story by Louis Simpson is offered twenty-six pages. Given the dense complexity of virtually all of Celan's poetry from the late '50s on (all of which is, on one level, saturated with the Holocaust), I began to notice the extent to which Forché's own rather conventional writing played a role in her selections. With the exception of Oppen, Levertov, and Leroi Jones, there are no American poets in the anthology associated with the various experimental fronts over the past fifty years. However, poets who would have been or were quite at home in the old *New Poets of England and America* anthology abound: Kunitz, Hugo, Simpson, Nemerov, Hecht, Dugan, Kinnell, Lowell, with Auden, Spender, and MacNiece a bit before them, and Fenton and Balaban a bit after.

Of course Forché is entitled to represent her view of significant poetry in any anthology she edits. But since this is not a general anthology but one in which there is a requirement for a careful assessment of what constitutes the most memorable poetry of witness in conditions of extremity, I believe that one's own poetics, taste, and companions in poetry must be made to yield to the project's obligations, to the field it proposes to engage. Say Forché simply does not care for Thom Gunn's poetry and would not include him in her version of a generalist twentieth-century anthology. That is fair enough. But: is it possible in the 1990s to edit an anthology of political witnessing and not include anything on AIDS? Or, for that matter, on the humiliating political conditions gay men and women have experienced, everywhere, throughout the twentieth century? And if it were simply a matter of page count, then, for example, I would feel obligated to leave Gertrude Stein out and put Gunn in. Stein is a major figure in many respects, but the fact that she lived in the occupied French countryside during the Second World War would not justify including poems by her that have little to do with witnessing in any trenchant sense. I would also have left out passages from Perse's poem *Exile*, since it could have been written in the nineteenth century.

Uncomfortable with what she takes to be a gap between the personal and the political, Forché attempts to bridge the two terms by suggesting that the space between them can be described as "the social," and that it is in "this social space" that we should situate poetry. An alternative to setting up a duality to be bridged is to see the personal and the political not as separate categories but as aspects of a singular, composite force that makes up poetic identity. Any poetic utterance is personal/political. When one thinks one is being apolitical, the chances are one is in agreement with the way things are, which is also a political stance. Any political poem is helplessly infused with one's own personality, one's language, one's feeling for oneself in a context that involves others.

Forché's editorial policy is less involved with bridging the personal and the political than with assuming that the personal must be directly invaded by the political for any significant witnessing to take place. How much terror must I experience to justify my speaking for someone who is in agony or who has died from torture?

The exile, in this respect, may be in less of a position to bear significant witness than someone who lived next door to a "disappeared," watched the person be stuffed into a car trunk, and who daily spoke to the "disappeared's" despairing wife or husband. In "Vocabulary," Ariel Dorfman writes: "But how can I tell their story / if I was not there?" He concludes: "Let them speak for themselves." Forché quotes these lines and understands them to mean that "the story belongs to those who have undergone the extremity."

Dorfman's last line evokes the paradox that while I can only speak for myself, I must also speak for those who cannot speak for themselves. Thus Aimé Césaire's monumental "Notebook of a Return to the Native Land," in which he speaks for himself, as a black Martinican exorcising his colonial poisoning, *and* for his fellow Martinicans, some of whom are dead and some of whom, being illiterate and uniformed, do not know how to speak for themselves. The amount of direct experience needed for imagined witnessing varies for every individual. It is a mistake to prioritize experience over imagination.

What I referred to as the new purgatory, or postmodernist DMZ, makes witnessing more and more complicated, at least when measured by the old standard of being there versus hearing about it. This DMZ is not simply a neutralizing zone between person and event but the technological spectacle that surrounds us and intersects human relationships. Once upon a time, a spectacle was public execution, or a sideshow, something one went to, and returned from, back into one's private sphere. The spectacle has now not only invaded the private sphere, but conquers it on a daily and nightly basis.

What we see through media is the world as spectacle run by a kind of Image Exchange, as if modeled upon the Stock Exchange, in which information is so intertwined with commodities that they are often indistinguishable. In myth, images were specific; they were not separated from what they revealed. In technology, commercial considerations have turned images into refuges; they can be relocated whenever and wherever it is convenient.

The challenge facing imagination today, at least in America and much of Western Europe, is that all things have come into their caricatures. Such requires the act of witnessing to come to terms with the fact that it too is part of the spectacle. In June 1994, millions of Americans stared for hours at the image of a white Bronco pursued by a flotilla of police cars. The formation's steadiness—no careening chases, no pileups—made the cars appear static and the wide freeway, as in a reverie, moving. The spectacle reminded one of a packed football stadium during pregame ceremonies: the police cars moved as a rectangular-shaped marching band. The Bronco played the role of the drum major, the head of the band. In this case, of course, the Bronco leading the show contained, we are told, a man with a gun to his temple and his mother on the phone. Alongside the freeway and the center divider, hysterical cheerleaders, fans, raised O.J. signs up and down.

For the past six months, millions, now following the trial game itself, have witnessed witnesses testifying for or against a celebrity that the camera angle generally presents as a bust. The trial is a caricature of a trial, a larger than life football opera, a thing we can and cannot grasp. What *are* we witnessing? A trial? A travesty of justice? The greatest show on earth? A long and boring proof of what we already know, that we can never know the absolute truth? That we are all seeing something slightly different and may have a closer view than someone who is actually there, sitting at the back of the courtroom? That we see more of what is going on than—is it possible—Simpson himself? What he mainly sees are twelve people—or are they disciples? Jurors become witnesses, not of the crime but of the spectacle of the trial, trying to assemble the pieces. Like us, they will only truly be witnesses of the puzzle of their own presence.

We know that every culture develops "distancing devices" to hide the facts about its bloody past. Now with digitally altered videos, one can totally change history. One can even show Germans smiling and making breakfast for the inmates of Auschwitz. Digital alteration takes the spectacle into a new and absolute dimension. Paradoxically, it might also release us from the spectacle as it will not only make indirect witnessing impossible but demonstrate the ability of lies to go undetected.

NOTES

1. After reading this piece when it appeared in *Sulfur,* Eliot Weinberger sent me ten pages of "footnotes." He mentions that the passage Palmer is citing is from Paz's *The Other Voice:*

> Political poetry was of major importance in the first half of the twentieth, but very few of the poems written in those years attained the universality of genuine poetry. Its authors were too close to news bulletins and much too far away from the events themselves. The news bulletin turns into mere propaganda, whereas the event itself is history suddenly making an appearance. Ours is a puzzling reality, and we must decipher it if we are not to be devoured. History devoured the so-called *poètes engagés.* They believed in justice and in the emancipation of humanity, but theirs was a blind faith, and they mistook oppressors for [liberators from] tyrants. What they lacked was insight—or, better put, vision. For this reason their poems have aged badly in less than thirty years.

My point is that potent and complex political poetry can be written from virtually any proximity to event (on the front lines—Owen—to watching tv—Duncan—to great historical distance—Jay Wright on Crispus Attucks). The poet's proximity in time and space to events neither guarantees nor precludes effective response. The political poem of Paz's that I recall most often, "Mexico: The XIX Olympiad," a response to the student massacres in Mexico City, was written in India (a translation of it appeared in the November 7, 1968, *New York Review of Books*).

2. Concerning my remark about Paz's conservative politics in the '70s and '80s, Weinberger writes: "Paz is essentially a European-style socialist: he has been personally close to Mitterand and Felipe Gonzalez, not Chirac and Thatcher. His anti-Communist polemics in the '70s and '80s were primarily a defense of individual freedoms, not capitalism, and had little to do with the former American religion of anti-Communism. He is repelled by the current moral agenda of the American (and Mexican) right. In the U.S., his political attacks have tended to appear in *Dissent*, not *The National Review*. In Mexico, his politics are more or less center-left. And his private life seems to have less contradictions than that of his 'leftist' contemporaries—for example Garcia Marquez, whose friendship with Castro is well-known, but whose vacations with Henry Kissinger are rarely mentioned."

3. Weinberger also writes that my comment concerning Aimé Césaire speaking for those who cannot speak themselves is "untrue and demeaning." He continues: "The only people who cannot speak are the dead and the infirm: the phrase has some meaning when applied, perhaps, to a writer who has survived Dachau or the Gulag. But there is no people, as a whole, who do not speak for themselves in the countless manifestations of a culture. Martinique, at the time Césaire began publishing, may have had a short history of printed words, but it had a long tradition of spoken and sung words. Césaire is a major poet; he may well be regarded by Martiniqueans as the best speaker among them; but he can only be perceived as speaking 'for' them by the First World. Poets speak out of the culture from which they are born, but they speak for themselves alone: to take an individual as the 'voice' of a culture is to reduce that culture to an individual expression. And writers who appoint themselves as representatives—as Césaire did not—particularly from the Third or Fourth Worlds, are nearly always no-talents, fostered by editors able to associate only one name at a time with any-

thing too foreign. A distinction must be drawn between belonging to a group, or subscribing to a cause, and embodying it. Césaire is not the African diaspora, and the African diaspora was never silent."

I had in mind such passages as the following from *Notebook of a Return to the Native Land*:

> At the end of daybreak . . . the martyrs who do not bear witness; the flowers of blood that fade and scatter in the empty wind like the screeches of babbling parrots; an aged life mendaciously smiling, its lips opened by vacated agonies; an aged poverty rotting under the sun; an aged silence bursting with tepid pustules, the awful futility of our raison d'être.

> And in this inert town, this squalling throng so astonishingly detoured from its cry as this town has been from its movement, from its meaning, not even worried, detoured from its true cry, the only cry you would have wanted to hear because you feel it alone belongs to this town; because you feel it lives in it in some deep refuge and pride in this inert town, this throng detoured from its cry of hunger, of poverty, of revolt, of hatred, this throng so strangely chatting and mute.

> I would go to this land of mine and I would say to it: "Embrace me without fear . . . And if all I can do is speak, it is for you I shall speak . . ."
> And again I would say:
> "My mouth shall be the mouth of those calamities that have no mouth, my voice the freedom of those who break down in the solitary confinement of despair."

Other passages could be cited from the same poem that would also justify my remark. Weinberger's argument is not with what I have claimed Césaire to have said, but with Césaire himself.

"What Is American About American Poetry?"

[Response to a questionnaire sent out by the Poetry Society of America]

1. Our amplification of Walt Whitman's panopticon (phrenology, Egyptology, opera, Hinduism, the poet as reporter *and* mystic, amative *and* adhesive, cultured *and* anarchic) and his "open road": the democratization of the whole person, the liberation of impulse and instinct from involuntary servitude, a new breath line based on vernacular and natural measures. We continue to operate under Whitman's charge.

2. Our invention of historical and prehistorical otherness: for Ezra Pound: ancient China; for H. D.: classical Greece; for Charles Olson: Maya and Sumer; for Gary Snyder: ancient India and Japan; for Judy Grahn: menarchic metaforms; for me: the Upper Paleolithic.

3. Our view of translation as an integral part of the poet's work. Examples: Pound's Cathay; Louis Zukofsky's Catullus; Kenneth Rexroth's Chinese and Japanese anthologies; Paul Blackburn's El Cid and Provençal troubadors; Cid Corman's Bashō, Montale, and Char; Richard Wilbur's Molière; Richard Howard's Baudelaire; Rosmarie Waldrop's Jabès; Jerome Rothenberg's Lorca (and his international anthologies); my Vallejo, Césaire, and Artaud; Bill Zavatsky's Breton; Ron Padgett's Cendrars and Apollinaire; Lyn Hejinian's Dragomoshchenko; Robert Pinsky's Dante, etc.

4. Our incorporation of multiple levels of language—the archaic, the "American idiom," the erudite, the vulgar, the scientific—along with sound texts, sublanguages, and typographical eccentricity, into the poem's textures. A sense of relentless excitement; say anything; all words can enter into play.

5. Our incorporation of the nonpoetic and the popular—report-age, history, dreams, songs, visions, libretto, chant, chance event, comic books, legal transcripts, agit-prop—as part of an ongoing, international "grand collage." *Everything is material.*

6. Our belief that poetry can be institutionalized and funded—degree writing programs, professorships for poets, archival purchases, endowment and foundation support—and remain authentic.

7. Our commitment to a radical, investigational poetry that is raw, unfinished, wayward, ineluctably *in* process; poetry as an intervention within culture against static forms of knowledge, against schooled conceptions and traditional formulations.

8. Our commitment to a conservative, univocal, episodic poetry employing a restricted vocabulary, grammar-book syntax, and traditional English verse forms; the world represented as it is; a poetry of "intimate, shared isolation."

9. Our vision that poetry must be political (in spite of the fact that no one in America takes the poet politically seriously), and confront racism, imperialism, ecological disaster, and war, as part of the poet's social responsibilities.

10. Our vision that the only genuine poetry is apolitical, sublime, victimized by a chronic belatedness, and thus is, at best, a revisionist palimpsest of predecessor poetry; distrust of the local and specific event; a belief that only poetry monumentally stripped of context can be great.

Nearly all current, seriously written American poetry draws upon varying aspects of the polarities proposed in points 7 and 8, and 9 and 10. Writing poetry is more complexly adversarial than in the past. The Dionysian/Apollonian, traditional/experimental, personal/public oppositions that have divided poets against their peers (and against themselves) have scattered into a kind of archipelago of sites.

One reason American poets have made contact with foreign poetries and "other" societies for materials and workings is because many of us feel that we cannot help but write an American poetry regardless of our thematic concerns. We are so saturated by media and commodity, so drenched in what might be called an imperialistic inscape, that regardless of what we intend we are walking pyramids packed with the impress of the daily blitz.

* * *

To speak internationally for a moment: poetry is always going nowhere and on one level to hell—on another, not to hell, but to the underworld, the pre-Christian subconscious. Poetry is fundamentally pagan and polytheistic, and would create assimilative space out of depth. One might say that a perpetual direction of poetry is its way of ensouling events, of seeking the doubleness in event, and an event's hidden or contradictory meaning. Each age produces some artists who, in their quest for authenticity, achieve their own truth by creating their own view of things. Such artists are never defined by movements of schools—their work may define or become the figurehead of a school, but as such they are never *of* the school they might be said to have created.

Individual poets are campers in the new technological wilderness, and at the periphery of the centers of social and political power. It does not matter what you say—or, it matters only to a very few. I am speaking here, of course, of the so-called "free world." In China and Iraq, for example, the "free world" situation is pulled inside out: your life depends on what you say or do not say.

Like alchemy, the poetry that matters to me faces the blackness in the heart of man and seeks to transform it into a product that attempts to become responsible for all a poet knows about himself and his world.

At the turn of the century, American poetry, with the compelling exceptions of Whitman and Emily Dickinson, was still filled with Victorian decorum and was a poetry of taste, on extremely restricted subjects, written almost exclusively by white males. As we approach the millennium, this picture has changed radically: written by American-American, Asian, Chicano, as well as white heterosexual and declared homosexual men and women, American poetry, as a composite force, has become human. Given the interest on the part of college students in writing poetry (often at the expense of reading the great dead), there are more people attempting to write poetry in American than ever before.

The archipelago of sites I mentioned earlier could also be described as a blizzard made up of academic poets, vagabond poets, student poets, Buddhist poets, eco-poets, surrealists, language poets, Neo-Formalists, haiku clubs, deaf signing poets, and poetry slams. In a fragmentary and confusing way, we are approaching what Robert Duncan called "a symposium of the whole."

Our situation today does not reveal—as the critic Harold Bloom would have it—that the barbarians are bursting through the ivory gates, but that the Anglo-American WASP stranglehold on the keep has disclosed its own only partially relevant center, and that those previously considered "barbaric" are now among the messengers displaying excluded energies, grounded information, and hybrid connections.

[1998]

The Lawless Germinal Element

It is surely possible that our massive American vocabulary contains in its magma and compost a loan-word-pidgin-slang libido that accounts for a crucial part of the American energy that, in the twentieth century, has enabled American poets to create arguably the most diverse, minority-inclusive poetry in the world.

From the beginning, on the *Mayflower* itself, when "the voices of Kent and Yorkshire and Devon, along with those of the East Anglian majority" began the process known as "accent leveling," we have been language mongrels. In 1619, a year before the Mayflower, the first shipload of West African slaves arrived in Virginia. Then and in the terrible years to come, language groups would be separated to minimize the possibility of rebellion. To be able to communicate, the slaves are said to have created a pidgin English based on the English of the sailors from such places as Liverpool and Bristol.

When I look at the origins of my American language, it returns me to "Baby's Book of Events," a scrap book my father compiled from the day of my birth until I was two years and eight months old. He appears to have kept a conscientious record of what I said as it occurred. Other than a few lists of words, he wrote out the entries as if I was speaking through him. Thus:

> April 20th, 1936—10 months, 3 weeks. "Dad-da" I called when the door would open or I thought it time for Daddy to be coming home. And then I added "car" one week later, April 28th—"Dad-da car." Even when I would hear an auto horn that sounded like Daddy's auto, I would jump up from my play pen, look at the door and say "Dad-da car Dad-da car."

This paper was presented at the panel discussion "What's American About American Language?" at the Poetry Society of America's *What's American About American Poetry? Festival* at the New School, NYC, November, 1998. It was subsequently published in *American Letters & Commentary* #11, 1999.

Glancing through my father's entries, I note that at sixteen months I could point out pictures of bow-wow, man, lady, chup-chup (for bird), cock (for clock), and Popeye. At twenty months, I identified myself not as Clayton Jr., or their nickname for me, Sonny, but as "He-hey," and when asked "What's your name?" replied "Cot-ju." At two years, I boldly stated: "Bok *old* Mamma, Tak-a *new* Mamma."

Without making too much of it, I'd like to suggest that some of the elements of my imprisonment and efforts to escape in language were even then falling in place. The Presbyterian God and my parents' anal compulsiveness were lining up on one side; and on the other were comic strips (my introduction to imagination and literature), and my impulse to rename myself and replace my mother. At around twelve, I recall playmates introducing me to swear words and daring me to repeat some out loud. I refused, but later, behind our garage, forced myself, terrified of the consequences, to blurt out: "Goddam black widows!"

As a teenager sitting at the dining-room table and having conversations with my parents that were not far from a bland Midwestern situation comedy, I was only vaguely aware that under our programmed exchanges was a vast cellar, as it were, of slang (as well as erudite language) sending up drafts and odors that I did not know how to access—and was afraid to access, for a few gusts of an emotionally spontaneous language told me that unless I were to break free of my behaviorial frame there would be no place to go.

Via playing the piano and entering the teenage fad fashion that included zoot suits and Mr. B. collars, I became aware of jazz and of Bud Powell's version of "Tea for Two." I murkily grasped that you didn't have to play the melody again and again but after stating it once, you could improvise, sort of make up your own tune. Consequently, I didn't have to play my parents' tunes all my life but could make up some of my own.

Soaking up a bit of the jazz world's improvisational spirit, tasting its alternative culture jargon, provoked me to blindly commit myself to poetry in my early twenties. I can see now that jazz, for me, was just an extension of my mother's church choir singing and the piano lessons she arranged for me when I was six. I could go so far with a discipline that was, in my case, on the leash of a fundamentally restrictive background.

Struggling to play jazz—especially during the summer of 1954 when I studied with Marty Paitch and Ritchie Powell in Los Angeles-—filled me with a desperate desire to improvise on my very life. I read and reread the jargon in the glossary to Mezz Mezzrow's *Really The Blues*. At the time I had no clue that jive talk actually had an African origin. *The African Heritage of American English* by Holloway and Voss informs the reader that the thousands of borrowings from Western and Central African languages (Bantu, Wolof, Mandingo, and Igbo, among others) include the words cool, chick, dig, jam, jazz, jive, to bad-mouth, bambi, to bug, chigger, bogus, booger, boogie-woogie, bozo, buckaroo, cootie, dirt, foo-foo, fuzzy, goober, guy, honkie, jelly, john (as a man easily exploited), kook, lam (as in on the lam), moola, okay, okra, palooka, phoney, poop, rooty-toot, ruckus, shucking, tote, yam, yackety-yack, and zombie.

The word "slang" is said to come from the Old English *slingan*, "to twist or wind," or *slincan*, "to slink." Slang words are prematurely cast, and another meaning of "to slink" is "to cast a calf prematurely." The word also appears to align with the Norwegian *slengja kjeften*, "to sling the jaw." Comparing the phrase "to sling hash" with the standard "to wait tables," the slang term suggests a greater familiarity with the referential object or idea. Such language is freckled or coarse with subconscious content that has yet to be ironed out into univocation.

In 1885, Walt Whitman wrote an article called "Slang in America," in which he proposed that slang stood for "Language in the largest sense"; that "Slang, profoundly consider'd, is the lawless germinal element, below all words and sentences, and behind all poetry, and proves a certain perennial rankness and protestantism in speech." "Slang, or indirection," Whitman argued, "is an attempt of common humanity to escape from bald literalism, and express itself illimitably, which in highest walks produces poets and poems, and doubtless in pre-historic times gave the start to, and perfected, the whole immense tangle of the old mythologies. . . .Slang, too, is the wholesome fermentation or eructation of those processes eternally alive in language, by which froth and specks are thrown up, mostly to pass away; though occasionally to settle and permanently crystallize."

Improvisational jazz, primarily an African-American phenomenon, is a kind of musical slang. The melody, in bebop, stated at the beginning and the end of a tune, is equivalent to standard American language; what happens in between is "the lawless germinal element"—slang, or poetry. The poetic equivalent of improvisational music would be a language that either discovers or invents its own parataxis in "the time of the moment of its own creation" or is capable, in revision, of reentering the original draft and treating it as material to be improvised upon again. Sometimes we get "it" right on the first take—more often, I believe, we have to reenter and reimprovise (thus Allen Ginsberg's motto "First thought best thought" is suspect advice: note that there are 18 "takes" to the superb Part Two of "Howl").

A great injustice has been done to the work of such musicians as Powell, Charlie Parker, and John Coltrane, in treating bebop and jazz as secondary forms of serious music. This prejudicial treatment probably stems from a distinction between performance and composition (a distinction, by the way, made in the nomination and induction policies of the American Academy and Institute of Arts and Letters: "Institute members in the department of music are composers rather than performers . . ."). Duke Ellington thus remains the only jazz artist ever fully inducted into the academy. The point is: there can be a lot of intellectual rigor in being hot. Deep in the slang cellar of the American language must be the word particles of Amazonian and African shamans whose entheogenic trances, filled with "language-twisting-twisting," represent the core out of which all subsequent improvisations in sound, language, and healing arise.

[1998]

Introduction to the Final Issue of
Sulfur *Magazine*

I had been talking with Jerome Rothenberg and Robert Kelly, among others, about the need for another *Caterpillar*-like magazine that would engage multiple aspects of innovative contemporary poetry in the context of international modernism. Because the California Institute of Technology is primarily dedicated to, and known for, research in science and engineering, I proposed in 1981, while Dreyfuss Poet in Residence and Lecturer in Creative Writing, that a literary magazine, sponsored by the Humanities Division, would draw attention to the humanities at Cal Tech. (I did so in somewhat the same spirit that Charles Olson, when rector, proposed to other faculty members at Black Mountain College in 1953 that a magazine might effectively advertise the nature of the college's program.) Roger Noll, an economist who was then Director of the Humanities Division at Cal Tech, liked my idea and arranged with President Goldberger for *Sulfur* to be supported initially for five years.

The word "sulfur" evokes the sulfur, a butterfly with black-bordered orange and yellow wings. On one level, the magazine is an evolution of *Caterpillar* (a magazine I founded and edited twenty issues of from 1967 to 1973). On other levels, the word denotes alchemical initiational combustion, and excited or inflamed language. The word was also attractive to me because it had not been used before as a literary magazine title. There is an extended note on the word at the beginning of *Sulfur* #24.

The magazine originally appeared three times a year but became a biannual in 1988. Its more than 11,000 pages of material have included around 800 contributors, some 200 of which are foreign writers and

This essay was written for the final issue of *Sulfur* Magazine, #45/46, Spring 2000.

artists. I began *Sulfur* with Robert Kelly as the sole contributing editor. Kelly disappeared due to a misunderstanding after the first issue appeared, and by the third issue, Michael Palmer, Rothenberg, and Eliot Weinberger had become contributing editors. Throughout *Sulfur's* run, Caryl Eshleman has been the managing editor; she took over the magazine's design from Barbara Martin with #37. She was also in charge of copyediting, proofreading, and she often read manuscripts and worked with author revisions. In short, her contribution was essential.

Over the years the masthead grew to its current sixteen members. Nearly all of this group have stayed on from the time they came aboard, and all, in one way or another, have contributed actively to what *Sulfur* has become (in contrast to the lists of well-known names that often decorate literary magazine mastheads). *Sulfur* is not, and has never been, a movement magazine. I invited people to join on the basis of believing that they were very good at their chosen focus, and took the chance that while there would be real disagreements among us (see #20 and #22 for the Language Poetry controversy), we had enough in common and were all sufficiently united against "official verse culture" (effectively examined by Charles Bernstein in #10) to be able to work together.

The magazine came close to being derailed on two occasions. In 1983, I was informed by President Goldberger that there was a crisis based on the following incident: he had been using discretionary funds from the Weingart Foundation in Pasadena to support *Sulfur.* At one point he proudly showed the Weingart Board of Trustees a copy of #4, which included twenty-two Paul Blackburn poems. One of these elderly trustees opened the magazine to Blackburn's "Birds chirp listlessly in the heat" and read it aloud to those assembled. They were outraged, and told Goldberger that *Sulfur* was pornographic. Not only did they not want their "discretionary" funds used to support the magazine, they wanted Cal Tech's name removed too. Goldberger told me that as much as he disagreed with this reaction, he had to honor it because of the Weingart Foundation's huge yearly donations to Cal Tech (mainly in the science area, I recall, but it should be mentioned that this foundation also funded a yearly "Humanities Conference" on campus). Goldberger, quite honorably I felt, offered to make good on his original five-year funding commitment via other sources, so *Sulfur* could continue either on its own for a few years or until it attracted a new sponsor. While the Blackburn poem is genuinely shocking, it is hardly pornographic by current standards. That a single poem by this shy, unassertive poet was sufficient to nearly eliminate a literary magazine on grounds of censorship in 1983 should keep us all alert to the fact that while things seem to change, on another level, they remain stuck, and the same.

Sulfur #9, which appeared shortly after the Weingart incident, was one of the two issues without a sponsoring organization. Issues #10 through #15 (1984–1986) were sponsored by the Writers' program in the UCLA Extension Program. In 1986, Karen Costello, who made the connection possible, left the program and the new director decided that *Sulfur*'s "office benefits" imposed too much of a burden on the program's budget. Thus #16 was published out of our home in West Los Angeles. In 1986, when I became a professor in the English Department at Eastern Michigan University, I brought *Sulfur* with me. From #17 on, EMU provided me with release time (one course per semester), a part-time graduate assistant, and "office benefits." These "benefits" have not included money for production, promotion, nor payments to authors and contributing editors. While the magazine's subscribers (around 700 at this point) and bookstore sales have offset some of these expenses, from the mid-1980s to 1996, the rest of the deficit was made up by thirteen grants from the National Endowment for the Arts. When we failed to get a grant in the last round of literary magazine support, we seriously considered ending *Sulfur*, but we did not want to be put out of business by the NEA. We have done issues #37 through #45/#46 on a reduced basis, cutting down the magazine's size and press run (which meant dropping distributors, which were costing us money), and stopping contributor payments. We are ending *Sulfur* now because we feel that the magazine has expanded and realized its initial purposes as much as is possible. I will turn sixty-five shortly and feel it is time to turn my focus solely on my own writing.

In regard to editing and content: associate editors regularly sent me their own work, or the work of others. More often than not, I published this work. When I was divided over such contributions (or material sent directly by would-be contributors), I sent it to three associate editors and abided by majority decision. This policy enabled work to get into the magazine via other editors—in particular, Palmer and Weinberger—through "lateral entry." It avoided many of the problems that occur with large editorial boards where a number of people vote on everything. Group editorial consensus tends to weed out the eccentric and the complex, filling issues with material that puzzles or offends no one.

While we occasionally published a piece of fiction when it seemed appropriate, for the most part we steered clear of fiction and drama, as it was not possible, given size restraints, to edit such material in a responsible way. The range of *Sulfur*'s interests in poetry, poetics, and some tangential fields made it difficult to keep issues under 200 pages. The amount of good material always determined the size of an issue; very little was held over for future issues. Here are our main focuses:

1. Translations of contemporary foreign-language poets and new translations of untranslated (or poorly translated) older works. We usually checked the accuracy of the work of unknown translators. Literary magazines that restrict themselves to a national literature deprive themselves of the international network of information and cross-fertilization that is at the heart of twentieth-century world poetry.

2. Archival materials—unpublished, significant writings—by earlier writers, in *Sulfur*'s case including Ezra Pound, William Carlos Williams, Hart Crane, Mina Loy, Basil Bunting, Lorine Niedecker, George Oppen, Charles Olson, Edward Dahlberg, and Francis Boldereff. Writers sometimes misevaluate or abandon significant works that if not destroyed end up in archival collections at university libraries (a great service to the literary community would be to have a checklist of all American archival holdings; the range and depth would astonish everyone). In the same spirit in which living poets share international affiliations, the living are also connected to, and continue to learn from, the "great dead." To include writers of the past as a dimension of the present openly affirms such affiliations.

3. The inclusion of several unknown and usually young poets in each issue. An effective literary magazine gives the impression that anyone, with the right goods, can be a part of it, and that when you turn a page you may find a poem by Karen Kelly or Dan Featherston facing one by Gary Snyder or Adrienne Rich. If the work of the "great dead" is to be included, then the work of the talented and untested should have a place too. A novice can learn something about his own efforts by scrutinizing them in a context with mature writers. Four of *Sulfur*'s authors—Jed Rasula, Eliot

Weinberger, August Kleinzahler, and John Yau—received General Electric Younger Writers' Awards in the 1980s.

4. Commentary, including poetics, notes, and book reviews (of a polemical as well as nondisputational nature). A crucial difference between a literary magazine and an anthology is that magazines comment on what is being published. Journals that do not publish reviews (or only publish pastel appreciations) evade revealing, and defending, a specific aesthetic viewpoint and become collection plates into which any contribution can be dropped. Certain aspects of poetry hone themselves on conflict and strife, and a literary magazine is an ideal site for the contestation of differing views.

5. Resource materials. Depending on the editor, and the availability, resource materials can vary widely. If poetry is the woof of a magazine, nonpoetic source material might be the warp. The idea here is that vital writing is always dependent upon materials outside of its own discipline for the renewal and deepening of content, of extending what might be called "the cleared ground of the art." Originality depends not only on voicing and technique, but on making writing responsible for previously excluded (and repressed) materials and experience. In *Sulfur*'s case, such materials included art, art criticism, archetypal psychology, anthropology, archeology, and political commentary.

These five areas of attention (along with poetry and prose by well-known American poets) made up what could be thought of as *Sulfur*'s personality. In a typical 225-page issue, there might be forty to sixty pages of commentary, several translation and art sections, and one or two archival or resource sections. Weinberger edited a special issue (#33), "Into The Past." Marjorie Perloff and Jenny Penberthy did a special issue on Anglophone Poetry and Poetics Outside the US and UK (#44). James Clifford edited and translated much of a large section on Michel Leiris (#15). Rachel Blau DuPlessis edited three presentations of George Oppen's working papers (in #25, 26, and 27). Jerry Glen edited a large section of and on Paul Celan (#11). Caryl and I put together a group of responses to the tragic death of Ana Mendieta (#22), and with Gyula Kodolanyi, I cotranslated and edited a section on Hungarian poetry (#21). Smaller sections were done on Blackburn (#4), Antonin Artaud (#9), Porfirio diDonna (#19), East German poetry

(#27), Peruvian photography (#34), and the Vancouver Robin Blaser conference (#37). *Sulfur* #32 (at 352 pages, the largest single issue) was filled with work and edited sections by the masthead. Caryl and I also worked with *Sulfur's* various art editors: John Yau, Pamela Wye, and Roberto Tejada. Over 600 paintings, drawings, photographs, and sculptures were reproduced in the magazine (and on the covers), in most cases with essays or notes.

The background against which *Sulfur* proposed itself is anchored in the Dionysian 1960s. As crazy as the period was, with its blissful and horrendous wave bands compounded of revolution, war, and mindful and mindless introspection, it was the richest period for American poetry since the 1920s. Many of the poets of my generation experienced visionary and political internationalism as a multifoliate force spinning itself out in translations, alternative presses and magazines, enthusiastic college audiences, Vietnam War protest, traditional magics, and a heady confidence articulated by Norman O. Brown at the end of his brilliant 1966 *Love's Body:* "The antimony between mind and body, word and deed, speech and silence, overcome. Everything is only a metaphor; there is only poetry." In fact, I'm sure that I am not alone in believing during the late 1960s that an American poetry based in international modernism, and signaled by Don Allen's "the new American poetry" but not restricted to his perimeters, might become the dominant poetry of the 1970s—in other words, that a world-aware, responsible avant-garde might overcome and peripheralize decades of dominant official verse culture. After all, the impact of the work of Charles Olson was equal in its own way to that of Francis Bacon, so why shouldn't Olson occupy a place in poetry equal to that of Bacon in painting?

Dionysian excess has, built within its boundary explosions, formlessness, violence, and despair. Dionysus must, at some point in his turmoil, find the hand of brother Apollo and swing with him, or be churned to flotsam. For me, there has always been a loose, sinister synchronicity between the crash of hippydom and popular culture (the Manson murders in Los Angeles, the debacle of the Rolling Stones' Altamont concert) and Olson's death in 1970, preceded by Robert Duncan's withdrawal and refusal to publish for the next fifteen years. The '70s flipped over, the energy dispersed.

Two obvious trends of the 1970s and 1980s were the ubiquitous spread of creative writing degree programs and Language Poetry. Of equal magnitude, but less discussed, was the development of a number of poets in their forties, fifties, and sixties. Women poets re/visioned not only the American canon but the heretofore unacknowledged patriarchal government of the history of poetry. There appeared a host of minority-oriented poetries: African-American, Indian, Chicano, gay, lesbian, performance, and many mixes, involving music and libretto, chants, and sound texts. What was once upon a time a Right and a Left Bank (the cooked vs. raw distinction, suspect even in the '60s) became an archipelago of sites.

One reason that Olson has not become a Bacon-like presence is that American (and English) poetry has depended upon academic sanction and support. What was true for Whitman, shunned by most of the "men of letters" of his time, is still true for almost all poets today. Students buy text anthologies and read poetry because it is part of the curriculum. Doctors and lawyers do not, in any noticeable sense, but many, in a very noticeable way, collect paintings—and not merely because wealth is involved, but because paintings (and most novels, plays, and films) offer more surface than poetry. They demand a less active response. One has to work hard to get anything out of *The Cantos, The Wasteland,* or *The Maximus Poems.* In such works, there is no plot, or color field to provide an entrance level that can be bypassed by the "ideal observer" or just relaxed into.

By creating a "poet-professor" middle class, the writing programs have played into the hands of poetry's traditional enemies: education and entertainment. The slams and open-mike readings are offsprings of, or reactions to, the creative writing class and courses based on Norton anthologies. It is wonderful for students to have contact with writers, but I continue to believe that such contact should not take place in workshops dominated by student work and response. All of a student's time in literature should be involved with getting a small percentage of it under his belt, and coming to terms with what, in my view, poetry is really about: the extending of human consciousness, making conscious the unconscious, creating a symbolic consciousness that in its finest moments overcomes the dualities in which the human world is cruelly and eternally, it seems, enmeshed.

While *Sulfur* has attempted to not support work that smacks of the creative writing workshops, we have published many Language Poets. An interesting anthology of Language Poetry, in fact, could be assembled from what has appeared in *Sulfur's* pages. Charles Bernstein is one of our correspondents, and other *Sulfur* editors are associated to varying degrees with the movement. I regard Language Poetry as a significant part of contemporary poetry but not as its primary force of focus (I don't think there is one; I think there are a couple dozen major figures today, and that they make up a crazy quilt of emphases and directions).

Sulfur's primary ambition, as I see it, has been to keep the field open and complex, with archival and contemporary writing, along with commentary, generating a multigenerational interplay. Besides advancing the work of a number of poets in their thirties and forties, the magazine has supported a range of those whose work has either held its significance or deepened during the 1980s and '90s. Along with certain *Sulfur* editors, such a range would include Robin Blaser, Adrienne Rich, Jackson Mac Low, Gary Snyder, Gerrit Lansing, Amiri Baraka, Philip Lamantia, Ron Padgett, Robert Duncan, Barbara Guest, and Gustaf Sobin.

For this last issue, I solicited work from 150 past contributors. In the case of artists, when it was possible, I simply asked for recent material. In the case of writers, I asked for unpublished things that they felt represented them well at the present time. No attempt was made to elicit testimonials. I asked everyone to try to hold their contribution to two *Sulfur* pages. I think it is a gala issue, and that in spite of some omissions (mainly due to death and disappearances), it projects a constellation that is true to *Sulfur*'s overall image.

D. H. Lawrence once wrote: "Living, I want to depart to where I am." As it has been able to, *Sulfur* has carried forth the ore in such a thought.

[January 2000]

VI

From an Interview with Duane Davis for Waste Paper *(1993)*

WP: Your use of language clearly violates many of the rules and restrictions imposed on poetic diction as taught in the academic setting or as accepted by the established poetry magazines and college journals. In some ways I see this as similar to efforts made in certain avant garde musics to re-introduce us to "noise," to words and sounds that have been taken away from us because they are dangerous and inappropriate to the kinds of expression regarded as acceptable and polite in our society. In your poem "The White Tiger" you note, "the imagination rejects even the most / filthy matter to its peril." What is that "peril" and why is it important not to reject it?

CE: Well, the so called "filthy matter" can come from a number of places. On a social plane it comes from anger, dissent, outrage, from, as it were, the way things are. For me, on a more interesting level, it would come from the dream or the unconscious and often involve material that is consciously censored which in our still quite Puritan society often constellates itself around the lower body. I find that if one closes off that lower fountain of material which appears to the rational mind to be incoherent one considerably reduces the grounds for poetry and for an expression of the soul. In other words, once you eliminate a particular area of sensation in language then you begin to pull into a rational focus what is proper as opposed to what is improper. I feel that one of the key thrills or meaningfullnesses of writing poetry is writing asleep awake. In other words, one should have access to as much of the mind as is possible so that one is writing in a kind of trance in contact with material that in dream is amoral, promiscuous, and packed with

This interview appeared in *Waste Paper* #33, a free "rock, rap, reggae, metal, hardcore, grunge, electronic, industrial and psychedelic" music magazine, Denver, 1993.

information. The attitude of rejecting that sort of material comes from a dislike of the unconscious. We still suffer in our society an attitude that unconscious equals chaotic, equals mad, equals utter disorganization and I don't believe that at all. I think that anyone who has shapely dreams or anyone who has dreams they are willing to accord as bringing them information that they are otherwise unable to get at realizes that the imagination has its own coherence and will trust that the coherence of the imagination often takes one into areas that from a rational, practical and "sensitive" viewpoint of self-regard seem to be obscene, nutty and incoherent. But then one goes back to this material and sees that it has its own way of working.

wp: You have said in regards to that particular area of Artaud's work that you admired that work but you felt there is a risk of becoming so mad you are unable to communicate at all. How do you yourself balance out a social awareness and a place in a social scheme with the kind of "I" you are given as a child while you try to get in touch with an unconscious out of which you think poetry has at least some of its power?

ce: In the spirit of some of Robert Duncan's remarks about madness, I would say that a writer such as myself must invent madness because I'm not clinically mad. (This said with a laugh.) I have to invent a madness in language to be able to unleash the imagination. In inventing a madness I'm a different kind of writer than Artaud was, who actually experienced and went through multiple personalities, inability to communicate, fecal obsession, etc. You suggested that I felt that Artaud's position was limited. I think that may have come from remarks I made in which I acknowledged that Artaud remained obsessed for the rest of his life after he began to write again. His obsessions inevitably wheel around certain major blocks of compulsive material. So to some extent one is constantly on the same merry-go-round with Artaud because he cannot release himself from certain powers that had literally shut him up for years. But I find that he is capable of penetrating areas that most writers have never allowed themselves to think about in public. And in that sense I find it heroic.

wp: This actually gets back to an area I'm curious about and that is the way in which you yourself handle language. One of your points in your introductory essay to Artaud's *Four Texts* is that Artaud was working within the context of a very restricted language, classical French, and the whole effort for maybe a hundred and fifty years before that of trying to weed out all the incorrect words. Obviously Artaud was struggling for a language that was outside of that. It sounds like you are talking about madness as a strategy in terms of trying to break through those language barriers and to incorporate other kinds of material. I really feel that the language you use is decidedly unpoetic as it would be defined in the University of Iowa MFA workshop.

ce: There is a cult that is pervasive throughout writing programs and is manifest in the publishing industry, for example, in books put out by Knopf or in APR. This cult maintains that the poet is a kind of hypersensitive being who is constantly registering a sensitivity to life which shows that he is a fine upstanding, moral citizen. It becomes PR for a poet as good guy. And it eliminates all these areas that I take to be the real areas of investigation for which poetry exists. What does Marvin Bell do if as he's writing, the line "I want to kiss Hitler's tits" comes in to his mind. He's not going to drop that in his poem about walking along the river, feeling the autumn and looking at the beeches. You have a real impasse there. That line comes in and unless one can be nimble enough to accommodate it or figure out where it's coming from and say "Wait, that is so weird and strange that it must carry important content; I will reject it at the peril of losing the information that I'm at the edge of in the poem right now." So if one lets this line about Hitler's tits drop into the poem at that point one might find that the acceptance has pushed one into an area one could not possibly have gotten to without "Hitler's tits." And had one cut it off there without the image, then Psyche—my fantasy is that there is some sort of magical creature in my mind someplace who's constantly playing tricks and games with me as I'm writing—so Psyche throws me "Hitler's tits" at this point and says "let's see what he's going to do with that one, that one's a curve." So if I say no to "Hitler's tits" at that point, Psyche says "Well fuck you, finish the poem yourself." And she goes away and I'm left with my dopey ego and my "subject," as it were, before me.

wp: You're left with an APR poem. In the figure of Bud Powell you seem to draw some important connections between music and sacrifice—clearly, music evokes these responses in you, but not just any music. What is it about Powell's music and jazz that resonates so strongly with you?

CE: It's an early and primary creative influence. My mother gave me piano lessons when I was about six years old and I had a typical neighborhood piano teacher in Indianapolis named Mrs. Brown. At about fifteen or sixteen I wandered into a record shop near my high school and heard some *Jazz at the Philharmonic* records which really interested me. I didn't understand it but there it was. And then *Jazz at the Philharmonic* came to Indianapolis, so with a few friends I went down and listened. I don't think Charlie Parker or some of the greats were there but it was still the Norman Granz group. At that point I began to order things through *Downbeat* magazine. At that time you could buy a 45-rpm record through the mail for about seventy-five cents and I ordered a 45 that had Lenny Tristano playing "I Surrender" on one side and Bud Powell doing "Tea for Two" on the other. I don't know if you know Powell's "Tea for Two," but it is one of the great versions—it'll never be better. He takes it at breakneck tempo and does all sorts of fantastic things with the melody and chord structure of the song. Somehow it got through to me in a very rudimentary way that these guys were not following the melody, but were changing it, improvising on it, which immediately suggested one could change the way one lived. In other words, I had been brought up in a very strict family where I was being programmed to be a xerox of my father and go into business school. But Powell was varying the melody, he was creating his *own* melody line. It translated into: you can vary your life, you can play variations on what you've been given. That was a massive sensation at that time, so I began to listen to a lot of Tristano and Powell. I could hear the chord structure and also hear the melody line of "I Surrender" and "Tea for Two" disappear and all of this poetry, as it were, coming in which these guys were thinking up *on the basis of* the chord structure. Powell and Tristano introduced me to improvisation and it also struck me that Powell was a more consummate and challenging pianist. But we haven't yet come to terms with Tristano. He had a rough life and he never really has gained his true listenership. You probably know something of Powell's background, his stays in asylums and how he once chalked up a keyboard on his cell wall and began to work out tunes.

WP: You use that image to powerful effect in your poem "The Bison Keyboard."

CE: I wrote it out originally as a formal sestina and then it didn't read right as a sestina so I wrote it as I wanted it to read and the sestina form disappeared into the new lines.

wp: Do you see a connection between Powell's keyboard chalked on a madhouse wall and another area of particular importance to your writing, the cave drawings from the Upper Paleolithic period found in southwestern France?

ce: A delicate, very delicate one. The man in the cave of his room refusing to be stopped by the circumstance of the hospital, scribbling these marks on the wall that might remind us of some of the marks in the caves that we have no way to read—there are so many marks and lines in the caves that seem to be improvisations around realistically depicted animals. As if Cro-Magnon person was searching for a keyboard, or the imaginative keys by which he could sound his world.

wp: You have written (in "Bud Powell 1925–1966") of how important suffering was to Powell's art and expression and even drawn carefully delineated correlations between your own suffering and that of someone like Powell (or, in another context altogether, with Sylvia Likens in "Foetus Graffiti" and "Manticore Vortex"). How does suffering relate to expression and in what way is poetry consciously therapeutic? Or can it be?

ce: Well, we could do a whole book on that. Let me take it step by step as I'm not quite sure where this will lead. Likens as a victim of torture, exploitation, a sort of Blakean Thel, marooned in an innocence which became, in the hands of her tormentors, hell. This struck a deep chord in me as an Indiana kid. The sons of Gertrude Baniszewsky wrote with a nail in her stomach, "I am a prostitute and am proud of it." A rather long sentence to have written in your flesh. This also evokes Kafka's Penal Colony in which the condemned has his sentence written in his back. At the time my fascination was probably stimulated by the fact that my father whipped me when I was a kid and I only became dimly aware of this in the sixties and seventies. Then I would have said "Oh yes, he hit me a few times" or something like that. But the extent to which the whippings were more devastating and programmatic didn't worm its way into my awareness until the eighties. So earlier I was making a kind of thwarted identification with Likens. And I was probably also roasting Indiana again for the soullessness of the place and its destruction of innocence. Which would also connect with my joining a fraternity. In other words, there was a movement from being beaten by the father to joining clubs in high school where you are humiliated but you want to be part of them because they are where the popular kids are. This naturally leads, I mean it's like a feeder, into the fraternity system. At least in Indiana in the fifties. So I was in the fraternity being paddled daily not realizing its connection to my father's beating me. We were the first class in the Phi Delta Theta Fraternity to go on strike because they would not initiate us, continuing to keep us in hell. But I still hung around the fraternity for a couple of more years. This destruction of the innocent person in the name of putting them through some sort of savage rite to make a man out of them is devastating for relations not only between men but also for the world. Robert Bly and the Men's Therapy Movement are trying to establish more comradely contact between men. It is also devastating for women, for all the guys back then were taking their brutalization out on women. The coeds in those days were icy virgins, or, if they allowed any sexual contact it became a feeding frenzy. The process turned the woman into an unpaid whore.

So this sense of the failed initiation is under my feelings for Sylvia Likens, who was a teenager from a poor family when she was boarded out to the Baniszewsky gang who were paid to take care of her! [As a kind of footnote, I recently read a horrifying account of the torture and murder of a twelve-year-old in Madison, Indiana, last January. Three girls, one sixteen and two seventeen, took this twelve-year-old who had become friendly with one of the seventeen-year-olds in such a way that the others felt competition with her, sodomized her with wrenches and tire irons and then they burned her alive. These are sixteen- and seventeen-year-old girls doing this to a twelve-year-old girl.]

WP: Your writing in recent years has dealt a great deal with a turn in the human psyche that you locate in the Upper Paleolithic era and the beginning of a recognizably human art. This seems to have been the point at which the human mind began to be organized, to become rational. Could you comment on what it is we lost, or gained, when we, as a species, first began to set up lines of definition for what is human and what is not?

CE: In a nutshell, the gain was culture as we know it today; the loss was the beginning of our severing our connection to the natural world. I see this as an almost simultaneous ascent and fall, and my notion as to why those images were placed on cave walls during the last Ice Age (roughly 35,000 to 10,000 B.C.) goes like this: certain "human" elements had been put in place long before Cro-Magnon began to paint and sculpt, basically rudimentary tools and fire (which made night life possible, and probably accelerated speech and conversation, as fire made it possible to engage what had happened that day and what might happen the next). With tools and fire, early people were beginning to disconnect with (improve upon) nature, and the first stirrings of a sense that humans and animals are different was set in motion. To then paint a realistic depiction of an animal on a cave wall was to project the animality that these people were losing, to clear their to-be-human heads of the last vestiges of what for Neanderthal must have been an unconscious web of human-animal interaction. The earliest art, then, was a making conscious of difference at the same time that, literally, a new world, or a world twin to the natural, came into being.

My attempt over the past 15 years has been to recognize Lascaux, say, dated at 17,000 B.C., as part of the back wall of image-making and culture (and by doing so to get beyond the false back wall of the Greeks and the early Neolithic). In other words, by 17,000 B.C. the first revolution, of consciousness, had been brought to a magnificent culmination. However, I must look at Lascaux, not only through tunnel upon tunnel of time, but as a person standing in the era of Auschwitz and Hiroshima. Perhaps it would be useful at this point to read from a work called "Placements I," the final paragraph, in which I try to sum up our situation relative to what I have been discussing here:

> As species disappear, the Upper Paleolithic grows more vivid. As living animals disappear, the first outlines become more clear, not as reflections of a day world, but as the primal contours of psyche, the shaping of the underworld, the point at which Hades was an animal. The "new wilderness" is thus the spectral realm created by the going out of animal life and the coming in, in our time, of these primary outlines. Our tragedy is to search further and further back for a common nonracial trunk in which the animal is not separated out of the human while we destroy the turf on which we actually stand.

The most recent forward thinking that I'm aware of on what that transformation might have involved is a book called *Blood Relations: Menstruation and the Origins of Culture* by an Australian named Chriss Knight who now lives in London. Knight believes that Cro-Magnon women at around 40,000 B.C. were able to synchronize their ovulation cycle. At this time, the men, the hunters, seem to have eaten their kill right at the site of the hunt and scraps were brought back to the so-called protofamily. The women apparently would refuse sex to those men who did not bring back anything from the hunt. Knight's evidence, and this is a huge book and I've only just started it, seems to indicate that the women began synchronizing their cycles so that they would menstruate while the men were out on the hunt. Then they would be fertile when the men came in and if they, the men, brought back meat then the men had sexual access to the women and could impregnate them. Knight ties this into the origins of culture. He sees body decorations, dance, timing, our relationship to periodicy, etc., all crystallizing at this point around 40 to 30,000 B.C., which is also the time when image-making begins.

The earliest images, other than meandering lines which are still unreadable, are generally vulvas or crude animals in conjunction with vulvas. Now this is very interesting from the point of view of the Knight thesis because if you have a large horse head gouged in rock and the neck of the horse head is intersected with a vulva that is the same size as the horse head then possibly a significant connection between sexuality and meat is being made. It is possible that the vulva is being empowered by being given this pictorial size, and that via Knight's speculations, we now have a way to start reading that image of the horse head intersected by the vulva. We know so little about Neanderthal. For example, at Drachenloch, 85,000 B.C., they have found bear skulls that have femurs inserted through them, which is a very creative kind of thing to do with a bear skull. And then the femur-loaded skulls are packed in slab boxes and the boxes are placed against red ochre at the back of the shelter. Red ochre, of course, suggests not only blood in general but can quite often evoke menstrual blood or blood of the womb or, in other words, blood with positive feminine properties so that those bear skulls are kind of being enwombed in the cave in hope of regeneration or as a power source for the people to draw upon.

So, one can make certain kinds of hypotheses that we are possibly much closer to Neanderthal than popular opinion might have it. But it seems as if the so-called cultural explosion really happens with Cro-Magnon, who in the past was thought to have magically appeared on the scene around 35,000 B.C.—though this is in dispute because of a dig in Israel where fairly firm evidence has been found of cohabitation between Cro-Magnon and Neanderthal at 90,000 B.C. If this is the case, Cro-Magnon is much older than we thought. It is certain though that Neanderthal does die out and it is Cro-Magnon who begins to make the first images on cave walls.

WP: How much does it matter that these kinds of speculations and investigations of a far distant time are really true? Is it more important perhaps that they provide us with strategies for thinking about who we are?

CE: Like you, I face a very uncertain future in the sense of eternity or perpetuity of the earth. Ecological disaster and warfare have given the earth, the future, and the present a much more transient feeling than in times past. We live today the loss of eternity. And I think its effect on art is incalculable still. This situation leads one to go back, as it were— if I can't take a step forward, then I take a step backward and survey where I am relative to that step. The twentieth century has been a massive comparative search for origins and for understanding of the rudimentary shape of the nature of the human mind. These activities translate as acts of incredible faith. If we can understand something basic about the nature of the mind, the provocation for human mind, it seems that this information could be made use of to avoid certain future disasters.

So in that sense there is something pedagogical in my going back to the caves. I'm not just going back there for the images. I'm going back there because it seems to me that Lascaux *is* the back wall. If one wants to be, as Charles Olson puts it, "responsible for an image of man," then one wants the largest contour possible.

WP: It seems that your work seeks a renewal of the body and to that end will not shy away from the grotesque or the repulsive. What is it that you are trying to say about the body and its relationship to language or its relationship to poetry?

CE: I want to admit sensations from these areas of the body that seem to be image domains. In other words, there is something that we might say is the soul of menstruation, the soul of urine, the soul of jism, the soul of intercourse, etc. All of these areas represent aspects of ensouling or of our learning more about our psychic makeup. They are side meanders of the mind in the sense of thinking of your mind as a kind of labyrinth or cave. I think dreams are extraordinarily physical. They have so many kinds of physical confrontations with the stuff that we filter out of our consciousness during the day. It then gets rehashed or reworked and that is an extremely physical domain.

WP: If the dreams are a working out of those things that occur to you during the day and that you can't deal with, is the writing of poetry then a kind of third step in the process?

CE: Yes, for me the dream mainly alerts me that it is there. When I was younger I thought dreams were poems. I don't think now that dreams are very good poems. I don't think you can take a dream and simply write it out and say "here's a poem." You are incapacitated while you're dreaming. Dreaming is not a total state because you don't have access to your rational mind, and I'd like that in the poem. I'd like to be self-critical as well as inspired. In other words I like to set up a kind of schizophrenic situation in which I am genuinely being moved by something that is irrational and not understood other than as it comes into language and yet at the same time I want to have a kind of mind running along the edge. If there is a horse galloping through a meadow, I want to encourage that horse, the powerful figure of the dream, to gallop through the meadow, but I want to be there running along next to it and inspecting it as it goes. I want to have critical access to the inspiration and you don't have critical access when you are dreaming. Or if you do it is so involved in the dream it won't tabulate with the situation.

WP: This goes back to what you were saying at the beginning which is that you want to invent your madness. You are saying at this point that you want to reinvent your dreams. Dreams are an invention of a certain part of your mind and what you are trying to do is reinvent the process of dreaming as a poem.

CE: And not just leave it at that but to work through to the point where the form is not simply reinvented dream but something more. I guess the traditional great word here is imagination and imagination seems to me to invoke a larger realm than just simply the dream. It includes dreams but encompasses a critical self. It not only includes Los in a Blakean sense but also Urizen, the rational monster that is constantly inspecting.

WP: This effort at balance of course brings up the problem of the communication of experience. What do you think is the impact of your work on someone who reads it, or can you even get outside your own reaction enough to feel what you want it to bring out in someone else, in the Other?

CE: I'm not audience oriented. I don't write for you, I write to understand something about my mind and my relationship with the world. I'm overjoyed if you can respond to it and I work very hard with my wife Caryl to create a kind of communicational flexibility with the work so that it doesn't remain obscure to the point that the reader is put in the position of having to go seventy-five percent of the way—something which is for me often the limitation of the Language poetries, the situation in which you have to more or less create your own poem out of a pile of words given to you. I want to direct the poem's impact. Caryl reads everything that I do and we talk about it and she says a lot about it. We've been working this way for the last twenty years. I initiate the piece and I finish it, but there is a so-called middle passage in there in which she is very actively involved as a sensitive, careful reader. So in that sense I'm very concerned about you and your response to the work but I don't have any intentionality as to how you should respond. I don't write that much about myself anymore as I'm more and more outraged by what goes on in the world around us. I feel that as I get older my work will become more and more what they used to call political. And certainly going back to the Paleolithic was one way to slip the Indiana noose and get away from that fix on personal emotion and background. But as to how someone would respond to the work, I guess the ideal response would be that the reader would write his or her own poem after reading something of mine or write a song or do something that was for him an imaginative act. The experience of the work should stimulate a chain reaction—that's the desire, to keep it in the imagination.

From an Interview with William Harmer
for Agenda *(1994)*

AGENDA: Your poetry seems to deal with animal nature on one hand and the human capacity for reason on the other. Can you comment on this?

ESHLEMAN: I think that animal nature is exactly what humankind lost in the process of discovering what we might call today the autonomous imagination, or art. In this sense, the beginning of art is a kind of animal undressing, and this *loss*, as it were, is embedded, at a very deep layer, in the nature of art. In fact, I'd say that the loss of animal spontaneity, which must be involved with the animal's unawareness of its own death, is felt by poets in the abyssal space between desire and the imaginative fulfillment of desire. What you refer to as "animal nature" in my poetry I'd call the extent to which my own image-making is tied into my ceaseless hauntedness over the out-prisoning of my animal nature, which I feel that I have only been able to contact, as a person, in extreme, emotional agitation, such as fear, or sexual orgasm. I am haunted by this image: that in lovemaking as one approaches orgasm, it is as if one is inching up a wall surrounding paradise, and the sensation is that at the moment of orgasm one will be catapulted over the wall and BE HOME—but as most of us know, this never happens. Man and woman penetrate this sacred precinct, and I can honestly say that I have felt it rush through me—but paradise, as home without outside, is, even when it is closest, at an imaginative remove, and while we can imagine it via other imaginations, the abyss between desire and the fulfillment of desire seems to be bottomless. Of course certain people have clever ways of denying the absoluteness of this abyss, putting bars over it, or wallpapering the bars, or splitting its size between heaven and hell, and so

This interview appeared in the Ann Arbor alternative news monthly, *Agenda*, #197, December 1994.

on, but I think that the poet must be the one (and here I am thinking of all artists as poets) who lives this abyss and who is not afraid to allow it to show through his imagination.

AGENDA: In the first poem in your new collection, *Under World Arrest,* you write:

> Begin with this: the world has no origin.
> We encircle the moment, lovers
> who, encircling each other, steep in
> the fantasy:
> now we know the meaning of life.

Would you care to comment on these lines?

ESHLEMAN: The paradox: one is always beginning anew, yet one is never at origin. We are haunted—that word again—by our seeking to be originators, to be instrumental, make things happen, to be as vital as van Gogh, say, in his twelve-candled hat under the starry infinite drawing the infinite into his own tiny grid so that it might implode in me, the viewer—and which, of course, as viewer I want to assimilate, compost, lose it in my own energy, turn that moment he has offered me into my own. Thus art goes on and on, a vast daisy-chain, each artist willy-nilly linked to others in something that is probably deeper than sexual connection. At this point, critics such as Harold Bloom tell us we are all helplessly belated. Origin is something that happened out of sight blinded from mind. I find this kind of thinking to be one dimensional, and *only* critical, in that its intention appears to be to trap me and shut down my workshop. If my poetry is only a faint, faint evocation of some original imaginative leap, why bother to write at all? So, going back to the poem whose opening lines you have quoted, I prefer to get rid of origin *at the same time that* I work with its splintered resplendence.

One may sense the truth of a moment, but "the meaning of life" is at once so absurd, painful, joyous, and strange as to be ineffable. And if, for a moment, we take origin and belatedness seriously, we realize that perhaps Cro-Magnon alone was original. We are all, Dante and Shakespeare included, in a towering juggernaut of pickabacks, standing on the shoulders of those who made the incredible breakthrough from no image of the world to *an* image.

I just recalled that Carl Jung once defined the meaning of life as a good companion, and that I used this statement as the epigram to a collection of poems—dedicated to my wife, Caryl.

AGENDA: In the Preface to *Under World Arrest* you speak of placing yourself under world arrest and refusing to release yourself. Could you elaborate on this?

ESHLEMAN: Your question, of course, evokes some notions that press about being under world arrest. To refuse to leave the world, in poetry, can also mean a desire to curtail escape from the world on the part of the reader. All art, on one level, is an escape from what one feels and knows of one's actual situation. Much art is little more than diversion, a pseudosophisticated form of entertainment. Yet while we are in our seats, drinking champagne and watching the cancan, we are aware that the beggars are freezing outside the nightclub, and if we look closely at the chorus line, we can see some of the lineaments of the actual lives of the women who have signed up for this basically humiliating work to pay their rent. Which is to say that in my poetry I want included the street and the beggars, and the condition of these women's lives, in the dance of the imagination. I must insist on the dance, because to only describe or plead on behalf of the beggars is to abandon the imagination as a force that enables one to see the thing *and* to see through it, around it, and to place it in an individual context, as a sharable aspect of my imagination.

Plus this: we live in the age of the death of eternity, in the age of mortal sky, mortal ocean, mortal earth. From the Tang Dynasty to late English Romanticism, artists, in spite of the never-ending terror of so-called mother nature, have sought refuge in a fantasy of the impermanent permanent, supported by the feeling that in spite of our almost weightless impermanence, such was underwritten by "something" that would always be, call it God, earth, or even eternal night. I place myself under world arrest because that is where I really am, where all of us really are. I have tried to adopt a viewpoint that is congruent with my fix, and then to work from that perspective, to imagine it and in that way to affirm it. I believe that what is left of life is worth living, but I want to test this affirmation against as much negation as my writing can accommodate.

From an Interview with Keith Tuma for Contemporary Literature *(1996)*

What to say to introduce Clayton Eshleman? First of all, perhaps, this: in my experience I have found few poets whose work generates—for other poets, for readers coming to it for the first time—such animated outbursts. It is a work of "a peculiar honesty, which, in a world too frightened to be honest, is peculiarly terrifying"—to use T. S. Eliot's words for William Blake's poetry, one of Eshleman's models. Surely there is little not capable of provoking controversy in this work, from the mythopoeic reading of the Upper Paleolithic that has informed and been advanced by Eshleman's poetry and prose since the early eighties to the idea of political poetry that some of the poems in Eshleman's most recent collection, *Under World Arrest* (1994), embody. Beyond such controversy there is now the considerable bulk of Eshleman's work to consider. And his is not a work easily excerpted—to follow it over time is to meet turmoil, self-negations, and self-projections; excavations in the rubble of gender, art, myth, event, and media spectacle; evolving encounters with a disparate body of cultural materials, exemplary persons, and personal friends; dreams and dream discourse; propositions shadowed by laughter, ecstasy, and farce; grotesque realism propelling a struggle for meaningful utterance and meaningful community. The work is cluttered with—is shaped by as it shapes—the wreckage, chance encounters, and developing passions of a middle-class, Indiana-born poet who has self-consciously dismantled his Indiana origins to wander among the possibilities that the never altogether emptied vessel of Indiana can be made to contain.

Walking into the household Clayton and Caryl Eshleman have made

This interview appeared in *Comtemporary Literature*, summer 1996, volume 37, #3.

for themselves in Ypsilanti, Michigan, across the street from a church, one is at first overwhelmed by the many paintings, drawings, prints, photographs, and sculptures covering nearly every inch of the walls. These are—to name just some of their creators—by Leon Golub, Nancy Spero, Nora Jaffe, William Paden, Irving Petlin, R. B. Kitaj, Wallace Berman, Jess, Robert Duncan, Hans Bellmer, Linda Jacobson, Jorge Perez-Roman, Susana Lago, Nina Subin, Wandjuk (an Australian aboriginal bark painter), Michel Nedjar, Dorothy Rossi, Caryl Eshleman, Kenward Elmslie, and Bob Cato. Mexican masks and anonymous folklore from the Oaxaca region, most of it pertaining to the Day of the Dead ceremonies, surround the dining room table. It's an idiosyncratic collection, and it takes shape as a testimony to a life. Many of the paintings are gifts, ultimately the products of—the story of—the community Eshleman has pursued beyond Indiana. What is not gift is discovery transformed by Eshleman's signature. Just so, the Day of the Dead joins the array of materials, customs, and ritual mulled over by the poetry—"Cempasúchil" in *Under World Arrest*. One needs no transition between the paintings and Eshleman's poetry. It is as if the poetry must be at least as complex and crowded—as agonized, hilarious, confused, lucid, derivative, singular, as full of farts, food, and ecstasies—as life itself. Melee and synthesis both, all the more valuable for its being uncategorizable, the work is what Eliot Weinberger calls "a series of imaginative confrontations with the 'other'—other humans, other species, the historical other, the geographical other, the personal other" (Introduction, *The Name Encanyoned River: Selected Poems 1960–1985* [Black Sparrow, 1986], 12), and it solicits a reader who seeks a confrontation with imagination "in extremis." This is not a poetry that wants to be "liked," but neither is it meant to "shock."

What follows is a text that took shape as I sent Eshleman questions directed at three aspects of his life in poetry since the early 1960s—his editing, particularly of *Caterpillar* (1967–1973) and *Sulfur* (1981 to the present), his translating, and his work in poetry from *Mexico & North* (1962) through *Under World Arrest*. While the written form of the interview made the spontaneity of immediate interaction impossible, it also allowed for more detailed questions and answers. The questions were composed in sets and over a period of several months, generated by different readings back and forth in Eshleman's poetry, translations, and journals, and in one case by Eshleman having mailed me the text of an essay he read at last summer's Vancouver conference in honor of

Robin Blaser, an essay in which Eshleman details at more length than ever before what he speaks of as a "vision" in Kyoto in the early sixties. Like so much else in his work, this text and the experience it addresses will no doubt tempt some to regard Eshleman as a "naïf, a wild man, a wild pet for the supercultivated," to quote again Eliot writing of the way Blake was often regarded. But Eliot suggested that a reading of Blake across his career made it impossible to take Blake in this way. Short of a reading the work itself, which deserves to be better known, or in the translations of César Vallejo, Antonin Artaud, and others, an interview seemed the best opportunity to allow Eshleman to suggest how it is that he would have one take him.

Q. I'm hoping that in this exchange we can discuss the several dimensions of your life in poetry—the editing of magazines, particularly *Caterpillar* and *Sulfur;* your work translating poets such as Artaud, Vallejo, Aimé Césaire, Michel Deguy, and others; and your own poems up through *Under World Arrest* and beyond. I'm guessing that you see your work as a poet, translator, and editor as essentially part of one, evolving project, as activities that inform one another, but for convenience's sake let's see if we can keep the editing, writing, and translating separate at least for a while.

In your essay on editing *Caterpillar* in *The Little Magazine in America* you write of a number of matters—of the influence of Cid Corman's *origin* on your thinking about a poetry magazine, of your desire to provide "a dependable and generous outlet" for the writing of Robert Duncan, Jerome Rothenberg, Louis Zukofsky, Paul Blackburn, Diane Wakoski, and others. You also suggest that doing a magazine can result in "meaningful conflict." Now it seems to me that your magazines have always manifested a degree of openness to the new and unknown, but they have surely never been exactly eclectic; you have always depended heavily on a number of key contributors. With *Sulfur,* some of these contributors—Michael Palmer, Rachel Blau DuPlessis, Eliot Weinberger, Pamela Wye, Jed Rasula—are on the masthead. I'm wondering how you reconcile your devotion to the work of such persons with what sounds like a Heraclitean idea that strife or conflict is meaningful, even productive. How do you see conflict manifesting itself in *Sulfur,* for instance? By conflict do you mean something more than the obvious, such as the exchange on Language Poetry between Weinberger, Michael Davidson, yourself, and DuPlessis several years ago?

A. A fine response to your question, focused on poetics rather than magazine editing, is provided by Robert Duncan in "Man's Fulfillment in Conflict and Strife," which first appeared in *Caterpillar* 8/9.

The exchange on Language Poetry in *Sulfur* is part of the magazine's ongoing commitment to including polemic. I am shocked by the lack of polemic in most other poetry magazines. I believe that one of the crucial differences between a magazine and an anthology is the inclusion of commentary that cuts both ways (nothing is risked in publishing polite, positive reviews of books; a lot is risked in attacking sacred cows). I recall how exciting it was to read polemical articles by Gilbert Sorrentino and Amiri Baraka in *Kulchur*. Polemic always carries, by implication, a strong affirmation of something else, and sometimes one can only grasp what one does strongly believe in by articulating what is wrong with something else. I suppose certain writer-editors do not publish material that is directly critical of established writers (there is no point in attacking young or hardly known writers) because they know that there is always a good chance that the criticized will be sitting on an award panel or be handed their next book for review. Critics especially believe they are beyond criticism (especially by poets—we are supposed to be grateful for any scraps they throw us). After *Sulfur* published Rothenberg's powerful attack on Harold Bloom in 1982, I was told by my department chairman at Cal Tech that Bloom had called the president and demanded an official apology. Even though I did not write the piece, I will be on Bloom's shitlist forever—as recently indicated by the fact that he could not bring himself to mention my name when he identified books that I had translated in his canonical "hit parade."

If you write political poetry, as I do, chances are you will want the political to be a significant facet in anything you edit. Thus the appearance of artwork in *Sulfur* by Leon Golub, Nancy Spero, Mel Edwards, and Joel-Peter Witkin gives a sensation of strife as inherent to what the magazine is about. On the other hand, *Sulfur* never has, to my knowledge, exploited suffering and violence. I think of the magazine as a whole as very affirmative—it is not snide, cynical, intentionally obscure, dedicated to famous names, or easy, for that matter.

Seven years ago, while I was editing number 19, an unusual conflictual issue came up. After accepting some poems by John Ashbery for publication, a totally dismissive review of his *Selected Poems* came in, written by Sven Birkerts, whose proposal to write the review I had accepted. It didn't seem right to print new poems by an author in the same issue in which his lifework was being dismissed. Yet it would have been worse to send the poems back and then print the review, and censorship to have rejected a review which I had OK'd. I resolved the situation the best I knew how by printing both poems and review, and responses to the review by four *Sulfur* editors (who tore it apart). Birkerts was profoundly offended, and Ashbery, who decided that I had set him up, has never offered material to *Sulfur* again.

Q. When you look back on *Caterpillar* now, and when you think of what is of course an ongoing project at *Sulfur*, what do you think of as the greatest accomplishments and failures of these two magazines?

A. In regard to accomplishment, both magazines have forwarded for their times a wide-ranging vision of international investigative poetics. By avoiding movements, on one hand, and eclecticism, on the other, both magazines have displayed unique, interactive combinations: for example, a range of writers that includes Frank Samperi, Norman O. Brown, Jackson Mac Low, Lorine Niedecker, Ryunosuke Akutagawa, Stan Brakhage, Wolfgang Giegerich, and Philip Lamantia. And these writers have not been published in a showcase fashion. Their work, and the work of some four hundred other writers, has been intersected and complexed by commentary, visual art, archival materials, and the writing of those just starting to tangle with what is out there. Both magazines have maintained a high quality of translation and have strongly implied that to be a significant American poet you have to read internationally.

As for failure, *Caterpillar* especially was very hit-and-miss when it came to criticism. More commentary should have appeared on writers whose work the magazine backed. While the magazine thrived on the heady atmosphere of the times, it also allowed itself occasionally to be undermined by current fads—for example, the lecture on Scientology published in number 5. I don't feel that there have been any major failures in the contents of *Sulfur*; I would stand behind just about everything in its thirty-seven issues to date.

However, there is a major failure in regard to both magazines, especially *Sulfur*: my inability to finance and base them in such a way that the contributors would reach the readership they deserve. With the proper support, I think the circulation could now be six thousand instead of two thousand. Ideally, *Sulfur* should also have generated a new press that would be publishing books by its contributors.

I may be wrong, of course. It may be that there are always only a couple of thousand people in America prepared to read, say, Jerome Rothenberg's *Khurbn*, but that there are twenty thousand eager to be entertained, in the name of poetry, by Bill Moyers and Robert Bly. I feel badly that I have not been able to figure out a way to test my notion that with effective publicity and distribution *Caterpillar* and *Sulfur* might have helped reverse the lamentable situation in American poetry in which the conventional continues to be the majority and the investigational the minority.

Q. Along with its publishing many translations from diverse traditions, one of the things that I most admire about *Sulfur* is what one might call its archival function. You've published, for instance, portions of the notebooks of George Oppen, fragments on religion by Mina Loy, other work by modernist writers long or recently dead. How do you see the archival materials as fitting in the magazine?

A. Publishing archival materials is not only a service to writers of the past (since significant pieces get overlooked by a poet during his or her lifetime and left in an archive if not destroyed): in the context of a mainly contemporary-oriented journal, it keeps an image of many generations alive, in interaction with each other. And this seems accurate to me, since no single generation represents the present. The great dead are never, imaginatively speaking, dead, and if I can validate instances of this by making otherwise buried material available, then everyone is ahead. Also, I think there is a value in younger writers finding themselves in a context that includes Oppen or Artaud or Olson. They may read their own work differently and move more resolutely into new areas that have not been mapped by their predecessors.

Q. In the introduction to your *Conductors of the Pit* (1988), the collection of translations of Rimbaud, Vallejo, Césaire, Artaud, and Vladimir Holan, you write: "All of the poets with whom I have spent long periods of translation—twenty-nine years, in the case of Vallejo—have drawn me because their poetry knew something that my poetry wanted to know. Besides attempting to make accurate, readable versions, I was also involved in a secondary plot or a subtext, wanting to shovel some of their psychic coal into my own furnaces." And a little later you mention an "assimilative space" opened in the process of translation. So in the space of a paragraph you offer at least one motive for translation—a motive more unabashedly personal than many translators would offer, I think—and take care to stress your concern for "accuracy"—you have worked with collaborators, and I have heard you on several occasions say how wrong such and such a translator has rendered such and such a poem. These two concerns—trying to do one's best struggling with the difficult otherness of the poem to be translated and straightforwardly acknowledging a desire somehow to consume it, to shovel it into one's furnaces—might seem to some opposed. But I'm guessing that your idea of an "assimilative space" means to articulate some relationship between them. I wonder if you would elaborate on this idea of an "assimilative space" forged in the act of translation.

A. By the psychic coal metaphor I was trying to get beyond a simplistic reading of "influence." The main problem with influence is that while it is necessary, it too often is mere absorption, the novice as sponge: squeezed, he issues only what he has taken in.[1]

"Assimilative space" is the continuum that exists between my first reading of a foreign poem and whatever I might do with it in a poem of my own. This space consists of notes, research, drafts, correspondence with scholars, etcetera, and I call it "assimilative" to contrast it with absorptive influence. Assimilation involves transformation, a translating of the translated, as it were, into materials whose identity is primarily *not* that of the precursor.

While a desire for translational accuracy may appear to be in contradiction with a desire to consume and transform what is being translated, such, while at first conflictual, turns out to be a process in which two directions pass through each other, with a gain at both ends. By refusing to treat the original as an Eshleman plaything, I make myself serve it and deny myself any immediate creative use of it. This creates a crisis in my psyche since it smells some action via the presence of a poem under translation. It feels that it has been invited to help turn the translation into a poem that pleases it. Over the years, I have trained my psyche to keep its hands off a poem under translation. The deal I make goes like this: if you leave me and Vallejo alone now, there will be a greater reward for you in the future, for the "assimilative space" material will trickle down to you, and I will call upon you to work with me with this material in an Eshleman poem where you can exercise your forces at large.

Accurate translating takes much longer than careless "poetic" translating. Difficult situations must be worked through, not covered up. This increased time enriches the "assimilative space," offering the psyche an active sediment.

"Assimilative space" is a silo or warehouse from which the translator-poet can draw a variety of materials. In the case of Vallejo, I see two basic categories: direct addresses to, or involvements with, the precursor (for example, the traditional "at the tomb of" poem),[2] or uses of one's own translations of the precursor (employing his forms, strategies, or nuances). Here is an example from the second category: I drew upon the following translation to write a poem of my own. The original, "El libro de la naturaleza" is dated October 21, 1937. I began to translate the poem in the early 1960s; here is a version from 1978:

The Book of Nature

Professor of sobbing—I said to a tree—
stick of quicksilver, murmurous
linden, at the bank of the Marne, a good student
is reading in your deck of cards, in your dead foliage,
between the obvious water and the false sun,
his three of hearts, his queen of diamonds.

Rector of the chapters of heaven,
of the ardent fly, of the manual calm there is in asses;
rector of deep ignorance, a bad student,
is reading in your deck of cards, in your dead foliage
the hunger for reason that maddens him
and the thirst for dementia that drives him wild.

Expert in shouts, conscious tree, strong,
fluvial, double, solar, double, fanatic,
knowledgeable in the cardinal roses, totally
embedded, until blood spurts, in stingers, a student
is reading in your deck of cards, in your dead foliage,
his precocious, telluric, volcanic king of spades.

Oh professor, from having been so ignorant!
Oh rector, from trembling so much in the air!
Oh expert, from so much bending over!
Oh linden! Oh stick murmuring by the Marne!

I think that Vallejo may have invented this form. It consists of an apostrophe which is extended for three lines, followed by a three-line response. This form is repeated twice, with new information, based on the original apostrophe, introduced in stanzas 2 and 3. The key metaphors are then addressed, line by line, in a four-line conclusion that evokes the envoy of a sestina.

I had been reading and translating Artaud, by the early 1980s, for a decade or so and had discovered some fascinating parallels with Australian aboriginal myth (which I first became aware of, via Joseph Campbell's *Masks of God*, while translating Vallejo in Kyoto). I decided to do a poem using Vallejo's "The Book of Nature" form, injecting Artaud in it as the subject to be apostrophized:

The Excavation of Artaud

> Shaman of obsession—I said at his tomb—
> excavated in electricity, opened between
> anus and sex. In the Australian outback of the soul,
> 3 dead men are fingering your anesthetized root support
> shining like a chain of sputtering lights, for the key to creation,
> between the bone they've drawn out and the bone they so desire.
>
> Priest of lethal phallic rites, of sparkings
> in foetid material, of remaining in antithesis
> with no hope of synthesis, priest of a genuine melee—
> 3 dead men are fingering your Muladhara Chakra, your amphimixis,
> as if, under the Christian gunk that clogged your focus,
> they could plug into your triangle and its twisting tongue of flame
>
> Pariah in silence, coprophilially
> squatting in the corner of your cell for years,
> sealed open, who only came when called by your mother's name—
> repressing their way in, to the point of anal cancer,
> 3 dead men, licking your electroshock-induced Bardo, have found
> your atomic glue, the Kundalini compost they must eat to speak.
>
> O shaman, from having been so masterfully plundered!
> O priest, from having been so fixed in antithesis!
> O pariah, from having been so desired by the dead!

Q. Perhaps especially in American poetry, this has been a century of translations and translators. In another interview (with Lee Bartlett) you have suggested that the "early" aesthetics of Ezra Pound strike you as outdated or useless—the question asked you involved not translation but the difference between "notebooks" and "finished work," the extraordinary stress on precision and exactness in early Pound. Pound, of course, also has had immense influence on the translating done by American poets in this century. I wonder how you might situate yourself within or beside or apart from the tradition of that influence, which is perhaps complex enough or poorly enough understood to have seemed to authorize some very different translations and translators.

A. The tradition you associate with Pound became available to me via Cid Corman and Paul Blackburn in the late 1950s and 1960s. Both poets, who are wonderful translators, were internationalized by Pound.

Corman was the first to give me hands-on direction as a translator when, in Kyoto, he suggested we translate some José Hierro poems together. Up to this point, I had been taking shortcuts. Corman's rigor, and respect for the original's knowing what it was about (that is, it does not have to be "educated" by the translator), made a lasting impression on me. I have never felt the need for any "translation theory" beyond what I learned from working, one on one on one, with Hierro and Corman.

Pound's influence, as I take it up, is less a method of translating than an admonition for the poet to become aware of foreign poetries (of the past as well as the present), and to view translation as part of one's service to the community of poetry at large—a parallel respect for self and other, almost as if for every poem one writes, one should translate a poem. It is one way of understanding Blake's aphorism that "the most sublime act is to set another before you."

Q. In the university recently, much of the attention paid to translation and translation theory has involved the politics of translation. I'm thinking in particular of theories of translation-as-empire in books such as Eric Cheyfitz's *The Poetics of Imperialism: Translation and Colonization from "The Tempest" to "Tarzan"* and Tejaswini Niranjana's *Siting Translation: History, Post-Structuralism, and the Colonial Context*. I don't know if you've read these books, and I don't want you to respond to them directly. But I do know from your essay "The Translator's Ego" in your prose collection *Antiphonal Swing* that you are conscious of the "somber implications" of a "first-world" translator working on—even "colonizing"—a "third-world" writer. As a practicing translator, and as a poet and editor dedicated to "internationalism" in the arts, how would you construct a defense of translation? Is there a point at which translation becomes an imperial or colonizing act, or is translation for an American always already implicated in the structures of global power now in place?

A. Since making my comments about "colonization" in "The Translator's

Ego," I have realized that one can push this notion too far, can use it to downgrade another translator's approach that differs from one's own. Blackburn's Provençal translations might appear to contest my sense of accurate translating, but there is no way to translate twelfth-century rhymed songs in a way that anyone today would want to read without considerably reshaping them.

Much of what one will allow a translator-poet is conditioned by how one feels about his poetry. I find Robin Blaser's "variations" on Gérard de Nerval's *The Chimeras* of interest in a way that I do not find Ben Belitt's "variations" on Pablo Neruda's poetry of interest, primarily, I think, because Blaser's sense of poetry engages me and Belitt's does not. At the same time, I prefer Robert Duncan's versions of the same Nerval poems to Blaser's. Why? Well, they are more like what I would do!

One must be careful not to literalize such terms as "colonialization" and "imperial act" in regard to literature. What Belitt has done to Neruda cannot in any significant way be compared to what The United Fruit Company to did to Chile.

"Translating" the American Donald Duck into prejudicial stereotypes rigged to appeal to millions of adult Latin American comic book readers is also something else. Of course, that is a different kind of "translation" (as are Tarzan and Caliban) than a strict literary translation. It is a direct attempt to exploit uneducated people, in a series of ripples that extend from the act of reading a comic book to misunderstanding revolution.

Q. As I understand matters, you were raised a Protestant, and all of the poets whom you have translated—Neruda, Vallejo, Artaud, and so on—come from very different, primarily Catholic cultures. And I think I can see how their work has influenced your own, drawing you away from and beyond those Indiana origins, toward "a poetry written *in extremis*" (to quote your introduction to *Conductors of the Pit*). I wonder—with your background, working toward the kind of poetry you want—what is it of these poets that you haven't been able to digest, as it were, what is it that you most envy them? Or maybe it's what you most "wonder at," or perhaps what you consciously leave behind as finally unassimilable?

A. There is no Neruda in *Conductors of the Pit*. He would not qualify for the concept of that book, plus the fact that he was someone I translated when I was a young poet and then abandoned. Like Jerry Rothenberg, David Antin, and Robert Kelly, I was attracted to Neruda's sensual,

surrealist poems of the late 1920s. I stopped reading Neruda after reading his longest poem—longer than the *Canto General* and bypassed by
all Neruda translators—"The Grapes and the Wind," in Lima in 1965.
For me, the undigestible in Neruda would be the blatant Stalinism in
this poem written in the 1940s.

As for Vallejo and Artaud, their lives attract me, given their radical
difference with my own background; at the same time, they are often
impossible to plumb. Vallejo's Andean mestizo background, for example, or his constantly grueling life in Paris the years when he wrote the
poems that quicksanded me in Kyoto. These poems opened up a new
and perilous vista on human consciousness to me, but they close off at
the level of daily experience. And sometimes the density of certain
poems still leaves me baffled, and I continue to be magnetized to these
densities because I do not think they represent willful obscurities.

With Artaud, the "finally unassimilable" is his madness. I'm hope-
lessly stark, raving sane, and I have resisted identifying with Artaud's
madness because such an identification would not only be false but
probably have negative consequences in translating him (as it did, I
think, for Jack Hirschman in the 1960s).

There is also this limitation which fits into your question: I have no
structured background in Peruvian or French literature, so there are
bound to be influences, associations, nuances, etcetera, that miss me,
and may interfere with the reading, and thus the translating, of a word
or phrase. It is very difficult to totally surround such figures as Vallejo,
Artaud (or Césaire and Deguy), *and* to translate them at length, *and* to
dedicate one's own life to writing one's own poems. There have to be
priorities—meaning infernal secondaries, too.

Q. Are there translators working today whom you especially admire?
Are there poets and/or poems badly in need of translation? Do you have
plans to translate more of the undertranslated—Holan for instance?

A. I very much admire—restricting myself to poets here—Corman's
Bashō, Kusano, Montale, and Celan; Blackburn's Provençal and *Poem
of the Cid*; Rothenberg's Lorca; Alastair Reid's Neruda; Rosmarie
Waldrop's Jabès; Weinberger's Paz, Huidobro, and Villaurrutia; Ron
Padgett's Apollinaire and Cendrars; Bill Zavatsky and Zack Rogow's
Breton; Andrew Schelling's Mirabai; and Pierre Joris' Celan.

Vladimir Holan is a very great poet, on a par with Rilke. He is woe-
fully undertranslated. I was fortunate to be able to work with the late

Frantisek Galan on Holan's masterpiece, "A Night with Hamlet," and also very fortunate to have Michael Heim with us for a whole week cross-checking our work. This situation will not recur, so chances are I will not cotranslate any more Holan.

Lezama Lima, as a poet, essayist, and novelist, is an undiscovered continent, the third of the great internationalist Latin American triad that includes Vallejo and Borges. James Irby has done fine translations of some of Lezama Lima's essays, but there is not much else. I am told that his novel, *Paradiso*, needs to be retranslated.

Among the poets I feel are absolutely deserving of more translating into American are Miguel Hernández, Pier Paolo Pasolini, Ferenc Juhász (the Hungarian Olson), Adonis, U'Tamsi, Duo Duo, Carlos Germán Belli, Margit Szécsi, René Depestre, and Inger Christensen.

Q. I'd like to begin now asking you about your poetry from a slightly oblique angle, reminding you of a comment Eliot Weinberger made in the introduction to your selected poems, *The Name Encanyoned River*: "It is surprising that no published critic seems to have noticed that Eshleman is, at times, extremely funny." I imagine that many readers, coming to it for the first time, are taken aback by the visceral, direct discourse of the "lower body" in your work—in one recent poem on translating Artaud you write of "subtle semen, crawling across the floor," for instance—and miss or neglect the Rabelaisian grotesquery and the puns and wordplay, sometimes playful, sometimes not, that are part of a poem like "Short Story," where you have phases like "Wordsworth's *recollection*: wreck election," and "Now is the tear and ear of terra's torn era," and the Eshleman neologism "abysscadabra." Your own evolving sense of self and desire are sometimes subject to something approaching satirical comment as well. How do you respond to Weinberger's remark? What is the place of satire and farce in your work?

A. I grew up in Indianapolis in the 1940s; comic strips and comic books were my introduction to imagination and literature. I drew my own cartoons and for a year took private cartoon lessons from a college art student. I was obsessed with practical jokes, like whoopee cushions and devices that would make someone's dinner plate jiggle (squeeze bulb attached to tube attached to small balloon placed under tablecloth and victim's plate). My parents took me to see Spike Jones, and Olsen and Johnson ("Hellzapoppin"). My whole sense of information about the world beyond our block was formed by Jack Benny, Burns and Allen, Charlie McCarthy, and Mortimer Snerd. With my pals, I would call people up on the phone and pretend that I was the emcee for a quiz program; after asking several very easy questions, I would inform the generally unsuspecting housewife that she had won a keg of horseshit. Doing this would drive all of us into fits of laughter.

While my parents were both very strict and never to my knowledge let go, my father, who was a deacon at the Fairview Presbyterian Church, occasionally wore a rubber rose in his lapel and while he shook hands with the churchgoers, manipulated a bulb in his trouser pocket with the other hand. When squeezed, the bulb expanded a green worm which then appeared in the rose.

The laughter in my work is ambivalent, and less involved with satire than with degradation and regeneration. That is, it mocks spiritual and intellectual pretense, dragging this stuff down to the material level of the lower body. My attitude is clearly expressed by Norman O. Brown in a passage from *Love's Body:* "Knowledge is carnal knowledge. A subterranean passage between mind and body underlies all analogy; no word is metaphysical without its first being physical; and the body that is the measure of all things is sexual; a penis in every convex object and a vagina in every concave one."

I find this ambivalence to be true to the subconscious (the eversmoldering hotbed of humor), whose vitality is depicted not only by the Maya underworld, say, with its simultaneous birthings and beheadings, but in Bugs Bunny—total mayhem as punctuation to ongoing action. For poetry to be truly open and accessible to the unknown, I feel it must contain a grotesque, carnivalesque body, forever unfinished, simultaneously senile and pregnant, in copulation with self and other, ignorant and wise, graceful and ugly. The fantasy of a wholeness moving through this must also include the absurdity of writing poetry today as well as the absurdity of being anything other than a poet today.

Q. To prepare the questions for this interview one of the things I've been doing is reading your poetry with some attention to the dates of its publication, trying to imagine it across time, as it were, watching the concerns that have come to the fore and then perhaps receded—the struggle with the Eshleman Indiana self as it came under the influence of Wilhelm Reich, Vallejo, and others in the earlier books, the poems on "woman" and Caryl Eshleman later on, the engagement with the Upper Paleolithic in *Hades in Manganese* and especially *Fracture*. I also know, from your book *Novices*, that you've thought about poetic careers. I want to give you the opportunity to talk about your sense of the movement or development of your work—your career—by mentioning an essay you wrote for the Robin Blaser conference in Vancouver. In that essay you mention what might be described as a hallucination or vision in Kyoto in 1962 or 1963 where you saw at Nijo Castle a spider the size of a human adult suspended forty feet above you, which you say that you took to be "a totemic gift" that "would direct your relation to poetry." Now, in rereading your poetry, I notice that the spider is all over the place: "The Crocus Bud" (1962) begins "The vise of Jung thrills me less than spider," and "The Physical Traveler" (1972) begins "I woke up pregnant by a wall / where a red spider watched me." And the spider is still present in *Under World Arrest*. But many will wonder how to take your remarks at the Blaser conference, how to take this "vision." Is this a case of you yourself rereading your own poems and finding (new) continuities and resources there—a process resembling that which Robert Duncan writes of in his second preface to the reissued *Caesar's Gate?* One thinks of Yeats, too. How literally are we to take this story?

A. My earliest spider experience was seeing, when I was about eleven, the film "Tarzan's Desert Mystery," which had Tarzan at one point battling a gigantic spider in a cave. Spider and cave. It is as if two major preoccupations in my life as a writer were initially sparked by that film.

About a year before my Kyoto spider vision in the fall of 1962—and it was a *vision*, very concrete, very real—I killed a large black spider that terrified my first wife in our house in Tainan, Taiwan. I felt terrible about this in a way that I did not expect to, and it may have set some of the stage for my supernatural sensitivity to the spider in the Okumura backyard.

I had been begging for a vision in Kyoto, convinced that if there was not some special confirmation of the validity of my desire to direct my life through poetry that I should stop writing poetry. I had no sense of how this validation would take place, even at the point I reacted to the disappearance of the spider in the backyard. As I said in "Spider Companion," "Something went through me that I can only describe as the loss of one deeply loved. I cried, and for several days felt nauseous and absurd." Assuming that all visions are in part projections, I suppose that I tore something open in my subconscious at the time—maybe knocking aside the Presbyterian boulder that had been blocking access—and set myself up for an envisioning of the spider in the sky over Nijo Castle.

Over the years I have noticed a lot of ramifications of having accepted the spider as my confirmational figure (and thus imbuing it with muselike qualities). I've reflected on the overlap between Arachne and Ariadne ("Placements II"), and the extent to which the web prefigures the labyrinth. This has led me to posit that there are archetypal, creative designs, and that one of the oldest must be that of the labyrinth (*Novices*, chapter 7). I believe that I make my poems out of my body in a way that is symbolically sympathetic with spider spinnerets issuing thread, and that I live and hunt in my poetry.

I not only give my heart to my poetry, but I eat my poetry as well (Artaud proposed that a poet should only do the former). Since my confirmational figure is lethal as well as constructive, it supports negation as well as affirmation, releasing me from the kind of idealism that permeates so much poetry. I relate to spider, web, and prey as a complex in which building, killing, attraction, and the apotropaic constitute a creative maze in which the way out, or resolution, can never be seen until one is right there. Without an overview, there are bound to be lots of dead ends, wrong turns, etcetera, which I accept as part of the creative process as I understand it.

There are alchemical shadowings within this maze, especially at the center, or moment of realization, where according to Fulcanelli, "the bitter conflict of the two natures takes place." Sulfur versus mercury. Theseus versus Minotaur, a tiny male spider in coitus with the much larger and ravenous female—the overlays here are amazing, and in the poem they must be felt as that moment in which, say, the Grail suddenly appears, hovering before one. The center has been reached—but what does one do now? What to do with this Grail? Now one must get out, bearing one's treasure, and this involves developing the poem to the point that it exhausts its material. All poets die in the labyrinth of their work. Some, like Blake, Artaud, and Stevens, die very close to the exit.

My second wife, Caryl, and I discovered the French Dordogne (and thus the Ice Age caves) in the summer of 1974. We rented an apartment in a farmhouse near the village of Les Eyzies, and soon became aware that we had an unexpected companion: a large lavender spider who lived under the stove. One could hear the spider walk on the linoleum at night. Caryl did not share my enthusiasm for this ally, and one day, while taking a walk in the fields, on noticing a spider I spontaneously popped it into my mouth and swallowed it to show her that spiders are not to be feared. Had I known that the spider was pregnant, I would have passed that one by. Several nights later I was suddenly awakened by Caryl's screams, to discover that baby spiders were crawling out of my ears, nose, and mouth. In spite of the bizarre outcome of this event, I was moved to have become part of a birthing that as a man I could certainly never have accomplished on my own. Over the years I have been tormented by a question similar to the one that vexed the Chinese philosopher Chuang-Tzu: am I a poet dreaming that he participated in the birth of spiders, or a spider dreaming that I was reborn through a poet? For the dollmaker Michel Nedjar, the fundamental creative question is, Of what is the spider dreaming?

Q. Along this same line of wanting to know how you hope to be read, I want to ask about the history and the continuing status of your reading in archetypal psychology as it intersects with your use of materials from the Upper Paleolithic. In some poems—"Notes on a Visit to Le Tuc d'Audoubert" (1982), for instance—your reading of the caves merges with fragments of an autobiographical narrative in which "I swear I sensed the disintegration of the backbone of my mother now buried 12 years," and the act of crawling through the cave becomes a metaphor for psychic birth or rebirth. To what extent do you stand by your readings of the Upper Paleolithic and the historical narrative of human consciousness these readings sometimes advance, and to what extent do these readings constitute an Eshleman autobiography—one of mythopoeic dimensions, perhaps—under construction?

A. In the late 1970s I read James Hillman's *The Dream and the Underworld* as a way to help me de-literalize the animals to be found on cave walls. Hillman was not concerned with prehistory, but what he had to say about dreams and the way we have used them suggested a way for me to think about cave art. Briefly, Hillman felt that modern man had interpreted his dreams and seen them as a reflection of daylight and daytime activity, thus denying them an autonomous realm, an archetypal place that corresponds with a distinct mythic geography—in short, an underworld that is not merely a reflection, that is, a diminution, of an empirical sense world.

Hillman's criticism of dream interpretation could be applied to the "sympathetic magic" (Salomon Reinach) and "hunting hypothesis" (Robert Ardrey) interpretations of cave art. In contrast, Hillman's own perspective on dreams as representing an autonomous realm could also be applied to cave art, and by doing this I was able to conceive of the earliest images as the first appearance of the autonomous imagination (in contrast to utilitarian "tool culture"), the beginning of art when what is human and what is animal were still bound together. I began to see image-making at 35,000 B.C. as the human-to-be separating out his/her animality and placing it on cave walls. Consciousness, as I am thinking of it here, seems to be the upswing of a "fall" from the seamless animal web, in which a certain amount of sexual energy was transformed into fantasy energy, the loss being partially and hauntingly compensated for by dreaming and imaging—processes not directly related to survival.

I stand by this approach or "reading" of cave art as one that is more encompassing and challenging than any others I know of (including the valuable work of André Leroi-Gourhan and Alexander Marshack). At the same time, when I crawl around in the caves, I don't shut down psychically and merely seek to reinforce my approach. There is still enough initial energy in cave imagery to stimulate my fantasy life, which is autobiographical as well as transpersonal, and all of this of course carries over into writing. While I am responding to what is there, I am also making things up. This situation was considerably brooded on by Olson in his work on what he called "muthologos."

We live in an eon that is marked by the disappearance of animal diversity and the coming in of what might be thought of as the primary outlines of the human story. As we try to assemble the rudiments of "initial mind," the ground is turning into an oil spill under our feet. When I crawl in an Ice Age cave I am in my skeleton in the skeleton of the Upper Paleolithic and the last years of the twentieth century. Whatever firstness that I can bring forward must make its presence felt in the jaws, as it were, of this triple consummation.

When I first met Alexander Marshack in the kitchen of our farmhouse apartment in 1974, he yelled at me, *What is a poet doing in the caves?* I don't recall how I answered him, other than by a guffaw. At this point I'd propose that solid research including extensive cave visiting brought to bear on active imagination may yield as much pay dirt on the deep past as theoretical and taxonomic archaeology.

Q. In its interest in and explorations of interiority, your work borrows from a range of twentieth-century psychologists and psychoanalysts— Freud, Sandor Ferenczi, Jung, Norman O. Brown, James Hillman, and beyond. Some readers criticize the traditions of discourse these names represent, perhaps especially those more closely affiliated with an "archetypal psychology," for their inscribing or reinscribing of essentialized gender binaries, for their efforts to locate—in nature, myth, or culture—a stable structure of "masculinity" or "femininity." Now, in your most recent book, *Under World Arrest,* you include a series of poems written in the "mask" of one Horrah Pornoff, a pseudonym for what you call in the book's notes "the feminine aspects of my personality" which had "fought over the years for their rightful place in my work." In the same notes you suggest that writers are "persona-infested" and that "wholeness consists of a circulation of negative as well as affirmative formations." I'm wondering about this "wholeness" you mention, and also about your investment in "masculine" and "feminine" "aspects." I can offer a concrete example to get you started. In "Under Louse Arrest"—one of those puns I mentioned earlier is in the title— you offer the following lines, which perhaps you could read for me in this context:

> We are at every moment in swill with nothingness,
>   in the awe of chaos bottled
> as the blood head of male nuclear destruction.
>   The Grail unidentifiable still
> because we have not created a common stone
>   fluidified with Kali's ichor.
>   I am anchored to Sonoran pronghorn,
>   to Queensland rat kangaroo,
>   to white-headed saki, to you,
>   disgusting plague of novelty,
> shield against which men have crushed the underworld.

A. While I have questioned aspects of Leroi-Gourhan's attribution of sexual significance to signs and animals in the caves (which would relocate your comments here to the origin of image-making), to my knowledge the first images are post-Mousterian (35,000 B.C.) cupules that are, by the Aurignacian (28,000 B.C.), associated with clearly defined vulvas which also appear in conjunction with specific animals. It is probable that ritual activities involving fire, killing, menstruation, and burial are older than the earliest images we have access to—but on the basis of image data, gender appears to be there at the start.

Horrah Pornoff's poems are a composite of my dreams of myself as a woman, feminist viewpoints, as well as material that might have sooner or later appeared in my own poetry. This is twilight-zone writing that may, from moment to moment, get something through that would otherwise have remained untapped. I might also mention that certain Horrah Pornoff poems are written in the style of other poets (Vallejo, Celan, and Adrienne Rich, for example).

What I am not, to the extent that I can imagine it, is not just a conscript in my sense of wholeness, but a force I must be willing to acknowledge in order not to set myself above and beyond what humankind is. In his essay "Man's Fulfillment in Conflict and Strife," Robert Duncan writes, "Reject Mae West as vulgar or Hitler as the enemy, reject them as fellows of our kind, and you have to go to battle against the very nature of Man himself, against the truth of things." I do not mean to imply that a wholeness is attained by enabling the personas who infest us to speak. We are all commanded in varying ways and at various times to address the Lear of ourselves, the Crazy Jane, or the Horrah Pornoff. I see Horrah as part of my gnomework.

I don't like glossing my own work, but here goes: "Under Louse Arrest" was originally called "Antinomian Windows." Caryl suggested the second title. To pick up on "antinomian" as the word relates to the poem: strong faith is clearly no obstacle to treating others cruelly. The amount of self-opposition humanity tolerates is truly unthinkable. Today man is out carousing with annihilation, hypnotized by his technological usurpation of nature. Instead of being a vessel of spiritual transformation available to all, the Grail (offered in the poem as a contrary to the atomic bomb) is an archaic relic one learns about in medieval history courses. Penelope Shuttle and Peter Redgrove, however, in *The Wise Wound*, offer a striking argument that the Grail is "an allegory of the feminine womb and vagina, the 'goblet' full of blood, the menstruation that contains many redeeming secrets." Rather than creating a "common stone," a common wealth, we cook up philosopher stones, ideals beyond the basic requirements for sane living. In the spirit of those who have chained themselves to fences at nuclear development sites, I anchor myself to endangered species (and am really anchored to these creatures whether I want to be or not; when they vanish, aspects of my humanness vanish too). Man's obsession with novelty seems to me to be the greatest plague of all, for it is involved with black magic that is unrestrained by any moral law. In the twentieth century, we have seen Hades, as a psychic realm, rendered meaningless and raised to the earth's surface as a kingdom—or death camp—solely on earth. I see myself as cross-tied between the Sonoran pronghorn and Donald Trump.

Q. A question about the phonotext in your work, about form rather than content, if we can hold them separate for a while—I know that Charles Olson's "Projective Verse" essay must have been a formative influence. I mention this issue because I'd like you to respond to Paul Christensen's suggestion in his book on your work *(Minding the Underworld: Clayton Eshleman and Late Postmodernism)* that your poetry can be understood as "variations on blank verse" with "line structures" intended "to distribute an orthodox metrical scheme over open ground, to liberate the lines as much as possible while ordering them from within by a partially concealed iambic tempo." How do you think about the shape of the poem, its smaller and larger units?

A. Olson's "Projective Verse" has always struck me as somewhat obscure and unwieldy as a manifesto. Christensen's description of my prosody is OK, but it doesn't say anything about what really happens in my lines. I have no theoretical approach to the line. I move word by word through the first several lines and at that point begin to get a sense of what the poem wants to look like, how it wants to *be* on the page. That is when I am typing (on a Swintec 1186 CMP); when I travel, I write in notebooks and pay little attention to line endings. The shape of one of my poems is often only determined via extensive revision (I figure I publish less than ten percent of what I write). To give you a concrete response to this question, I would have to look at a particular poem. The two stanzas of "Under Louse Arrest" that you quote are arranged on a very visual basis, balancing shorter phrases with longer phrases. Either a page looks right or it does not—if not, I move things around again and again until what I see meshes with what I hear.

Q. Clayton, would I be wrong to describe you as a moralist using your own life as an object lesson? I have before me your poem "Outtakes," from *Under World Arrest*, which begins "He wanted the synthesis *and* the mêlée" and contains the following lines:

> But did he have the sense to love himself?
> To respect what he disputed?
> To dispute what he loved?

Because he was tactless, he was an asshole.
As an asshole, he was never praised.
This baffled him and made him better.
As better, he was spat upon
because he was not entirely tactless.

A. I had no idea, writing "Outtakes," that the first line of the poem
(which you quote) was going to lead to those other eight lines that you
quote. The first line is a pretty precise linking of oppositional forces,
each of which some poets have staked their poetics on (for example,
Enslin on synthesis, Duncan on melee). The second stanza from which
you quote is a kind of shack full of fun-house mirrors. If both synthesis
and melee are taken seriously, there is going to be a lot of flopping back
and forth from frying pan to fire. I was laughing when I wrote those
eight lines you quote. I don't really find any moralizing in them (other
than some amused digs at myself for never getting my calculated and
spontaneous acts in sync).

There is, however, certainly a moral stance in what I write, as well as
amoral elements. Synthetically, I try to present a vision of reciprocity:
equal rights, equal time, eye to eye with the world. At the same time,
often in the same poem, I am also trying to let my subconscious have its
say. It adores contradicting my good intentions. Diego Rivera depicted
himself in one of his frescoes as a thirteen-year-old holding an umbrella
in one hand and, in the other, the "hand" of Madam Death. Were I to
paint a similar fresco, I would depict myself at twenty-seven holding
Caryl's hand in one hand, and in the other the pap of a red spider twice
my size.

NOTES

1. Here I would refer the reader to the passaage in "At the Locks of the Void,"
p. 142, concerning the difference between influence through translation and influence through reading masters who write in one's own tongue.
2. Concerning the first of these two categories, see the material on translating
Vallejo and extending this activity into my own life in "Companion Spider," p. 118.

Medusa *Dossier: Clayton Eshleman (1999)*

MEDUSA: Could you talk about your writing habits? What is your writing process and what stimulates you to write a poem? Do you use pencil, pen, typewriter, computer? Do you keep notebooks? Do you have a specific method or ritual that you follow? When and where do you write? Do you have "dry" periods, I mean, times in which you find it difficult to write?

CE: As a young poet, living in Kyoto, Japan, in the early 1960s, I forced myself to attempt to write daily, and often in the evening too. I would sit cross-legged on tatami before my low table and typewriter, sometimes staring at the page for hours. To sound like myself, whatever that might be, seemed impossible in those days. Moving from one line to the next seemed to involve crossing a continent.

From the late 1970s on, I have worked in a more flexible way, starting poems only when I felt a nudge from my subconscious. These days I write quickly (using a Swintec 2600 electronic typewriter at home, notebooks when traveling), and I set the draft aside immediately, no reworking for at least 6 months, sometimes 2 years. I am one of those bitches who eats her own pups if they are not taken away upon birth.

After time has passed, I show drafts to my wife, Caryl, who reads, comments, and even revises passages. Her intercession sometimes offers me detachment, sometimes changes my direction. When I start to revise, I carefully consider her suggestions, and we often work back and forth until I arrive at the finished piece. I do not think of this approach as traditional revision (polishing what has been done). My task

This interview was with Rodrigo Garcia Lopes for the Brazillian magazine *Medusa*. It appeared in an edited-down version in Samizdat 5, spring 2000.

is to explore what is worth keeping from the first draft. I often end up with twenty to thirty pages of worksheets for a two- to three-page poem.

Since I write lots of letters, and write essays and reviews as well as poems, and also translate a lot, I am not aware of ever having had a "dry" period. If I am having a problem with one genre, I just move to another. Translating and writing letters is a good way to keep my hand in, as it were, so that writing in some form or other is a daily practice.

MEDUSA: I've noticed that you are very critical of the "creative writing school" type of poem. Would you say that this is the dominant one written in America today? Since it seems to be a North American phenomenon, could you explain it for us? Being a professor of creative writing yourself, how do you position yourself concerning this type of workshop poem? How do you feel about these creative writing programs? Does "professionalism" of poetry represent a "curse" to the vitality and real "diversity" of American poetry (diversity here in terms of conflict, not bland variety)?

CE: Hundreds of creative writing degree programs in America exist today because they are popular at a time in which enrollment in traditional English Department classes is down. Students choose to "express themselves" instead of tackling arcane texts like *Paradise Lost* or *The Fairy Queen*, and universities oblige them by these offerings. In this sense, alas, writing workshops have become substitutes for reading.

Students sign up for such courses without any sense of how difficult it is to write genuine poetry (which must be based on an enormous amount of background reading). One reason that they do so is that "art" and "creativity" get a lot of media promotional hype here. Drive through any large city and you will find billboards promoting "the 'art' of banking" or "the 'art' of cooking." The Borders Bookstore chain recently, on my local radio station, encouraged people to experience "the 'art' of browsing" in their stores!

Students who do well in creative writing courses become candidates for undergraduate or graduate degrees in creative writing, pointing to a career as a professor-poet or -novelist. And to get tenure-track teaching positions, one must network and publish. There is undoubtedly much more poetry and fiction being published in America today than ever before—stimulated by governmental and private foundations that fund regional small presses—but much of it is chore work done to advance careers and self-esteem.

I accepted a professorship at Eastern Michigan University when I was fifty-one (in 1986). For the previous twenty-five years, I had lived in Mexico, Japan, Peru, and France, and when in America supported myself by part-time teaching, a few grants, and my wife's willingness at one point to work to support us. I wagered that at fifty-one the university environment would have no effect on me, for good or for bad, and that has turned out to be true. But I *am* part of the creative writing degree program system. I teach literature as well as creative writing, and require that my students in writing workshops read a lot—and I inform them of the limitations of such workshops.

There are always only going to be a handful of original, innovative poets in any generation. Such individuals are self-driven and self-initiated. The presence of writing programs, on one level, means nothing to such poets. However, I qualify that statement because the plethora of workshop-generated writing has created a publishing blizzard. It is much more difficult for a young poet today to figure out who he needs to read than it was for me, in the late 1950s, when William Carlos Williams and Charles Olson were a clear-cut alternative to Robert Frost and Robert Lowell. Today the workshop student poets read what they are told to read by professor-poets who are, unlike myself, products of the system and have never left school. This greatly waters down the ranges of experience that can be drawn on in writing poetry.

MEDUSA: In terms of an oppositional poetics, what do you think of the phenomenon of Language Poetry, which has found an important space in the pages of *Sulfur* (Michael Palmer being one of your Contributing Editors)? Do you think that Language Poetry, with the entry of many of its members in the academy, has lost its original insights, has become accommodated, tamed? Is it still possible to create a poetic movement today?

CE: Three poets directly or indirectly associated with Language Poetry are on the *Sulfur* masthead: Charles Bernstein, Clark Coolidge, and Michael Palmer. I invited them to participate in the magazine's direction because I think they are, at their best, writers whose individuality or voice is outside of what I consider to be the rather mechanistic range of most Language Poets.

When Language Poetry appeared in the 1970s, it was a mixed blessing for certain poets of my own generation. In its defiance of "official verse culture" it presented a back-turned, difficult language grid that shared some things with French Surrealism and the abstract word play one finds in Gertrude Stein and late Louis Zukofsky. However, I have always been suspicious of artists who gather under a conceptual canopy and move as a pack. For me, the two most valuable Surrealist poets are Artaud and Aimé Césaire. Artaud's force is in great part a reaction against Bretonesque Surrealism. Césaire, as a second-generation Surrealist, from Martinique, utilized aspects of Surrealism to express the suffering and anguish of black people everywhere. Like Bernstein, Coolidge, and Palmer, Artaud and Césaire will ultimately be known by their names, not by movements.

Looking at Language Poetry per se, its primary limitation is liquid thinking. Too much of the focus and significance of this poetry is left up to the reader to assemble for himself. Gary Snyder once remarked that authentic poetic experience was contingent upon the poet and the reader each going fifty percent of the way. Snyder's metaphor for this process was poem as campfire, reader as out in the night woods. The fire must extend its light—the reader must leave the woods and come to the firelight's edge. At the point they converge, art is active. In this sense, one could say that an authentic poem is a half-poem that must be completed by reader involvement. Language Poetry often only goes about twenty percent of the way and thus remains vague. It can "mean" too many things, which is to say that its nonreferential and non-sequitur nature might be an empty shell with no thinking behind it.

This not to imply that all non–Language Poetries are thoughtful and directed! The writing that comes out of the creative writing degree programs is more often than not posited on the writer's sensitivity, a formal or casual declaration that he has strong feelings about what he uses as material.

The fact that some Language Poets have gotten teaching jobs doesn't mean much. In fact, it makes sense that some of these writers become academicians because Language Poetry, in spite of its reader-unfriendly surface, does not directly propose anything that English Departments would find objectionable. What they do find objectionable, and resist, is someone like Amiri Baraka, whose politics are up front and abrasive. It happens that Baraka is in the Africana Department at SUNY-Stonybrook (on Long Island, New York). I bring him up here because he sought a tenured position at Rutgers, nearer his home in

Newark, New Jersey, and his appointment was blocked because, I believe, of the contentious nature of his writing.

There will always be poetic movements as long as society peripheralizes artists. Someone said: it is insane today to be an artist in America. And someone else said: it is the only sane thing to be. Regardless, to borrow the cliché about coal mining, making art is dark and lonely work, and many artists feel they can only gain momentum in numbers—look at the Beats, for example. Allen Ginsberg almost singlehandedly put them on the map as a "generation," implying in his unceasing promotion that they were *the* generation, that is, that they represented the most valid viewpoint of the times. This was Ginsberg's own way of attempting to create a literary dynasty with himself at the hub. Unlike Ginsberg, I am unsure of where my poetry belongs, unsure at times if it belongs at all. This is an exacerbating situation, but I feel that such bewilderment is true to the disaffiliation all artists today, with or without movements, experience.

MEDUSA: In a 1985 interview, you said: "One of the sad, hapless things about North American life is that there is no imaginative core—no psychic underworld—that enables people to express their fantasies in an astounding, carnivalesque way." Is that so because of the Puritan and Protestant heritage? You also speak of an "American grotesque" as an alternative to the two types of poetry mentioned above (workshop poetry and Language Poetry). Where can this "American grotesque" be found in specific poets, movements, and culture (Disneyland!)?

CE: For centuries poets have been making their ways through the forest of belief in the fatherhood of God, the literal existence of the Devil, the Bible (or Koran) as the only infallible source of truth, adamant distinctions between the elect and the damned (meaning eternal torment for nonbelievers), and human nature as wholly sinful. All of these judgments are in opposition to imagination as I understand it, and they have spawned a significant amount of Western art.

Religiosity has, in contemporary American society, been complexed with an obsession with entertainment, celebrity, scandal, and sex disguised as titillation. Our permissive environment is not restrictive at all in a religious sense, but this is not necessarily good news for artistic endeavor. For many, religiosity represents seriousness; after worship they are ready to be entertained, and thus outside of church, after work, they seek Elvis Presley or Marilyn Monroe. Serious art is like a leper at the door for such people, for art, when it is serious, refuses to allow diversion, confronting whoever looks at it or reads it with a gamut of real sensations including remorse and anguish.

I started thinking about an "American grotesque" in the early 1980s as a result of reading Mikhail Bakhtin's splendid meditation on "grotesque realism," *Rabelais and His World*. At the same time I was discovering that the tradition of the grotesque originates in Upper Paleolithic cave imagery, specifically in animal/human, or hybrid, images. To be a metaphor is to be grotesque (initially of the grotto). At the point that I conceived that "a single smoking road leads from Indianapolis to Lascaux" this road also seemed filled with the unending pileup of smashed automobiles that constitutes history. And contemporary American culture, which certainly includes Disneyland and Mickey Mouse, looked more and more grotesque, especially when you did not separate out the political from the comic book. I wrote a few poems that explored American grotesqueness (such as "The Tomb of Donald Duck" and "Manticore Vortex" in *Fracture*), but I never formalized the notion or tried to enlist others in its cause.

As a kind of spin-off of all of this, it occurred to me in the late 1980s that if the poets I had spent the most time translating—Vallejo, Césaire, Artaud, Holan—were to be cross-indexed, their superimposed configuration might identify all of them as "conductors of the pit." "Pit" here of course puns on "orchestra pit" and "abyss." I see all four of these poets as drawing their strength from the underworld of the psyche and producing a poetry written *in extremis*. The reader is led in and down, further and further into a thickening dark, glinting with marvelous shapings of the dark, but at core without resolution or release from the weight and transiency of the journey. I called a selection of my translations (or cotranslations) of these authors' work *Conductors of the Pit* (1988).

There are elements of the grotesque in such American poets as Allen Ginsberg, Jerome Rothenberg, Jayne Cortez, and Will Alexander.

MEDUSA: You have said in an interview: "I live in a society that is obsessed with the other on an extremely superficial level." This reminded me that when I was living here for the first time (1990 to 1992), specifically while the Gulf War was going on, *The Los Angeles Times* made a survey among university students across the U.S. and the result was that less than 10 percent were able to identify where Iraq and Kuwait were located on a world map. A classmate friend of mine, very bright, surprised me one day when he said: "Rodrigo, I was wondering . . . in what part of Africa is Brazil located?" As a North American poet, translator, and professor, and as someone deeply interested in other cultures, how do you see the American educational system as well as the privileged position of the United States in today's global scene, in economical, military, and cultural terms? Is "Globalization," in fact, a mere euphemism for "Americanization?" Why are North Americans, in general, and poets, specifically, so little and superficially interested in what occurs outside the U.S.?

CE: A complete response to this octopodal question would involve writing a book. I will do with it what I can.

When I was growing up in Indianapolis, Indiana, in the 1940s, I used to be fascinated by a ubiquitous advertisement for Atlas house paint. The sign had an image of a globe half-covered with paint running down around it. Under it was the slogan: "Atlas Paint covers the world." I think this identifies your metaphor: Globalization = Americanization.

As for our educational system: I don't know enough about it to give you a thoughtful answer. I know nothing about what goes on in our grade schools today, and only a little about what students learn in high school. I do know that the students in my Introduction to Literature: Poetry course at Eastern Michigan University (mostly freshmen from the midwest) have no background in literature. The first day of class I ask each student what poetry he has read or studied. About 70 percent of the class have either not read any poetry or do not recall what they have read.

But I don't teach the privileged. The privileged control and keep the rest of Americans in the same position as the rest of the world.

The North American artists and writers that I have had contact with over the past two decades *are* interested in what occurs outside of America, even if they do not directly manifest such in their work. As for other Americans, I know that via such magazines as *The Nation, Z,* and *The New York Review of Books* there is a well-informed minority. The poor, here as elsewhere, are so overwhelmed with daily survival that they are not up to much beyond entertainment when they have a little time to relax. Perhaps I am naive, but I suspect steady interest in the lives of people in other countries is a minority preoccupation everywhere.

MEDUSA: Continuing what I've asked but in a more specific sense. You have said, in an interview, that "to be a significant American poet you have to read internationally." North American poetry seems to have been, in great part, unaware of Latin American poetries. Even though geographically we are in the same continent—and correct me if I am wrong—North American poets have been more tuned in to European poetic traditions. *Sulfur*, in this sense, was very important for opening its pages to what was being done in other parts of the globe. You are a respected translator of Vallejo, Césaire, and Neruda. How do you see Latin American poetry and what impact have these authors had on your poetry? Who are the key names in Latin American poetry and why? What do you know about Brazilian poetry?

CE: Contrary to your assertion, quite a few American poets, representing a diverse poetics, have not only been aware of Latin American poetry—from the 1960s to the present—but have translated it. Such poets include Muriel Rukeyser, Thomas Merton, Paul Blackburn, Elizabeth Bishop, Ben Bellit, Mark Strand, Nathaniel Tarn, Alastair Reid (a Scot, but in residence here for many years), Robert Bly, Willis Barnstone, Philip Levine, James Wright, Margaret Randall, Galway Kinnell, Ed Dorn, W. S. Merwin, Carolyn Forché, Eliot Weinberger, and Forrest Gander. And these are just the ones who come immediately to mind. I am sure there are more.

My introduction to Latin American poetry took place around 1957 via Dudley Fitt's 1947 *Latin American Poetry* anthology. It included the work of 95 poets. I read it avidly, and immediately got involved with the poetry of Neruda and Vallejo. I bought a bilingual dictionary and tried to read their poems word by word, and then, discovering other translations of some of the poems, was dumbfounded by the differences. I spent the summers of 1958 and 1959 in Mexico (hitchhiking the first summer; riding down in the back of a truck the second one). I took a Neruda collection to Chapala in 1959 and rented a room from a retired American butcher who had a young Indian wife. While pigs wandered in and out of my room, we would sit on the bed and I would ask her about words in Neruda's poetry.

I completed my first little collection of translations—about 30 poems from Neruda's first two *Residencias en la tierra*—in Kyoto, 1962. I then turned, seriously, to Vallejo's *Poemas humanos* and was, as I have written elsewhere, quicksanded. Neruda's *Residencias* were a forest of curious hybrids and aromas; one walked on solid ground inspecting this and that. With Vallejo the little ground I had gained gave way. I was foundering in an abyss of contradictions and dissonance, in which absurdity, compassion, and anguish mixed like smoke. After several months of attempting to scale Vallejo's vertical walls, I determined that a translation of *Poemas humanos* that I could live with would be my apprenticeship to poetry. To make a long, complicated story short, Grove Press published a bilingual *Human Poems* in 1968. Several years later, I decided that the translation had to be redone and teamed up this time with the Spanish scholar José Rubia Barcia. *César Vallejo: The Complete Posthumous Poetry* was published in 1978 by University of California Press (since that time they have sold around 13,000 copies of the book). As you probably know, I returned to Vallejo in 1989 and spent three years translating *Trilce*, which was published bilingually by Marsilio in 1992, and reprinted by Wesleyan in 2001.

As a translator/reader I have always gone deep into a few individual poets, translating complete books when possible. This is also to suggest that I have no overall sense of twentieth century Latin American poetry, or European poetry, for that matter. I have preferred to read Vallejo, Césaire, and Artaud in depth rather than read lesser amounts of many writers. The collective resource offered by the poets I have translated has been one of permission—of giving me permission, in my own poetry, to say anything that would spur on my quest for authenticity and for constructing an alternative world.

I know very little about Brazilian poetry. I am so suspicious of the translations of others that it takes a special occasion for me to be reeled into a study of a poet's work in a language I do not read. And I don't read Portuguese. My one genuine experience with contemporary Brazilian poetry involved a long poem by Horacio Costa called "The Boy and the Pillow." Horacio was visiting us and showed me an English version of the poem that he had done via a Spanish version with an American poet in Mexico City. I read through the English version and immediately knew something was wrong. After questioning Horacio about the first two pages, word for word, we came to the same conclusion: the translation was inadequate and had to be redone. We spent the next five days redoing it and I ran the new version (signed by everyone who had worked on it) in *Sulfur* #36 (1995). I admire that poem very much, but had I looked at the first English version under different circumstances I would probably have put it aside after several pages.

MEDUSA: Pound has defined the poem as a vortex "from which, and through which, and into which, ideas are constantly rushing." In modern and postmodern poetry we observe a conscious attempt to conceive the poem as a kind of "black hole" that is able to suck up different discourses, traditions, times, into the body of the poem. Thus, the old concept of lyric and epic poetry has increasingly opened up to incorporate and assimilate materials that were formerly considered "nonpoetic." Your poetry, it seems, derives its energies not only from your own personal experiences, autobiography, with the struggle with the poets you have translated, but also from anthropology, psychology, etc. How would you define your poetics in this context?

CE: I don't care for the words "vortex" or "black hole" as terms for heterogeneous assimilation as they are basically destructive. The incorporation of different genres, and previously nonpoeticized information, into the poem is something else. I'm not sure what to call it. Northrop Frye referred to William Blake's multigenre "The Marriage of Heaven and Hell" as an "anatomy," and I have used that term to identify my research/book project on Ice Age cave imagery.

As you imply, the problem with much poetry is that it passes too effortlessly down the road in others' ruts. From the viewpoint of the eighteenth century, say, the twentieth, in terms of what has happened in poetry, must look like a millepedal nightmare. As Robert Duncan put it, reflecting on what he called "a symposium of the whole," his vision of the twentieth century range of the humanities, "all the excluded orders must be included. The female, the proletariat, the foreign; the animal and vegetative; the unconscious and the unknown; the criminal and failure—all that has been outcast and vagabond must return to be admitted in the creation of what we consider we are."

For the individual poet, the task is to cathect areas of experience that have yet to be "admitted," and to then make them part of what his poetry, and possibly poetry at large, is responsive to and responsible for. While many of the areas that Duncan cites have been engaged, it is stunning to ponder how many ranges of human experience—virtually all of the sciences—have yet to be assimilated into poetic visions.

How would I define my poetics? I've attempted to be responsible, in my poetry, for all I know about myself and the world. I've tried to splice a number of dualisms: to write for myself *and* to communicate; to engage inspiration and self-criticism; to practice a reality that is at once created *and* observed; and to fight self-censorship *and* self-indulgence. The idea is to turn these oppositional situations into folds, or (in the Blakean sense) contraries, in a poetry that is as Argus-eyed as it is porous.

I have also constructed a myth in the book on Ice Age art that primordial image-making was motivated by a crisis in which people began to separate the animal out of their about-to-be human heads and to project it on cave walls. The corollary to this intuition is that proto-shamanism may have come into being as a reactive swerve from this separation continuum, to rebind human being to the fantasy of a paradise that did not exist until the separation was sensed.

The task I've created for myself has been to travel to the origin of humanness—to a real backwall—while maintaining a focus on late-twentieth-century life. Besides exploring the basis for dualism (the separation and rebinding that in my view characterizes Ice Age image-making), I want to deal directly (and brutally) with political issues—for example, the El Mozote massacre in Salvador, the O. J. Simpson trial, the beating of Rodney King in Los Angeles, the Gulf War—as well as to "read" twentieth-century visual art: in *From Scratch* (1998) there are poems working with the imagery of such painters as Chaim Soutine, Willem de Kooning, and Nora Jaffe. These areas of attention occasionally intermingle, and this brings up the matter of methodology:

The art that engages me involves a dance between the artist's subconscious and conscious realms. The subconscious is Dionysian, the grounds of inspiration, teeming with conflict; the conscious is Apollonian, or the will to cohere, perceptive and self-critical. The challenge in this regard is to communicate while synthesizing within a melee. Sometimes I have a plan when I begin a poem, sometimes no plan whatsoever. I try not to anticipate myself, but to let each phrase or line generate the next. This is not "automatic writing" or "stream of consciousness" because inspiration is constantly shadowed by evaluation. I don't want the unknown to be fully translated into the known. I want the dream to have its life in the poem along with insights into its ramifications.

MEDUSA: Your poetry is aligned with a visionary tradition that goes back to ancestral times, and many of your contemporaries—such as Blackburn, Snyder, Corman, McClure, and Rothenberg—are also involved in peculiar types of *re*-vision. How would you situate your investigation in relation to these poets? Do you feel that you belong to a visionary North American poetics? How has this "looking back" to ancestral times affected your poetry?

CE: Blake would be the source of any alignment to be found in my poetry with a visionary tradition. There are moments of grandeur in all of these phases, from the pagan "Marriage of Heaven and Hell" to the

Christianity-encumbered "Jerusalem." Blake's attempt to translate Christianity into his own system is heroic, and because he revealed what it entailed I don't need to take it on. I can reject Christianity because Blake demonstrated that if you try to incorporate it in an altered form you will still end up identifying man with humanity and woman with nature. This is one of the errors, of nearly incalculable depth, that continues to hold humanity in its thrall.

Of the contemporary American poets that you mention, only Rothenberg and McClure could be thought of as participating in a visionary tradition. I feel some kinship with them, particularly with Rothenberg, whose blend of vision and political awareness is powerfully demonstrated in the poem "Khurbn." Blackburn and Snyder are more observational than visionary; both have a keen sense of how perceived materials can be aligned in language. I suppose a case could be made for Snyder as a visionary via his adherence to Zen Buddhism, which has some things in common with Blake's conception of art as creation designed to pull *the* Creation inside out. However, Snyder is so observationally engineered, so attuned to natural specificity and flux, that his visionary propensity is usually restrained. Corman is the least visionary of the poets you mention; he is a kind of haiku-minimalist whose vista is restricted by his unceasing obsession with dying, or "livingdying" as he puts it. However: he can cover more ground in eight or ten words than any other American poet alive today, and he is also a splendid translator (of Bashō, Celan, and Montale, for example), and he edited *the* seminal literary magazine of the 1950s and early 1960s, *origin*. I should also acknowledge here that Blackburn, Snyder, and Rothenberg are excellent translators too and that as an essayist, Snyder is our Thoreau. As an anthologist, Rothenberg has almost single-handedly reinvented the range of anthologies for our times.

I don't think that there is a visionary North American tradition in poetry. There are a few visionaries, but all are dependent upon either preindustrial tribal or Western European sources. The American Protestant-Capitalist complex does not support visionary poetics—as both Hart Crane and Charles Olson learned at crucial and tragic points in their careers.

My poetry of the late 1960s and early 1970s is very personal, pent upon excavating my Indianapolis "family romance" and background. When I chanced upon the Ice Age caves in the French Dordogne in the mid-1970s and realized that they were prime unpoetic material, I made a 180-degree turn in focus. I shifted from highly differentiated personal concerns to possibly the most undifferentiated transpersonal realm we know of. I don't mean to suggest that I simply jettisoned my personal life as material when I began to engage the caves. What they offered me was a shot at the origin of metaphor, or even the origin of poetry if one believes, as I do, that early shamans were proto-poets. The caves thus gave me a bedrock on which to stand. They solved, for me, the twentieth-century existential dilemma of: to whom do I belong? Do I belong to any place? Do I belong at all? In 1987, as the sensations of loss poured through me in the village of Les Eyzies (the epicenter of French prehistory), I realized that I was home. Whatever missing story I have had to create for myself has, since the late 1970s, taken place against an Upper Paleolithic background and the myths I have created in order to understand some of that background. The Dordogne was the gift of a lifetime.

MEDUSA: I'm fascinated by your research on Paleolithic imagination. Could you talk to us about this investigation and how it enters your poetry? What is "Juniper Fuse"? What did you learn from your study and actual experience with the caves?

CE: What I learned will be published in the upcoming work you mention, the full title of which is "Juniper Fuse: Upper Paleolithic Imagination & the Construction of the Underworld." Concerning the book's title: wicks made of 1/4-inch juniper branches were used in many of the 130 hand lamps found in Lascaux. Since the Upper Paleolithic, wick has become fuse as the conveyor of ignition for electrical purposes as well as for shells and bombs. "Juniper Fuse," then, is a metaphor connecting the flame by which cave imagery was made possible to its ignescent consequences in modern life.

Here is how the "Juniper Fuse" project began: at the suggestion of a friend, my wife and I rented an apartment in a farmhouse outside of Les Eyzies for the spring and summer months of 1974. After discovering the caves in the area, I discovered something of equal importance in regard to anything I might write: no poet had taken on the Upper Paleolithic and done what Charles Olson referred to as a "saturation job." Without knowing where such a project would lead, or even how I would go about it, I began to revisit the caves of the Dordogne, Lot, and Ariège regions, and to read what had been written about the Upper Paleolithic. Over the past twenty-five years, we have visited and revisited around forty caves, and I have read hundreds of books and articles.

As one might expect, studies of Ice Age image-making have been written by archeologists, in scholarly, objective prose, based on field-work, and often framed by a single theory to account for the "art." In the late 1970s, I became aware that cave imagery is an inseparable mix of mental constructs and perception. That is, there are "fantastic" animals as well as astutely perceived realistic animals. There are not only human figures representing men and women whose social roles cannot be determined, but others, with bird masks, bison heads, and peculiar wounds, that evoke an interior world, in some cases shamanism. So instead of solely employing rational documentation (as have the archeologists), it struck me that this "inseparable mix" might be approached using mental imagery as well as perception, or poetic imagination as well as thorough fieldwork and research.

Thus in the writing of "Juniper Fuse" I sought to be open to what I thought about and fantasized while in the caves or while meditating on their image environments—to create my own truth as to what they mean, respecting imagination as one of a plurality of conflicting powers. I also sought to be a careful observer, and to reflect on what others have written, photographed, and drawn. Sometimes a section is all poetry, sometimes all prose—at other times it is a shifting combination like a Calder mobile, with poetry turning into prose, prose turning into poetry.

I also decided to bring to bear on my "saturation job" a range of thinkers outside of archeology proper. While I studied the work of the Abbés Breuil and Glory, Annette Laming, André Leroi-Gourhan, S. Giedion, Max Rafael, Alexander Marshack, Jean Clottes, Margaret S. Conkey, and Paul Bahn, I also read C. S. Jung, Sandor Ferenczi, Geza Róheim, Mikhail Bakhtin, Weston LaBarre, N. O. Brown, Kenneth Grant, James Hillman, and Hans Peter Duerr. I sought to match my pluralistic theoretical approach with varying styles. "Juniper Fuse" is, as I mentioned earlier, an "anatomy," composed of poetry, prose poetry, essays, lectures, notes, dreams, and visual materials.

MEDUSA: Two phrases strike me when I think of poetic translation: "Poetry is what gets lost in translation" and "One never finishes a translation; one abandons it." How crucial is translation for a poet? What is your approach regarding translation? What are your criteria? What are your next projects in this area?

CE: I think your first question is possibly only relevant in regard to the translation of traditional rhyme and meter verse. You can't translate a sonnet *as a sonnet* without seriously distorting its meaning; to translate it for meaning alone means doing it as free verse, and losing most of its sonnet identity. I have never touched, as a translator, Vallejo's first book, *Los heraldos negros*, because I regard translating it as a no-win situation. Most of it is traditional verse. Once you strip the poems of their metrical uniforms in a free-verse translation they are not compelling. And if you offered them new English verse uniforms the result would inevitably be inaccurate and grotesque. However, most of Vallejo's complex poems written in Europe are, in my opinion, potentially translatable because they are intellectually geared, and without the musical veneer of regular meter and rhyme.

Your second quotation: I heard it years ago, in a slightly different version, attributed to Picasso! The story: "Picasso, how do you know when a painting is finished?" "I don't finish paintings, I abandon them."

Presented as a statement on translation, I find this quotation questionable. It is probably only true in the case of poems that have a very strong sound component (as in "sound poetry"), or words that the translator cannot track down—or neologisms that he cannot match in the second language. Let's put it this way: it is possibly true for certain poems by Paul Celan and Vallejo (I "abandoned" a half-dozen translations of poems in *Trilce*). But I don't think it would hold true for, say, Montale, Neruda, or Breton.

As a translator, I try to do accurate work—seeing myself as the servant of the original, not a performer using its space to dance—*and* to bring what I do, as much as is possible, up to the performance level of the original. Because my French and Spanish are not fluent, I often work with a cotranslator. In this regard, I have been lucky: I've worked with rigorously honest, demanding, capable people. I have avoided the situation in which a speaker of the original language prepares a trot in the second language and passes it along to the second-language person to be polished. With José Rubia Barcia, Annette Smith, and Bernard Bador, I have worked in tandem, spending countless hours with each of them, exploring, researching, debating, and checking our work.

I have no new translation projects.

MEDUSA: In the end of the beautiful poem "Short Story," you wrote: "Poetry's horrible responsibility: / in language to be the world." What can poetry do, in your opinion, in a world dominated by materialism, consumerism and the mass media, as well as in a world with increasing social injustices and deep economical problems? What is the poet's "mission" (if there is such a thing), in your vision? The Brazilian poet Paulo Leminski (1945–1989) had a motto: "In order to be a poet it is necessary to be more than a poet." Do you agree with that? How do you posit yourself, as poet, in the world?

CE: In *Love's Body* (in the chapter called "Fulfillment"), N. O. Brown writes: "The central feature of the human situation is the existence of the unconscious, the existence of a reality of which we are unconscious." He also proposes that "the axis of world history is making conscious the unconscious," and that "symbolic consciousness" (comprised of seeing and not seeing, of waking and sleep) overcomes dualities and is expressed as poetry. One could argue that of the language arts poetry is the one that is most involved with ensouling, or deepening meaning by admitting the unconscious to consciousness, by eliminating the literal floor of consciousness so that the basement becomes part of meaning's space. This activity is an essential ingredient in the process of becoming human and being human.

The kind of poetry that meets this definition faces formidable obstacles relative to being received and assimilated because it often moves into uncharted areas. Under the best of circumstances, a slim minority of the population performs the role of a supporting receiver for such poetry. In North America today, we have far from the best circumstances for such an exchange. Our culture is not only drenched in entertainment and media distraction but layered with art phobia. If an art is blasphemous, obscene, abrasively dissentaneous, or really demanding—that is, if it does not easily reflect the viewer/reader's immediate experience—it will be rejected. I am not talking about merely the uneducated viewer/reader, but the so-called "arbiters of culture." Editors, reviewers, gallery directors, university department heads, foundation officers, and award panels, as a conglomerate, determine what will see the light of day. Increasingly, I believe, such people are insensitive and hostile to original work. The trend here (and probably in Brazil too) is toward passive spectatorship, in which the film, book, or painting is expected to go ninety percent of the way. Global TV dissemination of sporting events has undoubtedly stimulated this passivity.

My experience as a professor and as a writer giving a half-dozen readings each year before university audiences is that the most "open" segment of the population is people in their thirties and forties who have some real life experience under their belts and who still think of themselves as part-time students. They are porous and curious, and willing to try something that may also make them uneasy. Such people constitute a very modest percentage of North Americans.

Difficult poetry offers less surface than most novels, plays, and paintings, and demands, therefore, a more active response; you have to work hard at it to get anything at all since there is seldom a plot, and never a color field, to provide an entrance level that can be bypassed or just relaxed into.

There always seem to be a small number of people who will work out their lives in poetry and be grateful for the opportunity to do so regardless of the paucity of response. Poetry in the twenty-first century could become like alchemy in the late nineteenth century: a handful of people working on what appears to others as arcane and pointless transformations. Such workers will need a Jung to justify their activities as part of an evolving symbolic consciousness. If this alchemy parallel is pertinent, however, the news is not good: to my knowledge, alchemy as a practice has ceased to exist.

Concerning Leminski's motto: one could say that translating and editing—activities I earlier identified as, on one level, services to the community of poetry—constitute "being more than a poet." Or perhaps Leminski had in mind the need to incorporate the nonpoetic into the poetic so as to not end up with aesthetic reruns. Or maybe he had Rimbaud in Africa in mind—though Rimbaud had severed all ties to poetry before going into regions no white man had penetrated before him. Perhaps a more appropriate image for our times would be Allen Ginsberg and Gary Snyder in India, in 1962, visiting ashrams, and discovering the depth of Far Eastern thought for Occidentals. I think Leminski's point is well, if ambiguously, taken: the poet must eternally incorporate the previously unincorporated into his holdings. And he does so as society at large directs the incorporated and the unincorporated into profit and fun.

About the author: Clayton Eshleman is Professor of English at Eastern Michigan University. The founding editor of two highly regarded literary magazines, *Caterpillar* (1967–1973) and *Sulfur* (1981–2000), Eshleman's poetry has been published by Black Sparrow Press since 1968; his twelve books of poetry include *The Name Encanyoned River: Selected Poems 1960–1985* (1986) and most recently *From Scratch* (1998). An earlier collection of his essays and interviews, *Antiphonal Swing* (McPherson & Co.), appeared in 1989. He is the main American translator of César Vallejo (with José Rubia Barcia) and of Aimé Césaire (with Annette Smith). Besides the seven collections of Vallejo and Césaire translations, he has also translated books of Pablo Neruda, Antonin Artaud, Vladimir Holan, Michel Deguy, and Bernard Bador. His 1978 cotranslation of Vallejo's *Complete Posthumous Poetry* was the first translation of modern poetry to win the National Book Award. He is also the recipient of a Guggenheim Fellowship in Poetry (1978), and several grants from both the National Endowment for the Arts and the National Endowment for the Humanities. In 2000, he received an honorary Doctor of Letters from the State University of New York at Oneonta.

His translations of *Trilce* by César Vallejo (2000) and *Notebook of a Return to the Native Land* by Aimé Césare (2001) are available from Wesleyan University Press.